The Institute of Chartered Accountants in England and Wales

TAX COMPLIANCE

For exams in 2019

Question Bank

www.icaew.com

Tax Compliance
The Institute of Chartered Accountants in England and Wales

ISBN: 978-1-50972-155-9
Previous ISBN: 978-1-78363-909-0

First edition 2013
Seventh edition 2019

British Library Cataloguing-in-Publication Data
A catalogue record for this book is available from the British Library

Contains public sector information licensed under the Open Government Licence v3.0.

Originally printed in the United Kingdom on paper obtained from traceable, sustainable sources.

Contents

The following questions are exam-standard. Unless told otherwise, these questions are the style, content and format that you can expect in your exam.

Title	Study manual reference	Marks	Time allocation Mins	Page Question	Answer
December 2017					
73 Sherazi LLP	1	7	10.5	89	305
74 Virgil Ltd	23, 24	13	19.5	89	306
75 Carrie	11-13, 15-17	25	37.5	90	308
76 Mathison Ltd	18-22	15	22.5	91	312
77 Saul	2-10, 13, 14	40	60	92	314
March 2018					
78 Janet and John	1	7	10.5	94	319
79 Skate Ltd	23, 24	13	19.5	94	320
80 Simon and Graham	11-13, 15-17	25	37.5	95	323
81 Salt Ltd	18-22	15	22.5	96	326
82 Amy	2-10, 13, 14	40	60	97	328
June 2018					
83 John	1	7	10.5	100	334
84 Kavitha	23, 24	13	19.5	100	335
85 Denzel and Marwan	11-13, 15-17	25	37.5	101	337
86 H Ltd	18-22	15	22.5	102	341
87 Ellie	2-10, 13, 14	40	60	103	344
September 2018					
88 Gustavo and Mike	1	7	10.5	106	349
89 Schrayder Ltd	23, 24	13	19.5	106	350
90 Walter	11-13, 15-17	25	37.5	107	352
91 Heissen Ltd	18-22	15	22.5	108	355
92 Jessie and Saul	2-10, 13, 14	40	60	108	358

Question Bank topic finder

Set out below is a guide showing the Tax Compliance syllabus learning outcomes, topic areas, and related questions in the Question Bank for each topic area. If you need to concentrate on certain topic areas, or if you want to attempt all available questions that refer to a particular topic, you will find this guide useful.

Topic area	Syllabus learning outcome(s)	Question number(s)	Study Manual chapter(s)
Capital gains tax			
- Capital losses	3a, d	20, 60, 65, 80	11
- Chattels	3a, d	19, 20, 21, 70	11
- Connected persons	3a, d	21, 22, 23, 50	11
- Entrepreneurs' relief	3b, d	20, 22, 55, 65	12
- Gift relief	3b, d	21, 55, 60, 70, 75	12
- Letting relief	3b, d	20, 45, 90	12
- Overseas	3c, d	18, 50, 65, 85	13
- Part disposal	3a, d	19, 40, 50, 80, 85	11
- Principal private residence relief	3b, d	20, 22, 45, 50, 55, 90	12
- Residential property	3a, d	20, 22, 45, 55, 80, 90	11
- Shares and securities	3a, d	18, 21, 23, 50, 55, 65, 70, 75, 85	11
Corporation tax			
- Adjustment to profit	4a, b, c, h	24, 25, 26, 27, 29, 41, 51, 56, 61, 66, 71, 81, 86	18
- Administration	4i	24, 25, 27, 28, 30, 61, 66, 76, 86	18
- Capital allowances	4c	24, 26, 27, 28, 30, 41, 46, 51, 61, 66, 71, 81, 91	7, 18
- Capital losses	4d, f, g	24, 25, 26, 29, 30, 46, 51, 66, 71	19, 21
- Deficit	4b, h	See Non-trade loan relationship deficit below	21
- Degrouping charges	4d, f, g	56, 76, 81	22
- Gains	4d	24, 25, 26, 27, 30, 41, 51, 56, 61, 71, 76, 81, 91	19
- Gains groups	4d, f, g	46, 51, 71, 81	22
- Group relief	4f, g, h	24, 46, 51, 66, 86	22

Topic area	Syllabus learning outcome(s)	Question number(s)	Study Manual chapter(s)
- Intangible fixed assets	4b, h	24, 26, 29, 61, 66, 86	20
- Loan relationships	4a, h	24, 25, 27, 28, 29, 41, 51, 56, 71, 81, 86	18
- Long period of account	4f, h	26	18
- Losses		See each type of loss: trade, non-trade, property, capital	21, 22
- Non-trade loan relationship deficit	4g, h	41, 61	21
- Overseas	4h	17, 29, 56, 91	20
- Property income/losses	4g, h	24	18, 20, 21
- Research and development	4a, c	24, 25, 28, 30, 51, 56, 71	20
- Rollover relief	4e	26, 27, 51, 71, 91	12, 19
- Share disposals	4d	28, 29, 30, 46, 76	19
- Substantial shareholding exemption (SSE)	4d	25, 27, 28, 29, 56, 66, 81, 86	19
- Trade losses	4f, g, h	26, 46, 66, 76	21
Ethics			
- Conflict of interest	1a	8, 63, 78	1
- Data protection	1b	1, 88	1
- Disclosure	1a	48, 68	1
- Errors	1b	5, 8, 9, 38, 43, 48, 68, 78	1
- Fundamental principles	1a	4, 5, 6, 7, 8, 36, 43, 53, 58, 68, 73, 78	1
- Money laundering	1b	1, 5, 6,8, 9, 36, 38, 43, 48, 58, 63, 78, 88	1
- Other	1	4, 7, 53, 73	1
- Planning, avoidance and evasion	1b	3, 5, 6, 10, 68, 83	1
- Professional Conduct in Relation to Taxation (PCRT)	1a	2, 38, 83	1
- Professional Indemnity insurance (PII)	1c	2, 7, 63, 68, 88	1

Topic area	Syllabus learning outcome(s)	Question number(s)	Study Manual chapter(s)
Income tax			
- Adjustment to profit	5a, b, c, o	31, 32, 33, 34, 36, 37, 42, 47, 52, 62, 67, 72, 77, 82, 87, 92	2, 6
- Badges of trade	5	57	6
- Basis period – opening year rules	5e, o	32, 34, 36, 37, 47, 62, 67, 77, 82, 87	6
- Basis period – closing year rules	5g, o	31, 52, 62	6
- Basis period – change of year end	5h, o	72	6
- Capital allowances	5c	31, 32, 35, 36, 37, 42, 57, 62, 67, 72, 77, 82, 87, 92	7
- Cash basis – trading profits	5c, o	35, 52, 82	10
- Cash basis – property income	5k, l, o	32, 34, 36, 47, 52, 57, 67, 77, 87, 92	3, 10
- Child benefit charge	5o	34, 92	2
- Employment income – accommodation	5j, o	31, 33, 36, 62	5
- Employment income – beneficial loan	5j, o	32, 33, 36, 47, 57, 67, 77	5
- Employment income - car benefit	5j, o	32, 33, 34, 36, 37, 42, 52, 62, 72, 87, 92	5
- Employment income – expenses	5j, o	34, 47, 52, 72, 77, 87, 92	5
- Employment income – fuel benefit	5j, o	31, 32, 33, 36, 37, 52, 72, 87, 92	5
- Employment income – loan of asset	5j, o	32, 33, 34, 42, 57, 67	5
- Employment income – medical	5j, o	32, 35, 52	5
- Employment income – SMRS	5j, o	32, 35, 47, 57, 77	5
- Fixed rate expenses	5c	33, 82, 92	5
- Marriage allowance	5o	34	2
- Overseas	5n, o	31, 35, 37, 42, 72, 77	13
- Partnerships	5d, o	31, 32, 35, 47, 52, 77	9
- Pensions	5m, o	32, 33, 34, 35, 36, 42, 52, 62, 72, 77, 82	4

Topic area	Syllabus learning outcome(s)	Question number(s)	Study Manual chapter(s)
- Pre-trading expenditure	5c	34, 36, 77, 92	6
- Property income – cash basis	5k, l, o	See cash basis – property income above	3
- Property income – property allowance	5k, l, o	32, 34	3
- Property income – rent a room	5k, l, o	33, 34, 57, 82	3
- Property income – losses	5k, l, o	67	3
- Trading allowance	5c	57, 87	6
- Trading losses – closing years	4i, o	37	8
- Trading losses – ongoing	4i, o	31, 37, 57, 67, 77	8
- Trading losses – opening years	4i, o	47, 82, 92	8
- Trading losses – restrictions	4i	31, 57, 77	8
Inheritance tax			
- Administration	3i, k	17, 70, 85	17
- Agricultural property relief (APR)	3j	19, 60, 80	17
- Business property relief (BPR)	3j	19, 20, 40, 50, 55, 60, 80, 85	17
- Charitable giving	3e, i	19, 20, 65, 75, 90	15, 16
- Exempt gifts	3e	23, 40, 90	15
- Fall in value relief	3j	20, 40, 50, 80	15
- Interaction of CGT and IHT	3	20, 23, 40	17
- Overseas	3f	19, 60, 65, 70, 80	17
- Quick succession relief (QSR)	3j	18, 22, 45, 75	16
- Residence nil rate band (RNRB)	3i	19, 20, 50, 65, 70, 75, 80	16
- Spouse/civil partner transfers	3	18, 21, 55, 90	16
- Transfer of unused bands	3	19, 20, 22, 50, 70	16
- Valuation rules	3	18, 19, 21, 22, 23, 45, 55, 60, 65, 70, 75, 80, 85, 90	16

Topic area	Syllabus learning outcome(s)	Question number(s)	Study Manual chapter(s)
National Insurance			
- Class 1 Primary	5q-t	32, 33, 34, 35, 36, 37, 42, 52, 82	14
- Class 1 Secondary and 1A	5q-t	33, 36, 37, 42, 57, 82, 87, 92	14
- Class 1B	5q-t	31, 34, 62, 72	14
- Class 2 and 4	5q-t	31, 32, 35, 36, 47, 62, 67, 72, 77, 82	14
Stamp duty			
- Administration	2i-k	14, 15, 17, 69, 89	24
- Groups	2i-k	43, 54, 79	24
- Leases	2i-k	11, 14, 16, 17, 59, 84	24
- Non-residential property	2i-k	15, 44, 49, 54, 64, 74, 79, 84, 89	24
- Residential property	2i-k	12, 13, 15, 39, 44, 49	24
- Shares	2i-k	12, 13, 69, 74	24
VAT			
- Calculation	2	13, 15, 39, 49, 74, 89	23
- Capital good scheme	2d	13, 15, 16, 64, 69, 89	23
- Flat rate scheme	2	17, 84	23
- Groups	2b	44, 54, 64, 79	23
- Option to tax (OTT)	2c	11, 13, 15, 16, 49	23
- Overseas	2f	11, 15, 16, 49, 74, 79	23
- Partial exemption	2e	12, 39, 59, 89	23
- Property transactions	2a	11, 13, 44, 49, 59, 79, 89	23
- Services	2g	11, 14, 16, 49, 74	23
- Single vs composite supplies	2h	11, 14, 59	23

Exam

Your exam will consist of:

5 questions	100 marks
Pass mark	55
Exam length	2.5 hours

The ACA student area of our website includes the latest information, guidance and exclusive resources to help you progress through the ACA. Find everything you need, from exam webinars, past exams, marks plans, errata sheets and the syllabus to advice from the examiners at icaew.com/exams.

Question Bank

Ethics and law

1 ABH LLP

You work as a tax assistant for ABH LLP, a firm of ICAEW Chartered Accountants. Your manager has left the following information on your desk:

Anti-money laundering procedures

The senior partner recently attended a seminar on money laundering and she is now concerned that our firm is not compliant with current anti-money laundering regulations. Other than having a vague awareness of money laundering, I am not sure that we have done anything to ensure compliance with the regulations. I have never had enough time to really look into it but now the senior partner is involved we need to take action fast.

Data protection

I know the rules about data protection changed recently but I don't know the detail. Can you tell me which types of businesses will need to comply with the new rules, what to do if there is a data breach and what the potential penalties might be for non – compliance?

Requirements

1.1 Prepare brief notes which set out the anti-money laundering procedures which the firm should implement in order to ensure compliance with anti-money laundering regulations.

(5 marks)

1.2 Explain the types of business which will need to comply with the new data protection rules, what a business must do if it identifies a data breach and outline the penalties which may be due for non – compliance. **(2 marks)**

Total: 7 marks

2 Dirk

2.1 Dirk is an ICAEW Chartered Accountant working as a tax adviser for a firm of accountants. Dirk has created a new tax planning scheme.

The scheme is likely to be particularly valuable to the firm because it can be applied to a particular group of clients without the need to tailor it to their individual needs.

Dirk accepts that his scheme is contrary to what parliament intended when the legislation was enacted. However, he disagrees with HMRC's stated view and therefore does not intend to explain to clients that the scheme is potentially contentious.

Dirk's scheme requires some highly artificial and contrived transactions in order to be implemented.

Requirement

Explain whether Dirk's scheme complies with the Standards for tax planning included in professional conduct in relation to tax (PCRT). Use the Client Specific and Tax Planning Arrangements Standards from PCRT to justify your answer. **(5 marks)**

2.2 Matilda is an ICAEW Chartered Accountant and operates as a sole practitioner in London. Matilda will retire at the end of December 2019. She intends to cancel her professional indemnity insurance as soon as she retires.

Requirement

Explain what action Matilda should take with respect to her professional indemnity insurance in order to comply with the ICAEW's Professional Indemnity Insurance Regulations.

(2 marks)

Total: 7 marks

3 Trent Ltd

You are an ICAEW Chartered Accountant, calculating national insurance contributions (NIC) for a client, Trent Ltd. In the process of performing this work, you discover paperwork which suggests that the directors of Trent Ltd have omitted many of their own taxable benefits from the annual P11D returns. Income tax and NIC have been underpaid as a result. This has happened for several years and is clearly deliberate. Furthermore, paperwork has been falsified to hide the benefits from HMRC.

Requirements

3.1 Explain the legality of tax planning and tax avoidance, and HMRC's distinction between tax planning and tax avoidance.

(2 marks)

3.2 Explain why the actions of Trent Ltd's directors constitute tax evasion; and outline the legal consequences for Trent Ltd's directors if the deliberately underpaid tax is not promptly disclosed and paid to HMRC.

(5 marks)

Total: 7 marks

4 Happy Ltd

You work as a trainee at PC & Co, a firm of ICAEW Chartered Accountants.

Happy Ltd

Sunil is the managing director of Happy Ltd which has been a tax client of PC & Co for a number of years. Sunil has just sent your manager, an ICAEW Chartered Accountant who is in charge of the Happy Ltd tax engagement, the following email:

'I know that you don't normally act for me personally but I'd really appreciate it if you could find time to prepare my wife's USA tax return and disclosures to the US Internal Revenue Service. The current accountants we use have been next to useless. They claim that because my wife has American income her affairs are too complicated for them to deal with.

I have faith in PC & Co and am sure you will be able to deal with it. If so, we'll be able to negotiate a good fee as after all I'm the person who decides how contracts are awarded at Happy Ltd and yours is up for renewal next year.'

Margaret

Margaret is a sole trader who became a client of PC & Co last year. Margaret previously kept paper records and filed a paper self-assessment tax return. However, with your manager's encouragement, she is now willing to start using electronic records and to file online. However, she wants to know how PC & Co will keep her electronic information safe.

Requirements

4.1 Explain the ethical issues your manager should consider before replying to Sunil's email.

(5 marks)

4.2 Identify two precautions advised by 'Professional Conduct in Relation to Taxation' or by HMRC's guidelines, to prevent unauthorised access to client information on computer or online.

(2 marks)

Total: 7 marks

5 Gothi Ltd

You work as a trainee ICAEW Chartered Accountant for Bishop & Co, where you are currently working on the VAT affairs of Gothi Ltd.

Gothi Ltd is a VAT-registered partially exempt trader, and is expecting a VAT control visit within the next couple of weeks.

You have been asked to help with preparation for the control visit. The work has progressed well and it has been suggested by the company's financial controller, Elsa King, that a job may be available for you at Gothi Ltd once you qualify.

At lunchtime you were chatting with Elsa. She told you that the company has failed to take account of the capital goods scheme when the use of a building changed three years ago. The building was originally used to make taxable supplies but since the change has been used to make exempt supplies, and as a consequence the company should have repaid some VAT to HMRC.

Elsa admitted to you that she had completely forgotten about the VAT implications until now. To avoid getting into trouble, it is her intention to tell HMRC at the control visit that the change in use has only just occurred.

Requirements

5.1 Identify which of the fundamental ethical principles are threatened in this situation and explain the category of threat the situation causes. **(2 marks)**

5.2 Explain whether Elsa's intentions amount to tax avoidance or tax evasion, and explain the actions that both Bishop & Co and you should take as a result of Elsa's disclosure. **(5 marks)**

Total: 7 marks

6 Pigeon Ltd

You are a trainee ICAEW Chartered Accountant working as an employee for Pigeon Ltd in its finance department. Pigeon Ltd is an unquoted, UK-based trading company.

You identified errors in the corporation tax return for the year ended 31 December 2017 which was filed on 31 December 2018. At your weekly progress meeting with your manager, you raised the errors as an issue. Your manager is also an ICAEW Chartered Accountant.

In the meeting your manager made it clear that her main concern was that if the errors were disclosed she would lose her job. She asked you not to discuss the errors with anyone else, explaining that the errors had caused only a small underpayment of tax overall. She also promised you that she would consider you for promotion if you agreed to say nothing about this. However, if you did disclose the errors she said she would ensure that it had long-term implications for your career.

Requirements

6.1 In relation to your manager's behaviour towards you at the meeting, identify which type of threat to the fundamental ethical principles arises here and explain which **three** of the five fundamental ethical principles are most threatened. **(4 marks)**

6.2 Discuss whether non-disclosure of the errors amounts to tax evasion. **(2 marks)**

6.3 Assuming it is tax evasion, explain the potential implications for you under the anti-money laundering regulations if you fail to disclose the errors. **(1 mark)**

Total: 7 marks

7 Lucy

Lucy Cavendish was appointed as finance director of Sunnyday Ltd two years ago, shortly after qualifying as a professional accountant. She received a substantial pay increase on her appointment. She was not a suitable candidate for the post, but her application form exaggerated her experience.

Lucy has recently resigned. This followed her disclosure to the board of directors of errors in the corporation tax return for the year ended 31 March 2018 that she had prepared, and the refusal by Sunnyday Ltd's bank to process payment of the corporation tax liability, due to insufficient available funds.

It was Lucy's sole responsibility to prepare the corporation tax return and arrange payment of the tax. The issues which arose were due to Lucy's lack of understanding of some technical issues and her inexperience rather than any dishonesty on her part. The corporation tax errors came to light when preparing for a meeting with the company's bankers.

The board of Sunnyday Ltd has now engaged Darwin LLP, a firm of ICAEW Chartered Accountants, to prepare corporation tax returns in future. The directors are keen to understand the safeguards in place to protect the company in case of any future problems with Darwin LLP's work.

Requirements

7.1 Identify the threats to fundamental principles that Lucy Cavendish faced on her appointment and in her role as finance director and explain which fundamental principles were threatened. **(5 marks)**

7.2 State the safeguards available to reassure clients in relation to the work of ICAEW Chartered Accountants. **(2 marks)**

Total: 7 marks

8 Geiger LLP

You work for Geiger LLP, a firm of ICAEW Chartered Accountants, which has been engaged by Mallory Ltd for many years to perform accounting and corporation tax work. Geiger LLP has also just agreed to perform all payroll functions for Mallory Ltd. In your review of Mallory Ltd's current payroll practices you have discovered that, on the instruction of the managing director, the company has recently started incorrectly paying the directors as consultants rather than employees. The amounts paid meet the definition of employment income. This has resulted in PAYE being understated. Mallory Ltd is a valuable client of Geiger LLP, and the engagement partner is a close friend of the managing director of Mallory Ltd.

Requirements

8.1 Explain the types of threat to fundamental ethical principles faced by Geiger LLP and identify which of the fundamental ethical principles are most threatened. **(3 marks)**

8.2 State the actions to be taken by Geiger LLP in relation to the issue you have discovered. **(4 marks)**

Total: 7 marks

9 Pear Ltd

You work as a trainee ICAEW Chartered Accountant for SM & Co, where you are currently working on the tax affairs of Pear Ltd.

You have just been approached by one of Pear Ltd's finance staff. He tells you that the company recently received a VAT refund of £63,000 from HMRC. He reported this immediately to the finance director, who told him to forget about it. He is concerned because Pear Ltd was not due any refund of VAT.

Requirements

9.1 Identify actions that your firm should take in line with the guidance given in 'Professional Conduct in Relation to Taxation'. **(3 marks)**

9.2 Assuming the refund is not repaid to HMRC, explain whether anti-money laundering legislation applies and identify any potential further steps that may be necessary for you and SM & Co to take in order to comply with that legislation. **(2 marks)**

9.3 Identify two defences against a charge of failure to report a suspicion of money laundering. **(2 marks)**

Total: 7 marks

10 PPA

You work as a trainee for PPA & Co, a firm of ICAEW Chartered Accountants. You have been asked to review part of a new client's file:

'I work for X plc as a director. A few years ago X plc set up a new payment scheme for the members of the senior leadership team. The scheme involves a complicated series of transactions designed to reduce our tax bills. Basically, the senior team are paid 75% less than we were previously via PAYE. We then receive various non-UK loans in Romania's currency, the lei, which give rise to non-taxable gains. Initially I was a bit worried about the whole non-taxable gains thing. However, the overall effect in cash terms for me is that I have reduced my liability to income tax and NIC by at least £100,000 pa for the past 10 years. I was assured that each step in the scheme is in itself legal, so I'm happy that my tax returns have been completed accurately.'

Requirements

10.1 Explain the difference between tax evasion and tax avoidance. **(2 marks)**

10.2 Explain whether the legality of each step in such a 'tax avoidance' scheme would be sufficient for the scheme to be held as valid by the courts. **(2 marks)**

10.3 If the scheme were held to be tax evasion, outline what the legal consequences for both you and your client would be if the underpaid tax were not promptly disclosed and paid to HMRC. **(3 marks)**

Total: 7 marks

Indirect taxes

11 Waxwell Ltd

You are working on secondment in your firm's indirect tax department. Your manager has asked you to deal with several client queries and has provided the following information. All figures below are shown exclusive of any VAT.

- Waxwell Ltd sells standard-rated goods. It has undertaken the following transactions in the quarter ended 31 December 2018:

Sales of goods to	£
UK customers	68,500
Private individuals in Italy	17,450

Purchases of	£
Legal services from a company resident in India	2,500
Standard-rated goods	25,000
Zero-rated goods	8,000

- Shaker Airways operates transatlantic flights (zero-rated supply). Each customer's ticket includes entitlement to in-flight catering (standard-rated supply). Shaker Airways is not contractually obliged to provide the in-flight catering, and no refund is issued for customers declining the in-flight catering.

- Badir Ltd makes wholly standard-rated supplies. Badir Ltd recently purchased a commercial building from an unconnected company, Polly Parrot Ltd, for £450,000. Polly Parrot Ltd had opted to tax the building in January 2004. No VAT was accounted for on the sale of the building and no mention of VAT was made in the sale and purchase agreement.

- Zeeson Bank Ltd was granted a six-year lease of a new office building on 1 December 2018. Zeeson Bank Ltd paid a premium of £88,888. The annual rental is £27,000.

All companies are UK resident and are registered for VAT where possible.

Requirements

11.1 Calculate Waxwell Ltd's VAT liability for the quarter ended 31 December 2018. Clearly show your treatment of each item. **(3 marks)**

11.2 Explain how Shaker Airways should calculate the VAT due on the sale of each ticket for a transatlantic flight. **(3 marks)**

11.3 Explain the VAT implications of the sale of the building by Polly Parrot Ltd. **(4 marks)**

11.4 Explain, with supporting calculations, the stamp duty land tax implications for Zeeson Bank Ltd in respect of the office building. **(3 marks)**

Total: 13 marks

12 Arthur

12.1 Arthur is a partially exempt VAT registered trader and sells only to UK customers. During the year ended 31 May 2019 he made the following supplies:

	£
Standard-rated taxable supplies (excluding VAT)	48,000
Exempt supplies	62,000
	110,000

Arthur's input tax for the year is:

	£
Wholly attributable to taxable supplies	16,000
Wholly attributable to exempt supplies	25,000
Non-attributable	12,450
	53,450

In addition to the above, during the year ended 31 May 2019 Arthur:

- purchased a company car for an employee for £10,500
- purchased a van for £6,000 for use only in the VAT-exempt part of the business
- sold plant for £10,000 which had been used in the taxable part of the business

Arthur was *de minimis* in the partial exemption year ending 31 May 2018. Therefore, he has been using the annual partial exemption test and during the year ended 31 May 2019 Arthur recovered all of his input tax suffered. Arthur has correctly calculated that he does not pass Simplified Test One for the year ended 31 May 2019.

All figures above are exclusive of any VAT.

Requirement

For the partial exemption year ended 31 May 2019, determine whether Arthur is *de minimis;* and calculate the amount of input tax payable to HMRC as a result of the annual adjustment.

(10 marks)

12.2 As part of his divorce settlement, Yami received 5,000 shares in XBit plc on 31 January 2019, when they were worth £15,000. A stock transfer form was completed. Yami also purchased 200 shares in Beep plc on 1 February 2019 for £2,200 via the CREST system.

Yami purchased a residential apartment for £210,000 on 23 March 2019, with the intention of renting it out. Yami already owns a house in which he lives.

Requirement

Calculate, with brief explanations, the stamp tax(es) payable by Yami in respect of these transactions. **(3 marks)**

Total: 13 marks

13 Salmon Ltd

The following four unrelated clients are UK resident. All the companies are VAT-registered traders making wholly standard-rated supplies. All figures below are exclusive of any VAT.

13.1 Salmon Ltd

On 1 January 2012 Salmon Ltd purchased a newly constructed commercial building for £1 million for use in its trade and incurred VAT on the purchase of £175,000. On 1 January 2019 it disposed of the building to an unconnected company for £2.5 million. Salmon Ltd has a VAT year end of 31 March and has not opted to tax the building.

Requirement

Calculate the amount of VAT payable to HMRC by Salmon Ltd in respect of its disposal of the property. **(3 marks)**

13.2 Kilmarnock Ltd

Kilmarnock Ltd is in the process of purchasing a new commercial building on which it will pay input tax of £1.5 million. Kilmarnock Ltd intended to use the building for trade purposes, however it now plans to rent it out as soon as the purchase is completed. Kilmarnock Ltd is considering whether to opt to tax the building.

Requirement

Explain the VAT implications if Kilmarnock Ltd opts to tax the building. **(4 marks)**

13.3 Trout Ltd

Trout Ltd has undertaken the following transactions in the quarter ended 31 December 2018:

Sales of standard-rated goods to:	£
UK customers	160,000
VAT-registered customers in Germany	35,000
Private individuals in France	45,000

UK purchases of standard-rated supplies	£
Expenses incurred related to the UK business	50,000
Expenses incurred related to the business in other EU countries	25,000
Car purchased for employee use with 90% business use	15,000
Machinery eligible for capital allowances	40,000

Requirement

Calculate Trout Ltd's VAT liability for the quarter ended 31 December 2018, showing your treatment of each item. **(3 marks)**

13.4 Yousef

Yousef purchased 1,000 shares in SBP plc on 1 January 2019 for £55,000 via the CREST system.

Yousef had owned a residential dwelling jointly with his brother, Salim, for a number of years. On 1 February 2019 Salim gifted his share of the dwelling to Yousef. Salim's 50% share in the dwelling was valued at £400,000 at the date of the gift. In return, Yousef took over Salim's £300,000 mortgage in addition to his own.

Requirement

Calculate Yousef's liability to stamp taxes for 2018/19. **(3 marks)**

Total: 13 marks

14 Roger

14.1 Roger operates an unincorporated business, offering boat cruises on the River Thames. He was not initially required to register for VAT but has decided to voluntarily register for VAT from 1 October 2019.

He is concerned that he has suffered significant input VAT on expenses incurred before his VAT registration. He would like to know whether he can recover this.

The costs incurred before registration include the following:

		£
May 2018	Legal advice on employment matters	1,200
June 2018	Purchase of a computer for 100% business use	2,400
July 2019	Entertaining suppliers	500

On his River Thames boat cruises, Roger provides a buffet for all customers at no extra cost. The customer pays one inclusive price irrespective of whether they eat any of the buffet food. Roger is not sure how he will treat his cruises for VAT purposes as he is aware that boat cruises in their own right are zero-rated supplies but the provision of a buffet is a standard-rated supply.

Requirements

(a) Explain whether Roger can recover the input VAT suffered prior to his registration on the three particular items detailed above. Assume that all amounts are inclusive of VAT.

(3 marks)

(b) Explain the **two** possible VAT treatments of the cruises offered by Roger, and state which treatment is likely to apply.

(6 marks)

14.2 On 1 July 2018 Thunder Ltd took out a 15-year lease on new manufacturing premises, paying a lease premium of £29,000 and annual rent of £20,000.

The land transaction form will be submitted and stamp duty land tax paid by the end of September 2019.

Requirement

Calculate the stamp duty land tax payable by Thunder Ltd on the new manufacturing premises and the maximum penalty for late filing of the land transaction form. **(4 marks)**

Total: 13 marks

15 Towers Ltd

15.1 Towers Ltd is a VAT-registered UK trading company making standard-rated supplies.

In August 2018 Towers Ltd purchased Roscoe House, a newly constructed freehold factory, for use in its trade for £2.6 million. This amount is stated exclusive of VAT.

Towers Ltd lost a large contract recently, but continues to manufacture goods that are standard-rated supplies. It no longer needs to utilise all of the factory space in Roscoe House.

The company intends to let 15% of the factory to a third party from 1 April 2020, for a rent of £50,000 pa. Towers Ltd has not opted to tax Roscoe House, and has a VAT year to 31 March.

Requirements

(a) Calculate the stamp duty land tax paid on the purchase of Roscoe House. **(2 marks)**

(b) Explain the VAT implications for Towers Ltd of letting out part of the factory, and how these would differ if Towers Ltd had opted to tax the factory. **(4 marks)**

15.2 Bactrian Ltd is registered for VAT and produces only standard-rated goods. In order to expand its business, the company has begun to sell its goods outside of the UK.

Figures for the quarter ended 28 February 2019 are as follows:

	£
Sales	
Supplies in the UK	39,500
Supplies to non-trading customers in other EU countries	12,900
Purchases	
Materials purchased in the UK	8,100
Computer advice from a non-EU supplier	190
Car purchased in the UK and used 80% for business purposes	6,280
Motor expenses including fuel costing £600 for employee Mary	1,750

All the above figures exclude any VAT.

Half of Mary's mileage was for work-related travel. The relevant VAT-inclusive fuel scale rate for the quarter is £384.

Requirement

Calculate the VAT payable by Bactrian Ltd for the quarter ended 28 February 2019, clearly showing your treatment of each of the above figures. **(5 marks)**

15.3 On 10 January 2019 Bilal sold land that he had held for investment purposes to his sister Priya for £120,000 when it was worth £185,000.

As the consideration was only £120,000, Bilal and Priya did nothing in respect of stamp duty land tax (SDLT) on the sale in January 2019. However, they have recently been told by a friend that HMRC should have been informed.

Requirement

Explain the consequences for SDLT administration of the land sale in January 2019. You should assume it is currently December 2019. **(2 marks)**

Total: 13 marks

16 Granate Ltd

16.1 For several years Granate Ltd, a VAT-registered UK trading company, has been producing and selling bespoke wooden products in England. This is a standard-rated supply.

At a recent trade fair, potential customers from overseas showed significant interest in Granate Ltd's products. The company now plans to supply its goods to business customers and private individuals elsewhere within the EU and in other parts of the world.

Granate Ltd recently made use of a German law firm based in Berlin to undertake some legal work. The law firm has sent Granate Ltd an invoice for the sterling equivalent of £20,000. No VAT has been charged even though the supply is standard rated both in the UK and in Germany.

All amounts are stated exclusive of VAT where appropriate.

Ben Jamieson, the finance director, is unsure how to treat these issues for tax purposes.

Requirements

(a) Explain the VAT treatment of Granate Ltd's planned supplies outside the UK. Differentiate between business and non-business customers within and outside the EU and identify any information that will need to be obtained by Granate Ltd for VAT purposes. **(4 marks)**

(b) Calculate the amount(s) to be included, if any, in Granate Ltd's VAT return in respect of the legal services supplied. **(2 marks)**

16.2 In order to raise cash, Granate Ltd has decided to dispose of a freehold factory to an unconnected third party, Marble Ltd, for £2,500,000 on 31 March 2019. Granate Ltd purchased the factory new for £750,000 on 1 April 2010. Marble Ltd will immediately lease the factory back to Granate Ltd on a 25-year lease. The annual rental will be £325,000 and there will be a lease premium of £400,000. Granate Ltd might opt to tax the factory before its disposal. Both Granate Ltd and Marble Ltd have a VAT year to 31 March.

All amounts are stated exclusive of VAT where appropriate and Ben is also unsure how to treat these issues.

(a) Explain, with supporting calculations, the implications of the capital goods scheme on the disposal of the freehold factory by Granate Ltd. **(4 marks)**

(b) Calculate the SDLT payable on the acquisition of the lease by Granate Ltd, assuming no option to tax has been exercised. **(3 marks)**

Total: 13 marks

17 Faizha and Tehira

17.1 Faizha is a VAT-registered sole trader making only standard-rated supplies. Her business category for flat rate purposes is financial services which has a flat rate percentage of 13.5%.

For the quarter ended 31 August 2019 Faizha will have sales of £25,000. So far, Faizha has spent £300 on the purchase of standard-rated goods for the quarter.

Faizha is considering purchasing a further £500 of standard-rated goods for use in her business before 31 August 2019.

All figures are stated exclusive of VAT.

Requirement

Calculate Faizha's net VAT surplus or deficit for the quarter ended 31 August 2019 assuming her purchases for the quarter:

- remain at £300
- increase to a total of £800. **(6 marks)**

17.2 On 1 January 2019 Tehira granted Jensen a 25 year lease of a commercial property located in Manchester for a premium of £140,000 plus annual rent of £8,000.

Tehira had opted to tax the property.

Jensen paid the stamp duty land tax (SDLT) due and filed his land transaction form on 1 April 2019.

Requirements

Calculate the amount of interest and maximum penalties payable by Jensen in relation to the SDLT which was paid and the land transaction form that was filed on 1 April 2019. Assume the interest rate on overdue SDLT is 3%. **(7 marks)**

Total: 13 marks

CGT and IHT

18 Finn

18.1 Finn was UK resident and domiciled at the date of his death on 6 January 2019. Finn's wife, Marian, is UK resident but non-UK domiciled and has made no election to become UK domiciled. At his death Finn's estate comprised:

- his home in London worth £1,600,000.

- 5,000 shares (0.1% holding) in Sitron plc, a UK quoted company. On 6 January 2019 the shares were quoted at 230 - 234p with marked bargains of 224p, 226p and 240p.

- a painting worth £500,000. This was part of the estate inherited from his mother when she died in June 2017. The value of her chargeable estate on death was £1.2 million and she left the entire estate to Finn. She had made no previous lifetime transfers.

- shares in Bulda Ltd, an unquoted investment company worth £115,000.

- cash and personal chattels of £180,000.

At his death Finn had credit card debts totalling £2,500 and his funeral costs amounted to £7,400. He had income tax payable for 2018/19 of £3,816. Finn left his home in London to his wife Marian and the remainder of his estate to his brother Olaf.

Finn's only previous lifetime transfers were:

- a gross chargeable transfer of £250,000 in January 2010.

- a gift of an investment property worth £285,000 to a new discretionary trust in October 2016. The trustees agreed to pay any tax due.

Requirement

Calculate the inheritance tax payable as a result of Finn's death. **(15 marks)**

18.2 Chris is domiciled in Utopia but has been resident in the UK for four years. He is a higher rate taxpayer. He made several capital disposals during 2018/19, as set out below:

- May 2018 - sale of a painting, located in the UK, for £6,600

  Chris's wife had given the painting to Chris in 2013 when it was worth £6,200. She had originally purchased it for £4,000 in 2004.

- August 2018 - sale of 10,000 shares in Weselton plc for £41,600

  Weselton plc is listed on the London Stock Exchange and Chris bought 9,000 shares in the company for £17,000 in June 2013. In August 2015 he took up his full entitlement of a 1 for 3 rights issue at £2.80 per share.

- February 2019 - sale of a Utopian commercial investment property for £425,000

  Chris purchased the property for £290,000 on 31 March 2003 (all prices quoted are sterling equivalents). Chris has kept all of the proceeds of the sale in his Utopian savings account. The Utopian tax paid on this disposal was £24,800.

Requirement

Calculate the capital gains tax payable by Chris for 2018/19, under each of the following alternative assumptions:

- He does **not** make a remittance basis claim (No RB); or
- He does make a remittance basis claim (RB). **(10 marks)**

Total: 25 marks

19 Kate

19.1 Kate died on 1 December 2018. Kate was UK resident and domiciled and owned the following assets at the date of her death:

- A villa in Spain with a sterling equivalent value of £90,000. Kate's personal representatives incurred additional costs in administering the foreign property of £6,450. Spanish death taxes of £11,250 had been paid.

- A house in London worth £1 million.

- Farmland in South West England farmed by a tenant, and worth £400,000 with an agricultural value of £275,000. Kate purchased in the land on 1 January 2014, and the tenant moved in immediately.

- 40,000 shares in TC plc, an investment company. On 1 December 2018 the shares were quoted at 152-178p with marked bargains of 171p, 175p and 176p.

- 12,000 shares in Pebbles Ltd, an unquoted trading company. Kate had bought the shares in January 2000 and on 1 December 2018 they were worth £125,000.

Kate bequeathed 10,000 of her shares in TC plc to Oxfam, a registered charity, and left the rest of her estate to her children.

At the time of her death Kate owed her local casino £6,000 in relation to gaming. Kate's funeral cost £8,500.

Kate's husband, Tom, died in January 2008 with a death estate valued at £600,000. Tom left £100,000 to his children and the rest of his estate to Kate. The nil rate band in 2007/08 was £300,000.

Requirements

Calculate the inheritance tax payable as a result of Kate's death, explaining whether reliefs are available in respect of the farmland. State the due date for payment of the IHT if interest is to be avoided and who is liable. **(16 marks)**

19.2 Isla has made the following capital disposals in 2018/19:

- Isla realised a chargeable gain of £40,000 in July 2018 on the disposal of a commercial investment property.

- Isla purchased five acres of land in January 2001 for £65,000 and sold two acres at an auction in January 2019 for £53,000 before auctioneer's fees of 10%. Isla had installed drainage to the land in January 2011 for £12,000. At the date of disposal the value of the remaining three acres was estimated at £60,000.

- Isla sold a vintage motor car for £25,000 in February 2019. It cost £12,000 in July 2004.

- Isla sold an antique vase for £9,000 in March 2019, incurring costs of disposal of £400. The vase cost £4,000 in January 2002.

Isla has taxable income in 2018/19 of £25,000.

Requirement

Calculate Isla's capital gains tax liability for 2018/19. **(9 marks)**

Total: 25 marks

20 John Robinson

20.1 John Robinson died on 1 January 2019. During his lifetime he had made three disposals:

(1) On 1 May 2008 John put assets into The Robinson Family Trust, with his daughter Emma, then 20 years old, as beneficiary. The gross chargeable transfer was £300,000.

(2) On 1 December 2011 John put further assets worth £266,000 into the trust.

(3) On 8 August 2018 John gave a painting worth £100,000 to Emma. John had bought this in July 2006 for £7,500. Emma sold the painting on 31 December 2018 for £95,000.

At John's death his estate comprised:

- his home in London worth £980,000

- 10,000 shares worth £50,000 in Rainy Ltd, an unquoted trading company, which John had acquired in August 2009

- cash and personal chattels of £420,000

- jewellery worth £500,000

John left his entire estate to his daughter Emma, with the exception of the jewellery, which was bequeathed to a UK-registered charity.

At his death John had paid his outstanding income tax for 2018/19 by self-assessment and was a higher-rate taxpayer.

John's wife died in 2003 and had used her nil rate band in full.

Requirement

Calculate the inheritance tax payable as a result of John's death. **(15 marks)**

20.2 During 2018/19, Simon made capital disposals as follows:

Newnham Cottage

Newnham Cottage was sold for £250,000 on 1 June 2018. Simon bought the cottage in December 2009 for £180,000.

The cottage was used as follows:

Dates	Months	Use of cottage
1 December 2011–31 May 2012	6	Occupied as Simon's home
1 June 2012–28 February 2013	9	Empty while Simon studied abroad
1 March 2013–31 May 2013	3	Occupied as Simon's home
1 June 2013–1 June 2018	60	Let to paying tenants while Simon shared another house with a friend
	78	

Antique table

Simon sold an antique table on 10 December 2018 for £7,200. The table had cost Simon £4,300 in July 2014.

Trinity Traders

On 10 January 2019 Simon sold his sole trade business, Trinity Traders for £600,000. He had set the business up in 2000 for £100,000 which he had inherited from his grandmother.

Requirement

Calculate the capital gains tax payable by Simon for 2018/19. **(10 marks)**

Total: 25 marks

21 John and Elizabeth

21.1 John disposed of a number of assets during 2018/19:

Factory – on 10 January 2019 John sold a factory that he had used in his business to his son Marcus for £185,000 when it was worth £205,000. The factory had cost John £100,000 on 31 March 1992.

Wilkes Ltd – on 3 February 2019: a gift of 6,500 shares in Wilkes Ltd, an unquoted trading company, to his son Jack. John subscribed for his shares at par in May 1993, but is not employed by the company. Wilkes Ltd has an issued share capital of 10,000 £1 ordinary shares which, just before the gift, were held as shown below.

	No. of shares
John	7,500
Ruby (John's wife)	2,000
Jack (John's son)	500
	10,000

The values of the shareholdings in Wilkes Ltd are as follows:

	Price per share £
Up to 25%	10
26%–50%	12
51%–74%	25
75%–100%	30

At 3 February 2019, Wilkes Ltd has the following assets:

	Market value £
Storage unit (Note)	40,000
Office building	150,000
Cars	25,000
Plant (Note)	60,000
Debtors	10,000
Cash	15,000

Notes

1 The storage unit was held as an investment but all other assets were used in the trade of Wilkes Ltd.

2 Each item of plant was worth more than cost and more than £6,000.

3 Wilkes Ltd had total net assets of £265,000 on 3 February 2019.

Painting – John bought a set of two paintings for £3,100 in February 1995. During March 2019 he sold one of the paintings to his friend Ernest for £4,200, when the other painting was valued at £4,500. John sold the second painting to Ernest's wife Frances in July 2019 for £5,000.

John was a higher rate taxpayer in 2018/19.

Requirement

Calculate John's capital gains tax payable for 2018/19, showing the amount(s) of any available reliefs and state the due date for payment. **(11 marks)**

21.2 Elizabeth died in December 2018. Elizabeth had always been UK domiciled. Her husband, Ricardo, is not UK-domiciled and has decided not to make an election to be treated as such. During her life, Elizabeth made a number of substantial gifts, as detailed below:

10 August 2008

£254,000 gross chargeable transfer for the benefit of her nephews.

19 May 2012

80,000 shares in Turing plc, a UK quoted company into a discretionary trust for the benefit of her sister. These shares represented a 1% shareholding. On 19 May 2012 the shares were quoted at 165p–173p, with marked bargains of 166p, 168p and 172p. The trustees agreed to pay any lifetime tax due.

10 June 2016

200 shares in Sturgeon Ltd, a UK unquoted investment company to her brother, William. Before the gift the shareholdings in Sturgeon Ltd were as follows:

Shareholder	Percentage holding	No. of shares
Elizabeth	45%	900
Ricardo	30%	600
William	25%	500
		2,000

The values of shareholdings in Sturgeon Ltd on 10 June 2016 were:

	Price per share £
Up to 25%	50
26–50%	60
51–74%	125
75–90%	150
91–100%	250

Elizabeth's total assets on her death, including the remaining Sturgeon Ltd shares are valued at £1.4 million. She also has allowable debts and funeral expenses of £100,000. She left her entire estate to her husband, Ricardo.

Requirement

Calculate the inheritance tax payable as a result of Elizabeth's death, showing the amount of any exemptions. **(14 marks)**

Total: 25 marks

22 Mary-Jane

22.1 Mary-Jane Parker died on 4 April 2019. Mary-Jane was domiciled in the UK and had lived in England. Mary-Jane's entire estate was left to her sister Gwen and comprised the following:

- Her home in London worth £550,000.

- 10,000 shares in Octo plc, a UK quoted company with 500,000 issued shares. On 4 April 2019 the shares were quoted at 180-188p with marked bargains of 179p, 182p and 187p.

- Cash and personal chattels of £180,000.

Mary-Jane had outstanding debts at the date of her death totalling £23,350. These were made up of her 2018/19 income tax liability of £9,250 and gaming debts of £14,100.

Mary-Jane's only lifetime transfer was a gift of £652,000 in cash to a discretionary trust set up in June 2017 for the benefit of her niece and nephew.

Mary-Jane received some antique furniture from her father-in-law, Jonah, on his death in February 2017. The antique furniture was worth £35,000. Jonah's chargeable death estate was worth £470,000, and he left the remainder of the estate to his daughter.

Mary-Jane's husband Ben, who was also domiciled in the UK, died in July 2008 leaving his entire estate to his daughter. Ben's estate was worth £234,000.

Neither Ben nor Jonah made any lifetime transfers or charitable bequests.

Requirement

Calculate the inheritance tax payable as a result of Mary-Jane's death. **(15 marks)**

22.2 Harry made disposals as follows during 2018/19:

- **Aranas Ltd shares**

  On 14 June 2018, Harry sold his 10% holding of shares in Aranas Ltd, an unquoted trading company, to his sister Stacy for £60,000. The shares had a market value at that time of £100,000.

  Harry had originally purchased the shares for £12,000. Harry had owned the shares for five years and had worked full-time for Aranas Ltd for 10 years.

- **Web Towers**

  On 15 July 2018 Harry made a gift of a commercial property worth £454,700 to a discretionary trust. The trustees will pay any inheritance tax due. Harry had purchased the property for £420,600 in May 2000 and had rented it out at a commercial rent from that date to Booth plc.

- **Cherry Tree House**

  Harry sold his home, Cherry Tree House, in December 2018 for £12,450,000. Harry originally purchased the house in December 1998 for £160,000. Harry has lived in the house since its acquisition except for a four-year period from December 2006 when he took time off work to travel, leaving the house empty.

Harry has taxable income for 2018/19 of £12,000 and has brought forward capital losses of £15,352 from previous years. Harry is domiciled in the UK, living in England.

Requirement

Calculate the capital gains tax payable by Harry for 2018/19. Clearly show the amount(s) of any relief(s) available. State the actions necessary to effect any claims. **(10 marks)**

Total: 25 marks

23 Jeff

23.1 During 2018/19 Jeff made the following disposals:

- Gift of a painting worth £100,000 to the Red Cross, a registered charity, on 1 July 2018. Jeff bought the painting for £60,000 in July 2008.

- Sale of an antique necklace worth £212,000 to his daughter for £76,500 on 1 August 2018. Jeff inherited the necklace from his mother on her death in July 2000 when it was valued for probate purposes at £145,000. His mother originally paid £12,000 for the necklace in 1985.

- Gift of 25,000 £1 ordinary shares in Sparks Ltd, an unquoted investment company, to the Rainy Discretionary Trust on 1 September 2018. Jeff subscribed for the shares at their par value of £1 per share in October 2000. Before this gift, the shares in Sparks Ltd were held as follows:

	No. of shares
Margot (who is Jeff's wife)	50,000
Jeff	25,000
Matilda (who is Jeff and Margot's daughter)	12,500
Bertie (who is Jeff and Margot's son)	12,500
	100,000

The values of the shareholdings in Sparks Ltd as at 1 September 2018 were as follows:

	Price per share £
1%–24%	2
25%–50%	3
51%–74%	5
75%	8
76%–100%	9

- Gift of 10,000 shares in Harps plc to the Sunshine Discretionary Trust on 31 December 2018. On 31 December 2018 Harps plc shares were quoted at 1,031p–1,043p with marked bargains of 1,035p, 1,040p and 1,042p. Jeff paid £1.91 per share in January 1991.

Jeff made a lifetime transfer in October 2011 when he gifted £194,000 in cash to a discretionary trust. His only previous lifetime transfer was in January 2005 when he made a gift with a gross chargeable transfer value of £177,000.

Jeff has taxable income for 2018/19 of £8,000.

Requirements

(a) Calculate Jeff's capital gains tax liability for 2018/19. **(7 marks)**

(b) Calculate the amount of lifetime inheritance tax, if any, arising on each disposal in 2018/19. **(11 marks)**

23.2 In April 2018 Alexandra gave her daughter, Isabelle, a building worth £5 million. The building has been used as the business premises of Cello Ltd since Alexandra purchased it in January 2002. Alexandra owns 100% of the shares in Cello Ltd, an unquoted trading company.

Alexandra is unwell and is not expected to live for more than five years.

Alexandra intends to keep the shares in Cello Ltd until her death.

Isabelle is considering selling the building as she wants to buy a house.

Requirement

Briefly explain the capital gains tax and inheritance tax implications of Alexandra gifting the building to Isabelle. You should explain any implications arising at the date of the gift and on Alexandra's subsequent death assuming she were to die on 1 April 2023. Calculations are not required. **(7 marks)**

Total: 25 marks

Corporation tax

24 Coe Ltd

24.1 Ovett Ltd is a UK resident, wholly owned trading subsidiary of Coe Ltd, which also owns 75% of Cram Ltd.

Ovett Ltd's adjusted trading profit before deduction of capital allowances for the year ended 31 March 2019 is £579,674. However, due to an error with the computer accounting system, the four items below were ignored in the preparation of the financial statements. Therefore any tax-allowable element of the following four items will need to be deducted, along with capital allowances, in arriving at the final tax-adjusted trading profit.

- Operating lease costs of £8,100 for a car used by the sales director. The car has a list price of £23,000 and CO_2 emissions of 85g/km. The car is used 75% of the time for business purposes. The lease was taken out on 1 May 2018.

- 20 free samples given to Ovett Ltd's biggest customer. The samples have a retail value of £12 each and cost £6 per item to manufacture.

- A trade-related patent royalty of £20,000. The royalty was paid to another UK company without any deduction of tax.

Ovett Ltd's capital allowances for the year ended 31 March 2019 comprise an annual investment allowance of £190,000 and writing-down allowances of £318,150 in respect of plant and machinery. All capital purchases were made in November 2018.

On 1 May 2018, Ovett Ltd sold a warehouse for £551,688 which it had purchased for trade purposes on 1 May 1999 for a total cost of £307,000. Since purchase, the property had been rented out to an unconnected company for an annual rent of £78,000, payable quarterly in advance.

At 1 April 2018, Ovett Ltd had a capital loss brought forward of £4,304. No group relief is claimed by Ovett Ltd.

Requirement

Calculate the corporation tax due from Ovett Ltd for the year ended 31 March 2019 and state the due date for payment of tax. **(7 marks)**

Note: Assume an RPI of 278.1 for December 2017 and 280.3 for May 2018. Ignore VAT and national insurance.

24.2 Jackie is the new financial controller of Coe Ltd. She has prepared a draft computation of taxable total profits for Coe Ltd for the year ended 31 March 2019.

Jackie is unsure of the treatment of some items. Her draft computation is as follows:

	Notes	£	£
Draft adjusted trading profits			400,190
Add:			
Interest on a loan to purchase a new lorry	1	930	
Interest on a loan to purchase a 2% shareholding in an unconnected company		790	
			1,720

	Notes	£	£
Less:			
Bank interest receivable	2		(2,845)
Capital allowances:			
Annual investment allowance on new lorry	1		(20,000)
WDA on main pool	3		(3,000)
Research and development	4		(40,000)
Tax-adjusted trading profit			336,065
Add: Dividend received from Cram Ltd			10,000
Less: Group relief from Cram Ltd			(336,065)
Taxable total profits			10,000

Notes:

1   The lorry cost £20,000 on 1 November 2018. Jackie made no deduction for the lorry in arriving at the draft adjusted trading profits of £400,190.

2   The figure of £400,190 includes the bank interest receivable of £2,845.

3   The tax written down value on the main pool at 1 April 2018 was £7,000.

4   £40,000 was spent in the year on qualifying research and development. Coe Ltd is classed as a small or medium sized enterprise for research and development purposes. No deduction for this cost has been made in arriving at the figure of £400,190.

5   Cram Ltd was purchased by Coe Ltd on 1 January 2015 and made a trading loss of £430,600 for the year ended 31 March 2019. It was agreed that the maximum possible loss should be surrendered by Cram Ltd to Coe Ltd.

Requirement

Using the information above and in part 24.1, redraft the corporation tax computation for Coe Ltd for the year ended 31 March 2019, correcting any errors you identify.   **(8 marks)**

Note: Ignore VAT.

Total: 15 marks

25 Clock Ltd

25.1 Clock Ltd was incorporated on 1 January 2016, deposited £500,000 in an interest bearing bank account on 1 February 2016 and commenced trading on 1 April 2016.

Clock Ltd prepared its first set of accounts for the 15 months ended 31 March 2017 and its second set of accounts for the nine months ended 31 December 2017.

In May 2017, Clock Ltd received notices from HMRC requiring it to file corporation tax returns for the periods ending in the 15 months to 31 March 2017. It is now June 2019 and the company has not yet filed any corporation tax returns or made any payments of corporation tax.

Requirements

(a)   In relation to corporation tax, state the dates of Clock Ltd's accounting periods falling between 1 January 2016 and 31 December 2017.   **(2 marks)**

(b)   In relation to the 15-month period of account ended 31 March 2017, state the dates by which Clock Ltd should have filed its corporation tax returns and explain what penalties are due in relation to their late filing.   **(3 marks)**

25.2 Clock Ltd is a trading company. Clock Ltd's draft tax-adjusted trading profits after
✓ deducting capital allowances for the year ended 31 December 2018 are £1,475,823. In
arriving at this figure Clock Ltd has adjusted the accounting profit in accordance with tax
rules by removing all non-trade items and adding back all disallowable expenditure.

However, further adjustments may be required in relation to the following two items:

- **Research and development expenditure**

  Clock Ltd has incurred the following costs since it began a qualifying research and
  development (R&D) project in April 2018:

	£
Staff directly engaged in R&D expenditure	99,500
Consumables	19,450
	118,950

  The £118,950 above has been deducted in arriving at the draft tax-adjusted trading
  profit of £1,475,823. Clock Ltd also spent £66,053 on the construction of a new
  laboratory (excluding land). Clock Ltd qualifies as a SME for R&D purposes.

- **Staff costs**

  On 1 December 2018, Clock Ltd finally paid its senior management bonus relating to
  the nine months ended 31 December 2017. The total bonus paid was £213,000
  (including employer NIC of £25,829).

  For accounting purposes, the bonus was treated as an accrued expense in the
  accounts for the nine months ended 31 December 2017.

  No adjustments have been made to the draft tax-adjusted trading profit of £1,475,823
  in relation to these staff costs.

In addition, the following items were not considered when calculating the accounting profit
figure as the bookkeeper was unsure of the correct treatment and no adjustments have yet
been made to the draft tax-adjusted trading profit.

(1) **Net interest payable**

	£
Bank overdraft interest payable	(20,350)
Interest payable on loan to acquire a 5% holding in Watch Ltd	(3,500)
Interest received on loans to employees	4,350
Bank deposit interest received	17,500
	(2,000)

(2) **Qualifying charitable donations**

Clock Ltd made its first charitable donation in August 2018 for £42,000. As at
31 December 2018 it had promised to make a further payment of £8,000.

(3) **Capital disposals**

Clock Ltd disposed of its entire 12% shareholding in Cuckoo Ltd in November 2018 for
£142,000. Clock Ltd had purchased the shares in January 2017 for £100,000. Cuckoo
Ltd is a trading company.

Clock Ltd sold a building in November 2018 for £238,000. Clock Ltd purchased the
building in April 2014 at a total cost of £156,000.

Clock Ltd had a capital loss brought forward at 1 January 2018 of £5,772.

Requirement

Calculate Clock Ltd's taxable total profits for the year ended 31 December 2018. **(10 marks)**

Note: Assume the RPI for December 2018 was 278.1 and November 2018 was 284.4. Ignore VAT.

Total: 15 marks

26 Powys Ltd

26.1 Powys Ltd has changed its accounting date from 31 December to 31 March, preparing accounts for the 15 months to 31 March 2019. Its forecast net operating profit for those 15 months is £2,050,000 after accounting for the following four items:

	Notes	£
Depreciation		151,000
Profit on disposal of lease	1	53,750
Dividends received	2	81,000
Patent royalties payable (accrued amount)	3	18,000

Notes

1 Powys Ltd bought some shop premises in January 2008 for £78,750. In January 2019 Powys Ltd sold the shop to an unconnected company for £125,000. Powys Ltd has always used the shop for trading purposes. In February 2020 Powys Ltd purchased a smaller shop for use in its trade for £110,000.

2 On 1 January 2018 Powys Ltd received dividends of £81,000 from a 7% shareholding in Conwy Ltd.

3 Powys Ltd paid patent royalties related to its trade of £7,200 every six months in advance commencing on 1 January 2018.

Capital allowances

Powys Ltd had a tax written down value for its main pool of £231,000 on 1 January 2018. In June 2018 Powys Ltd bought a car with CO_2 emissions of 45g/km for £22,000 and in February 2019 it sold an item of plant for £2,500 which it had originally cost £6,000.

Requirement

Based on the above information, calculate the corporation tax payable by Powys Ltd in respect of the 15 months ending 31 March 2019. **(10 marks)**

Note: Assume that the RPI for December 2017 was 278.1 and January 2019 was 286.9.

26.2 Red Ltd is an unquoted trading company and is not part of a group. Red Ltd's recent results and future forecast results are as follows:

	Year ended 31.3.18 £	Year ended 31.3.19 £	Year ended 31.3.20 £
Trading profit/(loss)	45,000	(662,500)	2,094,000
Rental income	33,000	–	–
Chargeable gains/loss	225,000	–	(12,000)
Non-trading loan relationships	–	12,000	6,000
Capital loss brought forward	(30,000)	–	–

Requirement

Calculate the taxable total profits for all three accounting periods assuming Red Ltd wishes to claim relief for losses as early as possible. State the date by which the loss relief claim(s) must be made and any losses left unutilised. **(5 marks)**

Total: 15 marks

27 Homerton Ltd

You work for a firm of ICAEW Chartered Accountants. You are preparing the corporation tax computation for Homerton Ltd, a VAT-registered UK resident trading company, for the year ended 31 March 2019.

Homerton Ltd's draft tax-adjusted trading income for the year ended 31 March 2019 is £339,575. However, items (1) to (3) below have not yet been fully considered and may require adjustment. Capital allowances have not yet been calculated.

(1)   On 24 February 2019 Homerton Ltd sold an office building, Smith's Plaza, used in its trade for £800,000. Smith's Plaza had been purchased on 31 March 2000 for £380,000. In calculating the draft tax-adjusted trading income of £339,575, solicitors fees of £2,000 relating to the sale have been deducted and the accounting profit on disposal of £24,000 has been added.

(2)   A letter was received from HMRC stating that the interest payable to 31 March 2019 in relation to the late-paid corporation tax for the previous year is £2,475. This has not been deducted in the calculation of the draft tax-adjusted trading income.

(3)   Interest payable of £3,750 on a loan to purchase Hughes Towers, a three-floor office building, was not deducted in arriving at the draft tax-adjusted trading income. Hughes Towers had been purchased in December 2018 for a cost of £900,000. The company uses two floors for its own business and lets out the third to an unconnected third party.

(4)   At 1 April 2018 the tax written down values were £16,500 on the main pool, and £25,100 on the special rate pool. During the year ended 31 March 2019 the company purchased machinery costing £45,000 and a car with CO_2 emissions of 131g/km costing £33,000 (both amounts are stated inclusive of VAT). The managing director uses the car 40% for business purposes. The company also sold an item of plant and machinery for £2,000 which had cost £8,000.

Income from subsidiary

Homerton Ltd had the following income from its wholly-owned subsidiary:

	Country of residence	Dividends received	Property income receivable
		£	£
Caius SA	Overlandia	11,890	31,200

Income from Caius SA is stated net of Overlandian withholding tax at 22%.

Other UK income/expenditure

Homerton Ltd had two other sources of income in the year ended 31 March 2019:

- £10,500 interest receivable on bank deposits; and

- UK property income of £12,750 in relation to surplus office space in Hughes Towers. This does not include rent of £4,250 for the quarter to 31 March 2019 which was received on 10 April 2019.

Homerton Ltd also paid £30,000 as a qualifying donation on 1 December 2018.

Requirements

27.1 Calculate Homerton Ltd's final tax-adjusted trading income for the year ended 31 March 2019 after capital allowances. **(6 marks)**

27.2 Calculate the corporation tax payable by Homerton Ltd for the year ended 31 March 2019. Assume that the RPI in December 2017 is 278.1 and in February 2019 is 287.3. **(9 marks)**

Total: 15 marks

28 Mallory Ltd

∨

Mallory Ltd has been a VAT-registered wholly-owned subsidiary of Ferriar Ltd for many years and is a small enterprise for the purposes of research and development. Both companies are UK trading companies making standard-rated supplies. Mallory Ltd had taxable total profits of £863,000 for the year ended 31 July 2018.

Mallory Ltd has a draft tax-adjusted trading profit before capital allowances for the eight months ended 31 March 2019 of £950,700. This is before adjustment for the issues considered below.

Research and development

The draft tax-adjusted trading profit includes a deduction of £50,430 in relation to a qualifying research and development (R&D) project as shown below:

	£
Staff costs	43,600
Consumables	5,630
Computer hardware	1,200
	50,430

Of the staff costs £14,500 relates to the total payroll costs of a member of staff working on the R&D project, who also spends 30% of her time working elsewhere in the company. All amounts are stated exclusive of VAT.

Share disposals

Mallory Ltd made two disposals of shares in unquoted trading companies during September 2018:

- Sale of the company's entire 2% shareholding in Lovell Ltd for £32,000. The shares were purchased in July 2002 for £10,300.

- Sale of the company's entire 17% shareholding in Crompton Ltd for £47,000. The shares were purchased in February 2012 for £24,500.

The draft tax-adjusted trading profit includes a profit on disposal of the shares of £44,200.

Interest

The draft tax-adjusted trading profit includes bank interest receivable of £41,492, and interest payable of £34,567 comprising interest on:

	£
Loan to purchase factory	34,105
Loan to purchase shares in Crompton Ltd	462
	34,567

Qualifying charitable donation

The draft tax-adjusted trading profit includes a deduction for a qualifying donation of £18,000 paid to a UK-registered charity in November 2018.

Capital allowances

The tax written down value of the main pool at 1 August 2018 was £100,648. During the eight months ended 31 March 2019 Mallory Ltd purchased various items of machinery for £110,940, inclusive of VAT at the standard rate. There were no purchases of cars.

Requirements

28.1 Calculate the corporation tax payable by Mallory Ltd for the eight months ended 31 March 2019. **(12 marks)**

28.2 State, and explain, the due dates and the amounts of the payments of Mallory Ltd's corporation tax in respect of the eight months ended 31 March 2019. **(3 marks)**

Note: Assume the RPI for December 2017 is 278.1 and September 2018 is 283.7.

Total: 15 marks

29 Oscoop Ltd

Oscoop Ltd is an unquoted, UK resident trading company which manufactures stationery products. Oscoop Ltd has draft profits for the year ended 31 March 2019 of £2,586,346 after accounting for the following items:

	Notes	£
Depreciation		75,400
Property income	1	232,875
Profit on sale of assets	2	204,500
Bank interest receivable		95,300
Interest payable	3	60,300
Qualifying charitable donation		270,000
Dividends received		6,327

Notes

1   During the year Oscoop Ltd received overseas property income of £232,875 from an investment property in Erehwon. The property income was received net of withholding tax of 25%. The UK has no double tax treaty with Erehwon.

2   On 10 November 2018 Oscoop Ltd sold a patent for £141,300, resulting in a profit of £68,700. The patent was acquired on 15 May 2009 for use in its trade.

The company also sold its entire holding of shares in the following trading companies in November 2018:

	Percentage holding	Date of purchase	Cost £	Sale proceeds £
Goblino plc	1%	10 May 1985	55,200	254,000
Electrobe Ltd	15%	29 Apr 2003	268,000	205,000

3   Interest payable comprises:

	£
Bank overdraft interest	42,100
Interest payable on a loan to purchase the patent (Note 2)	4,500
Interest payable on a loan to purchase shares in Electrobe Ltd	13,700
	60,300

4   Oscoop Ltd's accountant has correctly calculated the capital allowances for the year ended 31 March 2019 to be £141,000.

5   Oscoop Ltd has an unused capital loss of £12,000 brought forward from the year ended 31 March 2018.

Requirement

Calculate Oscoop Ltd's corporation tax payable for the year ended 31 March 2019, showing how you have offset the qualifying charitable donation.

Note: Assume a RPI for December 2017 of 278.1 and November 2018 of 284.4 and ignore VAT.

Total: 15 marks

30 C Ltd

30.1 C Ltd is a UK trading company, which is large for research & development (R&D) purposes.

Your manager has correctly calculated C Ltd's finalised tax adjusted trading profits before capital allowances to be £846,059 for the year ended 31 March 2019. This is after the deduction of qualifying R&D expenditure of £250,000. Your manager has given you the following information so that you can calculate the capital allowances and the chargeable gains figures in order to complete the corporation tax computation. C Ltd has elected for the tax credit regime to apply to their R&D expenditure.

Capital allowances

On 1 April 2018 C Ltd's tax written down values were: £423,000 for the main pool; £245,600 for the special rate pool; and £111,250 for a short-life asset.

C Ltd undertook the following acquisitions and disposals of assets in the year:

Purchases		Notes	£
1.5.18	Car	1	18,800

Disposals			
1.6.18	Printing press	2	55,000
1.9.18	Short life asset	3	51,000

Notes

1   The car was purchased new and has CO_2 emissions of 50g/km.
2   The printing press originally cost £12,000 on 1 June 2000.
3   The short life asset was purchased for £250,000 on 1 September 2015.

Share disposal

C Ltd held a 30% shareholding in the shares of Slab Ltd, an unquoted investment company, until it disposed of half its shares on 1 June 2018 for £45 per share. C Ltd originally purchased 10,000 shares in January 1995 for £10 per share. In January 2006 Slab Ltd made a 1 for 5 bonus issue.

On 1 April 2018 C Ltd had brought forward capital losses of £25,000.

Requirement

Calculate C Ltd's corporation tax liability for the year ended 31 March 2019. Ignore VAT.

(10 marks)

Note: Assume that the RPI for December 2017 was 278.1 and June 2018 was 280.9.

30.2 D Ltd always pays corporation tax by instalments. It prepared its most recent accounts for the period 1 July 2018 to 31 January 2019. D Ltd originally estimated its corporation tax liability for this seven month period to be £910,000 and paid the first instalment on its due date on that basis.

D Ltd later revised its estimate of its corporation tax liability to £1,050,000. D Ltd paid its second instalment accordingly along with the extra amount due in relation to the first instalment, on the due date for the second instalment.

D Ltd finalised its actual corporation tax liability for the seven months ended 31 January 2019 as £1,610,000. D Ltd paid its third instalment accordingly along with the extra amount due in relation to the first and second instalments, on the due date for the third instalment.

Requirement

For D Ltd's seven month accounting period ended 31 January 2019, state the due date for each instalment and calculate the amount of corporation tax actually paid on each date.

(5 marks)

Total: 15 marks

Income tax and NIC

31 Kim, Lien and Mai

31.1 (a) Kim, Lien and Mai have been trading in partnership for many years, running a chain of clothing shops. The partnership recorded an accounting profit for the year ended 30 June 2018 of £1,166,911 after accounting for the following items through the profit and loss account:

	Notes	£
Closing stock at 30 June 2018	1	321,450
Shop extension	2	80,600
Repairs	3	12,500
Overdraft interest payable		48,000
Legal fees	4	20,000
Lease rental on a car	5	2,600
Fines and penalties	6	750
Other expenses	7	1,000

Notes

1 The closing stock held at 30 June 2018 included in the balance sheet and deducted from 'cost of sales' in the profit and loss account was £321,450. This comprised the following at cost:

	Cost £
Children's clothes (market value £279,335)	121,450
Women's clothes (market value £108,750)	125,000
Men's clothes (market value £157,500)	75,000
	321,450

During the year, Kim took some children's clothes from stock for her personal use. The clothes cost £450 and had a sales value of £1,035. The cost of £450 is included in the 'cost of sales' charged to the profit and loss account, but no other accounting adjustments have been made to reflect this transaction.

2 In December 2017 the partnership expanded one of its shops by building an extension. The cost of the extension included as an expense in the profit and loss account was as follows:

	£
Labour and materials	39,820
Plant and machinery	34,130
Professional fees	6,650
	80,600

3 Repairs comprised of:

	£
Replacement of single glazed windows in one of the shops for double glazing	12,000
Redecoration of shop	8,000
	20,000

4 Legal fees comprised:

	£
Acquisition of shop in Bath acquired on 1 January 2018	4,150
Preparation of supplier contracts	9,335
Renewal of a 20-year lease on shop premises in Bristol	2,995
Preparation of employee contracts	3,520
	20,000

5   The lease rental related to a car provided to an employee which has a retail price of £35,000 and CO_2 emissions of 145g/km.

6   Fines and penalties includes £250 for a speeding ticket incurred by an employee and £500 for a parking fine incurred by Mai.

7   Other expenses comprises of £200 taking suppliers out for dinner and £300 on staff entertaining. The remaining £500 relates to £100 of trade samples given to potential customers and £400 on gifts to customers of chocolates costing £10 each with the partnership logo on the box.

Capital allowances

The tax written down value of the main pool of plant and machinery at 1 July 2017 was £337,115 and the tax written down value of the special rate pool at 1 July 2017 was £74,108. The partnership undertook the following transactions during the year:

Acquisitions:		£
10 September 2017	Machinery	164,000
1 October 2017	New car with CO_2 emissions of 70g/km	11,400
1 November 2017	New car with CO_2 emissions of 140g/km	28,450
10 February 2018	Electrical system (comprising air conditioning and heating)	118,370

Disposal:		
10 June 2018	A delivery van originally purchased for £8,000	1,400

Requirement

Calculate the tax-adjusted profit for the partnership for the year ended 30 June 2018. Ignore VAT.   **(12 marks)**

(b) Kim, Lien and Mai have divided the trading profits of the partnership in the same way for many years. Kim draws a salary of £64,000 pa. Interest on capital is payable at 6.5% pa. The balance of any profits is allocated in accordance with the profit sharing ratio as follows: 20% to Kim and 40% each to Lien and Mai.

The partners originally invested the following amounts of capital:

	£
Kim	500,000
Lien	750,000
Mai	1,000,000

Requirement

Using the information above and your answer to part (a), allocate the trading profits of the partnership for the year ended 30 June 2018 to each partner.   **(3 marks)**

(c) On 1 September 2019 Kim, Lien and Mai incorporated their partnership, transferring all the partnership assets and liabilities to a newly formed company, Felice Ltd. The partners therefore ceased to trade for income tax purposes on 31 August 2019. The partnership drew up its final set of accounts for the two months to 31 August 2019. Kim's share of the tax-adjusted profit for the last two accounting periods is:

	£
Year ended 30 June 2019	247,465
Two months ended 31 August 2019	42,532

Kim has not kept a record of her overlap profits from commencement. However, the partnership started to trade on 1 January 2003 and the partners drew up the first set of accounts to 30 June 2004. Kim's share of the partnership profit for this first 18-month accounting period was £37,440.

Requirement

Using the information above and your answer to part (b), calculate the taxable trading income for Kim for 2018/19 and 2019/20. Calculate Kim's NIC due for 2018/19.

(6 marks)

31.2 Berly is an additional rate taxpayer. His employer DUB Ltd provided him with a car for private use with a list price of £30,000 and CO_2 emissions of 153 g/km from January 2017. DUB Ltd has offered to start paying for Berly's private diesel from 6 April 2019. It currently costs Berly 12 pence per mile for diesel for the car.

Requirement

Calculate the number of private miles that Berly would need to drive in 2019/20 to be worth him accepting the offer of DUB Ltd paying for his private fuel. Use 2018/19 rates. **(3 marks)**

31.3 Paula has run her own unincorporated business 'Pointy Shoes' for many years and in 18/19 had trading profits of £72,000. During April 2019, Paula lost a major client whose contract normally generated a substantial amount of her profits. In order to revive her business, she decided to embark on a programme of expansion.

Paula made substantial acquisitions of assets qualifying for capital allowances during the remainder of 2019. As a result of this and additional costs of the expansion, she expects to make a trading loss of £60,000 for the year ending 31 March 2020 and then generate an estimated trading profit of £70,000 for the year ending 31 March 2021.

Paula has rental income of approximately £80,000 pa.

Requirement

Describe the ways in which Paula's trading loss for the year ending 31 March 2020 may be used. You are not required to calculate any tax liabilities. **(5 marks)**

31.4 Chase is UK resident, and has been for 15 years, but he is domiciled in Whereatania.

On 1 September 2018, Chase's UK employer, Spud Ltd, sent him on a three month secondment to the Whereatanian office. Chase's wife stayed in London for the duration of the secondment, apart from occasional trips to visit Chase in Whereatania.

Income

Chase's income and benefits from employment during 2018/19 were as follows:

- A monthly salary of £6,250 for his UK duties. This increased to £7,750 for the three months that he was on secondment. This was paid by the UK company.

- Accommodation in a one bedroom apartment in Whereatania for the duration of the secondment. The apartment cost Spud Ltd the equivalent of £1,250 per month.

- A return flight for the start and end of the secondment, plus a further flight to the UK to visit his wife costing £195 for each return ticket.

- Spud Ltd also paid for three return flights for Chase's wife to visit him during the secondment. Again, each return flight cost £195.

- Spud Ltd paid an amount equal to 1% of Chase's salary into his personal pension.

Chase also received the following income during 2018/19:

- UK bank interest of £4,250
- UK dividends of £1,200

He had overseas rental income of £150,000 during 2018/19 which Chase did not remit to the UK.

Chase makes a claim to use the remittance basis in 2018/19.

Requirement

Calculate Chase's income tax liability for 2018/19, showing your treatment of each item of employment income. **(9 marks)**

31.5 Trentino Ltd is a trading company. The summer party in 2018 cost Trentino Ltd £300 per employee and was attended by 20 employees, all additional-rate taxpayers. Trentino Ltd has agreed a PAYE settlement agreement with HMRC in respect of the summer party.

Requirement

Calculate the class 1B NIC in respect of the summer party for an additional-rate taxpayer and state the due date for its electronic payment. **(2 marks)**

Total: 40 marks

32 Charles

Charles has run his own unincorporated business, 'Ducal Traders', for many years. In addition he has recently invested in a newly formed partnership, Princely Partners. Charles also works one day a week for his wife's company, Cheval Ltd.

Ducal Traders

The draft accounts for the year ended 31 December 2018 show a net profit of £155,457 after deducting the following expenses:

	Notes	£
Depreciation		15,100
Utility bills and rent for office premises	1	54,500
Entertaining	2	15,680
Lease costs	3	1,600
Sundry expenses	4	164,359

Notes

1   Charles lives on the top floor of his office premises. The living area equates to approximately 20% of the building's total floor space.

2   Entertaining costs comprise the following:

	£
Staff party at a cost of £250 per person	1,500
Entertaining UK customers	10,180
Entertaining overseas customers	4,000
	15,680

3   Lease costs consist of £1,600 paid for the lease of car with CO_2 emissions of 135g/km.

4   Sundry expenses comprise the following:

	£
Replacing windows in the business area of office premises	6,450
Charles's salary	45,000
Millie's salary (Millie is Charles's wife. Other staff doing the same role would be paid £8,000)	12,000
A speeding fine paid for an employee while delivering goods	60
Various allowable expenses	112,909
	164,359

5   During the year Charles took goods from the business costing £1,000 for his own use. The goods had a resale value of £1,600 and the cost of goods had been recorded in the accounts as good taken for own use.

The tax written down values of Ducal Traders' plant and machinery at 1 January 2018 were:

	£
Main pool	52,400
Special rate pool	14,500
Short life asset	3,300
Private use asset – computing equipment with 25% private use by Charles	5,100

Charles purchased new plant and machinery in May 2018 for £26,700. He sold the short life asset in November 2018 for £5,000 (original cost £22,000 in 2013). On 1 December 2018 Charles purchased a car with CO_2 emissions of 100g/km for £14,000. The car is used 100% for business purposes.

Requirement

32.1 Calculate the tax-adjusted trading profit after capital allowances for Ducal Traders for its year ended 31 December 2018. **(10 marks)**

Princely Partners

William, Harry and Charles started to trade in partnership on 1 June 2018. The partnership agreement stated that Harry would receive an annual salary of £44,000 and all partners would receive interest on capital invested at 7% pa. The balance of profits is allocated to William, Harry and Charles in the ratio 3:3:4.

The partners invested capital as follows: William £100,000; Harry £200,000; and Charles £500,000.

For the year ended 31 May 2019 the partnership had a tax-adjusted trading profit of £55,000.

Requirement

32.2 Calculate Charles's share of Princely Partners' profit for its year ended 31 May 2019.

(4 marks)

Cheval Ltd

Charles works as a business consultant for Cheval Ltd, earning a gross salary of £12,000 pa before deduction of £4,500 income tax under PAYE. Charles received the following benefits in 2018/19:

- A company car with a list price of £31,000 and CO_2 emissions of 230g/km. Cheval Ltd also pays for all of Charles's petrol for both business and private use. The company car was unavailable for the whole of July and August 2018. For those two months, Charles drove 5,000 business miles in his own car and received £0.50 per mile as payment towards the cost of the petrol. Charles has not previously used his own car for business travel.

- Photographic equipment owned by Cheval Ltd has been used by Charles since 6 April 2017. At that date its market value was £10,000. Cheval Ltd gifted the equipment to Charles on 6 October 2018 when it was worth £6,000.

- On 6 June 2018 Cheval Ltd loaned Charles £20,000 at an interest rate of 1%. This loan remains outstanding.

- Charles was provided with private medical insurance throughout 2018/19. This cost Cheval Ltd £450 but would have cost Charles personally £550.

- In June 2018 Cheval Ltd paid £100 for Charles to have a medical check up.

- An employer contribution of £1,500 pa to Charles's personal pension scheme.

Requirement

32.3 Calculate Charles's employment income for 2018/19. Clearly show your treatment of each item.

Note: The fuel benefit rate for 2018/19 is £23,400 and you should assume that the official rate of interest throughout 2018/19 is 2.5%. **(10 marks)**

Other income and payments

During 2018/19 Charles started to rent out a beach hut which he had inherited from his grandfather. He rented out the hut for £100 a week and had tenants for 12 weeks over the summer period. He paid £100 in management fees to a local property business who helped him find tenants.

In January 2019 Charles received dividends of £85,000 from his holding in Burmese Ltd. Charles made Gift Aid donations in February 2019 of £30,000 and made payments totalling £20,000 throughout 2018/19 into his personal pension scheme.

Requirements

32.4 Calculate Charles's income tax payable for 2018/19. State the due date for any beneficial claims or elections to be made. **(11 marks)**

32.5 Calculate how much Charles pays in NICs for 2018/19. Ignore the NIC annual maxima rules.

(5 marks)

Note: Ignore VAT. **Total: 40 marks**

33   Jasper

33.1 Jasper runs a business, 'Jasper's Joinery', as a sole trader.

Trading profits

Jasper's accounting date is 31 March. He elected to join the cash basis for the first time for his year ended 31 March 2018. Jasper agreed with his accountant that he would provide her with a summary of his transactions this year rather than a box of invoices and receipts. He has started to prepare a simple profit and loss account for his year ending 31 March 2019 using cash accounting. Jasper's forecast profit for the year ending 31 March 2019 is £51,000. However, he has omitted the following items in the calculation of this figure:

- Donation of £55 to a local charity's recent fund raising campaign.

- Cutting machine purchased in July 2018 for £5,000.

- It cost £3,000 to lease a car for the period 1 April 2018 to 30 November 2018 exclusively for business use. The car had CO_2 emissions of 150g/km.

- Purchase of a new Peugeot car on 1 December 2018 for use in the business at a cost of £8,500. Business use is 75%. The Peugeot car has CO_2 emissions of 120g/km.

- Jasper intends to claim the fixed rate mileage allowance for the Peugeot car. He estimates that his business mileage will be 7,000 miles from 1 December 2018 to 31 March 2019.

- Jasper removed stock from the business which cost £400 and had a resale value of £500. The cost of £400 is still included in the total cost of sales figure.

Jasper deducted the following items from his draft profit figure even though he was unsure of their correct treatment:

- £600 for bad debts in respect of a customer who has been made bankrupt
- £800 interest paid on a business loan
- £200 for winter tyres for his Peugeot car and £1,050 in fuel costs for his business journeys

Other income and outgoings

On 6 April 2018, Jasper started to let a furnished room in his home to a friend. The weekly rent is £150. Jasper incurred expenses during 2018/19 of £2,500 relating to the letting.

Jasper also received the following income in 2018/19:

- Interest income of £28,000 on gilts
- Dividend income of £50,000

Jasper made a personal pension contribution of £6,000 in January 2019.

Requirements

(a) Calculate Jasper's forecast tax-adjusted trading profit for the year ending 31 March 2019, showing your treatment of each item. **(7 marks)**

(b) Calculate Jasper's income tax payable for 2018/19. **(10 marks)**

Note: Ignore VAT.

33.2 Dylan works for Pomme Ltd, having joined the company on 6 April 2018 as a director.

Dylan received the following remuneration package from 6 April 2018:

- Salary of £70,000 per year.
- A company car with a list price of £45,000 and CO_2 emissions of 156g/km. Pomme Ltd pays for all of Dylan's petrol for both business and private use.
- A box of chocolates, costing £15, on his birthday in September 2018.
- An interest-free loan of £7,000 for Dylan to pay his son's school fees, made available from 6 April 2018 and still owed at 5 April 2019.
- Living accommodation owned by Pomme Ltd provided for Dylan to live in as his main residence. The property originally cost Pomme Ltd £124,000 in April 2003. It was refurbished in January 2014 at a cost of £55,000. It had a market value of £345,000 in April 2018. The annual value of the property is £25,700.

  The property is provided with furniture which cost £20,000 in April 2018.

Requirements

(a) Calculate both Dylan's and Pomme Ltd's NIC liability in respect of Dylan for 2018/19, showing your treatment of each item. Use an official rate of interest of 2.5%. **(10 marks)**

(b) State the date by which Pomme Ltd must pay its class 1A NIC liability in relation to 2018/19. **(1 mark)**

33.3 Meg was 68 years old on 1 June 2018. On that date she decided to vest her pension benefits. Meg had a money-purchase scheme which was valued at £1,600,000 on 1 June 2018.

Requirement

Explain the tax consequences for Meg based on how she chooses to draw her pension benefits. Detailed calculations are not required. **(4 marks)**

33.4 On 1 January 2019, Martina set up her own unincorporated business as a designer and manufacturer of glassware.

Business options

Martina has decided to employ a part-time assistant from 1 January 2020 as she anticipates that her trading profit will rise substantially over the next year and she will become an additional rate taxpayer. The assistant will receive a salary of £12,900 pa and will have the use of a van, which will be leased by Martina. Martina will incur leasing and business fuel costs of £7,200 pa. The assistant will be allowed unlimited private use of the van, but will be required to pay for their own private fuel.

Martina's husband does not approve of the plan to employ an assistant as he thinks it is a waste of money and not tax efficient. He has offered to find time to do the same job for an annual salary of £15,000. He would not need the use of a van, but would use his own car to meet all delivery needs. He estimates that he would drive 5,000 business miles a year and would require a mileage allowance of 50p per mile. Martina's husband is a basic rate taxpayer.

Requirement

Calculate the cost to the business of each of the suggested business options. Include calculations to support your treatment of national insurance. **(8 marks)**

Total: 40 marks

34 Selwyn

34.1 Selwyn and Edmund have both worked for Downing Ltd for many years. Each has a basic salary of £2,500 per month.

Downing Ltd allows its employees to choose the remaining elements of their employment package. Selwyn and Edmund made the following choices for 2018/19:

Selwyn

- A company car with a list price of £21,000. He made a £6,000 capital contribution towards the cost of the car, which has CO_2 emissions of 138g/km and does not meet the RDE2 standards, when it was first provided on 6 July 2018. Downing Ltd does not pay for the diesel used in the car.

- Use of a laptop computer that cost £540. Selwyn used this purely for private purposes.

- Payment of £1,500 by Downing Ltd into its employees' occupational pension scheme on behalf of Selwyn.

- Childcare costs of £60 per week for Selwyn's daughters, paid by Downing Ltd to a local nursery. Selwyn has been a member of the scheme for the last eight years.

Selwyn paid £4,630 income tax via PAYE on his employment income.

Edmund

A bonus of £6,500 in December 2018.

Edmund personally pays an annual subscription of £300 to his professional body, which is relevant to his employment.

Edmund paid £6,950 income tax via PAYE on his employment income.

Requirement

Calculate the 2018/19 taxable employment income of:

- Selwyn; and
- Edmund. **(6 marks)**

34.2 In addition to their employment income Selwyn and Edmund had various other sources of income in 2018/19.

Selwyn

Selwyn is married to Clare. They were both born in 1986. Clare has not worked for three years since the birth of their twin daughters, for whom the couple received total child benefit of £1,788 in 2018/19. Clare has no other source of income.

Selwyn's other sources of income for 2018/19 include the following:

(1) Interest: Selwyn received an inheritance during the tax year which he has invested in various bank accounts. He received interest of £18,445, of which £345 was from an ISA.

(2) Dividends: Selwyn received dividend income of £5,750 from shares in Downing Ltd, which is an employee-controlled company. Selwyn also paid interest of £220 in 2018/19 on a bank loan to purchase these shares.

Edmund

Edmund is married to Alison. They were both born in 1943. Edmund's other sources of income for 2018/19 include the following:

(1) State pension of £5,881.

(2) Property income: Edmund let out a furnished room in his house to a tenant at a rent of £150 per week. Edmund incurred allowable expenses of £2,670 in relation to the let room.

(3) Interest income: Edmund and his wife receive £1,200 from their joint savings account.

During 2018/19 Edmund made gift aid donations totalling £14,200.

Edmund's wife, Alison, has total income of £5,600 for 2018/19.

Requirements

(a) Using the information from parts 34.1 and 34.2, calculate the income tax payable/repayable for 2018/19 by:

- Selwyn; and
- Edmund.

  Show your treatment of Edmund's property income. **(15 marks)**

(b) Calculate the national insurance contributions payable for 2018/19 by:

- Selwyn; and
- Edmund. **(2 marks)**

34.3 Edmund's sister Gertie has recently inherited a beach hut. She is considering renting it out for £100 per week over the Summer months and would like advice about how her income would be taxed. Gertie would incur no running costs in relation to the hut as these would all be covered by any tenant.

Requirement

Explain the implications of Gertie renting out the beach hut on the assumption that she either rents the hut out for 8 or 12 weeks over the 2018/19 summer season and claims any beneficial election. **(4 marks)**

34.4 On 1 July 2018 Sidney set up an unincorporated business, offering interior design services. He was not required to register for VAT.

Sidney prepared his first set of accounts to 30 April 2019, and will prepare accounts annually thereafter. He has not elected to use the cash basis.

The tax-adjusted trading profits for the 10 months ended 30 April 2019 are £14,500. However this is before any adjustment for the following expenditure:

(1) On 1 July 2018 Sidney leased a car with CO_2 emissions of 150g/km that he uses 30% for business purposes. The lease costs of £300 per month, and additional running expenses of £700 for the 10 month period have been deducted in full in arriving at the tax-adjusted trading profits of £14,500.

(2) Sidney incurred the following costs before commencing trading. He did not deduct these in arriving at the tax-adjusted trading profits of £14,500.

		£
April 2018	Legal advice on safety regulations applying to the business	1,394
May 2018	Purchase of a computer for 100% business use	2,150
June 2018	Entertaining estate agents with a hope of gaining future business	320

Sidney's business has grown significantly since May 2019, and he is expecting trading profits of approximately £51,000 for the year ending 30 April 2020.

Requirements

(a) Calculate Sidney's revised tax-adjusted trading profits for the 10 months ended 30 April 2019. Briefly explain your treatment of each item in (2) above. **(5 marks)**

(b) Calculate the trading income assessments for Sidney's first three tax years of trading. State the dates of the basis periods and the dates and amount of any overlap profits.

(5 marks)

34.5 During 2018/19, Lathe Ltd, a UK trading company, made a gift costing £70 to each employee on their birthday. These gifts are subject to a PAYE settlement agreement. Of the 50 employees, 36 are basic-rate taxpayers, and the rest are higher-rate taxpayers.

Requirement

Calculate the national insurance contributions payable by Lathe Ltd in respect of these gifts, stating the class of national insurance payable and the due date for payment. Ignore VAT.

(3 marks)

Total: 40 marks

35 Pierre

35.1 Pierre, who is 40 years old, came to the UK 10 years ago, having been born and brought up in the country of Erehwon, where his family have lived for many generations. Shortly after coming to the UK he met and married Madge, who is UK-resident. Pierre is treated as UK-resident but not UK-domiciled for income tax purposes.

Requirement

Explain why Pierre is treated as non-UK domiciled, and state any actions that he must take to become UK domiciled for income tax purposes. You do not need to consider the deemed domicile rules.

(2 marks)

35.2 Pierre is UK-resident but domiciled in the country of Erewhon. He is employed by Rutherford Ltd, a UK company, as the sales and marketing director. His remuneration arrangements are as follows:

(1) Salary of £27,000 pa

(2) Rutherford Ltd pays Pierre a bonus based on the results for each year ended 31 December:

Accounts to year ended	Bonus £	Date approved at AGM	Date received
31 December 2017	11,300	25 March 2018	28 April 2018
31 December 2018	9,100	24 March 2019	30 April 2019

(3) Pierre is not provided with a company car but he travelled 12,000 business miles in his own car during 2018/19 and was paid 50p per mile for this.

(4) Pierre has had the use of a bicycle since 1 October 2017 as part of a scheme open to all employees. The bicycle had been bought for £600 by Rutherford Ltd. On 1 July 2018 Pierre bought the bicycle from Rutherford Ltd for £40, when it was worth £130.

(5) Rutherford Ltd paid £410 in private medical insurance for Pierre. If Pierre had purchased it himself it would have cost £520.

(6) Pierre's PAYE deducted for 2018/19 totalled £5,000.

Requirements

For 2018/19, calculate Pierre's:

(a) Taxable employment income **(6 marks)**

(b) Class 1 primary national insurance contributions **(3 marks)**

Other income and expenses

Pierre received dividends from Rutherford Ltd of £5,650 in January 2019.

He also had two sources of income relating to 2018/19 from Erehwon received after deduction of tax at source at the rates shown below:

	Received £	Overseas tax rate
Bank interest	3,444	30%
Property income	6,160	45%

The UK has no double tax treaty with Erehwon and Pierre decided not to make a remittance basis election.

Pierre also contributed £4,160 into his personal pension scheme during 2018/19.

Requirements

For 2018/19, calculate Pierre's:

(c) Income tax payable **(13 marks)**

35.3 Emmeline and Richmal have been trading in partnership for many years, preparing tax returns using the accruals basis. The partnership is not VAT-registered.

For the year ended 31 December 2018 the partnership had turnover of £73,156, and tax-adjusted trading profits before deduction of capital allowances of £53,194.

At 1 January 2018 the tax written down value on the main pool was £2,490, and there was a tax written down value of £1,524 in relation to a Ford car with CO_2 emissions of 170g/km used by Richmal 30% for business purposes. During the year ended 31 December 2018 the partnership paid £1,560 for new machinery and £9,200 for a Nissan car with CO_2 emissions of 140g/km to be used 30% for business by Richmal. The Ford car used by Richmal, which originally cost £10,450, was sold for £1,800.

Amounts are stated inclusive of VAT where appropriate.

Emmeline and Richmal originally shared profits equally. However Emmeline increased her working hours and the profit-sharing arrangement changed from 1 October 2018 to be:

	Emmeline	Richmal
Salary (pa)	£8,000	£Nil
Profit sharing ratio	55%	45%

Requirements

(a) Calculate the tax-adjusted trading profits after deduction of capital allowances for the partnership for the year ended 31 December 2018. **(5 marks)**

(b) Calculate the trading income assessment for each partner for 2018/19. **(2 marks)**

(c) Calculate Emmeline's national insurance contributions for 2018/19. **(2 marks)**

35.4 Emmeline and Richmal intend to elect to use the cash basis to calculate the partnership's tax-adjusted trading income for the year ending 31 December 2019.

The accounts for the previous year to 31 December 2018 had included:

(1) debtors totalling £598 for which the money was received in April 2019
(2) accountancy fees of £860 accrued at the year end but paid in May 2019

In September 2019 Emmeline and Richmal took goods from stock that had cost the partnership £350, but would have been sold to customers for £670. In the same month the partnership purchased a computer costing £430 and a car for use in the business costing £10,000.

The partnership will voluntarily register for VAT from 1 January 2020.

Requirements

(a) State how the partnership will make the election for the cash basis to apply, and explain the tax treatment of items (1) and (2) above on the change of basis. **(3 marks)**

(b) Explain how the transactions in September 2019 are treated in calculating tax-adjusted trading income using the cash basis, and whether their treatment would have differed under the accruals basis. **(3 marks)**

(c) State the basis which should be used by the partnership to account for VAT from 1 January 2020. **(1 mark)**

Total: 40 marks

36   Peter

36.1 Peter Osborn worked as a project manager for Bugle Ltd for many years before leaving his employment on 31 October 2018. Peter's remuneration package in 2018/19 until the day he left employment was as follows:

- Monthly salary of £2,500.

- Provision of a mobile telephone for both business and private use. The line rental from 6 April to 31 October 2018 was £175. Peter used the mobile 50% for private use with private calls costing a total of £68 in 2018/19.

- An interest-free loan of £16,000 extended to Peter in 2014, which was written off by Bugle Ltd on 31 October 2018.

- Provision of a petrol-fuelled company car with a list price of £25,000 and CO_2 emissions of 95g/km. Business fuel, insurance and repairs cost Bugle Ltd £2,460. The car was unavailable to Peter for the whole of August 2018 as it needed to be repaired. Bugle Ltd paid for all of Peter's private fuel.

- Furnished accommodation which cost £85,000 in January 2005. By the time the accommodation was first provided to Peter on 1 April 2014 it had increased in value to £250,000. The accommodation has an annual value of £15,000. The furniture cost £12,000 when first provided to Peter on 1 April 2014. Peter paid rent of £625 per month until he moved out on 31 October 2018.

In addition, Peter received business entertaining expenses totalling £843.

In 2018/19 Bugle Ltd contributed £3,100 to its group personal pension scheme on Peter's behalf.

Requirements

For 2018/19, calculate:

(a) Peter's taxable employment income; and **(8 marks)**
(b) Peter's employee class 1 national insurance contributions. **(4 marks)**

Note: The official rate of interest throughout 2018/19 was 2.5% pa, and the fuel benefit charge fixed amount is £23,400.

36.2 On 1 November 2018 Peter started trading as 'Edderkop Apps', preparing his first accounts to 30 April 2019. 'Edderkop Apps', which designs applications for smartphones and tablets, became VAT registered on 1 January 2019. The tax-adjusted trading profits before capital allowances for the six months ended 30 April 2019 are £45,095.

On 1 October 2018 Peter had bought computer equipment costing £9,840 (inclusive of VAT) ready for use in the new business, which makes standard-rated supplies.

Other purchases of plant and machinery are shown below inclusive of VAT at the standard rate:

		£
10 January 2019	Car (CO_2 emissions 142g/km)	14,880
14 February 2019	Furniture	3,000

Peter's car, purchased on 10 January 2019, was used 60% for private use.

Requirements

(a) Explain the capital allowances treatment of the computer equipment purchased on 1 October 2018. **(2 marks)**

(b) Calculate the tax-adjusted trading profits of Edderkop Apps for the six months ended 30 April 2019. **(4 marks)**

(c) For 2018/19:

- calculate Peter's taxable trading income;

- state the dates of the basis period; and

- calculate the national insurance contributions (NICs) relating to his self-employment.

Note: Do not consider NIC maxima. **(3 marks)**

36.3 Peter's brother, Liam, has recently started renting out a second home he has bought in Padstow, South West England. He previously was a basic rate tax payer with only £40,000 employment income and is concerned about his extra tax responsibilities and would like advice. PAYE suffered on Liam's salary was £5,630. Peter has asked whether your firm would consider acting as Liam's tax advisors.

Liam started renting out the Padstow house from 1 June 2018 at a monthly rent of £1,200. The rent was paid on the 1st of each month except for the amount due 1st April 2019 which has not yet been received.

The expenses paid in 2018/19 in relation to the house were:

	£
Repairs	1,306
Refrigerator (note)	150
Replacement refrigerator (note)	840
Property management fees	605
	2,751

Note: The fridge which Liam paid for along with other fixtures and fittings in the holiday home was broken very quickly by tenants. The replacement refrigerator included a separate freezer and ice dispenser, which the old one did not have. A similar model to the old refrigerator would have cost £240. Included in the cost of £840 was a fee of £10 for disposing of the old refrigerator, scrapped for nil proceeds.

In addition to the expenses above, Liam paid for insurance for the house. He paid £300 on 1 June 2018 to insure the property for period to 31 December 2018 and then he paid £550 on 1 January 2019 to insure the property for the year end 31 December 2019.

Requirements

(a) Calculate Liam's property income assessment for 2018/19. **(4 marks)**

(b) Calculate Liam's income tax payable for 2018/19. **(3 mark)**

(c) Explain the money laundering procedures you should follow prior to agreeing to act as Liam's tax advisor, identify the fundamental principle threatened by taking Liam on and outline steps which could be taken to mitigate this threat. **(3 marks)**

36.4 Peter's wife, Mildred, is aged 51 and is considering how much to contribute to her personal pension for 2018/19. Mildred anticipates that for 2018/19 she will have total income of £115,000 made up of employment income of £12,500 and £102,500 of rental income from investment properties.

Mildred has already made charitable donations via Gift Aid of £2,000 in 2018/19 and her employer makes no pension contributions on Mildred's behalf.

Requirement

Calculate how much Mildred's income tax liability would reduce by if she were to make the maximum possible tax-relievable personal pension contribution in 2018/19. **(9 marks)**

Total: 40 marks

37 Sunil

37.1 Sunil has been resident in the UK since 2009/10 but is domiciled in Norway.

Trading income

Sunil started to trade as a publisher in the UK on 1 January 2018 preparing accounts for the 15 months to 31 March 2019. Sunil calculated his profit for the 15 months to 31 March 2019 as £144,975 after taking account of the following items:

	Notes	£
Client entertaining		2,556
Staff costs	1	14,950
Interest received on business bank account	2	150
Property repairs for Sunil's office	3	15,400
Depreciation		5,500
Sunil's car expenses	4	24,850
Gift Aid donation in July 2018 to MSF, a charity		500
Gift of leather handbags to 12 key customers		8,340

Notes

1 Staff costs comprise the following:

	£
Gross salary for Marwan, the sole employee	12,500
Petrol for business miles in van provided to Marwan	2,000
Job-related training course for Marwan	450
	14,950

From the date his employment commenced on 6 April 2018, Marwan was provided with a van for both business and extensive private use. Sunil paid the list price of £8,500 for the van which has CO_2 emissions of 145g/km.

Sunil has lost the payroll paperwork and cannot remember the amounts of national insurance contributions (NIC) paid for Marwan since he joined. As a result, no deduction has been made for employer's NIC in arriving at Sunil's profit figure of £144,975.

2 Interest income of £150 was received in January 2019.

3 Property repairs for Sunil's office comprise the following:

	£
New hot water heating system	1,500
Decoration of premises	3,400
Replacement of windows broken in January 2019	10,500
	15,400

4 Sunil's car expenses figure is made up of £18,500 for the cost of a new car with CO_2 emissions of 145g/km which he purchased on 1 January 2018, £3,000 for a three-year car servicing and repairs plan paid for in advance, £2,000 for fuel and £1,350 for running costs. Business use is 75%.

Requirements

(a) Calculate the employer's and employee's NIC due in respect of Marwan's 2018/19 employment. Clearly show the amount due for each class of NIC. **(4 marks)**

(b) For the publishing business, calculate Sunil's tax adjusted trading profits after capital allowances for his 15 month period ended 31 March 2019. Ignore VAT. **(11 marks)**

Other income and outgoings

Sunil owns a rental property in Norway. In 2018/19 Sunil received gross rents of £34,000 and paid rental costs of £7,400. In addition Sunil replaced furniture for the property at a cost of £6,250. Sunil paid taxes of £500 in Norway on his rental income which he remitted in full to the UK.

Sunil received dividends from UK companies totalling £163,000 and UK bank deposit interest of £17,855. Sunil also received £250,000 of dividend income from shares held in Switzerland, none of which was remitted to the UK.

Sunil made a personal pension contribution of £8,000 in January 2019.

Requirement

(c) Calculate Sunil's income tax payable for 2018/19 assuming he claims the remittance basis. **(10 marks)**

37.2 Harish works for XYZ Ltd. During 2018/19 Harish had the following remuneration package from XYZ Ltd:

- Basic salary of £15,000 pa.

- For the last nine months of 2018/19 Harish was provided with a company car with a list price of £13,000 and CO_2 emissions of 85g/km. Harish made a £2,500 one-off contribution towards the cost of the car. In addition Harish paid his employer £50 per month towards the private use of the car. XYZ Ltd paid for all Harish's petrol for which Harish contributed a notional £10 per month.

- XYZ Ltd made a contribution of 10% of Harish's basic annual salary to an occupational pension scheme. Harish made a further contribution of 5% of his basic annual salary.

- Luncheon vouchers with a total value of £2,225. The vouchers were exchangeable for meals. The vouchers only actually cost his employer £2,069.

- Harish received a silver clock worth £500 in February 2019 in recognition of him serving 10 years with XYZ Ltd.

Harish attended a number of social events paid for by his employer during 2018/19. Only employees were allowed to attend the events. Harish went to the annual year-end ball at a cost to XYZ Ltd of £130 per person. He also attended the summer ball at a cost to XYZ Ltd of £60 per person and the firm's annual barbecue at a cost to XYZ Ltd of £75 per person.

Requirement

Calculate Harish's employment income for 2018/19. **(7 marks)**

37.3 Dhruthi ceased to trade on 31 October 2019. Her recent results are:

	2015/16 £	2016/17 £	2017/18 £	2018/19 £	2019/20 £
Trading profits/(loss)	102,000	31,000	10,000	7,000	(105,000)
Rental income	14,000	14,000	14,000	14,000	14,000
Chargeable gains					33,000

Dhruthi prepared accounts to 31 March each year until her final set of accounts which were prepared for the seven months to 31 October 2019.

Dhruthi has unrelieved overlap profits from commencement of £23,450.

Requirements

(a) Calculate the total amount available for terminal loss relief. **(2 marks)**

(b) Show how Dhruthi could utilise the loss under the terminal loss relief rules and state the date by which a claim for terminal loss relief must be made. **(3 marks)**

(c) State how Dhruthi could utilise any loss which cannot be set-off under the terminal loss relief rules. **(3 marks)**

Total: 40 marks

38   Amy and Kath

38.1 Amy is an ICAEW Chartered Accountant working in practice as the owner of a small accountancy practice. Amy has a vague awareness of anti-money laundering requirements and remembers that she did register with ICAEW as her supervisory body about eight years ago. However, Amy has never implemented any specific procedures to ensure compliance with the regulations. Amy has been notified that ICAEW, as her supervisory body, will be conducting a monitoring visit.

Requirement

Prepare brief notes which set out the anti-money laundering procedures which Amy should implement in order to ensure compliance with anti-money laundering regulations. **(4 marks)**

38.2 Kath, one of your clients, has just disclosed to you in your role as her tax adviser that she misrepresented some of the figures relating to her business and her personal income in her 2017/18 return. She admits that she has charged her son's school fees of £12,000 as a business expense. In addition she has not disclosed that whenever she is away she rents out her home to tourists. For 2017/18 this generated rental income of £8,000.

Requirement

Briefly explain what action you should now take in accordance with ICAEW's guidance as set out in Professional Conduct in Relation to Taxation. **(3 marks)**

Total: 7 marks

39   Pict Ltd

39.1 Pict Ltd is a VAT registered manufacturing company. Pict Ltd's records show the following sales and purchases for the quarter ended 31 December 2018. All figures are stated exclusive of VAT.

	Notes	£
Standard-rated sales to UK customers		345,150
Exempt sales to UK customers		25,260
Sales to EU customers outside of the UK	1	75,000
Total sales		445,410
Standard-rated costs relating to:		
Taxable supplies	2	89,150
Exempt supplies		8,875
Overheads for the whole business		26,290
Purchase of delivery van	3	28,800
Purchase of car for a director	4	20,000

Notes

1   One third of the sales made to EU customers are to VAT registered customers. The remaining sales are to customers who are not VAT registered. If the sales had been made in the UK they would have been made at the reduced rate.

2   Expenses of £2,500 were incurred without the receipt of a valid VAT invoice from the supplier.

3   The delivery van is used for delivering taxable supplies only.

4   The director is responsible for standard-rated products sold to UK customers. The car is available for the director's private use.

Requirement

Calculate the net VAT payable by or repayable to Pict Ltd for the quarter ended 31 December 2018. Show the VAT treatment of all items. **(10 marks)**

Note: Ignore the simplified partial exemption tests.

39.2 On 1 July 2018 Edith purchased her first home in London for £1.25 million from Wilma.

Requirement

Calculate the amount of stamp duty land tax due on the purchase of the house and state when it was due to be paid. **(3 marks)**

Total: 13 marks

40 Tracey, Fred and Matthew

40.1 Tracey lives in London, and has always been resident and domiciled in the UK. On 1 July 2018 she:

- sold 12 hectares of land from a holding of 23 hectares. Tracey sold the 12 hectares for £42,000 and incurred disposal costs of £1,450.

  Tracey paid £76,000 for the 23 hectares of land in January 2001 and incurred acquisition costs of £2,400.

  The market value of the remaining 11 hectares was £60,000 on 1 July 2018.

- sold a Jaguar E-type, a classic car, for £25,000. Tracey purchased the car in January 2011 for £6,000.

In December 2018 Tracey sold a commercial investment property realising a chargeable gain of £147,000.

For 2018/19 Tracey has employment income of £25,615.

Requirement

Calculate Tracey's capital gains tax liability for 2018/19. Clearly show your treatment of each asset. **(6 marks)**

40.2 Fred has a life-limiting medical condition which means he is unlikely to live beyond 2024. Fred is domiciled in the UK and lives in England. During his lifetime he has made the following gifts:

- 1 April 2011: gross chargeable transfer of £307,000.

- 1 February 2018: house with a market value of £240,000 to a discretionary trust. At the date of Fred's death the house is expected to have a market value of £119,000.

- 1 March 2018: gifts of £250 each to his two grandchildren.

In addition, since 1 September 2015, Fred has paid £25,000 for his grandchildren's school fees on 1 September each year. Fred has always used his pension income to pay the fees and the payments have not affected Fred's standard of living.

Fred owns the following assets which he intends to leave to his son when he dies. The value of these assets is not expected to change in the future.

- A holding of 75% of the shares in an unquoted trading company. The shares have a market value of £2 million. Fred has owned the shares since January 2015.

- Cash and personal effects with a market value of £1 million.

Requirement

Calculate the inheritance tax that would be payable as a result of Fred's death assuming he dies on 1 December 2024. Clearly show your treatment of each item. **(12 marks)**

40.3 Matthew owns 10,000 shares in an unquoted trading company. He has owned the shares since 1 January 2013 when he joined the company as managing director.

Matthew intends to give the shares to his daughter on 1 July 2019, but is concerned about the tax implications of the gift, especially if he were to die within a few years of making the gift.

The shares will have a market value of £10 million on 1 July 2019.

Both Matthew and his daughter are UK resident and domiciled, living in England.

Requirement

Assuming Matthew gifts his shares to his daughter on 1 July 2019, briefly explain the capital gains tax and inheritance tax implications arising:

- at the time of the gift; and
- on Matthew's subsequent death if he were to die in five years' time.

Note: Calculations are not required. **(7 marks)**

Total: 25 marks

41 Pietra Ltd

Pietra Ltd is a UK resident trading company. Pietra Ltd's accounting profit for its year ended 31 December 2018 is £4,000,000. The items in Table 1 below have been added or deducted in arriving at the accounting profit.

Table 1	Notes	£
Depreciation		130,000
Profit on disposal of lease	1	340,000
Rental income	2	20,000
Interest income	3	800
Interest expense	4	43,350
Charitable donations	5	50,000

Notes

1 On 1 August 2018 Pietra Ltd sold a warehouse for £550,000. Pietra Ltd paid £210,000 for the warehouse on 1 August 2007 and had extended it in July 2010 for £124,000. The warehouse, has been used for trading purposes throughout.

   In December 2018 Pietra Ltd bought a new warehouse for £535,000 to use within its trade.

2 Pietra Ltd has rented out one floor of its factory for the past five years. The factory has five floors in total. The tenant pays annual rent of £20,000.

3 The interest income is in respect to a small balance on Pietra Ltd's current account.

4 The interest expense figure comprises:

	£
Interest on loan to purchase the factory (Note 2)	23,400
Interest on loan to purchase fixed assets used in the business	18,500
Incidental costs of arranging loan to purchase fixed assets	1,450
	43,350

5 Pietra Ltd paid qualifying charitable donations of £40,000 during the year ended 31 December 2018 and had a closing accrual of £10,000 at the year end.

Capital allowances

On 1 January 2018, Pietra Ltd had tax written down values of £386,000 for its main pool and £283,000 for its special rate pool. On 1 June 2018 Pietra Ltd spent £242,000 on new lifts for its head offices and £664,000 on new equipment for its warehouse. On 1 September 2018 Pietra Ltd purchased a new fleet of company cars costing £135,000 in total. The cars have CO_2 emissions of at least 150g/km.

Requirements

41.1 Calculate Pietra Ltd's tax-adjusted trading profit for the year ended 31 December 2018. Start with the accounting profit of £4,000,000 and show all items given in Table 1, using a zero for any that require no adjustment. **(8 marks)**

41.2 Calculate Pietra Ltd's corporation tax liability for the year ended 31 December 2018.
(7 marks)

Notes

1   Assume the RPI for December 2017 is 278.1 and August 2018 is 283.3.
2   Ignore VAT and stamp taxes.   **Total: 15 marks**

42   Anka

42.1 Anka runs a clothes manufacturing business, Silk Traders, as a sole trader.

Anka has calculated an accounting profit figure of £112,000 for the year ended 31 December 2018. This is after deducting costs including the following items:

- Depreciation of £8,450.

- Anka's pension contributions of £80 per month in cash.

- Client entertaining of £550.

- Leased car costs of £3,000. The car is leased for an employee who uses it 50% for private use. The car has CO_2 emissions of 145g/km.

- Loss of £2,000 on disposal of a machine used in the business. The machine was originally purchased for £10,000 and was sold for £6,000.

- £100 given to the local children's hospital, a registered charity, for its latest fundraising appeal. The donation was listed in the hospital's magazine.

- Legal and professional costs

	£
Legal fees for renewal of a five year lease of business premises	1,200
Fees for preparing Anka's tax return	400
Fees incurred in recovery of a trade debt	365
	1,965

- Bad debt expense

	£
Trade debts written off	1,800
Loan to former employee written off	250
Increase in provision for specific trade debts	300
Recovery of loan to former employee previously written off	(100)
	2,250

- £700 being the cost of stock taken by Anka from the business for her own use. The stock had a resale value of £1,000. No other record has been made in the accounts of the stock being withdrawn from the business.

Capital allowances have not yet been calculated. Tax written down values as at 1 January 2018 were:

	£
Main pool	44,000
Anka's car with 80% business use (purchased in 2015 with CO_2 emissions of 110g/km)	12,000

Requirement

Calculate Anka's tax-adjusted trading profit for the year ended 31 December 2018. Show your treatment of each item. **(11 marks)**

Note: Ignore VAT.

42.2 Xanthe and Gandalf are employed by Holm Ltd.

Gandalf

For 2018/19 Gandalf has a salary of £50,000. In addition he drove 8,000 business miles in his own car and received a payment of £0.35 per mile from Holm Ltd. Gandalf also received shopping vouchers from Holm Ltd worth £2,500. The vouchers cost Holm Ltd £2,400.

Xanthe

For 2018/19 Xanthe has received the following remuneration package:

- Basic salary of £60,000.

- A diesel company car with CO_2 emissions of 109g/km. The car cost Holm Ltd £28,000 although its list price was £31,000. Xanthe made a contribution to the capital cost of the car of £6,000 when it was first provided in 2015. Holm Ltd pays for the diesel fuel for both business and private use. Xanthe pays Holm Ltd £20 per month towards the cost of private fuel. Holm Ltd spends at least £50 per month on Xanthe's private fuel.

- Use of sound recording equipment which was purchased specifically for Xanthe's private use from 6 November 2018. The equipment was worth £5,520 when it was first provided to Xanthe. Xanthe pays £75 per month as a contribution towards its use.

- Provision of a car parking space in a public car park near Xanthe's place of work. Holm Ltd pays £1,500 pa for the parking space.

Xanthe paid 10% of her basic salary into her occupational pension scheme. Holm Ltd made a further contribution of 2.5% of her basic salary. These pension contributions do not exceed Xanthe's pension annual allowance for 2018/19.

Xanthe has significant investment income and therefore pays income tax at 45% on her employment income from Holm Ltd.

Requirements

In relation to the tax year 2018/19:

(a) Calculate Holm Ltd's liability to class 1 secondary national insurance contributions (NIC) in respect of Gandalf. **(3 marks)**

(b) Calculate Holm Ltd's liability to class 1A NIC in respect of Xanthe. **(6 marks)**

(c) Calculate Xanthe's net disposable income in respect of her employment. **(7 marks)**

Note: Ignore the employment allowance.

42.3 Mack lives in London and is UK resident and domiciled.

Mack received the following income in 2018/19:

- Gross UK employment income of £25,385. Income tax of £2,957 was deducted at source via PAYE.

- UK dividends received in cash of £13,000.

- Interest received on a UK bank account of £2,680.

- Gross overseas debenture interest of £9,450 (includes overseas tax of £2,200).

- Gross overseas rental income of £15,000 (includes overseas tax of £8,000).

Requirements

(a) Calculate Mack's income tax liability for 2018/19 before taking account of any double taxation relief available. **(4 marks)**

(b) Calculate the amount of double taxation relief available to set against Mack's income tax liability for 2018/19. **(9 marks)**

Total: 40 marks

43 Lyra

Lyra is an ICAEW Chartered Accountant working as a sole practitioner. One of Lyra's clients, Hat plc, has just received a tax repayment of £1 million from HMRC in error. The finance director of Hat plc has told Lyra that he will only repay the £1 million if HMRC realises its mistake.

Requirement

State and explain the steps Lyra should take in this situation to deal with HMRC's error. Your answer should include an explanation of Lyra's duty of confidentiality to Hat plc. **Total: 7 marks**

44 Hammer Ltd

44.1 Hammer Ltd owns 100% of Nut Ltd, 100% of Bolt Ltd, 75% of Screw Ltd, 52% of Nail GmbH, and 49% of Tack Ltd. All the group companies are UK resident trading companies except Nail GmbH which is resident in Germany.

Hammer Ltd and Tack Ltd make wholly standard-rated supplies in the UK.

Nut Ltd sells goods to private individuals in EU countries other than the UK. If the goods were sold in the UK they would be standard-rated supplies.

Bolt Ltd makes wholly zero-rated supplies in the UK.

Screw Ltd makes wholly exempt supplies in the UK.

Nail GmbH sells all of its goods outside of the EU. If the goods were sold in the UK they would be standard-rated supplies.

Requirement

Explain why Hammer Ltd and Nut Ltd, but none of the other companies, should be included in a single VAT group. **(6 marks)**

44.2 On 1 July 2018 Burro Ltd sold two newly constructed properties:

- A commercial property to Pane Ltd for £150 million
- A residential property to Abigail for £825,000

Both properties are located in London. All amounts are stated exclusive of any VAT.

Burro Ltd and Pane Ltd are UK resident, VAT registered, trading companies.

Burro Ltd is not connected with Pane Ltd or with Abigail. Abigail does not currently own any other residential properties although she is not a first time buyer.

Requirements

(a) Briefly explain whether any input VAT incurred in relation to the construction of each property is recoverable by Burro Ltd. **(2 marks)**

(b) Calculate how much stamp duty land tax is due on each purchase. **(3 marks)**

(c) Briefly explain how much stamp duty land tax would be due on the purchase of the commercial property if Pane Ltd were a wholly owned subsidiary of Burro Ltd.

(2 marks)

Total: 13 marks

45 Emma and Tom

45.1 For 2018/19 Emma was resident in the UK. Emma has always been domiciled in the UK.

On 1 July 2018 Emma sold her house in Manchester, England, for £330,000. Emma purchased the house for £153,000 on 1 January 2007. Emma incurred stamp duty land tax of £1,530 and also paid legal fees of £600 relating to the purchase. Emma occupied the house as follows:

- Emma lived in the house for the first 18 months until 1 July 2008 when she was sent to London by her employer to work on a client project.

- Emma spent five years working on various client projects in London and finally returned to live in her own home on 1 July 2013. For the five years she was in London Emma let the house to tenants.

- Emma lived in the house again for six months from 1 July 2013 to 31 December 2013.

- Emma decided to go travelling and left the UK on 1 January 2014. While she was overseas the house was let to tenants.

- Emma returned to the UK on 1 April 2018 and has been living at her sister's house since her return. Emma's house was left empty from 1 April 2018 to its sale on 1 July 2018.

In October 2018 Emma sold a commercial property, realising a chargeable gain of £50,000. In January 2019 Emma sold an antique clock for £15,000 which she purchased in January 2011 for £10,000.

For 2018/19 Emma had employment income of £22,500.

Requirement

Calculate Emma's capital gains tax liability for 2018/19. Clearly show your treatment of each asset. **(10 marks)**

45.2 Tom died on 1 January 2019. At the date of his death Tom was domiciled in the UK and lived in England. Tom's death estate comprised:

- cash and other personal effects worth £350,000.

- a life assurance policy taken out on his own life with a market value of £55,000 at the date of his death. The proceeds payable on death were £150,000.

- 10,000 units in a unit trust. On 1 January 2019 the bid price of a unit was £1.55 and the offer price was £1.58.

At the date of his death Tom had an outstanding bank loan of £20,000 and owed HMRC £17,000.

On his death Tom left £5,000 to a UK political party and the remainder of his death estate to be divided equally between his children. At the last general election one MP for this political party was elected to the UK parliament, with 500,000 votes being cast for candidates of this party.

During his lifetime Tom made the following gifts:

- 1 January 2010 – gross chargeable transfer of £275,000
- 1 February 2012 – gift of £250,000 in cash to a discretionary trust

In February 2017 Tom's father died leaving Tom his entire death estate valued at £500,000. Tom's father had made no lifetime gifts.

Requirement

Calculate the amount of inheritance tax arising as a result of Tom's death. **(15 marks)**

Total: 25 marks

46 Bagno Ltd

John Smith owns 100% of the shares in both Bagno Ltd and Acqua Ltd. Bagno Ltd had the following shareholdings on 1 April 2018:

Bagno Ltd

85%   4%   85%

Doccia Ltd   Tappo SpA (Italian resident trading company)   Onda Ltd

75%

Ponte Ltd

Results for the year ended 31 March 2019 for the UK resident trading companies are:

	Acqua Ltd £	Bagno Ltd £	Doccia Ltd £	Onda Ltd £	Ponte Ltd £
Trade profits/(losses)	1,000,000	(5,000,000)	1,000,000	1,000,000	2,200,000
Property income	–		–	1,900,000	–
Chargeable gains/(losses)	–	See below	160,000	(900,000)	–
Qualifying charitable donation	–		–	(400,000)	–
Trading loss b/f (incurred in y/e 31 March 2018)	–	(200,000)	–	(500,000)	–

Ponte Ltd

Ponte Ltd's trading profit of £2,200,000 is stated before any deduction for capital allowances:

- The tax written down values brought forward at 1 April 2018 were:

  - £875,450 for the main pool
  - £345,600 for the special rate pool
  - £42,000 for a short life asset

- The short life asset was sold for £76,000. The short life asset originally cost £100,000.

- Ponte Ltd purchased a new machine for £300,000 which has a useful economic life of 30 years.

- Ponte Ltd purchased a new machine for £100,000 which has a useful economic life of 12 years.

- Ponte Ltd spent £500,000 on a new science laboratory for its research and development activities. The purchase price represents £350,000 for the cost of the land and £150,000 for the buildings.

Bagno Ltd

On 1 March 2019 Bagno Ltd sold its 4% shareholding in Tappo SpA for £860,000. Bagno Ltd originally purchased these shares on 1 January 1995 for £265,000.

Group policy on losses

Group policy is to utilise capital losses in priority to trading losses, using all losses as quickly as possible.

Requirements

46.1 Calculate Ponte Ltd's final tax-adjusted trading profit for the year ended 31 March 2019.

(5 marks)

46.2 Regarding group relationships for corporation tax purposes:

- state which companies are members of Bagno Ltd's loss relief group; and
- state which companies are members of Bagno Ltd's chargeable gains group. **(2 marks)**

46.3 Assuming the companies utilise losses in accordance with group policy:

- explain how the capital losses should be utilised;
- calculate the taxable total profits for all five UK companies for the year ended 31 March 2019; and
- clearly show the amount(s) of any losses carried forward. **(8 marks)**

Notes

1 Assume the RPI for December 2017 is 278.1 and for March 2019 s 288.1.
2 Ignore VAT and stamp taxes. **Total: 15 marks**

47 Indira

47.1 Indira runs a clothes manufacturing business, Silk Outfitters, in partnership with her two sons Chakor and Sanjeev.

Silk Outfitters trading profits

Indira has calculated a draft tax-adjusted profit figure of £171,000 for the year ended 31 December 2018. However, this is before deducting any amounts in respect of the following:

- The partnership leased new business premises on 1 June 2018 as part of a plan to expand the business and incurred the following associated costs:

  - The partnership paid rent of £24,000 annually in advance to lease the premises.

  - To assist with the expansion a bank loan of £200,000 was drawn down with an annual interest rate of 5%.

  - The new premises were in a poor condition and some of the windows had to be replaced before the premises could be used. The new windows cost the partnership £10,000.

  - Legal fees of £2,000.

- The partnership spent the following amounts on marketing:

	£
Adverts in newspapers	7,012
Staff party (£200 per employee)	1,000
Corporate hospitality to entertain clients at local sporting events	6,300

  Indira knows that there is a liability to class 1A national insurance contributions (NIC) in respect of the staff party. However, as Indira does not know how to calculate the NIC, she has not deducted it from the draft tax-adjusted trading profit.

- The partnership paid a £60 parking fine incurred by Chakor while delivering stock to a customer.

- Indira took clothes costing £240 out of the business for her own use. These would have sold for £500 and no accounting adjustment has been made.

- The partnership gave away 100 silk scarves costing £982 to locals in an attempt to generate some sales contracts.

Capital allowances have not yet been calculated. Tax written down values as at 1 January 2018 were:

	£
Main pool	76,500
Indira's car with 75% business use (purchased in 2015 with CO_2 emissions of 140g/km)	18,000

The partnership purchased a new car for Sanjeev on 1 June 2018 for £25,000. The car has CO2 emissions of 50g/km. The car's business use is 60%. Plant and machinery costing £12,000 was purchased on 12 July 2018 to help get the new premises functional.

Allocation of partnership profits

Indira and Chakor had been running Silk Outfitters in partnership for a number of years sharing profits equally. Sanjeev joined Silk Outfitters as a partner on 1 June 2018.

After Sanjeev joined the partnership, the profit sharing agreement was changed to pay Indira a salary of £15,000 pa with the balance of profits shared 2:2:1 to Indira, Chakor and Sanjeev respectively.

The partnership has forecast its tax-adjusted trading profit for the year ended 31 December 2019 to be £115,000.

Requirements

(a) Calculate the final tax-adjusted trading profit for the partnership for the year ended 31 December 2018. Show your treatment of each item. Ignore VAT and stamp duty land tax. **(12 marks)**

(b) Calculate each partner's share of the tax-adjusted trading profit for the year ended 31 December 2018. **(3 marks)**

(c) Calculate each partner's assessable trading profit for 2018/19. **(3 marks)**

(d) Calculate Indira's liability to national insurance contributions for 2018/19 with respect to her share of the partnership profits. **(3 marks)**

47.2 Meera works for Limo Ltd as an employment law specialist. For 2018/19 she received the following remuneration package:

- Salary of £45,000.

- £2,500 of shopping vouchers which cost Limo Ltd £2,250.

- A loan of £100,000 at an annual rate of interest of 1%. Meera took out the loan on 1 January 2019 and has not repaid any of the capital.

- General round sum allowance of £8,000. Meera spent £6,375 of the allowance on client entertaining and the rest on clothes for herself for work purposes.

Meera drove 12,000 business miles in her own car in 2018/19. Limo Ltd paid her £0.25 per mile.

Meera personally paid £250 as her annual subscription to the Chartered Institute of Personnel & Development, which is on HMRC's list of approved professional bodies.

Limo Ltd operates a Give as You Earn scheme which is an approved payroll giving scheme. Meera donates £50 per month to charity via the scheme.

Other income

During 2018/19 Meera received £15,000 in rent from a property she rents out to unrelated tenants and incurred allowable property costs for the year of £7,300. Rent of £3,000 relating to February and March 2019 remained unpaid at the year end. Meera anticipates that she will be paid the outstanding rent.

During 2018/19 Meera also received bank deposit interest of £8,125 and dividends of £7,800.

Meera won £9,000 on the lottery.

Meera makes monthly cash contributions of £100 to her personal pension scheme.

Requirements

(a) Calculate Meera's taxable employment income for 2018/19. Show your treatment of each item. **(7 marks)**

Note: Assume that the official rate of interest throughout 2018/19 is 2.5% pa.

(b) Calculate Meera's income tax liability for 2018/19. **(6 marks)**

47.3 Sunil's tax liabilities for 2016/17 were:

	£
Income tax	25,000
Class 4 NIC	3,000
Capital gains tax	3,800

Sunil planned to retire during 2017/18 and therefore made a claim to reduce his payments on account for 2017/18 to £10,000 each.

Sunil made the following payments to settle his actual income tax and class 4 NIC liabilities for 2017/18:

		£
First payment on account	31 January 2018	10,000
Second payment on account	1 September 2018	10,000
Balancing payment	1 June 2019	19,000

Requirement

Calculate the interest payable in respect of Sunil's payments on account for 2017/18. For each payment on account state when each payment was due and the period for which interest is payable. **(6 marks)**

Note: Assume an interest rate of 3% pa and work to the nearest month and pound.

Total: 40 marks

48 Teresa

Teresa is an ICAEW Chartered Accountant working as a sole practitioner with no employees. Anthony is one of Teresa's tax clients and is a sole trader.

In January 2019, while preparing Anthony's personal tax return, Teresa noticed a £50,000 tax repayment from HMRC on Anthony's bank statement. At the time Anthony explained that this related to a period before he became one of Teresa's clients. Teresa had not been made aware of this by Anthony's previous accountant so she advised Anthony to check with HMRC whether this was an error. He refused to do so, stating that he was certain it was correct. Teresa reluctantly accepted his explanation and took no further action, although it should have been apparent to her that HMRC had made a mistake. Anthony has since been charged with money laundering offences in relation to events leading up to the repayment.

Requirements

48.1 State the possible consequences for an ICAEW Chartered Accountant of failure to disclose money laundering. **(2 marks)**

48.2 State **two** potential defences available to an ICAEW Chartered Accountant who is charged with failure to disclose. **(2 marks)**

48.3 Explain what actions Teresa should have taken regarding the HMRC error. **(3 marks)**

Total: 7 marks

49 Star Ltd

49.1 Star Ltd is a UK VAT-registered company manufacturing goods which are standard rated when supplied in the UK. The company sells its goods within and outside the UK to both private individuals and VAT-registered businesses, and retains full documentation for all transactions. The following figures relate to the quarter ended 31 March 2019:

Sales	£
All sales figures exclude any VAT.	
Sales in the UK	385,000
Sales elsewhere in the EU:	
To other businesses	32,000
To individuals	15,400
Overseas sales outside the EU:	
To other businesses	20,000
To individuals	5,000

Purchases and expenses

All figures below are the cash amounts paid directly to the suppliers, inclusive of any VAT where appropriate.

	£
Materials – all standard-rated goods:	
From UK suppliers	105,000
From suppliers in China (outside the EU)	78,000
Car purchased for private use by the managing director	24,000
Overhead costs – all standard rated	42,000
Professional services – from consultant in China	7,200

Star Ltd does not pay for the fuel for the managing director's car.

Requirement

Calculate the VAT payable by Star Ltd for the quarter ended 31 March 2019. Show the output tax and/or input tax for each item. **(6 marks)**

49.2 Caitlin is VAT registered and owns many residential and commercial properties. She has recently received a substantial sum of money that she wishes to invest in her property business. She then intends to rent any property purchased to tenants. She will purchase one of the following properties located in London, directly from the builder, paying £200,000, plus VAT where appropriate:

- A new residential property
- A new freehold commercial property

Requirements

(a) Explain the VAT implications of the purchase and renting out of each of the properties, including the impact on Caitlin of opting to tax where possible. **(4 marks)**

(b) Calculate the stamp duty land tax (SDLT) payable by Caitlin on each of the purchases. **(3 marks)**

Total: 13 marks

50 Carmen

50.1 Carmen lives in London. She has been resident in the UK since 2004/05 but is non-UK domiciled, having been born and brought up in Ruritania.

Carmen intends to return to Ruritania permanently on 5 April 2020 and has been selling some of her assets to raise money in preparation for her move. During 2018/19 she sold the following assets:

- 4,500 of her shares in Widmore Ltd, an unquoted UK investment company. Carmen sold these to her brother for £36 each when the market value was £45 each. Carmen had purchased 6,000 shares for £90,000 in August 2007. The shares were the subject of a 1-for-4 rights issue at £20 per share in July 2009 and she took up all of her rights.

- Seven out of 10 hectares of land in Ruritania. Carmen sold the seven hectares for £520,000 less auctioneer's fees at 3%. At the date of sale the remaining three hectares were valued at £150,000. She had purchased the full 10 hectares in November 1999 for £120,000. She has paid Ruritanian tax of £63,100 on the disposal, and will keep the remaining proceeds in her Ruritanian bank account until she returns to live there.

The UK has no double tax treaty with Ruritania.

For 2018/19 Carmen's only source of income was UK employment income of £52,600.

Carmen will continue to live in her house in London until she moves back to Ruritania in April 2020 and immediately becomes non-UK resident. She will then wait two years before selling it, to ensure that she is happy to make her move permanent. She originally purchased the house in April 2005 for £180,000 and has lived there since then, except for a nine-month period in 2012 when she took time off work to travel around Europe. The house was worth £375,000 on 5 April 2015. Carmen will benefit from principal private residence relief but will not make any election in respect of the gain on the property.

Requirements

(a) Calculate Carmen's capital gains tax liability for 2018/19, assuming:

- Carmen does not make a remittance basis claim; and
- Carmen does make a remittance basis claim.

Present your answer in two columns using headings:

(1) No claim; and
(2) Remittance basis claim. **(11 marks)**

(b) Calculate the chargeable gain on Carmen's house, assuming it is sold on 5 April 2022 for £450,000. Show the amount of any available reliefs and exemptions. **(3 marks)**

50.2 You are a tax assistant at a firm of ICAEW Chartered Accountants. Hugo was a client of your firm until his death on 28 December 2018.

During his lifetime Hugo made the following gifts:

- June 2010 – gift of £342,000 in cash to a discretionary trust.

- January 2012 – gift of shares in a quoted investment company worth £98,000 to his daughter Claire. The shares were valued at £78,000 on Hugo's death.

In his will, Hugo left the following assets:

- His house in London worth £860,000 with a mortgage secured on it of £350,000.

- Cash and other personal effects worth £290,000.

- Shares in Lapidus Ltd, an unquoted trading company with a market value of £140,000. Hugo inherited the shares on the death of his wife Kate in February 2018. Kate had owned the shares since August 2015. On her death Kate left her entire estate to Hugo with the exception of jewellery worth £400,000, which she left to Claire.

At the date of his death Hugo had outstanding tax payable and a bank loan totalling £15,300. Hugo left his entire estate to Claire.

Requirement

Calculate the amount of inheritance tax payable as a result of Hugo's death. Show the amount of any reliefs and exemptions. **(11 marks)**

Total: 25 marks

51 Faraday Ltd

The Faraday Ltd group comprises Faraday Ltd; Straume Ltd, in which Faraday Ltd has an 80% shareholding; and Rutherford Ltd, in which Straume Ltd has a 75% shareholding.

All three companies prepare accounts to 31 March each year. The group always uses losses as early as possible. Both losses and capital allowances are claimed within Faraday Ltd as far as possible.

Trading profits

Faraday Ltd has draft tax-adjusted trading profits before capital allowances for the year ended 31 March 2019 of £621,400. However this is before any possible deduction in respect of the following three items:

- Research and development (R&D) expenditure

	£
Computer hardware	2,900
Computer software	3,700
Staff costs – R&D workers	48,000
	54,600

The R&D workers are provided by an agency which is an unconnected company.

Faraday Ltd is a small company for R&D purposes.

- Finance costs

	£
Interest payable on a loan to purchase the shares in Straume Ltd	1,100
Arrangement fee for a loan taken out on 30 March 2019 for the purchase of new machinery	400
	1,500

- The tax written down value of the main pool at 1 April 2018 is £158,000. Faraday Ltd purchased new machinery on 31 March 2019 costing £40,000.

Other income and gains

In addition to trading profits, Faraday Ltd has other sources of income and made some capital disposals during the year ended 31 March 2019. These have all been treated correctly in calculating the draft tax-adjusted trading profits.

- Faraday Ltd had interest receivable of £1,560 from loan stock which is a qualifying corporate bond. The company sold the loan stock in January 2019 for £46,000. The loan stock was purchased in June 2017 for £38,000.

- Faraday Ltd sold its office building, Austen Towers, in January 2019 for £580,000. Austen Towers had been purchased in July 1998 for £210,000. Faraday Ltd purchased a replacement office building, Burke Place, in September 2018 for £300,000.

Faraday Ltd will defer all possible gains.

Other group issues

- Straume Ltd had also purchased two properties during the year ended 31 March 2019; a factory used in its trade for £150,000 and a retail unit for investment purposes for £70,000.

- Rutherford Ltd has had a difficult year and has trading losses of £75,000 and capital losses of £29,000 for the year ended 31 March 2019.

Requirements

51.1 State which companies are members of Faraday Ltd's:

- Loss relief group; and
- Chargeable gains group. **(2 marks)**

51.2 Calculate Faraday Ltd's corporation tax payable for the year ended 31 March 2019. Show the amount of any available reliefs and exemptions. **(13 marks)**

Note: Assume an RPI for December 2017 of 278.1 and January 2019 of 286.9. Ignore VAT and stamp taxes.

Total: 15 marks

52 Omar, Pierre and Sayid

52.1 Omar, Pierre and Sayid have traded in partnership for many years as 'Oceanic Cases', manufacturing luggage. The partnership made a draft profit for the year ended 31 January 2019 of £413,633 after accounting for the following items:

	Notes	£
Depreciation	1	42,100
Car lease costs	1	4,000
Fines	2	2,575
Legal and professional fees	3	5,700
Repairs	4	18,000

Notes

1   The total depreciation charge of £42,100 includes depreciation on vehicles that were acquired for use by Omar and Sayid on 1 February 2018:

- Omar has use of an Audi car with CO_2 emissions of 162g/km. It cost the partnership £26,000. Omar uses the car 40% for business purposes.

- Sayid has use of a Ford van with CO_2 emissions of 150g/km. It cost the partnership £15,000. Sayid does not use the van for private purposes.

Pierre also has use of a BMW car with CO_2 emissions of 144g/km. On 1 February 2018 the partnership took out a three-year lease on the car at a cost of £4,000 pa. Pierre uses the car 30% for business purposes.

The partners' previous vehicles were disposed of in January 2018.

2   Fines of £2,575 are made up of a £2,500 fine for breach of health and safety regulations, and a £75 parking fine incurred by an employee when visiting a client.

3   Legal and professional fees:

	£
Recovery of bad debts	600
Costs of registering a patent	3,000
Legal costs re purchase of factory (Note 4)	2,100
	5,700

4   Until this year the partnership has leased factory premises however, as the business is expanding a larger factory has been purchased.

Repairs:

	£
Repairs to the chimney of the new factory. These were required for the factory to be operational	10,000
Redecoration of the partnership offices	2,000
New double glazing to the partnership offices (replacing single glazing)	6,000

5   Capital allowances have not yet been calculated. Tax written down values as at 1 February 2018 were:

	£
Main pool	35,000
Special rate pool	23,000

In addition to the vehicles mentioned in Note 1, the partnership incurred other capital expenditure in January 2019 when the business moved to the new factory premises:

	£
Machinery – new machine to improve efficiency	140,000
Permanent internal wall built to divide factory floor	20,000
Additional thermal insulation for the new factory	75,000

In addition to these items Omar took suitcases from the partnership costing £1,200 for his own use. There would have sold as a mark-up on cost of 40% and no entry was made in the accounts.

Pierre made a £500 payment to a supplier from his personal bank account which has yet to be reflected in the partnerships accounts.

Omar, Pierre and Sayid's original partnership agreement provides for all partners to receive interest on capital at 4% pa based on the balance at the start of the accounting period. The partners' capital accounts at 1 February 2018 were £50,000 each for Omar and Pierre, and £100,000 for Sayid. Omar receives a salary of £20,000 pa. The balance of any profits is shared 30% to Omar, 50% to Pierre and 20% to Sayid.

Sayid left the partnership on his 50th birthday on 31 July 2018, to take early retirement. From that time Omar and Pierre agreed to share profits and losses equally, with no salary or interest on capital for either partner.

Sayid has overlap profits brought forward of £5,000.

Omar and Pierre have heard about the 'cash basis of accounting' for tax purposes. They have been told that it can simplify tax reporting, but are not sure whether it could apply to their business. The partnership anticipates that trading profits will continue at approximately the same level for the next few years.

Requirements

(a) Calculate the tax-adjusted trading profit for Oceanic Cases for the year ended 31 January 2019. **(14 marks)**

(b) Calculate each partner's share of the tax-adjusted trading profit for the year ended 31 January 2019. **(4 marks)**

(c) Calculate Sayid's taxable trading profit for 2018/19. **(1 mark)**

(d) Identify the types of business that can elect for the cash basis of accounting, and determine whether the partnership is eligible to use this basis. **(2 marks)**

Note: Ignore VAT.

52.2 Regina works for Cortez Ltd as a promotion and marketing manager and received the following employment package for 2018/19:

- Salary of £3,200 per month.

- A general round sum allowance of £200 per month. During 2018/19 Regina spent £2,170 of the allowance on entertaining clients.

- A car with a list price when new of £25,000, although Regina paid a contribution of £5,000 towards this when she received the car in June 2017. The car has CO_2 emissions of 93g/km. Cortez Ltd pays for all of the petrol for the car.

- Private medical insurance that cost the company £400.

- Christmas present of vouchers to use in a local department store to purchase goods up to the value of £280. However, the vouchers cost Cortez Ltd only £230.

- Contributions equal to 5% of Regina's salary paid by Cortez Ltd into Regina's personal pension scheme. Regina herself pays 6% of her salary into the scheme.

Regina also pays a subscription of £200 each year to the Institute of Promotional Marketing, an HMRC-approved body. Cortez Ltd does not reimburse her for this.

Other income and payments

Regina owns a furnished house that she let throughout 2018/19 for rental income of £12,000. Her costs of letting were as follows:

	£
Insurance premiums	
Paid on 1 July 2017 for the year to 30 June 2018	200
Paid on 1 July 2018 for the year to 30 June 2019	240
Interest on a mortgage to buy the property	400
Replacement of sofa with similar model	1,170

During 2018/19 Regina received dividend income of £610; including £110 of dividends from her ISA.

Holiday plans

Regina will be 40 years old in March 2019, and she intends to use all remaining 2018/19 income, after payment of tax and other expenses, to pay for a special holiday. She spent £16,000 on household bills and personal expenses during 2018/19.

Requirements

(a) Calculate Regina's taxable employment income for 2018/19. Show your treatment of each item. **(5 marks)**

(b) Calculate Regina's primary class 1 national insurance contributions for 2018/19. **(3 marks)**

(c) Calculate Regina's income tax liability for 2018/19. **(5 marks)**

(d) Calculate the post-tax cash available to Regina to pay for her holiday. **(6 marks)**

Total: 40 marks

December 2016 exam questions

53 Johanna

Lucy works in the tax department of DB LLP, a firm of ICAEW Chartered Accountants. Johanna has been one of DB LLP's clients for many years, and Lucy prepares Johanna's VAT returns.

Johanna disagrees with Lucy's treatment of some items in her most recent VAT return. Johanna is refusing to allow Lucy to submit the VAT return, which is now late, and Johanna has not paid the VAT Lucy has calculated. The following is an extract from an email sent by Johanna to Lucy:

'I don't think that you have spent enough time on my return and I am seriously considering reporting your firm to ICAEW. If there are problems with HMRC I expect you to sort these out as you are responsible for my VAT.'

Lucy's manager, Gordon, has initiated a conflict resolution process. He has followed DB LLP's internal procedures and believes that Lucy has acted appropriately throughout, but may have been subjected to undue pressure from Johanna to change the return. Gordon has discussed alternative courses of action with Johanna, but the matter is still unresolved.

Requirements

53.1 Identify one fundamental principle threatened in this situation and explain the nature of the threat. **(2 marks)**

53.2 Explain who is responsible for the accuracy of Johanna's VAT return, and who will be liable to HMRC if an incorrect return is submitted. **(3 marks)**

53.3 Identify any further action that it would be advisable for DB LLP to take in relation to the conflict. **(2 marks)**

Total: 7 marks

54 Yemi Ltd Group

The Yemi Ltd group has the following structure:

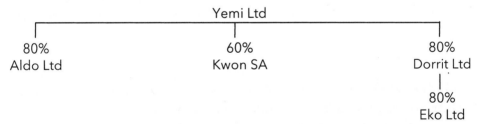

All companies are UK resident except Kwon SA, which is resident in Spain. The companies make supplies as follows:

Yemi Ltd   Standard-rated supplies
Aldo Ltd   Exempt supplies
Kwon SA   All supplies are made in Spain (in the EU), but would be standard rated if made in the UK
Dorrit Ltd   Zero-rated supplies
Eko Ltd   Standard-rated supplies

All companies that are able to VAT register have done so individually. However the directors are considering forming a VAT group from 1 January 2020 so that they can complete a single VAT return each quarter.

Yemi Ltd owns a freehold office building in Birmingham which it uses for its trade. The newly-constructed building was purchased in October 2017 for £140,000 plus VAT. The directors intend to sell the freehold of the building to either Dorrit Ltd or Eko Ltd for its current value of £200,000, plus VAT if appropriate. The purchasing company will then lease the property back to Yemi Ltd for a market rent. The sale is expected to take place on 21 January 2020. There is no option to tax in place on the building, and the purchasing company does not intend to opt to tax it.

Requirements

54.1 State the conditions to be satisfied if two or more companies wish to form a group for VAT purposes. **(2 marks)**

54.2 Explain why Yemi Ltd and Eko Ltd, but none of the other companies, should be included in a VAT group. **(4 marks)**

54.3 For Yemi Ltd and Eko Ltd, explain the VAT consequences of the sale of the building if sold to Eko Ltd, assuming:

- Eko Ltd is in a VAT group with Yemi Ltd;
- Eko Ltd is not in any VAT group. **(2 marks)**

54.4 Explain, with supporting calculations, the liability to stamp duty land tax (SDLT) on the purchase of the freehold office building by:

- Dorrit Ltd;
- Eko Ltd, if it is in a VAT group with Yemi Ltd; or
- Eko Ltd, if it is not in a VAT group with Yemi Ltd.

State the due date for payment of any SDLT and by whom it is paid. **(5 marks)**

Note: Throughout this question, assume rates and rules applying in 2018/19 continue to apply in future.

Total: 13 marks

55 Ruby and Todd

55.1 For 2018/19 Ruby had taxable income of £45,000. She made the following disposals:

- 1 August 2018: Sale of her home for £458,000. Ruby purchased the property for on 1 February 2008 for £200,000, and had lived in the house the whole period of her ownership except for a 4 year period from 1 January 2010 when she travelled around the world.

- 20 September 2018: A gift of 300,000 ordinary shares in Crust plc, a trading company, to her brother Ozzy. Ruby and Ozzy have agreed to make an election for gift relief and Ruby will make a claim for entrepreneurs' relief.

  The 300,000 shares gifted represent a 6% holding in Crust plc. Ruby was a director of Crust plc from 2007 until her retirement at the end of September 2018. On 20 September 2018 the ordinary shares in Crust plc were quoted at 560p–574p with a marked bargain of 564p. Ruby purchased the shares in October 2004 for a total cost of £400,000.

  On 20 September 2018 Crust plc had assets with the following values:

	£'000
Freehold property used in the trade	20,000
Leasehold property held for investment purposes	5,000
Plant and machinery (Note)	1,500
Stock	600
Debtors	500
Cash	1,300
	28,900

Note: Plant and machinery includes several items valued at £1 million in total, each of which cost more than £6,000 and are valued at more than the cost of purchase. All other items are cars used in the trade.

Requirement

Calculate Ruby's capital gains tax liability for 2018/19. Show the amount of any available reliefs and exemptions. **(9 marks)**

55.2 Todd is expected to die within the next few years. He has made the following gifts during his lifetime:

- 31 August 2014 – a gross chargeable transfer of £300,000 to a discretionary trust.

- 16 March 2019 – a gift of 40,000 £1 ordinary shares in ABC plc, a quoted trading company, to a discretionary trust. On that day the shares were quoted at 460p–476p with marked bargains of 461p, 463p and 471p. ABC plc has a total issued share capital of 50 million £1 ordinary shares. Todd has owned the shares since January 2013.

- 24 March 2019 – a gift of 2,000 shares in XYZ Ltd, an unquoted trading company, to his brother Finn. Finn intends to keep his shares in XYZ Ltd for many years. The shareholdings for the 25 years prior to the gift of shares were as follows:

	Number
Todd	5,500
Lynn, Todd's wife	3,000
Dee, Todd's niece	1,500
	10,000

The value of the XYZ Ltd shares at 24 March 2019 was as follows:

Holding	Price per share
Up to 25%	£21
26%–50%	£30
51%–74%	£38
75%–100%	£45

The shares are expected to remain at this value for the next few years. Todd also has other assets worth £2 million of which £1.5 million (including the family home) will be left to Lynn. His XYZ Ltd shares and the remaining assets will be left to Dee.

Requirements

(a) Calculate the amount of inheritance tax arising as a result of Todd's death, assuming that he dies on 1 December 2021 and that the shares remain at the March 2019 value. Show the amount of any available reliefs and exemptions. **(13 marks)**

(b) Explain, with supporting calculations, the inheritance tax implications of Finn changing his intentions and selling his shares in XYZ Ltd prior to Todd's death. **(3 marks)**

Total: 25 marks

56 Scissor Ltd

Scissor Ltd is a UK-resident trading company which is a large company for the purposes of research and development. For many years the company had two wholly-owned subsidiaries: Crop Ltd, a UK-resident trading company, and Divisi SpA, a company resident in Elixia. All three companies prepare accounts to 31 March each year.

For the year ended 31 March 2019 Scissor Ltd's draft tax-adjusted trading profit before deduction of capital allowances is £20,795,000. However the four items below may still require adjustment:

(1) The draft tax-adjusted trading profit includes a profit on disposal of the shares in Crop Ltd of £241,000. Scissor Ltd purchased the shares on 1 June 2004 for £442,000 and sold them on 20 May 2018 for £683,000.

   At the time of the share disposal, Crop Ltd owned a property worth £300,000 that was transferred to it on 18 November 2014 by Scissor Ltd. The property was originally purchased by Scissor Ltd on 29 April 2003 for £80,000 and was worth £240,000 on 18 November 2014.

(2) Interest payable of £28,900 has been deducted in arriving at the draft tax-adjusted trading profit, comprising:

	£
Interest on a loan to purchase a 5% shareholding in Brush Ltd	11,900
Interest on a loan to purchase new machinery	3,000
Bank overdraft interest	14,000
	28,900

(3) Research and development expenditure, as detailed below, has been deducted in arriving at the draft tax-adjusted trading profit:

	£
Salaries of laboratory staff	92,000
Computer hardware	3,000
Computer software	4,500
Consumables	12,000
	111,500

   Scissor Ltd has elected for the tax credit regime to apply to its R&D expenditure.

(4) Scissor Ltd's capital allowances for the year ended 31 March 2019 are correctly calculated as £29,850 but before considering the information in items (1) to (4).

Other income

Scissor Ltd's other income in the year ended 31 March 2019 was:

- bank deposit interest receivable of £16,200;

- £2,700 of exempt dividends received from Brush Ltd, and £28,800 of exempt dividends received from Divisi SpA; and

- property income of £77,900 from renting out an office building in Elixia.

All income from Elixia is stated net of withholding tax at 18%.

Requirements

56.1 Explain the gains implications of the disposal of the shares in Crop Ltd. Calculate the total proceeds on disposal to be used in the gain calculation. **(5 marks)**

56.2 Calculate Scissor Ltd's final tax-adjusted trading profit for the year ended 31 March 2019 after capital allowances. **(6 marks)**

56.3 Calculate the corporation tax payable by Scissor Ltd for the year ended 31 March 2019. **(4 marks)**

Note: Ignore VAT and stamp taxes. The retail price index for December 2017 is 278.1 and May 2018 is 280.3 (assumed).

Total: 15 marks

57 Nellie, Ben and Judd

57.1 Nellie runs a luxury food business, 'Perfect Pies', as a sole trader. She prepares accounts to 31 March each year.

Recent years' tax-adjusted trading profits have been as follows:

Year ended 31 March	£
2015	60,000
2016	80,000
2017	90,000
2018	82,000

For the year ended 31 March 2019 Perfect Pies had a tax-adjusted loss of £24,000 before deduction of capital allowances.

The business is expected to make profits again in the future.

Capital allowances

Capital allowances for the year ended 31 March 2019 have not yet been calculated. Tax written down values as at 1 April 2018 were:

	£
Main pool	96,500
Special rate pool	900
Nellie's Ford car: 25% business use, CO_2 emissions 200g/km	4,220

During the year ended 31 March 2019 Nellie made the following purchases and a disposal:

		£
Purchases:		
25 October 2018	BMW car for Nellie:	
	30% business use, CO_2 emissions 146g/km	24,600
13 November 2018	Lift fitted within the factory building	74,040
10 December 2018	New small building to store raw materials	94,000
2 February 2019	Machinery	62,400
Disposal:		
25 October 2018	Nellie's Ford car (original cost £10,020)	3,500

Nellie is registered for VAT. All figures above are stated inclusive of VAT at 20% where relevant.

Nellie: other information

In recent years Nellie has had the following income and expenses:

	Notes	2017/18 £	2018/19 £
Rental income	1	13,650	13,650
Costs relating to the letting	1	(400)	(320)
Interest on NS&I Direct Saver account		6,500	6,800
REIT income	2	78,560	Nil

Nellie also had substantial chargeable gains in 2017/18, but none in 2018/19.

Notes

1 Since 6 April 2016 Nellie has let a furnished room in her house to a family friend receiving annual rental income of £13,650. She intends to make any election available to minimise her property income.

2 Nellie is a shareholder in a REIT and this dividend was received from the tax-exempt property income within the REIT.

Requirements

(a) Calculate the tax-adjusted trading loss after claiming maximum capital allowances for Perfect Pies for the year ended 31 March 2019. **(8 marks)**

(b) Explain the options available to Nellie for relieving the trading loss you have calculated in part (a). Use net income figures where available to illustrate your answer, but do not calculate any tax liabilities. **(8 marks)**

57.2 Ben has been employed as a sales and marketing manager by Boilt Ltd since 6 April 2018. Ben's employment package for the year ended 5 April 2019 was as follows:

- A salary of £45,000.

- A lump sum payment of £1,500 made to Ben to assist with solicitors' fees for purchase of a new house when relocating to London for his new job. This is 200 miles away from his previous home in Manchester.

- Photography equipment costing £4,000. The equipment was first provided to Ben for private use on 6 April 2018. On 6 October 2018, Ben purchased the equipment from Boilt Ltd for £2,500. At that time it was worth £3,000.

- Pension contributions: Boilt Ltd pays an amount equal to 2% of Ben's salary into Ben's personal pension scheme. Ben pays 4% of his salary into his personal pension scheme.

- An interest-free loan of £11,000. The loan was made to Ben on 6 April 2018 and he has not repaid any of the capital.

- A mileage allowance of 50p per mile paid for the 13,000 business miles travelled by Ben during 2018/19.

Ben paid an annual fee of £148 for his membership of the Institute of Sales and Marketing Management, an HMRC-approved body.

Requirements

(a) Calculate Ben's employment income for 2018/19. Show your treatment of each item.

(9 marks)

Note: The official rate of interest throughout 2018/19 is 2.5%.

(b) Calculate the national insurance contributions (NICs) payable by Boilt Ltd in respect of Ben's employment, identifying each class of NIC. State the due date for each class of NIC **(5 marks)**

Note: Ignore the employment allowance.

57.3 Judd, who is employed working in a second hand book shop, inherited a large collection of books from his grandmother in December 2018. He plans to sell these books via the internet as soon as possible. Some of the books are damaged and so he will get them rebound before selling them on. He plans to advertise in the local paper and anticipates cash receipts of between £800–£1,500 in 2018/19 and to incur minimal costs.

Requirements

(a) Discuss whether the profits made from Judd's proposed sale of books via the internet will be liable to either income tax or capital gains tax. **(6 marks)**

(b) Assuming that it is deemed that Judd is trading, explain how Judd's taxable trading profits will be calculated dependant on whether his cash receipts are £800 or £1,500. Explain any election available to allow Judd to minimise the income tax due. **(4 mark)**

Total: 40 marks

March 2017 exam questions

58 Mita and Ruth

58.1 Mita has been asked to take over as the money laundering reporting officer (MLRO) at her firm of ICAEW Chartered Accountants. She is enquiring about the role before deciding whether to accept.

Requirement

State the responsibilities of the MLRO with regard to reporting. **(3 marks)**

58.2 Ruth is an ICAEW Chartered Accountant employed by Sparks plc.

Sparks plc is preparing a database of employee qualifications and has asked Ruth to submit her qualifications.

The database will be used to find suitable candidates for a new project team. All team members will receive a 25% pay rise and a two-year secondment to the New York office.

Ruth wants to join the new project team but she does not have all of the qualifications required. She has decided to submit false information about her qualifications to ensure she gains a place on the new project team.

Sparks plc's policy is to dismiss employees who misrepresent their qualifications.

Requirement

Explain two of the fundamental principles that are threatened when Ruth submits the false information about her qualifications and identify the threat. **(4 marks)**

Total: 7 marks

59 Andy, Jim and Lamb Ltd

59.1 Andy is a doctor in a private medical practice. Andy is VAT registered. He charges patients a single fixed fee that pays for both the medical consultation (an exempt supply) and any medicine provided (a standard-rated supply). The fee remains the same even if no medicine is provided.

Requirement

Explain how Andy should determine the VAT due on his fees. **(4 marks)**

59.2 On 5 April 2019 Jim was granted a 30-year lease of a commercial property in London. Jim paid a premium of £261,500 and agreed to pay an annual rent of £5,500. This is Jim's first property purchase.

Requirement

Calculate Jim's stamp duty land tax liability from the grant of the lease. **(3 marks)**

59.3 Lamb Ltd is a VAT-registered company which is partially exempt. For the year ended 31 March 2019, Lamb Ltd failed both Simplified Test One and Simplified Test Two. Lamb Ltd needs to make an annual partial exemption adjustment calculation.

Lamb Ltd's supplies of goods in the year ended 31 March 2019 were:

	£
Standard-rated taxable supplies (excluding VAT)	562,562
Exempt supplies	68,821
	631,383

Lamb Ltd's input VAT for the year ended 31 March 2019 was:

	£
Wholly attributable to standard-rated supplies	100,100
Wholly attributable to exempt supplies	12,600
Non-attributable	26,780
	139,480

The input VAT recovered during the year ended 31 March 2019 was £125,532.

Requirement

Calculate any annual adjustment required to the input VAT recovered by Lamb Ltd for the year ended 31 March 2019. **(6 marks)**

Total: 13 marks

60 Clara and Simon

60.1 Clara is aged 55, lives in London and has always been resident and domiciled in the UK. In February 2019 she:

- realised a gain of £75,000 on the disposal of a painting.

- sold her entire holding of shares in XYZ plc for £12,000. Clara purchased the shares for £8,000 and held them in an ISA until their disposal.

- sold some jewellery at auction. Clara paid the auctioneer 5% of the £23,000 proceeds. Clara inherited the jewellery from her mother 10 years ago when it was valued for probate purposes at £16,000. Her mother paid £7,600 for the jewellery in 1983.

- sold shares in Garden Ltd, an unquoted trading company to her sister for £200,000 when the shares were worth £260,000. Clara had bought the shares in February 2010 for £150,000 and has never been employed by the company.

At 6 April 2018 Clara had a capital loss brought forward of £8,450.

For 2018/19 Clara has rental income of £3,600 and trading income of £13,500 from her business.

Clara's business made a tax-adjusted trading loss of £34,500 for 2019/20. Clara will utilise this 2019/20 loss as early as possible by offsetting it against her income and gains for 2018/19.

Requirements

(a) State the latest date by which Clara must submit a claim to offset her 2019/20 trading loss against her 2018/19 income and capital gains. **(1 mark)**

(b) Calculate Clara's capital gains tax liability for 2018/19. **(10 marks)**

60.2 Simon was born in America and is American domiciled. He became tax resident in the UK in 2002/2003 when he moved to London. During 2018/19 Simon made the following gifts of assets located in England:

- In May 2018 Simon gave £25,000 to his daughter.

- In June 2018 Simon gave 20,000 shares in PQR Ltd, an unquoted trading company, to the Cloud Discretionary Trust. Simon had owned the shares for 10 years.

At the time of the gift Simon owned 60,000 of the 100,000 shares in issue and the shares were valued at:

Shareholding	Price per share
1%–24%	£18
25%–50%	£25
51%–75%	£36
76%–100%	£46

PQR Ltd had total assets less current liabilities worth £5.8 million. Included in total assets was an investment property worth £600,000. PQR Ltd had a long-term bank loan of £400,000 outstanding.

- In August 2018 Simon gave a farm to the Wind Discretionary Trust. Simon rented the farm to tenants under a tenancy granted in January 2006. The farm's total agricultural value was £500,000. The farm's open market value of £850,000 is much higher because it takes account of planning permission attached to some of the land.

Simon's previous lifetime gifts were:

- July 2006 – gross chargeable transfer value of £263,000.
- July 2011 – cash gift of £125,000 to the Rain Discretionary Trust.

Requirements

(a) For inheritance tax purposes, state and explain the date from which Simon began to be treated as domiciled in the UK. **(2 marks)**

(b) Calculate the amount of any lifetime inheritance tax arising on each disposal in 2018/19. Show the amount of any available reliefs and exemptions. **(12 marks)**

Total: 25 marks

61 Cup Ltd

61.1 Cup Ltd owns 100% of Saucer Ltd, which owns 100% of Teaspoon Ltd. All three companies are UK-resident trading companies.

Saucer Ltd's draft accounting profit for its nine-month accounting period ended 31 December 2018 is £5,298,000. The items in Table 1 below have already been added or deducted in arriving at the draft profit.

Table 1	Notes	£
Net intangible fixed assets expense	1	25,000
Dividends received from Teaspoon Ltd		800,000
Profit on disposal of land	2	145,000
Rental income	3	72,000
Interest expense	4	93,750

Notes

1 The net intangible fixed assets expense figure comprises:

	£
Profit on disposal of trade-related copyright	(32,000)
Goodwill impairment expense	57,000
	25,000

2 On 1 August 2018 Saucer Ltd sold some land for £450,000. It purchased the land for £305,000 in January 2000.

3 Since 1 September 2018 Saucer Ltd has rented a commercial building to tenants. Prior to 1 September 2017 the building was used for business purposes. The monthly rent is £6,000. The tenants paid a full year's rent in advance on 1 September 2018.

4 The interest expense figure comprises:

	£
Interest on loan to purchase shares in Teaspoon Ltd	75,750
Interest on loan to purchase commercial building (Note 3)	18,000
	93,750

Capital allowances

On 1 April 2018, Saucer Ltd had tax written down values of £648,500 for its main pool and £256,000 for its special rate pool. On 1 June 2018 Saucer Ltd spent £525,000 on thermal insulation for its office premises and £250,000 on new machinery. Saucer Ltd is the only company in the group that purchases fixed assets.

Requirements

(a) Calculate Saucer Ltd's tax-adjusted trading income after capital allowances for the nine months ended 31 December 2018. Start with the draft profit of £5,298,000 and show all items given in Table 1 including the notes, using a zero for any item that requires no adjustment. **(8 marks)**

(b) Calculate Saucer Ltd's corporation tax liability for the nine months ended 31 December 2018. **(4 marks)**

Note: Assume an RPI for December 2017 of 278.1 and August 2018 of 283.3. Ignore VAT.

61.2 Cup Ltd owns 100% of Saucer Ltd. Saucer Ltd purchased 100% of Teaspoon Ltd on 1 October 2018. All three companies are UK-resident trading companies.

Teaspoon Ltd's results are:

Year ended	Taxable Total Profits £	Corporation Tax Liability £
28 February 2019	1,855,000	353,996
29 February 2020	685,000	130,150

Requirement

State and explain the dates by which Teaspoon Ltd should pay its corporation tax liability for the year ended 29 February 2020. **(3 marks)**

Total: 15 marks

62 Chitra

62.1 Chitra Nehru is aged 50. Chitra runs a UK manufacturing business, Ergo Containers, as a sole trader.

Ergo Containers

Chitra has calculated a draft accounting profit of £121,500 for her year ended 31 December 2018. However, this does not include the following items, as she was not sure how to treat them:

- Chitra took out a loan many years ago to purchase a building which comprises her business premises and the flat above. Interest of £14,000 pa is payable on this loan.

  Chitra lives in the flat above the business premises with her husband, Rajiv. The flat represents 15% of the building's total floor space.

- Staff salaries:

	£
Chitra	12,000
Chitra's niece who works full time in the business as an accounts assistant	20,000

The draft profit figure already includes a deduction of £15,000 for the staff costs of the other full-time accounts assistant.

- A fine of £3,500 for breach of Health & Safety regulations in the workplace.

- A gift to a local school of stock worth £2,300.

Chitra has yet to make any necessary adjustment to stock following a flood in October 2018 which damaged some containers. Chitra included the damaged containers in her closing stock figure at their original cost of £15,600. The containers had a market value before the flood of £20,800. After the flood their market value was £10,100.

Capital allowances have not yet been calculated. Tax written down values as at 1 January 2018 were:

	£
Main pool	56,755
Special rate pool	895
Chitra's car with 35% private use	21,000

The car was purchased in 2013 and has CO_2 emissions of 125g/km

Other income and payments in 2018/19

Chitra received building society deposit interest of £3,600 and dividends from EFG plc of £9,440. Chitra gave £4,000 in cash to a registered charity as a Gift Aid donation.

Requirements

(a) Calculate Chitra's tax-adjusted trading profit after capital allowances for Ergo Containers for the year ended 31 December 2018. Show your treatment of each item. Ignore VAT. **(8 marks)**

(b) Calculate Chitra's income tax liability for 2018/19. **(6 marks)**

(c) Calculate Chitra's liability to national insurance contributions on her business profits for 2018/19 and state the due date for payment. **(4 marks)**

62.2 Saina Nehru works as the finance director for BK Ltd, a fashion retailer. For 2018/19 Saina has received the following remuneration package:

- Salary of £86,000

- Use of a furnished company flat near the office. The flat has an annual value of £18,000. It cost BK Ltd £200,000 in January 2003. The flat had a market value of £425,000 in February 2013 when Saina first moved in. The flat was completely refurbished in January 2018 at a cost of £68,000. The furniture in the flat cost £26,000.

- Use of a company car with a list price of £21,000 which only cost BK Ltd £18,750. The car has CO_2 emissions of 134g/km. In September 2018 BK Ltd spent £2,455 on repairs to the car. Saina pays for her own petrol.

- Attendance at a training course on how to compose music which cost BK Ltd £2,400.

Alternative to company car

For 2020/21 BK Ltd has offered Saina an alternative to her existing company car scheme. If she were to accept the alternative, Saina would return her company car on 5 April 2020 and receive a car allowance of £1,000 (gross) per month instead. Saina would then lease a car privately at a cost of £675 per month. Saina would also need to pay £1,750 per year for its running costs, excluding petrol. Saina would continue to pay for her own petrol. The cost of Saina's fuel would be the same regardless of which alternative she chooses.

Saina will be an additional rate taxpayer in 2020/21.

Requirements

(a) Calculate Saina's taxable employment income for 2018/19. Show your treatment of each item. **(6 marks)**

(b) Calculate the after-tax cost to Saina of keeping her existing company car and the after-tax cost of choosing the car allowance instead. Use 2018/19 rates and allowances. **(4 marks)**

Note: Assume that the official rate of interest throughout 2018/19 was 2.5%.

62.3 Arun Nehru has been in partnership with his father Rajiv and brother Braj for a number of years. The partnership stopped trading on 30 November 2018. Arun's share of the partnership profits for the last two accounting periods is:

	£
Year ended 31 May 2018	30,264
Six months ended 30 November 2018	7,156

The partnership started trading on 1 August 2003 and prepared its first set of accounts for the 22 months to 31 May 2005. Arun's share of the partnership profits for this first accounting period was £75,020.

Requirements

Calculate Arun's assessable trading profits for 2018/19. **(4 marks)**

62.4 Rajiv Nehru is aged 53 and has made regular contributions to his personal pension scheme since 2014/15. In 2018/19 Rajiv had total employment income of £62,000, partnership income of £15,000, and rental income of £71,000.

Rajiv contributed the maximum possible tax relievable contribution to his personal pension scheme for 2018/19 using his unused allowances brought forward of £5,000 in addition to his annual allowance. Rajiv is wondering how much tax he saved as a result.

Requirement

Calculate the following:

- The maximum possible tax relievable pension contribution Rajiv could have made in 2018/19; and

- How much Rajiv's 2018/19 income tax liability was reduced by as a result of making the personal pension contribution. **(8 marks)**

Total: 40 marks

63 Liz, Kira and Jane

63.1 Liz is an ICAEW Chartered Accountant and operates as a sole practitioner in London. Liz will retire at the end of June 2019. She intends to cancel her professional indemnity insurance as soon as she retires.

Requirement

Explain what action Liz should take with respect to her professional indemnity insurance in order to comply with the ICAEW's Professional Indemnity Insurance Regulations. **(2 marks)**

63.2 Kira is an ICAEW Chartered Accountant employed by a large accountancy firm in London. Kira is being seconded to work for HMRC for a six-month period. After this, Kira will return to work for her employer.

Requirement

Explain what should be done to ensure that no conflict of interest arises during or after Kira's secondment. **(3 marks)**

63.3 Jane is an ICAEW Chartered Accountant employed in practice. Jane gave a new client legal advice about the taxation of his offshore income. The client admitted to Jane that he had not been declaring his offshore income to HMRC. Jane advised him to declare the income to HMRC and to pay the tax owed, together with any interest and penalties due. Jane did not check that the client had followed her legal advice. She did not consider making a report to her money laundering reporting officer.

Jane's client has now been convicted of money laundering. Jane is concerned that she may face prosecution for failure to report.

Requirement

Explain which defence Jane could use against a charge of failure to report a suspicion of money laundering. **(2 marks)**

Total: 7 marks

64 Mela Ltd and Pesca Ltd

64.1 Mela Ltd owns 100% of Neem Ltd, 100% of Pear Ltd, and 80% of Quince Ltd. All four companies are UK trading companies. Pear Ltd is very small as it only recently began to trade. Pear Ltd makes exempt supplies. The other three companies make wholly standard-rated supplies both to each other and to external customers.

All four companies are run separately with each company organising its own accounting and tax affairs.

Quince Ltd has made losses for six years and has suffered cash-flow issues for three months.

The group is considering making an application to form a single VAT group made up of Mela Ltd, Neem Ltd, Pear Ltd and Quince Ltd with Mela Ltd as the representative member.

Requirement

Explain the implications, advantages and disadvantages of forming a single VAT group made up of all four companies. **(5 marks)**

64.2 Pesca Ltd is VAT registered and makes taxable supplies. Pesca Ltd purchased a newly constructed office building for use in its business on 1 January 2016 for £2 million.

In the year ended 31 December 2016 Pesca Ltd used the entire building for trade purposes.

From 1 January 2017 to 28 February 2019 Pesca Ltd rented out approximately 30% of the building's floor area to Zucca Ltd, an unconnected company. Zucca Ltd vacated the building on 28 February 2019.

On 1 March 2019 Pesca Ltd sold the entire building for £3.5 million to Cipolla Ltd, an unconnected company.

Pesca Ltd's VAT year for capital goods scheme purposes runs to 31 December. Pesca Ltd had not opted to tax the building. The above amounts are stated exclusive of any VAT.

Requirements

(a) Explain, with supporting calculations, the VAT treatment of the office building under the capital goods scheme over the period of ownership by Pesca Ltd.   **(6 marks)**

(b) Calculate the stamp duty land tax payable by Cipolla Ltd on the purchase of the office building in 2019, and state when it must be paid.   **(2 marks)**

Total: 13 marks

65 Anne and Johan

65.1 Anne is aged 55. Anne has been UK resident since 2015/16, living and working in London.

She is domiciled in France.

In July 2018 Anne carried out the following transactions in relation to assets located in England:

- Sold her 10% holding of shares in an unquoted trading company, Mast Ltd, for £125,000. Anne paid £34,000 for the shares in May 2015 when she joined Mast Ltd's London office as a full-time employee.

- Sold a painting, realising a gain of £152,000.

- Sold 1,000 shares in Petal Ltd, an unquoted trading company for £83,000. Anne had bought 1,000 shares in January 2000 for £20,000. In June 2005 there had been a 1 for 2 bonus issue and then in December 2010 Anne had taken up all her shares offered in a 1 for 3 rights issue at £42 per share. Anne has never been employed by Petal Ltd.

In August 2018 Anne realised a gain of £350,000 from the sale of a commercial property in France. She has not remitted any of the proceeds from this to the UK.

Anne had total employment income in 2018/19 of £50,000. At 6 April 2018 Anne had a brought forward capital loss of £7,950 relating to the sale of an asset located in London.

Anne has made a claim for the remittance basis for 2018/19.

Requirements

(a) Explain why Anne will not suffer a remittance basis charge in 2018/19.   **(1 mark)**

(b) Using the remittance basis, calculate Anne's capital gains tax liability for 2018/19 in respect of the above disposals and state the due date for payment. Clearly show your treatment of each asset. Ignore stamp taxes.   **(9 marks)**

65.2 Johan died on 1 March 2019. Johan owned the following assets at the date of his death:

- A house in London worth £3.5 million subject to a mortgage of £1.5 million held by the London branch of a UK bank.

- Cash of £1 million held on deposit at the London branch of a Danish bank.

- 50,000 shares in Sam Inc, an investment company listed on the New York Stock Exchange, which maintains its register of shareholders in Delaware in the USA. At the time of Johan's death Sam Inc had 900,000 issued shares quoted at 255p–274p with marked bargains of 258p, 263p and 273p (sterling equivalents).

- A £500,000 life assurance policy taken out on his sister's life. At the date of Johan's death the market value of the policy was £48,000. Johan's sister lives in Sweden. The proceeds of the policy are payable in London.

In July 2012 Johan gave £100,000 to his daughter on the occasion of her marriage. Johan's only previous lifetime gift was in January 2007 when he made a gross chargeable transfer of £400,000 to a discretionary trust.

Johan bequeathed £425,000 to a UK-registered charity, £500,000 to his wife and the remainder of his estate (including his house) to his children.

Johan's wife and children are all domiciled in the UK. However, Johan's executors are currently in dispute with HMRC as to where Johan was domiciled.

Requirements

(a) For each of the four assets Johan owned at the date of his death, explain in which country it is located for the purposes of UK inheritance tax. **(3 marks)**

(b) Assuming Johan was always UK domiciled, calculate the inheritance tax due as a result of his death. **(12 marks)**

Total: 25 marks

66 Sedia Ltd and Tog Ltd

66.1 Sedia Ltd owns 100% of Letto Ltd, which owns 100% of Doccia Ltd. All three companies are VAT-registered, UK-resident trading companies.

Letto Ltd's accounting profit for the year ended 31 March 2019 is £6,500,000. The items in Table 1 below have already been added or deducted in arriving at the accounting profit.

Table 1	Notes	£
Amortisation of patents used in its trade		365,000
Loss on sale of patent	1	26,000
Profit on sale of shares	2	379,000
Loan finance costs	3	472,500
Charitable donations	4	60,000

Notes

1. On 1 April 2018 Letto Ltd sold a patent used in its trade for £34,000. Letto Ltd paid £120,000 for the patent on 1 April 2013.

2. On 1 April 2018 Letto Ltd sold its 11% shareholding in NOP Ltd for £879,000, which it purchased in February 2012 for £500,000. NOP Ltd is a trading company.

3. On 1 April 2018 Letto Ltd issued a new debenture to raise funds to expand its trade. The loan finance costs comprise £52,500 in incidental costs of issuing the debenture and £420,000 of interest on the debenture.

4. The charitable donations figure of £60,000 includes a closing accrual of £10,000.

Capital allowances

On 1 April 2018, Letto Ltd had a tax written down value of £850,233 for its main pool, and £443,000 for its special rate pool. In July 2018 Letto Ltd spent £90,000 including VAT on new zero-emissions goods vehicles and £83,450 excluding VAT on a new air conditioning system for its offices.

The group's annual investment allowance has already been fully claimed by Doccia Ltd.

Losses

Letto Ltd has a trade loss of £100,000 incurred in its year ended 31 March 2018 which was unused and is carried forward as at 1 April 2018. It also has a capital loss carried forward as at 1 April 2018 of £423,200.

Sedia Ltd has a trading loss for its year ended 31 March 2019 of £4.5 million and has trade losses carried forward from year ended 31 March 2018 of £225,000. It has no other income or gains to be able to utilise its own losses against. Sedia Ltd has therefore agreed to surrender the maximum possible loss to Letto Ltd after Letto Ltd has used its own losses to the fullest extent.

Requirements

(a) Calculate Letto Ltd's tax-adjusted trading profit after capital allowances for the year ended 31 March 2019. Start with the accounting profit of £6,500,000 and show all items given in Table 1, using a zero for any that require no adjustment. **(7 marks)**

(b) Calculate Letto Ltd's corporation tax liability for the year ended 31 March 2019. Clearly show your treatment of the losses. **(4 marks)**

Note: The RPI for December 2017 is 278.1 and for April 2018 is 279.1.

66.2 Tog Ltd prepared accounts for the 15 months to 31 March 2019. Tog Ltd does not pay corporation tax by instalments.

Requirements

For the 15 months ended 31 March 2019, state and explain the corporation tax filing and payment deadlines applicable to Tog Ltd. **(4 marks)**

Total: 15 marks

67 Anushka

67.1 Anushka runs a UK clothes manufacturing business, as a sole trader.

Clothes manufacturing business

Anushka has calculated a draft accounting profit figure for the year ended 31 March 2019 of £63,000 after accounting for the following items:

- Samples of clothing which cost £4,890 and which were sent to potential retailers to promote the business.

- Food costing £2,400 for Anushka's personal use paid for with the business credit card.

- A subscription to a trade association costing £500.

- An increase of £2,650 in the general provision for future repairs to equipment.

- Interest of £200 received on the business bank account.

- Legal fees of £925 relating to the purchase of Anushka's new home. Anushka uses 10% of the house for storage for the business.

Anushka was on holiday in December 2018 when the roof of her business premises required urgent repairs costing £2,100. She used her personal credit card to pay for the repair and has not reflected the repair in the draft accounting profit figure.

Tax written down values as at 1 April 2018 were:

	£
Main pool	26,879
Special rate pool	12,450
Computing equipment with 30% private use by Anushka	6,420

In January 2019 Anushka sold a car for £10,000 which had originally cost £20,000 in January 2016. The car had CO_2 emissions of 60g/km and was used only for business purposes by employees.

Other income and gifts in 2018/19

Anushka received building society interest of £20,175 and dividends from EFG plc of £9,960. Anushka donated shares in XYZ plc to a registered charity. At the date of the gift, the shares were listed on the London Stock Exchange and were worth £12,000. Anushka is aged 50 and is registered blind.

Requirements

(a) Calculate Anushka's tax-adjusted trading profit for the year ended 31 March 2019. Show your treatment of each item. Ignore VAT. **(8 marks)**

(b) Calculate Anushka's income tax liability for 2018/19. **(6 marks)**

67.2 Jasminder is employed by AZ Ltd.

2018/19 remuneration package

Jasminder received the following remuneration package:

- Salary of £18,000.

- A mobile phone paid for by AZ Ltd, which cost £140 and is used 50% for work calls.

- A £60,000 interest-free loan from AZ Ltd issued to Jasminder on 6 April 2018. Jasminder repaid £20,000 of the loan on 6 August 2018.

- Furnished job-related accommodation. The furniture cost AZ Ltd £4,000 when Jasminder first occupied the accommodation six years ago. During the year AZ Ltd paid for the following expenses associated with the accommodation:

	£
Rent	12,000
Utility bills	750
Cleaner	2,080
Redecoration	950
	15,780

Jasminder pays for safety clothing which AZ Ltd requires her to wear for work. This cost Jasminder £500 in 2018/19.

2019/20 relocation package

In 2019/20 AZ Ltd required Jasminder to relocate from London to Manchester. AZ Ltd paid Jasminder a relocation allowance of £15,000 for her removal expenses on 30 April 2019. Jasminder is a basic-rate taxpayer in 2019/20.

Requirements

(a) Calculate Jasminder's taxable employment income for 2018/19. Show your treatment of each item. **(7 marks)**

(b) Calculate the net cash Jasminder received from the £15,000 relocation allowance. **(3 marks)**

Note: Assume that the official rate of interest throughout 2017/18 is 2.5%.

67.3 Daniel rents out a property he owns in Cornwall. He rents the property out for £1,400 per calendar month which is paid monthly in advance although the payment due 1 April 2019 was paid late on 15 April.

During 2018/19 he paid the following expenses:

	£
Management expenses	1,000
Interest on a loan to buy the property	500
Capital repayments on the loan	2,500
Council tax and water rates	1,000
Insurance paid 1 January 2018 for year ended 31 December 2018	500
Insurance paid 1 January 2019 for year ended 31 December 2019	550
A new lawnmower	200
Replacement sofa (Daniel had to pay £20 to scrap the old sofa)	950
	15,780

He has a brought forward property loss of £300 from 2017/18.

Requirement

Calculate Daniel's taxable property income for 2018/19. **(6 marks)**

67.4 Steve and Louis have traded in partnership for many years.

Roger

Roger joined the partnership on 1 January 2017. Roger's share of the partnership profits or losses for his first three accounting periods are:

Year ended 31 December 2017   Loss of £43,500
Year ended 31 December 2018   Profit of £117,000
Year ended 31 December 2019   Profit of £145,000

Steve

Steve's allowable partnership loss for 2017/18 is £29,000 which he intends to use as soon as possible.

Steve's assessable partnership trading profits for 2018/19 are £78,000 and for 2016/17 are £2,000.

Steve has net property income each year of £12,000.

In 2018/19 Steve received a dividend from an American listed company. An amount of £3,000 was paid into Steve's UK bank account after the deduction of £1,500 of American withholding tax from the dividend.

Requirements

(a) Calculate Roger's assessable trading profits or allowable losses for his first three tax years as a member of the partnership. **(3 marks)**

(b) Calculate Steve's taxable income for 2016/17, 2017/18 and 2018/19 assuming he uses his allowable loss as early as possible. **(3 marks)**

(c) Calculate Steve's liability to Class 4 national insurance contributions for 2018/19. **(4 marks)**

Total: 40 marks

68 Flash LLP

Flash LLP is a firm of ICAEW Chartered Accountants. Eddie Allen, a professional accountant, is employed by Flash LLP and is currently on sick leave. On a review of Eddie's correspondence in his absence the following have been found:

- An email from Iris West, a client, which includes the following:

  'When preparing my 2014/15 tax return you said that no tax was payable on the termination payment of £80,000 from my former employer so it was not included in the return. I am extremely stressed as I have just received a 'discovery assessment' from HMRC demanding substantial tax plus interest relating to the termination payment. I cannot afford this and I hold your firm entirely responsible for paying it.'

- A letter from HMRC querying a P11D submitted by Flash LLP in July 2019.

  Eddie prepares all P11Ds on behalf of the firm and HMRC's query relates to Eddie's own P11D. On review, you discover that Eddie has omitted details of his company car in this P11D and in previous forms, although other employees' cars are correctly shown on their forms.

Requirements

68.1 Explain the steps Flash LLP should take to resolve the issue Iris has raised. **(3 marks)**

68.2 Explain the ethical and legal issues for Eddie surrounding his P11D form, and the actions that the firm should now take. **(4 marks)**

Total: 7 marks

69 Fleet Ltd

Fleet Ltd is a UK-resident, VAT-registered company preparing accounts annually to 31 March. It is a partially-exempt trader, with a VAT year to 31 March.

On 1 June 2015 Fleet Ltd purchased a new freehold commercial building in London, Sheer Heights, for £1.5 million plus VAT. At that time 60% of the building was used for taxable purposes. Because of declining sales, the exempt trade has decreased, and since 1 April 2019 Sheer Heights has been used 85% for taxable purposes.

The board of Fleet Ltd intends to sell Sheer Heights and trade from leased premises in future. A purchaser has been identified and Fleet Ltd is expected to sell the building in November 2019 for £2.5 million. The sale will realise a taxable gain of £760,000.

Fleet Ltd did not opt to tax Sheer Heights.

Fleet Ltd will set aside £140,000 from the sale of Sheer Heights for operational costs, and use the remainder to purchase shares as follows:

- 5,000 shares in Lopp Ltd via a stock transfer form for £514,600; and then

- Shares in Pemmican plc, which are currently trading on the London Stock Exchange at £50.24 per share. Fleet Ltd will buy as many shares as possible using the remaining post-tax proceeds.

Requirements

69.1 Show, with the aid of calculations, the VAT treatment of Sheer Heights from its purchase to sale under the capital goods scheme. Show whether the VAT amounts are payable or recoverable. **(5 marks)**

69.2 Identify and explain the payment dates for stamp taxes due from Fleet Ltd on the two share purchases. **(2 marks)**

69.3 Calculate the amount of stamp duty payable on the purchase of the Lopp Ltd shares. **(1 mark)**

69.4 Calculate the maximum number of shares in Pemmican plc that Fleet Ltd will be able to purchase. **(5 marks)**

Total: 13 marks

70 Nora and Linda

70.1 Nora Allen is resident in England and UK-domiciled. In 2018/19, Nora had taxable income of £27,800 and made the following disposals:

Shares in Snart Ltd

On 1 August 1991 Nora became a full-time working director of Snart Ltd, an unquoted trading company. On the same day she purchased a 20% shareholding in the company for £35,000. On 30 June 2018, Nora retired as a director and gave her shares to her daughter when they were worth £254,000. At the date of the gift Snart Ltd had the following assets:

	Market value 30 June 2018 £
Office building – held as an investment	300,000
Factory – used by Snart Ltd	600,000
Goodwill	250,000
Plant and machinery	
Items over £6,000 each	40,000
Items less than £6,000 each	30,000
Other net current assets	80,000
	1,300,000

Painting

On 25 January 2019 Nora sold a painting at auction for £5,000 less auctioneers' fees at 2%. She inherited the painting from her mother in June 2014 when it was valued at £9,000. It had originally cost her mother £6,500 in November 2012.

Shares in Ramon plc

On 22 September 2018 Nora sold 5,000 £1 ordinary shares in Ramon plc, a quoted investment company, for £24,000.

Nora had purchased 4,000 £1 ordinary shares in Ramon plc for £10,000 in June 2010. On 29 April 2013 the company made a 1-for-2 rights issue at £3.20 per share. Nora took up all of her rights.

Requirement

Calculate Nora's capital gains tax liability for 2018/19, clearly showing the amount of any reliefs available. **(12 marks)**

70.2 Linda died on 20 March 2019. She had been resident in the UK since 1981, when she moved to England to get married. She was born in Italy to Italian-domiciled parents. It had always been Linda's intention to return to Italy prior to her death, but she died before being able to do so.

Linda's death estate comprised:

- Her UK home worth £600,000.

- A holiday home in Italy worth £250,000. Italian death taxes of £80,000 have been paid in respect of the holiday home.

- 4,000 shares in Nimbus Ltd, an unquoted investment company, representing a 40% shareholding. Linda's son Henry owns 45% of the shares and the remaining 15% are owned by a charity. Linda gave the 15% holding to the charity in 2009. The shares were valued as follows at Linda's death:

	Value per share
	£
0–25%	50
26–50%	60
51–74%	80
75–90%	100
91–100%	130

- Cash and other personal effects worth £270,000.

Linda's husband Ronnie died in June 2008, leaving assets worth £234,000 to their son Henry and the remainder of his estate to Linda. Neither Linda nor Ronnie made any lifetime gifts. Linda has left her entire estate to Henry.

Requirements

(a) Explain Linda's domicile status for inheritance tax purposes since her arrival in the UK in 1981. **(2 marks)**

(b) Assuming Linda is treated as UK domiciled at the time of her death, calculate the amount of inheritance tax arising as a result of her death. **(10 marks)**

(c) State who must pay the inheritance tax on Linda's death estate and when it must be paid by in order to avoid interest. **(1 mark)**

Total: 25 marks

71 Bolt Ltd

Bolt Ltd is a wholly-owned subsidiary of Girder Ltd. Neither Bolt Ltd nor Girder Ltd has any other shareholdings and both companies prepare accounts to 31 March.

Bolt Ltd's trading profit

Bolt Ltd has draft tax-adjusted trading profits of £683,000 for the year ended 31 March 2019. However this is before deducting capital allowances or making any other necessary adjustment in respect of the following five items:

(1) Bolt Ltd sold its factory, Mardon Place, on 30 November 2018 for £300,000, less professional fees - see (4) below. The factory had cost £110,000 in June 1995. The factory has always been too large for Bolt Ltd and 20% of the factory has been let to an unconnected company throughout the period of ownership. A profit on disposal of £234,000 is included in the draft tax-adjusted trading profits.

(2) Bolt Ltd qualifies as a SME for research and development purposes and the following research and development costs have been deducted in arriving at the draft tax-adjusted trading profits:

	£
Salaries of two full-time research staff	32,000
Computer software	600
Consumables	1,000
Power, water and fuel incurred in the laboratory	600
Allocation of overheads to the research laboratory	800
	35,000

(3) Interest payable of £6,300 has been deducted in arriving at the draft tax-adjusted trading profits. The interest relates to:

	£
Loan to purchase Mardon Place	5,000
Loan to acquire machinery - see (5) below	400
Bank overdraft	900
	6,300

(4) Professional fees of £13,500 have been deducted in arriving at the draft tax-adjusted trading profits. They are costs in connection with:

	£
The sale of Mardon Place	12,000
The purchase of new machinery – see (5) below	1,500
	13,500

(5) The tax written down value of the main pool at 1 April 2018 was £45,000. Bolt Ltd purchased new machinery on 10 February 2019 for £19,000. The machinery has an expected economic working life of 30 years. Girder Ltd has fully utilised the group's entitlement to the annual investment allowance.

Bolt Ltd's other income

In the year ended 31 March 2019 Bolt Ltd's only other sources of income are property income of £8,300 from Mardon Place, and bank interest receivable of £5,700. These have both been correctly adjusted for in arriving at the draft tax-adjusted trading profits.

Girder Ltd

Girder Ltd has a capital loss brought forward at 1 April 2017 of £22,000 and incurred a trade loss of £100,000 in the year to 31 March 2019. It has no other income or gains and the group's objective is to utilise losses as early as possible.

In April 2020 Girder Ltd purchased a new warehouse for £210,000.

Requirements

71.1 Calculate Bolt Ltd's final tax-adjusted trading profit for the year ended 31 March 2019.

(7 marks)

71.2 Assuming Bolt Ltd maximises its use of all available reliefs, calculate its corporation tax liability for the year ended 31 March 2019. **(8 marks)**

Total: 15 marks

Note: RPI for December 2017 is 278.1 and November 2018 is 284.4. Ignore VAT and stamp taxes.

72 Martin Stein and Pattie

72.1 Martin Stein is a sole trader. He has run a manufacturing business, Gotham Fabrics, for many years, preparing accounts to 31 December each year. Martin recently made a valid change of accounting date to 31 March, preparing a set of accounts for the 15 months ended 31 March 2019.

Martin has an accounting profit of £361,700 for the 15 months ended 31 March 2019 after deducting the following items in the profit and loss account:

	Note	£
Depreciation		70,860
Staff costs	1	192,000
Gifts	2	1,800

Notes

1   The staff costs figure includes the following:

	£
Employee wages and national insurance contributions	139,600
Martin's wages	50,000
Small benefits covered by PAYE settlement agreement	2,400
	192,000

The £2,400 included in small benefits represents a cost of £300 for each of eight employees. Seven of the employees are basic-rate taxpayers and one is a higher-rate taxpayer. Martin has not accounted for the amounts due to HMRC in respect of the PAYE settlement agreement.

2   The gifts figure comprises £1,000 for trade samples, each costing £20, given to 50 customers; and £800 for Christmas gifts of food hampers, each costing £16, to the same customers.

Capital allowances

Tax written down values as at 1 January 2018 were:

	£
Main pool	120,300
Special rate pool	48,000
Computer equipment (purchased March 2015): short life asset election	1,465

During the period there were the following purchases and disposals:

		£
Purchases:		
Jun 2018	Van for use in the business	21,000
Oct 2018	Car for use by an employee:	15,600
	40% business use, CO2 emissions 143g/km	
Feb 2019	New electrical system	282,000
Disposal:		
Jan 2018	Computer equipment: short life asset from March 2015	720

All purchases and disposals are stated inclusive of any VAT at the standard rate.

Gotham Fabrics had a tax-adjusted trading profit of £40,000 for the year ended 31 December 2017. Martin has three months of unrelieved overlap profits totalling £9,500.

Requirements

(a) Calculate Martin's tax-adjusted trading profit after deduction of capital allowances for the 15 months ended 31 March 2019. **(13 marks)**

(b) Calculate Martin's assessable trading profits for 2017/18 and 2018/19. State the dates of the basis periods. **(3 marks)**

(c) Calculate Martin's liability to Class 2 and Class 4 national insurance contributions for 2018/19. **(3 marks)**

72.2 Pattie, who was born in June 1956, works for Spivot Ltd as a production director and has always lived in Birmingham. For 2018/19 she received the following employment package:

- Salary of £80,000.

- Round sum allowance of £2,400 of which Pattie spent £1,200 entertaining local suppliers; and £695 on train travel to the offices of another group company. The train travel took place when she was on a three-month secondment from 1 September to 30 November 2018 to the other company.

- Company car with CO2 emissions of 97g/km and a list price of £10,875. The car was available to Pattie throughout 2018/19. The company also paid for all petrol, except for the duration of the secondment, when Pattie opted out of the arrangement and paid for her own fuel.

- Employer contributions into Pattie's personal pension totalling £15,000. In addition to Spivot Ltd's contributions, Pattie herself paid £20,000 into her pension during 2018/19.

Pattie donates £40 every month to charity via Spivot Ltd's approved payroll giving scheme.

In addition to her employment income for 2018/19, Pattie also received:

- Interest of £6,240, including income tax repayment interest of £40, the rest being bank interest.

- Dividend income of £8,400.

- French property income of £8,000 on which 20% foreign tax has been suffered.

- Spanish interest income of £2,000 on which £200 of foreign tax has been suffered.

Requirements

(a) Calculate Pattie's taxable employment income for 2018/19. **(5 marks)**

(b) Calculate Pattie's income tax liability for 2018/19. **(13 marks)**

(c) Calculate Pattie's total cash saving if she had reduced her own personal pension contributions from £20,000 to £10,000 for 2018/19. Do not change your answer to part (b). **(3 marks)**

Total: 40 marks

December 2017 exam questions

73 Sherazi LLP

Sherazi LLP, a firm of ICAEW Chartered Accountants, recently tendered for tax compliance and advisory work for Javadi Ltd, a marketing company.

Sherazi LLP has received notice that the tender was successful. The partners in the firm are pleased as they already have another marketing company, Higgins Ltd, as a client and the firm intends to become specialists in this business sector.

Requirements

73.1 Identify the fundamental principles that are threatened if Sherazi LLP accepts Javadi Ltd as a client, and set out the safeguards that can be put in place to manage the threats to those fundamental principles. **(4 marks)**

73.2 Assuming the threats are sufficiently reduced, explain any other steps Sherazi LLP should take before accepting Javadi Ltd as a client. **(3 marks)**

Total: 7 marks

74 Virgil Ltd

Virgil Ltd is a UK-resident, VAT-registered company manufacturing goods that are standard-rated in the UK. For many years Peter owned all of the shares in the company.

Quarter ended 31 January 2019

Virgil Ltd had the following transactions in the quarter ended 31 January 2019. All amounts are stated exclusive of VAT, where relevant:

	£
Sales	
Supplies to UK customers	258,000
Supplies to Italy (in the EU):	
To registered businesses	53,000
To individuals	32,000
Supplies to USA (not in the EU):	
To registered businesses	74,000
To individuals	25,000
	442,000
Purchases and expenses	
Purchases and expenses in UK – standard rated	135,000
Rent paid in UK – exempt	25,000
Legal fees re trading contract – solicitor in Italy	8,400
Purchase of a car for private use by Peter	24,000
Purchase of machinery	12,000
	204,400

Sale of shares and property

On 31 March 2019 Peter personally sold the following assets:

- Shares in Virgil Ltd for £874,600 to Walden Ltd, an unconnected company.

- A commercial property in London for £400,000 to Sam, an unconnected individual. Peter had purchased the property in June 1990. Peter made no option to tax the property.

Requirements

74.1 Explain Virgil Ltd's VAT treatment of the legal fees. State the impact on this treatment if the solicitor had been located in the USA. **(3 marks)**

74.2 Calculate the VAT liability for the quarter ended 31 January 2019. Show your treatment of each item. **(6 marks)**

74.3 Calculate the amount of stamp duty and stamp duty land tax payable on the sale of the shares and the property. State the due dates and by whom the amounts were payable.

(4 marks)

Total: 13 marks

75 Carrie

Carrie died on 20 March 2019. During her lifetime she made the following disposals:

June 2011 – shares in Quinn Ltd, an unquoted investment company

Carrie gave shares in Quinn Ltd to a discretionary trust, when the shares were worth £256,000.

May 2018 – cash to her son Otto

Carrie gave £220,000 cash to Otto on the occasion of his marriage.

September 2018 – shares in Brody plc, a quoted trading company

Carrie sold 100,000 £1 ordinary shares, a 6% holding, to her nephew for £150,000. At the date of sale the shares were quoted at 308–316p with a marked bargain of 309p. Carrie paid £80,000 for the shares in July 1990. Carrie never worked for Brody plc.

On her death Carrie had total assets of £1.3 million. These included her home worth £600,000 and a painting worth £300,000 that she had inherited from her brother Simon in October 2017. At that time the painting was worth £240,000 and Simon's executors paid inheritance tax of £62,000 relating to the painting.

Carrie, a higher rate taxpayer, had unpaid income tax of £20,000 at 20 March 2019 and her funeral expenses were £9,500.

Carrie left £100,000 of her estate to a UK-registered charity and the remainder of her estate, including her home, to Otto.

Requirements

75.1 Calculate the capital gains tax payable as a result of the events in 2018/19. Show your treatment of each event. **(5 marks)**

75.2 Calculate the inheritance tax payable as a result of Carrie's death. **(16 marks)**

75.3 Calculate the after-tax net cash saving or net cash cost, if the charitable donation on Carrie's death had been £162,000 instead. Clearly state whether it is a net cash saving or a net cash cost. **(4 marks)**

Total: 25 marks

76 Mathison Ltd

76.1 Mathison Ltd is a trading company with one wholly owned subsidiary, Galvez Ltd, an investment company.

For the year ended 31 March 2019, Mathison Ltd had a tax-adjusted trading profit of £980,000. In addition the company had interest receivable on debentures of £20,000 which included £3,000 received on 3 April 2019.

On 1 November 2018 the company paid both a donation of £2,600 to a UK-political party and a qualifying donation of £4,500 to a UK-registered charity.

At 1 April 2018 the company had a trading loss brought forward of £37,200. The trading loss had been incurred in the year ended 31 March 2018.

Capital disposal

On 10 January 2019 Mathison Ltd sold the entire holding of shares in Galvez Ltd for £400,000.

Mathison Ltd purchased the shares for £150,000 in August 2008.

The sale of the shares does not qualify for the substantial shareholding exemption.

At the date of the share sale, Galvez Ltd owned an investment property that it purchased from Mathison Ltd in April 2016 for £200,000, when the market value of the property was £340,000. Mathison Ltd purchased the property for £60,000 in June 1990.

Requirements

(a) Calculate the degrouping charge arising as a result of transactions relating to Galvez Ltd. **(2 marks)**

(b) Calculate Mathison Ltd's corporation tax payable for the year ended 31 March 2019. Assume a claim is made to utilise trade losses as early as possible. **(7 marks)**

Notes

1 RPI for December 2017 is 278.1 and January 2019 is 286.9.
2 Ignore VAT and stamp taxes.

76.2 Lockhart Ltd prepared accounts for the seven months ended 31 October 2019, having previously prepared annual accounts to 31 March. For many years, the company has had a wholly-owned subsidiary, Beren Ltd, and a 5% shareholding in another company, Sonny Ltd.

Lockhart Ltd had the following sources of income for the seven months ended 31 October 2019:

	£
Tax adjusted trading profit	775,000
Dividend received from Sonny Ltd	12,000

In the year ended 31 March 2019 Lockhart Ltd had a taxable total profit of £1.1 million.

Requirements

(a) Explain, with supporting calculations, why Lockhart Ltd is required to pay corporation tax in instalments for the seven months ended 31 October 2019. **(3 marks)**

(b) State the due dates for payment of the instalments and the amount payable at each date. **(3 marks)**

Total: 15 marks

77 Saul

77.1 Saul is UK-resident and UK-domiciled. He is employed by Faisel Ltd as a researcher at the head office of a pharmaceutical company. His employment package for 2018/19 was:

- annual salary of £25,000.

- bonus of £790 received on 26 March 2019, relating to Faisel Ltd results for the year ended 31 December 2018. Saul received a bonus of £800 relating to the company results for the year ended 31 December 2017 on 29 April 2018.

- reimbursement of entertaining expenditure of £250. Saul kept receipts to support all of the entertaining expenditure, which relates to taking suppliers out for meals.

- payment of 52p per mile for 12,000 business miles in Saul's own car when travelling to other offices of his employer. Saul also takes a colleague on each of the business journeys and receives 6p per mile from Faisel Ltd for doing so.

- Faisel Ltd contributed the equivalent of 5% of Saul's basic salary into the company occupational pension scheme. Saul also contributed 2% of his basic salary into the scheme.

- an interest-free loan of £1,500 made to Saul several years ago was written off on 5 October 2018.

Saul paid subscriptions of £320 to the Medical Research Society, an HMRC approved professional body.

In addition to his employment income for 2018/19, Saul also received interest on his NS&I Direct Saver account of £1,400 and dividend income from UK quoted companies of £6,000.

Saul owns a house in Erehwon, an overseas country. The house was let out to a local family for gross rent of £13,000 during 2018/19. Saul's expenditure on the property during the year was:

	£
Repairs and insurance	1,100
Cleaning	450
New dining room furniture – see below	1,200

The new dining room furniture is made out of excellent quality oak. It replaces poor quality plastic furniture that lasted for only two years and was scrapped. Similar plastic furniture would have cost £300. Saul paid tax in Erehwon of £1,900 on the property income.

Requirements

(a) Calculate Saul's taxable employment income, showing your treatment of each item.

(8 marks)

(b) Calculate Saul's income tax liability for 2018/19. Show full workings for double taxation relief.

(11 marks)

Note. There is no double tax treaty between the UK and Erehwon.

77.2 On 1 January 2019 David, Mike and Nicholas started trading in partnership as DMN Marketing (DMN). David and Mike work at least 35 hours per week for DMN, but Nicholas kept his job at a publishing company and works for the partnership only one day each week ie around eight hours.

For the six months ended 30 June 2019 DMN's draft tax-adjusted trading profit before deduction of capital allowances was £22,000. The partners were not sure how to deal with the following six items so no deduction has been made in respect of these in arriving at the figure of £22,000.

(1) In December 2018, prior to starting the business the partners incurred the following expenditure:

	£
Legal advice regarding standard contracts for clients	20,000
Legal advice on the lease of business premises	2,500
	22,500

(2) On 1 January 2019 DMN took out a six-year lease on business premises. The rent payable was £6,000 per annum.

(3) In January 2019 on the launch of their business DMN sent gifts of mobile phone chargers to 100 potential clients. The chargers had the DMN logo and phone number printed on them and they cost the company a total of £1,000. They also donated £300 to their local church, a charitable organisation.

(4) In January 2019 David paid the partnership's insurance bill of £340 for the year ended 31 December 2019 from his own personal bank account.

(5) Throughout the six month period, Mike has been taking goods for his own use. No entry has been made in the accounts. The goods cost the business £100 but would have sold for £140.

(6) During the period £1,000 was spent on entertaining. This was for an evening meal for the 3 members of staff and 7 of their key clients.

Capital allowances

During the six months to 30 June 2019 DMN made the following purchases:

		£
January 2019	Specialist computer equipment	170,000
January 2019	Air conditioning and ventilation system for the offices	35,000
February 2019	New car for use by David:	25,400
	10% business use, CO_2 emissions 143g/km	
February 2019	New car for use by Mike:	17,000
	20% business use, CO_2 emissions 44g/km	

David, Mike and Nicholas share profits in the ratio 20:40:40 respectively, after allocating a salary to David of £90,000 per annum and £10,000 per annum to Mike.

DMN won a major client contract in August 2019 and after allocating profits to each partner, Mike is expected to have tax-adjusted trading profits of £140,000 for the year ending 30 June 2020.

Requirements

(a) Calculate DMN's tax-adjusted trading profit/(loss) after deduction of capital allowances for the six months ended 30 June 2019. **(11 marks)**

(b) Calculate the tax-adjusted trading profit/(loss) for each partner for the six months ended 30 June 2019. **(3 marks)**

(c) Calculate Mike's assessable trading profits for 2018/19 and 2019/20. **(3 marks)**

(d) Calculate Mike's liability to Class 4 national insurance contributions for 2018/19 and 2019/20. **(2 marks)**

(e) Explain the restriction on the use of trading losses by Nicholas, assuming he has other income of £35,000 each tax year. **(2 marks)**

Total: 40 marks

Note. Ignore VAT and stamp taxes.

78 Janet and John

78.1 Janet and John have been married for many years and have two young children. Together they have asked your firm for tax advice about their joint wills.

Janet and John disagree about some of the decisions that need to be made. Janet thinks the whole estate should pass to the surviving spouse absolutely. John thinks the whole estate should be placed into trust for the surviving spouse for life and then pass to the children absolutely. John's idea would ensure protection of the assets for the children.

Requirement

Explain the nature of the conflict of interest for your firm, and how this could be managed.

(4 marks)

78.2 You are aware that your client, Idris, has received a repayment of £1,000 from HMRC in error. Your engagement letter does not include an authority to disclose such matters to HMRC.

Requirement

Explain what action you should take in relation to the error. **(3 marks)**

Total: 7 marks

79 Skate Ltd

Skate Ltd owns:

- 95% of Tuna Ltd,
- 80% of Velvet Ltd, and
- 49% of Whale Ltd.

Tuna Ltd owns 75% of Unicorn Ltd.

All five companies are UK-resident trading companies. Skate Ltd, Tuna Ltd and Unicorn Ltd are registered together in a VAT group. Velvet Ltd and Whale Ltd are registered individually for VAT.

Skate Ltd, Tuna Ltd and Whale Ltd make wholly standard-rated supplies within the UK.

Velvet Ltd makes wholly zero-rated supplies within the UK.

Unicorn Ltd sells its goods to customers located elsewhere in the EU all of whom are private individuals. If Unicorn Ltd's goods were sold in the UK, they would be standard rated.

Skate Ltd sold a warehouse to Cat plc, an unconnected company, on 1 January 2019 for £200,000. Skate Ltd purchased the newly constructed warehouse on 1 January 2018. Cat plc makes wholly standard-rated supplies in the course of its business.

Requirements

79.1 Explain the benefits for Skate Ltd, Tuna Ltd and Unicorn Ltd of being grouped for VAT, and why Velvet Ltd and Whale Ltd have been excluded from the group. **(4 marks)**

79.2 Explain why Unicorn Ltd and Whale Ltd are not in a group with Skate Ltd for stamp duty land tax (SDLT) purposes. **(2 marks)**

79.3 Explain, with supporting calculations, the VAT charged and stamp duty land tax payable (SDLT) on the sale of the warehouse to Cat plc. Explain how your answer would differ if the warehouse had been sold to Tuna Ltd instead. **(5 marks)**

79.4 Assuming the warehouse is sold to Cat plc, briefly explain in what circumstances Cat plc would be able to recover any VAT payable on the purchase. **(2 marks)**

Total: 13 marks

80 Simon and Graham

80.1 Simon has always lived in Bristol, England. Simon is resident and domiciled in the UK. In March 2019 he:

- sold a sculpture realising a chargeable gain of £100,000.

- sold a vintage Aston Martin motor car for £250,000 which originally cost £15,000.

- sold two acres of land for £50,000 less auctioneer's fees of 2.5%. Simon originally purchased 10 acres for £18,000 plus legal costs of £1,500. At the time of the disposal the remaining eight acres had a market value of £43,000.

- sold a flat, 17 Richmond Place, for £250,000. Simon purchased 17 Richmond Place exactly 10 years before the sale for £150,000. Simon paid stamp duty land tax of £1,500 at acquisition. The flat was rented to an unconnected tenant.

At 6 April 2018 Simon had a capital loss brought forward of £23,450.

For 2018/19 Simon has employment income of £25,000.

Requirement

Calculate Simon's capital gains tax liability for 2018/19. Ignore VAT.

Total: 10 marks

80.2 Graham and his son Jim, both UK resident and domiciled, had lived for many years in a house in Bristol.

On 1 May 2018 Graham died aged 101 owning the following assets located in England:

- The house in Bristol that Graham and Jim lived in as their main home with a market value of £400,000.

- 1,000 shares in Sparks plc, a listed company with 200,000 issued shares. At the time of Graham's death the shares were quoted at 410p-418p per share with marked bargains of 407p, 411p and 414p.

- 100 acres of farmland which Graham had farmed for many years. The farm had an agricultural value of just £0.5 million but a market value of £1 million because of planning permission relating to some of the land.

- A 25% share in the 'Flhim Flam' partnership worth £20,000. The partnership was set up many years ago. The partnership agreement provides that, on death, a partner's share in the partnership will be purchased in equal shares by the other partners.

Graham also owned a holiday home in Utopia worth £347,000. Overseas death duties of £208,000 are payable in respect of the holiday home. The personal representatives of Graham's estate incurred additional administration costs of £21,000 due to the holiday home being in Utopia.

At the time of his death Graham owed HMRC £148,000 in unpaid taxes.

Graham's only previous lifetime gift was a painting transferred to a discretionary trust in January 2016 when it was valued at £1,123,000. It has since been discovered to be a forgery and is now valued at £235,000.

Graham had never married. He left his entire estate to his son Jim.

Requirement

Calculate the inheritance tax payable as a result of Graham's death, showing the amount of any available reliefs and exemptions. State why business property relief is not available on the 25% share in the Flhim Flam partnership.

Total: 15 marks

81 Salt Ltd

81.1 Salt Ltd is a UK-resident trading company with no related 51% group companies. Salt Ltd had the following results for the year ended 31 December 2018:

	Note	£
Tax-adjusted trading profit before interest and capital allowances	(1)	622,000
Bank interest receivable		42,000
Debenture interest payable	(2)	27,000
Profit on sale of debenture stock	(3)	16,400
Charitable donations payable	(4)	34,000

Notes:

1 Salt Ltd had a tax written down value brought forward of £485,000 in the main pool on 1 January 2018. Salt Ltd purchased £150,000 of plant and machinery on 1 April 2018. It sold an item of plant on 1 October 2018 £1,200. This was less than the original cost of the plant.

2 The debenture interest payable comprises:

	£
Interest on loan to purchase shares in Xylo SpA	12,000
Interest on loan to purchase a factory for use in the trade	15,000
	27,000

3 On 1 January 2018 Salt Ltd sold debenture stock for £32,400 which it had purchased for £16,000 on 1 January 2011.

4 Charitable donations accrued were £5,000 as at 31 December 2017 and £19,000 as at 31 December 2018.

Requirement

Calculate Salt Ltd's corporation tax liability for the year ended 31 December 2018.

Note: Ignore VAT and stamp taxes. **(6 marks)**

81.2 The Asp group consists of Asp Ltd and Boa Ltd which are both UK-resident trading companies with a year end of 31 December.

In January 2001 Asp Ltd purchased 75% of the shares in Boa Ltd for £236,000.

In February 2016 Asp Ltd sold a building to Boa Ltd for £500,000 when its market value was £2 million. Asp Ltd paid £333,000 for the building when it was first purchased in May 1995.

In March 2018 Asp Ltd sold half of its shares in Boa Ltd for £1.5 million. Boa Ltd still owns the building which is now worth £3.4 million.

Requirements

(a) Briefly explain how the sale of the building to Boa Ltd in February 2016 would have been treated for tax purposes in the year ended 31 December 2016. Calculations are not required. **(2 marks)**

(b) Calculate the taxable gains arising from Asp Ltd's disposal of half its shares in Boa Ltd before any potential exemptions. **(5 marks)**

(c) Briefly explain whether, and if so to what extent, the gains arising from Asp Ltd's disposal of half of its shares in Boa Ltd are exempt. **(2 marks)**

Note: The RPIs in December 2017 was 278.1 and in March 2018 was 278.3. Ignore VAT and stamp taxes.

Total: 15 marks

82 Amy

82.1 Amy, who is resident in London, England, had the following income for 2018/19:

- Total employment income of £30,000

- Property income of £10,000 from renting out a furnished room in her home. Amy incurred rental expenses of £850

- Building society interest of £2,000

- Dividends from UK companies of £17,000

- Betting winnings of £300

- Amy contributes £1,000 pa to her employer's occupational pension scheme and a further £1,500 pa to a personal pension scheme.

Requirement

Calculate Amy's income tax liability for 2018/19 assuming any beneficial elections are made. **(7 marks)**

82.2 Fred started to trade on 1 December 2017. Fred runs a UK manufacturing business, Pie City, as a sole trader. Fred voluntarily registered for VAT on 1 December 2017 and makes wholly standard-rated supplies.

Fred's forecast accounting profit is £545,504 for the sixteen months ending 31 March 2019. Expenses deducted in calculating the accounting profit include the following:

(1) Depreciation of £36,000.

(2) Staff costs:

	£
Fred's salary	15,000
Running costs for Fred's car	3,000
Staff salary costs paid and accrued	52,800
	70,800

Fred purchased his Toyota car on 1 December 2017 for £16,450. Fred drove 15,000 miles during the sixteen months ending 31 March 2019 of which 11,250 miles were for business purposes. Fred intends to claim fixed rate expenses in respect of the car.

Fred recruited his two employees on 6 April 2018. For the period 6 April 2018 to 31 March 2019, each employee was paid £24,000 plus an employer pension contribution of 10% of salary. No deduction from the accounting profit has been made for national insurance contributions.

The total pension contribution of £400 for March 2019 will not be paid until April 2019.

(3) Advertising costs:

	£
Charitable donation to local hospital	200
Gifts to customers	
100 sets of glasses bearing the business logo	5,500
Entertaining UK clients	3,780
	9,480

Capital allowances have not yet been calculated. Fred purchased the following items:

		£
1 December 2017	Machinery	292,292
1 January 2018	Air conditioning units	40,000
6 April 2018	Car for employee	15,000

The employee uses the car for both business and private use and pays for her own petrol. The car has CO_2 emissions of 170g/km.

All amounts are stated exclusive of VAT.

Requirements

(a) Calculate Fred's tax-adjusted trading profit after capital allowances for Pie City for the sixteen months ending 31 March 2019. Show your treatment of each item. **(14 marks)**

(b) Calculate Fred's taxable trading income for 2017/18 and 2018/19. State the dates of the basis periods for each tax year. **(2 marks)**

82.3 Saj started to trade on 1 January 2018. Saj's results for the year ended 31 December 2018 are:

	Note	£
Sales invoices issued to customers who pay in cash	(1)	27,840
Sales invoices issued to credit customers	(2)	28,000
Materials paid		21,000
Bank interest received		124
Office rent payable	(3)	1,500
Public liability insurance	(4)	245
Car expenses	(5)	1,350

Notes

(1) In addition, a further invoice was issued and paid in December 2018 for £4,500 for work carried out in January 2019.

(2) On 31 December 2018 sales invoices totalling £12,000 were unpaid.

(3) Saj rented office space on 1 August 2018 for £300 per month. The rent is payable every six months in advance.

(4) On 1 October 2018 Saj purchased public liability insurance for the 12 months to 30 September 2019 at a cost of £980.

(5) On 1 January 2018 Saj purchased a new car for £8,000 with CO_2 emissions of 120g/km. He drove 3,000 business miles and 2,000 private miles during the year. In total, he spent £1,350 on running costs for the car.

In addition Saj purchased a machine for use in the business for £2,500 on 1 May 2018.

Saj is not eligible for Universal Credit.

Saj has made an election to use the cash basis to prepare his tax-adjusted trading profits.

Requirements

(a) Explain why Saj is eligible to make an election to use the cash basis and how long the election will apply for.   **(3 marks)**

(b) Calculate Saj's tax-adjusted trading profit using the cash basis for the year ended 31 December 2018. Show your treatment of each item.   **(6 marks)**

Note: Ignore VAT.

82.4 Leroy is employed by Light Ltd and lives in London, England. Leroy receives the following remuneration package:

- Salary of £35,000

- Use of a company van with a list price of £18,000 which cost Light Ltd £16,000. The van has CO_2 emissions of 120g/km. Leroy pays for his own petrol and uses the van for significant private use.

Alternative business structure

Leroy has considered becoming self-employed for many years. He estimates that if he became self-employed he would generate fee income of £60,000 each year but he would need to provide his own van which would cost him £5,500 pa to run and lease. He estimates business use of the van to be 60% and it would have CO_2 emissions of 120g/km.

Other income

Leroy receives annual rental income which means that his employment income or trade profits will be taxed at the additional rate.

Requirement

Calculate Leroy's net disposable income for 2019/20, assuming:

- Leroy remains an employee of Light Ltd
- Leroy becomes self-employed.

Use 2018/19 rates and allowances.   **(8 marks)**

Total: 40 marks

83 John

John is an ICAEW Chartered Accountant working as a senior tax adviser for a firm of accountants. John has created a new tax planning scheme which he intends to promote to non-UK domiciled individuals.

John's scheme can be promoted to all non-UK domiciled clients without the need to tailor it to their individual needs. The scheme utilises a previously unexploited loophole in tax legislation by implementing a number of highly contrived and artificial steps.

In his research John has discovered that:

* although HMRC's interpretation of the relevant tax legislation is contrary to what the scheme proposes, HMRC's interpretation has never been tested before the Courts and is not specifically supported by the legislation, and

* while the relevant tax legislation does not specifically deal with this exact situation, it is clear that this scheme would be contrary to what Parliament intended when the legislation was enacted.

John disagrees with HMRC's interpretation and therefore does not intend to explain to potential clients that the scheme might be challenged by HMRC.

Laura, John's manager and the firm's managing partner, has reviewed the scheme. She has concluded that its promotion by an ICAEW member could put that member in conflict with the Standards for Tax Planning included in Professional Conduct in Relation to Taxation (PCRT).

Requirement

Identify and explain three Standards for Tax Planning from PCRT which best support Laura's conclusion.

Total: 7 marks

84 Kavitha

84.1 Kavitha is a VAT-registered sole trader making only standard-rated supplies. She uses the VAT flat rate scheme. Kavitha's business category for flat rate purposes is advertising.

For the quarter ending 30 June 2019 Kavitha expects to have sales of £15,000. So far this quarter, Kavitha has spent £200 on the purchase of standard-rated goods for use in her business.

Kavitha normally buys most of her purchases in December each year. However, Kavitha is concerned that her flat rate percentage now depends on the level of her costs in each quarter. Therefore she is considering spreading her purchases more evenly over the year. Kavitha anticipates spending a further £250 on standard-rated goods for use in her business before 30 June 2019.

All figures are stated exclusive of VAT.

(a) Calculate the VAT payable to HMRC by Kavitha for the quarter ending 30 June 2019 assuming:

* a total cost of goods purchased of £200
* a total cost of goods purchased of £450.

In each case, clearly show whether Kavitha is a limited cost trader.   **(5 marks)**

(b) Explain whether bringing forward the timing of Kavitha's purchases in order to lower the amount of VAT payable would be treated as tax evasion. **(3 marks)**

84.2 Bertie, Jeeves and Madeline are unconnected individuals.

On 1 January 2019 Bertie transferred a residential property to his wife, Georgiana, when it was worth £1.5 million. The transfer was made as part of their divorce settlement and is Georgiana's only property.

On 1 February 2019 Jeeves purchased a newly-constructed commercial property for £1 million.

On 1 March 2019 Madeline was granted a 30-year lease over a newly-constructed commercial property. Madeline pays an annual rental of £12,000 for the term of the lease.

All properties are located in England. All figures are stated exclusive of VAT where applicable. No options to tax have been exercised.

Requirement

Calculate the VAT and stamp duty land tax, if any, due on each transaction. **(5 marks)**

Total: 13 marks

85 Denzel and Marwan

85.1 Denzel has lived in London and been UK resident for 10 years but remains domiciled in Arendelle, an overseas country.

In December 2018, in relation to UK assets, Denzel:

- realised a chargeable gain of £45,200 on the disposal of a sculpture.

- sold 14,000 shares in EFG plc for £55,000. In December 2010 Denzel purchased 12,000 shares in EFG plc for £1.25 per share. In December 2014 he took up his full entitlement of a 1 for 4 rights issue at £2.50 per share. EFG plc is listed on the London Stock Exchange and has 2.5 million issued shares.

- sold a vintage car for £48,000 which he originally purchased for £32,000 in January 2011.

On 1 January 2019 Denzel sold 8 acres of a 10 acre plot of land located in Arendelle for £1.5 million. The proceeds were liable to taxation of 15% in Arendelle. The remaining two acres were valued at £750,000. The land originally cost £125,000 in January 1990. Denzel remitted £1.1 million of the proceeds to the UK in March 2019. All figures are the sterling equivalent.

For 2018/19 Denzel has UK trading income of £16,500.

Denzel is not automatically entitled to the remittance basis. He has decided not to make a claim for the remittance basis for 2018/19. The UK has no double tax treaty with Arendelle.

Requirements

(a) Calculate Denzel's capital gains tax liability for 2018/19. Ignore VAT and stamp taxes. **(9 marks)**

(b) Briefly explain what impact a remittance basis claim would have on Denzel's UK tax liabilities for 2018/19. Calculations are **not** required. **(4 marks)**

85.2 Marwan, who was UK domiciled, died on 1 April 2019. Marwan died owning no assets, having sold all his assets to pay medical bills. Marwan made the following lifetime transfers:

- On 1 January 2012 Marwan made a gift to a discretionary trust. The gross chargeable transfer value was £175,000.

- On 1 January 2014 Marwan gifted his entire 60% holding of shares in J plc, a quoted trading company, to his son. Marwan had owned the shares in J plc for many years. On 1 January 2014 Marwan's shares were valued at £2 million. Marwan's son still owned the shares at the time of Marwan's death.

- On 1 January 2018 Marwan gifted 10,000 shares in Z plc, a quoted investment company, to a discretionary trust.

At the time of the gift Marwan owned 22,500 of the 50,000 Z plc shares in issue and the shares were valued at:

Shareholding	Value
20%	£197,500
25%	£250,000
45%	£472,500
100%	£1,250,000

Requirements

(a) Calculate the inheritance tax arising as a result of Marwan's death. Show the amount of any available reliefs and exemptions. **(10 marks)**

(b) State who is liable to pay the inheritance tax due as a result of Marwan's death and the date by which it should be paid. **(2 marks)**

Total: 25 marks

86 H Ltd

Since 1 January 1990:

- H Ltd has owned 100% of A Ltd and 75% of Y Ltd.
- Y Ltd has owned 75% of Z Ltd.

All four companies are UK-resident trading companies which prepare accounts to 30 June.

On 1 September 2017 H Ltd sold its 100% shareholding in A Ltd for £500,000. H Ltd paid £550,000 for the shares on 1 January 1990.

The tax accounts and payment dates for the year ended 30 June 2018 were prepared by a trainee using new software. The directors of H Ltd are concerned about the accuracy of the trainee's work and have asked you to review the tax files and amend the figures if necessary.

For the year ended 30 June 2018 the trainee calculated H Ltd's taxable total profits as follows:

	£	£
Tax-adjusted trading profits (Note 1)		496,450
Net gains		
Chargeable gain	60,000	
Less loss on disposal of A Ltd	(50,000)	
		10,000
Non-trading loan relationships		48,550
Qualifying charitable donation (Note 2)		(25,000)
Less group relief from Z Ltd		(75,000)
Taxable total profits		450,000

Notes

1 The trainee had made the following adjustments to the accounting profit in order to calculate the tax-adjusted trading profit of £496,450:

- Depreciation expense of £43,400 and amortisation expense of £15,000 were added back to the accounting profit. The amortisation expense related to a patent royalty.

- Client entertaining of £23,450 and staff entertaining of £5,000 was added back to the accounting profit.

- Overdraft interest of £1,450 and interest on a loan used to invest in shares of £500 was added back to the accounting profit and deducted from non-trading loan relationships instead.

2 The donation was paid to a political party.

Payment dates

The trainee decided that H Ltd had two related 51% group companies for the year ended 30 June 2018. Including H Ltd this meant there were three related 51% group companies and therefore H Ltd filed its corporation tax return and paid corporation tax of £85,500 on 1 April 2019.

H Ltd had taxable total profits of £2 million for the year ended 30 June 2017.

Requirements

86.1 Briefly explain why H Ltd is not eligible to claim group loss relief from Z Ltd.　**(2 marks)**

86.2 Briefly explain why there are four related 51% group companies for the purposes of determining when H Ltd's corporation tax liability for the year ended 30 June 2018 is payable.　**(2 marks)**

86.3 For the year ended 30 June 2018:

- prepare a revised computation of taxable total profits amended for the errors made by the trainee, clearly showing your treatment of each item;

- calculate the correct amount of corporation tax due; and

- briefly explain when the corporation tax liability should have been paid.　**(11 marks)**

Note: Ignore VAT and stamp taxes.

Total: 15 marks

87　Ellie

87.1 Ellie was employed by JL Ltd for the first five months of 2018/19. JL Ltd operates a private school. Ellie left her job at JL Ltd on 31 August 2018 and started her own business as a sole trader on 1 September 2018.

Employment income

For 2018/19 Ellie received the following remuneration package:

- Salary of £5,000 per month.

- A free place for her daughter at the school. In 2018/19 her daughter spent one term at the school which normally costs £5,500 per term. The marginal cost to the school of providing the place for Ellie's daughter for this term was £530.

- A parking space in a public car park near her place of work which cost JL Ltd £690 for the period 6 April to 31 August 2018.

- Use of a diesel company car with a list price of £36,616 plus £1,000 for optional extras requested by Ellie. Ellie made a capital contribution of £2,500 to the cost of the car. The car had CO_2 emissions of 170g/km and does not meet RDE2 standards. JL Ltd also paid for all Ellie's private fuel. Ellie returned the car to JL Ltd on 31 August 2018.

- Ellie contributed 3% of her salary to JL Ltd's occupational pension scheme and JL Ltd contributed the equivalent of 5% of her salary.

Ellie spent £620 entertaining JL Ltd's clients and then claimed the £620 back from JL Ltd as reimbursed expenses.

In May 2018 Ellie paid £300 for her annual subscription to her professional institute, which is on HMRC's approved list.

Business income

Ellie started her business, E Traders, on 1 September 2018. Ellie's draft results for her first set of accounts for the nine months ended 31 May 2019 are:

	Note	£
Gross trading profit		85,714
Less:		
Ellie's salary		(4,000)
Repairs and renewals	(1)	(13,500)
Car expenses	(2)	(845)
Rent	(3)	(8,100)
Other expenses	(4)	(2,000)
Profit for the period		57,269

Notes

1 Repairs and renewals comprise:

	£
Purchase of external solar shading	2,400
Office redecorating	3,200
Purchase of moveable partition walls	7,900
	13,500

2 Ellie purchased a new car on 1 September 2018 for £13,000. It has CO_2 emissions of 125g/km. Ellie drives it 70% of the time for business purposes. Ellie spent £845 on an annual insurance policy and annual car tax on 1 September 2018.

3 Ellie began renting a new premises on 1 September 2018. The agreement requires Ellie to pay rent of £8,100 pa in advance on 1 September each year starting on 1 September 2018.

4 Other expenses include a speeding fine of £100 incurred by one of Ellie's delivery drivers.

Capital allowances have not yet been calculated. In September 2018 Ellie spent £4,100 on new office equipment and £1,000 on energy saving combination heat and power equipment.

Other income

During 2018/19 Ellie:

- received bank interest of £1,200 and dividends of £8,000;

- paid a contribution of £1,300 to a personal pension scheme;

- received gross rental income of £5,000 from a residential property. Her tenant still owed her £200 in rent for March 2019 as at 5 April 2019. Ellie incurred £4,000 of mortgage interest and £300 of allowable rental expenses in relation to the let property; and

- received £600 for doing some exam invigilation for a friend who works in a school.

Requirements

(a) Calculate Ellie's taxable employment income from JL Ltd for 2018/19. Clearly show your treatment of each item. **(9 marks)**

(b) Calculate Ellie's tax-adjusted trading profit after capital allowances for the nine months ended 31 May 2019. Start with the profit for the period of £57,269 and clearly show your treatment of each item. Ignore VAT. **(9 marks)**

(c) Calculate Ellie's income tax liability for 2018/19. Clearly show your treatment of the property income. **(12 marks)**

87.2 Cheryl runs her own business as a sole trader making significant profits. She is an additional rate taxpayer. Cheryl needs to employ a new delivery driver. She already has several employees and her liability to employer's national insurance contributions exceeds the employment allowance.

Cheryl is considering how best to structure the remuneration package for the new delivery driver and is looking at two options:

Option One

Annual salary of £13,500 plus the use of a car with CO_2 emissions of 100g/km provided by the business. The car has a taxable benefit of £3,000 pa. Cheryl will lease the car at a cost of £4,000 pa and incur associated running costs (including petrol for business deliveries) of £2,300 pa. The new delivery driver will pay for any private petrol.

Option Two

Annual salary of £8,300 plus shopping vouchers of £100 per week. The new delivery driver would use his own car for deliveries instead of a car provided by the business. The business pays 60p per business mile and Cheryl estimates that the delivery driver would need to drive 6,000 miles pa to complete all the deliveries.

Under either option the new delivery driver will have no other income.

Requirements

For each option:

(a) Calculate the annual employer's national insurance contributions payable by Cheryl in respect of the new delivery driver. **(4 marks)**

(b) Calculate the annual after-tax cost to the business. **(6 marks)**

Assume the new delivery driver's employment starts on 6 April 2020 and use 2018/19 rates and allowances.

Total: 40 marks

88 Gustavo and Mike

Gustavo and Mike are in the process of setting up in partnership as ICAEW Chartered Accountants offering tax compliance services. They will advertise for clients once they have completed all necessary steps to set up the firm.

Requirement

State the money-laundering and other regulatory requirements for tax practices which Gustavo and Mike must fulfil before starting in business.

Total: 7 marks

89 Shrayder Ltd

Schrayder Ltd makes both taxable and exempt supplies.

The following information relates to the quarters ended 31 March 2019 and 30 June 2019 for the company:

Quarter ended 31 March 2019

	£
Supplies:	
Standard-rated supplies, excluding VAT (Note)	90,000
Zero-rated supplies	10,000
Exempt supplies	24,000
	124,000
Input tax:	
Wholly attributable to taxable supplies	8,400
Wholly attributable to exempt supplies	1,400
Non-attributable	2,300
	12,100

Note: Standard-rated supplies include a sale of machinery for £9,000 excluding VAT.

Quarter ended 30 June 2019

On 10 May 2019 Schrayder Ltd purchased a newly-constructed freehold factory in London for £1.2 million excluding VAT. The factory is used for both taxable and exempt purposes. The partial exemption fraction for the quarter ended 30 June 2019 is 90%.

Requirements

89.1 Show that Schrayder Ltd cannot fully recover input tax for the quarter ended 31 March 2019 using only partial exemption Simplified Tests 1 and 2. **(2 marks)**

89.2 Using the standard partial exemption calculation, calculate the net VAT payable by Schrayder Ltd for the quarter ended 31 March 2019. **(7 marks)**

89.3 In relation to the freehold factory purchased in the quarter ended 30 June 2019:

- State the VAT implications for Schrayder Ltd of the purchase; and

- Calculate the stamp duty land tax payable by Schrayder Ltd and state the date by which it is payable. **(4 marks)**

Total: 13 marks

90 Walter

Walter sold his house in London on 1 February 2019 for £1.5 million. He had purchased it for £240,000 on 1 February 1984, a few years before his marriage to Marie.

Walter lived in the house for the whole of his 35 years of ownership except for the following two periods:

- 10 years from 1 February 1996 when his employer required him to work in Newcastle, 270 miles away from his home. During this time the house was let out.

- The last two years of ownership, when Walter and Marie went to live with their daughter Carmen.

Walter's only other capital disposal in 2018/19 was a sale of antique furniture, which realised a gain of £38,000. Walter's taxable income for 2018/19 was £225,000.

Walter died on 25 March 2019. Walter had outstanding income tax payable of £23,600 and the capital gains tax for 2018/19 was still outstanding at his death. Walter also had other debts of £2,000 relating to credit card bills and £1,000 of gaming debts.

During his lifetime Walter made the following gifts:

- **Annually since 2010 – school fees**

  Payment of school fees for his grandchild. The fees are currently £30,000 pa. Walter had £150,000 of disposable income each year.

- **June 2011 – cash into trust**

  A gross chargeable transfer of £300,000, for the benefit of Walter's grandchild.

- **October 2015 – shares to Carmen**

  Walter gave Carmen 2,000 of his shares in Froing Ltd, an unquoted investment company. Prior to the gift Walter owned 6,000 shares in Froing Ltd and Marie owned the remaining 4,000 shares. The agreed share valuations at October 2015 were:

Number of shares	£ per share
2,000	12
4,000	18
6,000	24
8,000	48
10,000	60

Walter's total assets on death were valued at £1.9 million. Funeral expenses were £10,200.

Walter left £550,000 to Marie, £170,000 to a UK-registered charity and the balance of his estate to Carmen.

Requirements

90.1 Calculate the capital gains tax payable on Walter's disposals in 2018/19. **(8 marks)**

90.2 Explain why the payment of school fees by Walter is exempt for inheritance tax purposes. **(3 marks)**

90.3 Calculate the inheritance tax payable as a result of Walter's death. **(14 marks)**

Note: Ignore stamp taxes.

Total: 25 marks

91 Heissen Ltd

Heissen Ltd, a UK-resident company, has tax-adjusted trading profits before capital allowances for the year ended 31 March 2019 of £86,000.

Factories

On 10 November 2018 Heissen Ltd purchased a 55-year lease of a factory for a total cost of £240,000. The company also purchased new moveable machinery costing £47,000 and paid £3,000 for alterations to the factory necessary to install the machinery.

On 1 December 2018 Heissen Ltd sold a freehold factory for £250,000. The company acquired the factory on 1 February 2010 for £180,000. Heissen Ltd traded from this factory throughout its period of ownership.

Overseas income

During the year ended 31 March 2019, Heissen Ltd had two sources of overseas income:

(1) Dividends received of £16,000 from an 18% holding in Webern SA, resident in Maltovia. The dividends are not exempt from corporation tax in the UK and were received after deduction of 20% withholding tax.

   The dividends were paid out of Webern SA's profits for its year ended 30 September 2018. Webern SA's accounts for that year showed distributable profits of £120,000 and tax payable of £9,600.

(2) Income from a property in Borduria. Income receivable was £90,000 after deduction of 10% withholding tax.

Other information

The capital allowances main pool at 1 April 2018 was £90,000, and the special rate pool was £12,000. The only additional capital purchase in the year was a car with emissions of 158g/km for £25,000. The car is used 35% privately by the managing director.

The company made a qualifying charitable donation of £35,000 on 1 May 2018.

Requirements

91.1 Calculate the chargeable gain on disposal of the freehold factory. Show the amount of rollover relief and the base cost of the new factory. **(3 marks)**

91.2 Calculate Heissen Ltd's corporation tax payable for the year ended 31 March 2019, showing how you have offset the qualifying charitable donation. **(12 marks)**

Note: The retail price index for December 2017 is 278.1 and for December 2018 is 286.7.

Ignore VAT and stamp taxes.

Total: 15 marks

92 Jessie and Saul

92.1 Jessie invested in a cottage in south-west England in 2000 and has been renting out the home since. In 2018/19 she rented the cottage out for £1,000 per month. She received her rent on the 1st of each month except that her tenant made the April rent payment 10 April 2019 following some cash flow problems.

During 2018/19, Jessie paid £5,600 towards her mortgage which comprised of £4,000 capital payments and £1,600 of interest. She paid £100 to an agent to manage the property and £500 for insurance. She also replaced a broken washing machine with a washer-dryer costing £150. A similar washing machine to the one being replaced would have been £100. Jessie paid £10 for the old washing machine to be scrapped.

Jessie is employed as the marketing director of Goodman Ltd. She received the following employment package during 2018/19:

- Salary of £59,000 pa. Jessie's salary has been reduced from £60,000, as part of a new salary sacrifice arrangement for a car park season ticket (see below). The PAYE deducted on her salary was £14,100.

- Car park season ticket. Goodman Ltd purchased a season ticket costing £1,000 for a space in a car park close to the company's office. Jessie has sole use of the season ticket.

- Round sum allowance of £1,200 for the year. Jessie spent £700 on entertaining customers and £400 on car parking when visiting customers for meetings.

- Company car with a list price of £36,000 and emissions of 139g/km. Jessie made a capital contribution of £6,000 towards the cost of the car. Goodman Ltd pays for all of the diesel used in the car which does not meet the RDE2 standards.

During the year Jessie also paid subscriptions of £155 to the Chartered Institute of Marketing, an HMRC-approved body.

During 2018/19 Jessie received £600 of interest on her savings, £838 of dividends and child benefit of £1,076.

Requirements

(a) Calculate Jessie's income tax payable for 2018/19. **(17 marks)**

(b) Calculate the Class 1 secondary and Class 1A national insurance contributions payable by Goodman Ltd in relation to Jessie. Show the earnings for each class of contribution.
(4 marks)

92.2 On 1 October 2018, Saul, aged 35, started a business alone as a training provider. He is not required to be VAT registered. Saul prepared his first accounts for the six months to 31 March 2019. The draft tax-adjusted trading profit for the period is £13,000. However Saul did not know how to deal with the following items and has made no deduction for them:

(1) **Pre-trade costs**

		£
Feb 2018	Legal advice on sales contracts	800
Jun 2018	Insurance, 12 months to 31 May 2019	1,200
Aug 2018	Entertaining potential customers	1,000

(2) **Car**

On 1 October 2018, Saul took out a lease on a car with emissions of 160g/km. During the six months to 31 March 2019 he travelled 15,000 miles of which 12,000 were business miles. Lease costs for the period to 31 March 2019 were £2,000 and fuel costs were £2,800.

(3) **Capital expenditure**

During October 2018, Saul purchased office furniture for £15,000 and had a lift fitted in the business premises costing £210,000.

Before setting up his own business, Saul was employed by another training provider. His other income in recent tax years has been:

	2014/15 £	2015/16 £	2016/17 £	2017/18 £	2018/19 £
Employment	38,000	35,000	39,000	40,000	20,000
Property	3,100	3,200	3,000	2,900	See below
	41,100	38,200	42,000	42,900	

During 2018/19, Saul let a residential property for annual rent of £4,200. However the tenants left the premises on 2 April 2019 having not paid rent for the last two months. Saul has been unable to trace the tenants. During the year he paid mortgage interest of £900 and repair costs of £350.

Requirements

(a) Explain the extent to which each of the pre-trade costs in (1) above is deductible by Saul when adjusting his draft trading profit for the six months ended 31 March 2019.

(3 marks)

(b) Prepare **two** calculations of the allowable deduction in relation to the leased car, using:

- the actual costs incurred; and
- a claim for fixed-rate expenses based on mileage. **(4 marks)**

(c) Assuming that Saul makes a claim for fixed-rate expenses in relation to the leased car, calculate the tax-adjusted trading loss for the six months ended 31 March 2019.

(5 marks)

(d) Calculate Saul's taxable income for 2014/15 to 2018/19, assuming he claims the earliest possible relief for the tax-adjusted trading loss calculated in part (c). Show the order in which losses are relieved. **(7 marks)**

Total: 40 marks

Answer Bank

Ethics and law

1 ABH LLP

			Marks
1.1	Register with supervisory authority	½	
	Appoint MLRO	½	
	Implement internal reporting procedures	½	
	Train staff	1½	
	Establish internal procedures re risk assessment	½	
	Customer due diligence	1	
	Verify identity of new clients	1	
	Report to NCA using SAR	1	
		6½	
	Max		5
1.2	Organisations holding data of EU citizens	½	
	Report breach within 72 hours of coming to light	½	
	Tiered fines	½	
	Max higher of 4% of turnover and €20 million	1	
		2½	
	Max		2
			7

1.1 Anti-money laundering procedures

The firm should do the following to ensure compliance with anti-money laundering regulations:

- Register with an appropriate supervisory authority (eg, ICAEW)

- Appoint a Money Laundering Reporting Officer (MLRO)

- Implement internal reporting procedures

- Train staff to ensure that they are aware of the relevant legislation, know how to recognise and deal with potential money laundering, how to report suspicions to the MLRO, and how to identify clients

- Establish appropriate internal procedures relating to risk assessment and management to deter and prevent money laundering, and make relevant individuals aware of the procedures

- Carry out customer due diligence on any new client and monitor existing clients to ensure the client is known and establish areas of risk

- Verify the identity of new clients and maintain evidence of identification and records of any transactions undertaken for or with the client

- Report suspicions of money laundering to the National Crime Agency (NCA), using a suspicious activity report (SAR)

1.2 Data protection

Every organisation that holds data on EU citizens needs to comply with the new General Data Protection Regulation (GDPR).

Where there is a breach of data likely to result in a risk to the rights and freedoms of individuals the breach needs to be reported within 72 hours of it first coming to light. For organisations in breach of the GDPR there can be tiered fines of up to a maximum of 4% of annual global turnover or €20million, whichever is higher.

2 Dirk

			Marks
2.1	Scheme unlikely to comply	1	
	Contrary to intention of Parliament	1	
	Highly artificial/contrived	1	
	Exploit shortcomings	1	
	Does not comply with tax planning arrangements Standard	½	
	Should be specific	1	
	Alert clients to wider risks	1	
	Does not comply with client specific Standard	½	
		7	
	Max		5
2.2	Two years	1	
	Preferably six years	1	
	Minimum cover (any one of three bullets)	1	
		3	
	Max		2
			7

2.1 Compliance with tax planning standards

The scheme is unlikely to comply with the tax planning Standards within PCRT.

Tax planning arrangements

Members must not create, encourage or promote tax planning arrangements or structures that:

- set out to achieve results that are contrary to the clear intention of Parliament in enacting relevant legislation; and/or

- are highly artificial or highly contrived and seek to exploit shortcomings within the relevant legislation.

Dirk's scheme clearly does not comply with this standard.

Client specific

Tax planning must be specific to the particular client's facts and circumstances. Clients must be alerted to the wider risks and the implications of any courses of action.

Dirk's scheme does not appear to be specific to individual clients and therefore it does not comply with this Standard.

2.2 **PII**

As a qualified member of ICAEW in public practice and resident in the UK, Matilda should maintain cover for at least two years after her retirement, preferably for at least six years.

The minimum recommended level of cover is:

- £100,000;
- 2.5 times fee income if fee income is higher than £100,000;
- preferably higher if Matilda's recent fee income has exceeded £600,000 pa.

---

3 Trent Ltd (March 2014)

Marking guide

				Marks
3.1	Legal		½	
	HMRC view of avoidance and planning		2	
	No distinction in law		½	
			3	
		Max		2
3.2	Deliberately misleading HMRC		1	
	Therefore not tax avoidance		½	
	Suppressing and providing false information		2	
	Tax evasion consequences		1	
	Money laundering and consequences		1½	
			6	
		Max		5
				7

3.1 Tax planning and tax avoidance are legal. There is no intention to mislead HMRC. HMRC make a distinction between tax planning – using tax reliefs for the purpose for which they were intended for example claiming tax relief on capital investment – and tax avoidance, which involves bending the rules of the tax system to gain a tax advantage that Parliament never intended. However, this distinction is not made in law.

3.2 The directors' actions include deliberately misleading HMRC and cannot therefore be tax avoidance.

They have both suppressed information (hiding), omitting relevant figures from returns, and also provided false information (lying), altering the records to hide the benefits.

Tax evasion is a criminal offence punishable by penalties, fines and/or imprisonment.

The unpaid tax becomes the proceeds of crime as it arises from tax evasion which is a criminal offence. Therefore money laundering issues arise which could lead to a criminal conviction for the directors.

Examiner's comments

The examiners were pleased to see that most answers demonstrated that students have learnt the ethics part of the syllabus and could apply it in a standard scenario.

---

4 Happy Ltd (June 2014)

				Marks
4.1	Whether to act	½		
	Skills	½		
	Threats to objectivity	2		
	Who reply to/confidentiality	1		
	Deal with wife	1		
	ML checks and engagement letter	1		
	Whether existing engagement can continue	$\frac{1}{7}$		
	Max			5
4.2	Access credentials	1		
	Change password	1		
	Report unusual activity to HMRC	1		
	Forward suspicious emails	$\frac{1}{4}$		
	Max			$\frac{2}{7}$

4.1 The manager must consider whether to agree to act for Sunil's wife.

The engagement should not be accepted unless either PC & Co has the internal skills to provide the advice required or such specialist advice is sought from a third party.

Consideration should also be given as to whether to act at all given the potential threats to compliance with the fundamental principles. The fundamental principle of objectivity is at stake, given that future work appears dependent on agreeing a good fee for this work.

Consideration should be given to who any reply should go to. The request comes from Sunil, but any engagement would mean dealing with Sunil's wife directly. Neither are currently clients. Any dealings with Sunil's wife would be confidential from Sunil unless she agreed otherwise.

If the firm is going to agree to act, the following will be needed:

- Money laundering checks including ID
- An engagement letter outlining the scope of the services offered

Consideration should also be given to whether the Happy Ltd engagement can continue if the manager's trust in Sunil is compromised.

4.2 Access credentials such as passwords should be kept safe from unauthorised use and computers should be physically secure.

Passwords should be changed regularly: HMRC recommends at least once every three months.

Any unusual or unexpected activity on clients' online HMRC records should be reported to HMRC immediately.

Suspicious emails appearing to be from HMRC should be forwarded to HMRC's phishing team and it is important to avoid clicking on links in these, or opening attachments.

5 Gothi Ltd (December 2014)

Marking guide

				Marks
5.1	Fundamental principles		1½	
	Threat		1	
			2½	
		Max		2
5.2	Suppression of information		½	
	Tax evasion		½	
	Illegal		½	
	Engagement letter		½	
	Actions in respect of client		2½	
	Written record		½	
	Money laundering		1	
	Refuse job offer		½	
			6½	
		Max		5
				7

5.1 The three fundamental principles that are threatened by this situation are objectivity,
integrity and professional behaviour.

You suffer a self-interest threat as a result of the job offer.

5.2 The company intends to deliberately suppress information to which HMRC is entitled, which
amounts to tax evasion which is illegal.

Your firm should check the engagement letter to ensure that it gives authority to make a
disclosure to HMRC.

Your firm should refer the matter to the client and the client should be:

- asked to advise HMRC of the incorrect treatment

- asked to pay the money due to HMRC

- warned of the possible legal consequences of refusal to give authority (including
interest and penalties and possible criminal prosecution)

- advised that if consent is not given or HMRC are not advised by the client, the firm will
cease to act for the client

A written record of all advice given to Gothi Ltd should be kept by the firm.

As this amounts to tax evasion it falls within the definition of money laundering. You should therefore contact your firm's MLRO who should consider submitting a SAR to NCA.

You should not take the job if offered by Gothi Ltd due to the poor ethical stance taken by the company in its dealings with HMRC, unless you are satisfied that Elsa and the company will proceed with full disclosure.

Examiner's comments

5.1 Students generally performed well on this part.

5.2 A small number of students thought that because the error made was originally unintentional, this was a case of tax avoidance, despite the individual then intending to withhold information from HMRC. More detail relating to the actions to be taken was required from a large number of students, with many only considering money laundering issues.

6 Pigeon Ltd (March 2015)

Marking guide

		Marks
6.1	Threat	1
	Objectivity	1
	Integrity	1
	Professional behaviour	1
		4
6.2	Tax evasion	½
	Misleading HMRC	½
	Deliberate	½
	Supression of information	½
		2
6.3	ML failure to disclose implications	1
	Disqualification from ICAEW	½
		1½
	Max	1
		7

6.1

> **Tutorial note**
>
> There is no single right answer to the first part. Students should be given credit for selecting either threat and explaining why it is relevant. Suitable answers might be one of the following.

There is a self-interest threat as the manager has promised to consider me for promotion if I remain silent.

There is also an intimidation threat as the manager is my supervisor and I am only a trainee.

The fundamental principle of objectivity is threatened here because the manager is trying to influence my behaviour.

The fundamental principle of integrity is threatened here because the manager wants me to behave in a way that is not straightforward and honest.

The fundamental principle of professional behaviour is threatened here because the manager wants me to behave in a way that is potentially not compliant with relevant laws and may discredit the profession.

6.2 This is tax evasion because it is misleading HMRC by deliberately suppressing information that we now know about the errors.

6.3 Tax evasion may have money laundering implications. I have a duty to report a suspicion of money laundering otherwise I may be guilty of failure to disclose which can result in a custodial sentence of up to five years.

For such dishonest behaviour I could face being disqualified as a member of ICAEW.

Examiner's comments

6.1 Answers were rarely very high scoring, although most students managed to demonstrate a basic understanding of ethics and gain more than half marks overall across the whole of the question. Generally students did manage to identify the relevant fundamental principles threatened, although could not always articulate why.

6.2 Some answers as to whether the non-disclosure of the errors amounted to tax evasion were interesting. One candidate thought that tax evasion was legal and tax avoidance was illegal. A number of students thought that a deliberate under-payment of tax could only amount to tax evasion if the amount under-paid was material. A number of students also thought that if there was no original intention to deceive, then subsequent non-disclosure of errors once they had been discovered could not be tax evasion.

6.3 Answers were rarely very high scoring, although most students managed to demonstrate a basic understanding of ethics.

7 Lucy (September 2015)

Marking guide

			Marks
7.1	Self-interest threat	1	
	Self-review threat	1	
	Professional competence and due care	1	
	Objectivity	1	
	Professional behaviour	1	
	Integrity	1	
		6	
	Max		5
7.2	Safeguards ½ per safeguard	2	
	PII	½	
		2½	
	Max		2
			7

7.1 On appointment Lucy suffered a self-interest threat, as she received a substantial increase in pay on her appointment.

During her time as finance director she faced a self-review threat as her earlier judgements in relation to the corporation tax return needed to be re-evaluated.

The fundamental principles threatened by her accepting the job were:

Professional competence and due care – as Lucy had not attained sufficient professional competence before accepting the job.

Objectivity – the fact that she was still willing to undertake the job despite insufficient experience suggests that her objectivity was compromised by self-interest.

Professional behaviour – as Lucy made exaggerated claims about the experience that she had previously gained.

Integrity – it appears she was knowingly associated with a corporation tax return that was furnished recklessly.

7.2 The safeguards that should reassure the directors in relation to the work of Darwin LLP are:

- continuing professional development requirements
- ICAEW professional standards
- regulatory monitoring
- ICAEW complaints procedure which will be detailed in the engagement letter

ICAEW also requires members to hold professional indemnity insurance.

Examiner's comments

7.1 Most students recognised the issues in this part – identifying at least one of the threats (usually self-interest) and two or three of the fundamental principles. Marks were lost for not correctly explaining why the facts of the scenario caused a threat to specific fundamental principle or not accurately identifying the fundamental principle (eg, professional **diligence** and due care).

7.2 Few marks were scored on this part. Students had not learnt the list of safeguards from the learning materials. Most did not focus on the safeguards as a result of the new accountants being members of ICAEW. The most common valid point that was mentioned was the CPD requirement.

8 Geiger LLP (December 2015)

Marking guide

		Marks
8.1 Self-interest threat	½	
Self-interest threat linked to 'valuable client'	½	
Familiarity threat	½	
Familiarity threat linked to 'close friend'	½	
Three correct principles (½ each)	1½	
	3½	
Max		3

		Marks
8.2	Ask directors to correct treatment in future	½
	Check engagement letter for authority	1
	Ask directors to disclose	½
	Cease to act, inform HMRC, do not give reasons	1
	Keep written record	½
	Money laundering	½
	Consider submitting a SAR to NCA	1
		5
	Max	4
		7

8.1 Geiger LLP suffers a self-interest threat as Mallory Ltd is identified as a 'valuable client'.

There is also a familiarity threat as the partner is a close friend of the managing director.

The three fundamental principles that are threatened by this situation are integrity, objectivity and professional behaviour.

8.2 Geiger LLP should ask the directors to treat the payments correctly going forward.

Geiger LLP should check whether the engagement letter allows them to disclose the issue to HMRC.

If the engagement letter does not give the power to disclose, the directors should be asked to advise HMRC of the incorrect treatment and pay the PAYE due.

If the directors refuse to disclose this matter, Geiger LLP should cease to act for Mallory Ltd. Geiger LLP should inform HMRC that they are ceasing to act but give no reason.

A written record of all advice given to Mallory Ltd should be kept by Geiger LLP.

As this amounts to tax evasion it falls within the definition of money laundering, Geiger LLP's MLRO should consider completing a SAR and submitting it to NCA.

Examiner's comments

8.1 This part was often well answered with many students scoring full marks.

8.2 In contrast to the previous part this was not well answered. Many students slightly missed the point and answered as though the engagement partner had performed the payroll process incorrectly, rather than the director at the client doing this. This led to much discussion of changing the partner on the job, new engagement team rather than correction of the error. Students also failed to address the specific requirement to state actions, and instead wrote at length about tax evasion generally.

9 Pear Ltd (Sample Paper 1)

			Marks
9.1	HMRC error	½	
	Engagement letter	½	
	Refer to client	½	
	Advise HMRC	½	
	Return money	½	
	Legal consequences	1	
	Cease to act	½	
	Written record of advice	½	
		4½	
	Max		3
9.2	Theft and proceeds of crime	1	
	MLRO	½	
	NCA using SAR	1	
	Do not tip off	½	
		3	
	Max		2
9.3	No knowledge or suspicion of ML	1	
	Privilege reporting exemption	1	
	Reasonable excuse	1	
	ML occurring outside UK	1	
		4	
	Max		2
			7

9.1 It appears that HMRC has made an error in relation to the company's VAT.

Your firm should check the engagement letter to ensure that it gives authority to advise HMRC of the error.

As the amount involved is not immaterial your firm should refer the matter to the client and the client should be:

- asked to advise HMRC of the error (or to authorise the firm if authority is not given in the engagement letter)

- asked to return the money to HMRC

- warned of the possible legal consequences of refusal to give authority (including interest and penalties and possible criminal prosecution)

- advised that if consent is not given or HMRC are not advised by the client, the firm will cease to act for the client

A written record of all advice given to Pear Ltd should be kept by the firm.

9.2 If the VAT refund is not returned it amounts to theft, and the refund becomes proceeds of crime.

You should report this to your firm's money laundering reporting officer (MLRO) on an internal report.

The MLRO, taking all matters into account, should decide whether to report his suspicions to the National Crime Agency (NCA) using a suspicious activity report (SAR).

Both you and other members of your firm must take care not to tip off members of staff at Pear Ltd.

9.3 **Any two from:**

I did not actually know or suspect money laundering had occurred and I had not been provided by my employer with the training required.

The privilege reporting exemption: An accountant who suspects or has reasonable grounds for knowing or suspecting that another person is engaged in money laundering is exempted from making a money laundering report where his knowledge or suspicion comes to him in privileged circumstances (the privilege reporting exemption).

I had a reasonable excuse for not making a report. Although there is no money laundering case law on this issue, it is unlikely to apply here as it is anticipated that only relatively extreme circumstances, such as duress and threats to safety, might be accepted.

It is known, or reasonably believed that the money laundering is occurring outside the UK, and is not unlawful under the criminal law of the country where it is occurring.

10 PPA (Sample Paper 2)

Marking guide

		Marks
10.1 Tax evasion	1½	
Tax avoidance	½	
		2
10.2 Tax avoidance not always successful	½	
Courts strike down if no commercial purpose	2	
Substance if artificial elements ignored	1	
GAAR	1	
	4½	
Max		2
10.3 Penalties and interest	1	
Criminal prosecution and consequences	1½	
Accountants failings under ML	2	
Disqualification from ICAEW	½	
	5	
Max		3
		7

10.1 Tax evasion is the deliberate intention to mislead HMRC and is illegal.

Tax evasion takes place where information is suppressed (hiding), or false information is provided (lying).

Tax avoidance is any legal method of reducing one's tax burden.

10.2 Tax avoidance is not illegal but it does not necessarily mean that it will work to successfully reduce a tax bill.

The courts have struck down certain tax avoidance schemes which have no commercial purpose or effect. This has been done by ignoring the elements of the scheme which have no commercial purpose.

Ignoring the artificial elements of the transaction, the courts could infer that the loans were in substance income from employment which is subject to income tax and NIC.

HMRC could also use the GAAR as a means to challenge the scheme.

10.3 Failure to disclose underpaid tax to HMRC may result in the payment of penalties to HMRC in addition to the unpaid tax and interest thereon.

If it is deemed sufficiently serious, tax evasion can lead to criminal prosecution resulting in fines and/or imprisonment.

Tax evasion may also have money laundering implications. If I fail to report a suspicion of money laundering to the firm's MLRO then I may be guilty of failure to disclose which can result in a custodial sentence of up to five years.

For such dishonest behaviour I could face being disqualified as a member of ICAEW.

Indirect taxes

11 Waxwell Ltd (March 2014)

		Marks
11.1 UK supplies	½	
Non-registered EU customers	½	
Legal services – output	½	
Legal services – input	½	
Purchase of standard-rated goods	½	
Purchase of zero-rated goods	½	
	3	3
11.2 Single supply vs multiple supply	1	
Single zero-rated supply	1	
Ancillary/incidental	1	
No offer of lower price if no meal	½	
No contractual obligation to supply food	½	
	4	
	Max	3
11.3 >3 years, exempt	½	
Option to tax – standard rated	1	
VAT (included in price)	1½	
VAT due from Polly Parrot	1	
Issue of invoice, VAT reclaimed	1½	
If agree exclusive of VAT price	½	
	6	
	Max	4
11.4 SDLT payable on lease premium and NPV rentals	½	
Premium – amount payable	½	
NPV of rentals – amount payable	1½	
Land transaction form and payment in 30 days	1	
	3½	
	Max	3
		13

11.1 VAT – quarter ended 31 December 2018:

	£
Output tax	
UK supplies £68,500 × 20%	13,700
Supplies to non-registered EU customers £17,450 × 20%	3,490
Legal services (reverse charge) £2,500 × 20%	500
Input tax	
Legal services (reverse charge) £2,500 × 20%	(500)
Purchase of standard-rated goods £25,000 × 20%	(5,000)
Purchase of zero-rated goods	0
VAT payable	12,190

11.2 Single and multiple supplies

How the VAT should be calculated depends on whether the supply is a single supply with a single VAT rate, or a multiple supply with multiple VAT rates.

Whether a supply is in fact a single or a multiple supply depends on the circumstances. Shaker Airways should treat the sale as a single zero-rated supply because the facts here are similar to the British Airways case in which the Court of Appeal ruled there was a single zero-rated supply being the supply of a flight.

This was for the following reasons:

- The supply was in essence a flight, with an ancillary/incidental supply of food. Where a supply is ancillary there is a single supply.

- The supply was a single economic supply as the customer was not offered a lower price if the meal was not required.

- The fact there was no contractual obligation to supply the food also indicated that this was a single supply.

11.3 VAT on property

As the building is more than three years old, ordinarily it would be exempt from VAT.

However, as an option to tax had been exercised in respect of the property, it should have been a standard-rated supply and VAT is therefore due.

As VAT was not mentioned in the sale and purchase agreement, the price paid will be treated as being the VAT inclusive price. Therefore VAT is due of £450,000 × 1/6 = £75,000.

This VAT is due from Polly Parrot Ltd.

Providing Polly Parrot Ltd issues a VAT invoice, Badir Ltd could reclaim this VAT as it makes wholly standard-rated supplies.

Polly Parrot Ltd and Badir Ltd could agree to treat the net proceeds as being the £450,000. In which case Badir Ltd would then need to pay over and subsequently reclaim VAT of £90,000.

11.4 SDLT

SDLT is payable on both the lease premium and the net present value of the lease rentals as follows.

On the grant of a non-residential lease for a premium between £0 and £150,000, there is no SDLT on the lease premium element.

On the net present value of the lease rentals (ignoring discounting), where the NPV exceeds £150,000 but is less than £5 million, the SDLT is [(£27,000 × 6) – £150,000] × 1% = £120.

A land transaction form must be submitted to HMRC and the associated SDLT paid by Zeeson Bank Ltd within 30 days of the lease agreement.

Examiner's comments

11.1 Generally answers to this part were good, although it was surprising how many students calculated input VAT on the purchase of zero-rated goods. The output element of the reverse charge was, not surprisingly, generally missing.

11.2 Most students arrived at the right answer and stated that it would be a zero-rated supply. The most common point made was that the catering was an ancillary supply. Very few students mentioned that there was no contractual obligation to supply the food.

11.3 Generally, answers to this part were good although a surprising number of students thought that the capital goods scheme was relevant.

11.4 [These comments have been edited for changes to the rules on SDLT – only the comments still relevant remain.] Answers to this part were not generally very good with most students clearly still lacking knowledge on stamp duty land tax. Some added the premium and the NPV of rent together. There were only a few students who referred to the 30 day time limit.

12 Arthur (June 2014)

		Marks
12.1 Test Two – assessment	1	
Conclusion on test two and consequence	1	
Car	1	
Van	1	
Recoverable amount %	1½	
VAT exclusive amount	1	
Non-capital items	1	
Apply to non-attributable input tax	1	
De minimis test	½	
Adjustment required	1	
		10
12.2 Divorce exemption	1	
SDRT	1	
SDLT at additional rates	2	
	4	
Max		3
		13

12.1 **Has Arthur passed Test Two?**

Is the monthly average of total input tax incurred less input tax directly attributable to taxable supplies £625 or less?

Monthly average = (£53,450 + £1,200) – £16,000/12 = £3,221

Test is not met

Is the value of exempt supplies not more than 50% of the value of total supplies?

£62,000/£110,000 = 56%

Test is not met

Both parts of Test Two are not met and therefore need to use the standard test

Standard test	Taxable £	Exempt £	Total £
Wholly attributable input tax:			
Taxable supplies	16,000		16,000
Exempt supplies		25,000	25,000
Car – irrecoverable as some private use			–
Van – £6,000 × 20%		1,200	1,200
Non-attributable input tax:			
Recoverable amount % is:			
48,000/110,000 = 44% (rounded up)			
Attributable to taxable supplies = 44% × £12,450	5,478		5,478
Attributable to exempt supplies = 56% × £12,450		6,972	6,972
	21,478	33,172	54,650

(1) Is the monthly average of attributable to exempt supplies £625 or less?

Monthly average = £33,172/12 = £2,764
Test not met

(2) Is the proportion of VAT on exempt supplies not more than 50% of all input VAT for the period?

£33,172/£54,650 = 61%
Test is not met

Both parts of the test are not met and therefore input tax attributable to exempt supplies is not *de minimis* and all the exempt input VAT recovered, £33,172, must be repaid.

12.2 There is no stamp duty payable on a transfer as part of a divorce settlement, so stamp duty on the XBit plc shares is nil.

Yami has to pay stamp duty reserve tax on the Beep plc shares of £2,200 × 0.5% = £11.

The purchase of the residential apartment is subject to SDLT at increased rates because this is an additional property:

£125,000 × 3% = £3,750
(£210,000 – £125,000) × 5% = £4,250
Total SDLT = £8,000

Examiner's comments

12.1 There were some very confused and messy answers to this partial exemption question, with some exam panic perhaps setting in at this late stage of the exam. Most students (those who were able to stay calm and continue) were able to gain some marks, mainly for the main test. Frequently students interpreted the VAT amounts given as being the amount of supplies, charged VAT on VAT, included output tax as input tax and vice versa, and finally tried to perform a calculation of output tax less input tax to work out the annual adjustment itself.

There was confusion as to what Test One (referred to in the question) and Test Two were, some thinking that these were the two parts of the standard test.

12.2 There are no examiner comments as this requirement was not part of the original exam question.

13 Salmon Ltd (March 2015)

		Marks
13.1 Disposal	1	
Capital goods scheme	1	
VAT claw back	1½	
	3½	
Max		3
13.2 VAT on rent	1	
Recovery of input VAT	2	
Implications for tenants	1	
Option irrevocable, cooling off period	1	
Sale of building	1	
	6	
Max		4
13.3 Output VAT – ½ per entry	1½	
Input VAT – expenses	½	
Car	½	
Machinery	½	
		3
13.4 SDRT	1	
SDLT	2½	
	3½	
Max		3
		13

13.1 Capital goods scheme

Disposal is exempt – no VAT due

Capital goods scheme applies to claw back some of original input VAT recovered.

An exempt disposal in interval eight means some of the VAT will be clawed back:
£175,000 / 10 × 2 = £35,000

13.2 VAT on property

If Kilmarnock Ltd opts to tax the building then:

- VAT must be charged at 20% on rent

- Kilmarnock Ltd will be able to recover the input tax of £1.5 million on the purchase of the building in addition to any other input VAT incurred in relation to the rental of the property. It would not otherwise be able to recover the VAT suffered as property rental is an exempt supply

- any of the tenants who are VAT registered will be able to recover the VAT charged on the rent as input VAT

- however, those tenants who are exempt from VAT will not be able to recover the VAT charged on the rent as input VAT which will make the property rental more expensive for them

- the option to tax is irrevocable for 20 years

- the option to tax can however be revoked during the 'cooling-off' period ie, within the first six months after it becomes effective

- a sale of the building within 20 years will be standard rated potentially making the sale price of the building higher than other similar buildings if the purchaser cannot recover the VAT as input VAT

13.3 VAT – quarter ended 31 December 2018:

	£
Output tax	
UK supplies £160,000 × 20%	32,000
Supplies to VAT-registered EU customers	0
Supplies to non-registered EU customers £45,000 × 20%	9,000
Input tax	
Expenses (£50,000 + £25,000) × 20%	(15,000)
Car – irrecoverable if any private use	0
Machinery £40,000 × 20%	(8,000)
VAT payable	18,000

13.4 SDRT

SDRT @ ½% = £55,000 × ½% = £275

SDLT

Not a gift as liability for a debt is assumed, so the liability assumed (ie, £300,000) is subject to SDLT:

£125,000 × 0% = £0
(£250,000 – £125,000) × 2% = £2,500
(£300,000 – £250,000) × 5% = £2,500
Total SDLT = £5,000

Examiner's comments

13.1 Answers were generally poor. Most students failed to recognise that the capital goods scheme applied. Many decided to deduct the original input VAT from an output VAT charged on sale (not appreciating that the disposal itself would be exempt), to give a nonsense figure.

13.2 Answers were generally good with most students able to make at least some relevant points about the option to tax. Marginal students could often demonstrate their knowledge of the rules as to how long the cooling off period lasted and how long the option itself lasted, but clearly still do not really understand that without the option to tax property rental would be an exempt supply. Whereas, if the building were used in Kilmarnock's trade it would be a taxable supply and the input VAT would be recoverable in any event. There were some interesting answers.

13.3 Answers were generally very good. This reflected the fact that the calculation was very basic and most students were able to gain full or nearly full marks.

13.4 Most students did badly. A significant number of students cannot calculate ½% of something and calculated 5% instead – again assumed to be exam nerves rather than a lack of mathematical ability, but incorrect none-the-less, although as always students who showed clear workings did not lose marks for a purely arithmetical error. Very few students knew how to treat the gift and assumption of mortgage.

14 Roger (September 2015)

		Marks
14.1 (a) Services – six months	½	
Application to legal services	½	
Goods – four years and still on hand	1	
Application to computer	1	
Entertaining	½	
	3½	
Max		3
(b) Single supply explanation	1½	
VAT treatment of single supply	1	
Multiple supply explanation	1½	
VAT treatment of multiple supply	1	
Methods of apportioning VAT	1	
Conclusion on this scenario	1½	
	7½	
Max		6
14.2 SDLT on lease premium	½	
SDLT on rent	1½	
3 month penalty	1	
12 month penalty	1	
		4
		13

14.1 (a) Input VAT can be recovered on services supplied in the six months before registration.

As the legal services in May 2018 were more than six months before registration then the input tax cannot be recovered.

Input VAT can be reclaimed on goods purchased in the four years before registration, provided they were supplied for business purposes and are still on hand at the date of registration.

It is likely that Roger still uses the computer for business purposes at 1 October 2019, and so VAT of £400 (1/6 × £2,400) will be recoverable.

Input tax on entertaining of suppliers cannot be recovered.

(b) HMRC could treat the supply as a 'single' (or composite) supply. This would be the case if one part of the supply is merely incidental, or ancillary to the main element, or a means of better enjoying the main element.

In this case the VAT rate applying to the main supply would apply to the whole supply.

Alternatively HMRC could treat the supply as a 'multiple' (or combined/mixed) supply. This would be the case if the elements are separate and clearly identifiable, but have been invoiced together at an inclusive price for both elements.

In this case each element is considered separately, so Roger would account separately for VAT on the different elements (boat cruise and buffet), by splitting the total in a fair and reasonable manner.

The main methods for apportioning the VAT include splitting the amount based on:

- cost to Roger of each element
- the open market value of each element

HMRC are likely to treat Roger's business as making 'multiple supplies.'

Note: This follows the decision in case law Durham River Trips.

14.2 SDLT on the lease premium

There is nil SDLT on the lease premium as this is less than £150,000.

SDLT on NPV of rentals:

Total NPV of rentals = 15 × £20,000 = £300,000

£150,000 × 0% = £0
(£300,000 – £150,000) × 1% = £1,500
SDLT on NPV of rentals = £1,500

As the land transaction form is due to be submitted more than three months late a fixed penalty of £200 is imposed.

There may also be a tax-geared penalty of up 100% of the SDLT due ie, £1,500 as the form will be submitted more than 12 months after the due date.

Examiner's comments

14.1 (a) The VAT rules were not well known. Students often confused these with the pre-trading expenditure rules. Often if the rule was stated eg, with regards to services, it was then incorrectly applied to the information.

(b) Many students did identify that this requirement concerned single v multiple supplies, although most only discussed the former at any length, despite the latter being in point. Good marks were gained by discussing both options. Some confused zero-rated and exempt supplies, and so answered this requirement as if it concerned partial exemption.

14.2 Students' answers were generally sufficient if not very good with marks frequently scored either on the SDLT calculations, or on the penalties, but not both.

15 Towers Ltd (December 2015)

		Marks
15.1 (a)	VAT inclusive price	½
	SDLT	1½
		2
(b)	VAT exempt	½
	CGS applies	1
	Annual repayment required	½
	Calculation of repayment	1
	Rent vatable if OTT	½
	Recover input VAT if OTT	½
	No CGS adjustment	½
		4½
	Max	4
15.2	UK supplies	½
	EU supplies	1
	Computer advice – reverse charge	½
	Fuel scale charge	1
	Materials	½
	Computer advice	½
	Car acquisition	½
	Motor expenses	½
	VAT payable	½
		5½
	Max	5
15.3	No SDLT due	½
	Land transaction form required	½
	Submitted by Priya	½
	Within 30 days	½
	Penalty	½
		2½
	Max	2
		13

15.1 (a) SDLT on purchase of freehold non-residential property

SDLT is paid on the VAT inclusive price of a property. A purchase of a new freehold commercial property is standard rated.

So the VAT inclusive price £2.6m × 120% = £3,120,000

SDLT	£
£150,000 – 0%	0
£(250,000 – 150,000) × 2%	2,000
£(3,120,000 – 250,000) × 5%	143,500
	145,500

(b) As Towers Ltd has not made an option to tax Roscoe House the rent of £50,000 is VAT exempt.

As the factory was purchased in the last 10 years, for in excess of £250,000, then the capital goods scheme applies.

So annually from y/e 31 March 2021 VAT will be repaid to HMRC

(100 – 85)% × £520,000 × 1/10 = £7,800

If Towers Ltd opts to tax the building then VAT at the standard rate will be charged on the rental income ie, £10,000 (£50,000 × 20%) each year.

Towers Ltd will be able to recover VAT on any costs of letting.

As the building will be used wholly for standard-rated supplies no adjustment for use will be required.

15.2

	£
VAT – quarter ended 28 February 2019	
Output tax	
UK supplies £39,500 × 20%	7,900
Supplies to non-registered EU customers £12,900 × 20%	2,580
Computer advice (reverse charge) £190 × 20%	38
Fuel scale charge £384 × 1/6	64
Input tax	
Materials £8,100 × 20%	(1,620)
Computer advice £190 × 20%	(38)
Car acquisition – irrecoverable as private use	–
Motor expenses £1,750 × 20%	(350)
VAT payable	8,574

15.3 As the actual consideration was below £150,000 stamp duty land tax was not payable on disposal.

However Priya should still have submitted a land transaction form to HMRC within 30 days of the sale.

As the form is more than 3 months late a fixed penalty of £200 is imposed.

Examiner's comments

15.1 (a) Many students scored full marks on this part. A common error for those not scoring full marks was to omit the VAT. A surprising number of students misread their tax tables and stated that there was no SDLT payable as the property transaction was more than £500,000.

(b) This part was often poorly answered. Many students did not answer the question asked and focussed on the original purchase of the building rather than letting out the property. The interaction with the capital goods scheme was often omitted. Written explanations were often inaccurate or vague.

15.2 There are no examiner comments as this requirement was not part of the original exam.

15.3 Most students thought that SDLT was payable on the market value – however knowledge of the admin aspects of SDLT, as demanded in the requirement, was reasonable. The main omission was failure to address who is responsible for completing the administration ie, the purchaser.

16 Granate Ltd (Sample Paper 1)

		Marks
16.1(a)	**EU**	
	Business customers (VAT registered)	2
	Business customers – not registered	½
	Private individuals	½
	Other parts of world	1½
		4½
	Max	4
16.1(b)	Output VAT	1
	Input VAT	1
		2
16.2(a)	No VAT >3 years old	½
	CGS	½
	Original input recovered	½
	CGS adjustment	1½
	Option to tax – standard rated, no CGS adjustment	1
	Purchase price depending on purchaser OTT	½
	Rent exempt	½
		5
	Max	4
16.2(b)	SDLT on premium	1½
	SDLT on lease rentals	2½
		4
	Max	3
		13

16.1(a) The treatment differs depending on whether the supply is to elsewhere in the EU or other parts of the world.

EU supplies:

To business customers

The supply to a customer is zero rated if:

- the supply is to a registered trader

- Granate Ltd quotes the customer VAT number on the invoice

- Granate Ltd holds evidence that the goods were delivered to another member state

Otherwise it is standard rated (ie, the same as a UK supply).

To private individuals

The supply is standard rated.

Supplies to other parts of the world

Exports going outside the EU are zero rated provided that HMRC are satisfied that the goods have been exported. This is unaffected by whether the customer is in business.

Granate Ltd will need to retain relevant evidence of the export (eg, shipping documents).

16.1(b) Supply of services from German legal firm

Output VAT payable = £20,000 × 20% = £4,000 (B2B so supplied in UK, reverse charge)

Input VAT recoverable = £20,000 × 20% = £4,000 (used to make taxable supplies, so recoverable)

16.2(a) Capital goods scheme

As the factory is more than three years old and assuming the option to tax was not exercised, there is no VAT to be charged on the sale. However, as the building is only nine years old and originally cost more than £250,000, it falls within the capital goods scheme. Therefore on an exempt disposal before 1 April 2020 there will be a claw back of some of the initial input VAT recovered:

Original input VAT recovered = £750,000 × 17.5% = £131,250

The sale adjustment under the capital goods scheme will be:

(£131,250/10) × (0% – 100%) × (10 – 9) intervals = £13,125 repayable to HMRC

Option to tax

Granate Ltd could opt to tax the building before its disposal. This would make the sale a standard-rated supply. There would then be no sale adjustment under the capital goods scheme.

However, this may affect the purchase price payable by Marble Ltd, depending on whether Marble Ltd is prepared to opt to tax the building in order to recover the input tax paid. As Marble Ltd will be renting out the property it will be an exempt supply and the input tax would be irrecoverable unless Marble Ltd also opted to tax the building.

16.2(b) SDLT on acquisition of lease

SDLT on premium:

£150,000 × 0% = £0

(£250,000 – £150,000) × 2% = £2,000

(£400,000 – £250,000) × 5% = £7,500

SDLT on premium = £9,500

SDLT on NPV of rentals:

Total NPV of rentals = 25 × £325,000 = £8,125,000

£150,000 × 0% = £0

(£5,000,000 – £150,000) × 1% = £48,500

(£8,125,000 – £5,000,000) × 2% = £62,500

SDLT on NPV of rentals = £111,000

Total SDLT on lease = £9,500 + £111,000 = £120,500

17 Faizha and Tehira (Sample Paper 2)

		Marks
17.1 VAT flat rate for a limited cost business		
Input VAT	1	
Output VAT	½	
Flat rate paid to HMRC	1	
Net VAT deficit surplus	1	
Limited cost trader test	1½	
VAT liability if purchases < £600	2	
VAT liability if purchases > £600	1	
	8	
	Max	6
17.2 SDLT premium	1½	
SDLT rentals	2½	
Interest	2	
Penalty	1	
		7
		13

17.1 VAT flat rate for a limited cost business

	Limited cost £	Financial services £
Input VAT suffered = £300 × 20% / £800 × 20%	(60)	(160)
Output VAT collected = £25,000 × 20%	5,000	5,000
Flat rate VAT paid to HMRC (W)	(4,950)	(4,050)
Net VAT deficit surplus	(10)	790

WORKING

Faizha's flat rate will depend on whether she is a limited cost trader. She will be a limited cost trader if her VAT inclusive costs for the quarter are less than either:

- 2% of VAT inclusive turnover for the quarter = £25,000 × 1.2 × 2% = £600; or
- £1,000 / 4 = £250

With purchases of less than £600 she will be a limited cost trader and her VAT liability will be:

- £25,000 × 1.2 × **16.5%** = £4,950

If Faizha's purchases exceed £600 then her VAT liability will be calculated using her industry percentage:

- £25,000 × 1.2 × **13.5%** = £4,050

17.2 SDLT

SDLT on premium:

SDLT payable on VAT inclusive price = £140,000 × 1.2 = £168,000
£150,000 × 0% = £0
(£168,000 – £150,000) × 2% = £360
SDLT on premium = £360

SDLT on NPV of rentals:

Total (VAT inclusive) NPV of rentals = £8,000 × 1.2 × 25 = £240,000
£150,000 × 0% = £0
(£240,000 – £150,000) × 1% = £900
SDLT on NPV of rentals = £900

Total SDLT on lease = £360 + £900 = £1,260

Interest due

Payable within 30 days = 30 January 2019
Actually paid = 1 April 2019
2 months late
2/12 × £1,260 × 3% = £6

Penalties

Filed less than 3 months late = fixed penalty of £100

CGT and IHT

18 Finn (December 2014)

	Marks
18.1 CLT October 2016 - Lifetax	
Property less AEs	1
NRB	1
Lifetime tax	½
CLT October 2016 – Death tax	
Gross chargeable transfer	½
NRB	1
Death tax less lifetime tax	1
Death estate assets	1½
Less deductions	1½
Spouse exemption restricted as non UK-domiciled	1
NRB	1
Death tax less QSR	1
Share valuation (W3)	1½
IHT on mother's estate (W4)	1
QSR	1½
	15
18.2 Gains with no remittance basis claim	½
AEA	½
CGT	½
DTR	2
Gains with remittance basis claim	½
No AEA	½
Painting (W1)	2½
Gain on shares (W2)	½
Cost of shares	1½
Gain on Utopian property (W3)	1
	10
	25

18.1

	January 2010 CLT £	October 2016 CLT £	January 2019 Death (W2) £
Stage 1 - Transfers			
Transfer		285,000	
Less exemptions			
Annual		(3,000)	
Annual b/f		(3,000)	
		279,000	
Stage 2 – Lifetime tax			
Less remaining NRB (W1)		(75,000)	
		204,000	
IHT@ 20%		40,800	
Gross chargeable transfer	250,000	279,000	
Stage 3 – Tax on death			
Gross chargeable transfer	More than 7 years	279,000	2,067,834
Less remaining NRB (W1)		(75,000)	(46,000)
		204,000	2,021,834
IHT @ 40%		81,600	808,734
Taper relief (<3 yrs) 20% chargeable		81,600	
Less lifetime tax paid		(40,800)	
Less QSR (W4)			(198,333)
Tax payable on death		40,800	610,401

WORKINGS

(1) **Remaining nil rate band**

	Januray 2010 CLT £	October 2016 CLT £	January 2019 Death £
Stage 2 – Lifetime			
Lifetime NRB		325,000	
Less chargeable in previous 7 years		(250,000)	
Remaining NRB		75,000	
Stage 3 – On death			
NRB at death	N/A	325,000	325,000
Less chargeable in previous 7 years		(250,000)	(279,000)
Remaining NRB		75,000	46,000

(2) **January 2019 – Death estate**

	£
London home	1,600,000
Sitron plc shares 5,000 × £2.31 (W3)	11,550
Painting	500,000
Bulda Ltd shares	115,000
Cash and chattels	180,000
	2,406,550
Less credit card bills and funeral costs (£2,500 + £7,400)	(9,900)
Less income tax payable for 2018/19	(3,816)
	2,392,834
Less spouse exemption (non-domiciled)	(325,000)
	2,067,834

(3) Valuation of Sitron plc shares

The shares are valued at the lower of:

Quarter up   230 + ¼ × (234 – 230) = 231
Mid bargain ½ × (224+240) = 232 ie, 231

(4) QSR

June 2017 – Mother's Death Estate	£
Death estate	1,200,000
Less nil rate band	(325,000)
	875,000
Tax £875,000 × 40%	350,000

QSR (1-2 years)

80% × £350,000 × £(1,200,000 – 350,000)/£1,200,000	198,333

18.2

Capital gains tax - No RB	UK gains £	Overseas gains £
Painting (W1)	1,000	
Weselton plc shares (W2)	20,433	
Utopian property (W3)		135,000
Total gains	21,433	135,000
Annual exempt amount (against UK gains first)	(11,700)	
Taxable gain	9,733	135,000
CGT liability @ 20%	1,947	27,000
		28,947

Less DTR: lower of
UK tax on overseas gains = £135,000 × 20% = £27,000
Overseas tax on gains = £24,800

	(24,800)
	4,147

Capital gains tax – RB	£
UK gains only as overseas gains not remitted	21,433
No annual exempt amount – remittance basis claim	
CGT liability @ 20%	4,287

WORKINGS

(1) Painting

	£
Proceeds	6,600
Less cost (wife's cost – transferred at NGNL)	(4,000)
Gain	2,600
Restricted to 5/3 × (£6,600 – £6,000)	1,000
ie	1,000

(2) Weselton plc shares

	£
Proceeds	41,600
Less cost	(21,167)
Gain	20,433

	Number	Cost £
June 2013 purchase	9,000	17,000
August 2015 rights issue (1 for 3 at £2.80)	3,000	8,400
	12,000	25,400
Disposal August 2018	(10,000)	(21,167)
	2,000	4,233

Utopian property

	£
Proceeds	425,000
Less cost	(290,000)
Gain	135,000

Examiner's comments

18.1 Generally excellent answers with many scoring close to full marks. The lifetime tax calculation and death tax on the property were well attempted as well as the death estate. Most also recognised that QSR applied to the inheritance however the most common approach was to calculate the relief by reference to the value of the painting rather than the whole estate.

18.2 The CGT gains calculations in this question were generally answered well, with the gain on the Weselton plc shares being particularly well handled. The most challenging gains calculation proved to be the chattels. In addition students generally had no problems calculating the DTR in respect of the capital gains tax.

19 Kate (March 2015)

Marking guide

		Marks
19.1 Villa	1	
House	½	
Farmland – no APR	1	
Farmland – no BPR	1	
Shares – TC plc	2	
Shares – Pebbles Ltd	1	
Allowable debts and expenses	1	
Charity exemption	1	
Own Residence nil rate	½	
Spouse's RNRB	½	
Own NRB	½	
Spouse's NRB	2	
IHT	½	
DTR	2	
Who pays	½	
Due date	1	
		16
19.2 Disposal of land		
Proceeds	½	
Cost	2	
Enhancement	½	
Car	½	
Chattel	2½	
Taxable gain	1	
BRB remaining	1	
CGT	1	
		9
		25

19.1

Death estate	£	£
Villa	90,000	
Less expenses capped at 5%	(4,500)	
		85,500
House		1,000,000
Farmland – no APR, no BPR		400,000
Shares in TC plc – valued at lower of:		
Quarter up = 152 + ¼ (178 – 152) = 158.5		
Average bargains = 171 + 176 / 2 = 173.5		
Valuation = £1.585 × 40,000		63,400
Shares in Pebbles Ltd	125,000	
Less 100% BPR	(125,000)	
		0
Less allowable debts and expenses		
Gaming debt	0	
Funeral	8,500	
		(8,500)
		1,540,400
Less charity exemption (£63,400 × 25%)		(15,850)
Chargeable estate		1,524,550
Less residence nil rate band (max) and unused spouse's RNRB		(250,000)
Own NRB	325,000	
Plus unused spouse's NRB		
£300,000 – £100,000 / £300,000 = 2/3		
2/3 × £325,000	216,667	
		(541,667)
		732,883
IHT @ 40%		293,153
Less DTR: lower of		
Overseas tax sufferered £11,250		
UK tax on the overseas asset		
293,153/1,524,550 × £85,500 = £16,441		(11,250)
IHT due		281,903

Agricultural property relief is not available on the farmland, as Kate had not owned it for seven years, the required time period for a tenanted farm.

Business property relief is also not available as Kate did not farm the land herself.

Personal representatives of the estate are liable to pay the IHT which is due on delivery of the IHT account, with interest running from 30 June 2019.

19.2

	£
Disposal of land	
Proceeds less auctioneer expenses = £53,000 × 90%	47,700
Less cost	
£53,000 / £53,000 + £60,000 × £65,000	(30,487)
Less enhancement	
£53,000 / £53,000 + £60,000 × £12,000	(5,628)
	11,585
Vintage car	
Exempt	–
Chattel	
Proceeds	9,000
Less costs of sale	(400)
Less cost	(4,000)
	4,600

Maximum = 5/3 × (£9,000 – £6,000) = £5,000

	£
Gains = £11,585 + £4,600 + £40,000 (investment property)	56,185
Less AEA	(11,700)
Taxable gains	44,485

Basic rate band remaining = £34,500 – £25,000 = £9,500

£9,500 @ 10%	950
£(44,485 – 9,500) @ 20%	6,997
CGT liability	7,947

Examiner's comments

19.1 Overall, most answers were good. However, very few students treated the gaming debts and property expenses correctly. A surprising number rounded their answers to the share valuation and applied a rate of 159p to the number of shares. A lot of students used a share valuation of 30,000 shares and then still deducted a charitable donation for the balance of 10,000 shares even though they had effectively already deducted the donation by using a valuation based on 30,000 shares. This may imply a lack of basic mathematical ability but it was probably just a result of exam pressure.

19.2 Overall most students produced very good answers achieving most of the marks available. The most common errors were to tax a gain on the vintage car; and to deduct the personal allowance from the taxable income figure given when determining the amount to be taxed at 10%. A few used net not gross proceeds in the 5/3 chattel calculation. Many dealt well with the part disposal although sometimes the £12,000 was deducted in full and occasionally included in the A/A+B fraction.

20 John Robinson (September 2015)

		Marks
20.1	Value of August 2018 lifetime gift less annual exemptions	1
	Fall in value relief	½
	NRB	1
	IHT	½
	Death estate – home and chattels	½
	BPR on shares	1
	Jewellery	½
	Capital gains tax deduction	½
	Charity exemption	½
	NRB	1½
	IHT @ 36%	1
	Value of transfer less annual exemptions (W1)	1
	Residence nil rate band	½
	Unused spouse's RNRB	½
	NRB	1
	Lifetime tax	½
	Gross chargeable transfer	½
	No IHT on death	½
	Gain on painting (W2)	1
	AEA	½
	CGT	½
		15
20.2	AEA including priority of allocation	1
	CGT calculations	1
	Gain on Newnham Cottage (W1)	½
	Less PPR	½
	Less letting relief	1½
	Use of Cottage ½ per period (W2)	2½
	Gain (W3)	½
	Chattel restriction	1
	(W4)	1½
		10
		25

20.1

August 2018: lifetime gift	**£**
Potentially exempt transfer	100,000
Less annual exemptions 2018/19 and 2017/18	(6,000)
	94,000
Less fall in value relief (£100,000 – £95,000)	(5,000)
	89,000
Less nil rate band (£325,000 – £318,750) (W1)	(6,250)
	82,750
Tax on death £82,750 × 40%	33,100

January 2019 – Death estate

	£
London home	980,000
Cash and personal chattels	420,000
Rainy Ltd shares – 100% BPR	–
Jewellery	500,000
	1,900,000
Less: capital gains tax liability (W2)	(16,160)
	1,883,840
Less charity exemption	(500,000)
	1,383,840
Less residence nil rate band (max)	(125,000)
Less spouse's unused RNRB	(125,000)
Less remaining nil rate band (£325,000 – £94,000)	(231,000)
Chargeable estate	902,840
Tax @ 36% (charitable donation clearly in excess of 10%)	325,022

WORKINGS

(1) **CLT 1 December 2011**

	£
Transfer	266,000
Less annual exemptions 2011/12 and 2010/11	(6,000)
	260,000
Less nil rate band (£325,000 – £300,000)	(25,000)
	235,000
Lifetime tax £235,000 × 20/80	58,750
Gross chargeable transfer £260,000 + £58,750	318,750

(2) **Gain on painting**

	£
Sale proceeds (Market value)	100,000
Less cost	(7,500)
	92,500
Less annual exempt amount	(11,700)
	80,800
Capital gains tax £80,800 × 20%	16,160

20.2 **Simon's capital gains tax payable – 2018/19**

	Gains qualifying for ER	Gains on other assets £	Gains on residential property £
Newnham Cottage (W1)			5,384
Antique table (W3)		2,000	
Trinity Traders (W4)	500,000		
	500,000	2,000	5,384
Less annual exempt amount (vs residential gains first then gains not qualifying for ER then ER gains)	(4,316)	(2000)	(5,384)
Taxable gains	495,684	–	–
CGT @ 10%/ 20% / 28%	49,568	–	–

CGT payable = £49,568

WORKINGS

(1) **Sale of Newnham Cottage – PPR**

	£
Proceeds	250,000
Less cost (MV on transfer)	(180,000)
Chargeable gain	70,000
Less PPR £70,000 × 36/78 (W2)	(32,308)
	37,692

Less letting relief
Lower of:
PPR £32,308
Letting gain £37,692

	£
£40,000 ie, £32,308	(32,308)
	5,384

(2) **Use of Newnham Cottage**

	Exempt	Taxable
1.12.11 – 31.5.12 Actual occupation	6	
1.6.12 – 28.2.13 Part of 3 years for any reason	9	
1.3.13 – 31.5.13 Actual occupation	3	
1.6.13 – 30.11.16 No exemption (not even part of 3 year any reason as no actual occupation following absence)		42
1.12.16 – 1.6.18 Last 18 months rule	18	
	36	42

> **Tutorial note**
>
> Remember to clearly show your PPR workings. Use a table as shown here to itemise the time period, reason for your treatment and whether it's actual/deemed occupation or taxable.

(3) **Antique table**

	£
Proceeds	7,200
Less cost	(4,300)
Gain	2,900
Restricted to: 5/3 × (£7,200 – £6,000)	2,000
	Ie, £2,000

(4) **Trinity Traders**

	£
Proceeds	600,000
Less cost	(100,000)
Gain	500,000

This gain qualifies for entrepreneurs' relief as a sole trade business which Simon has had for over one year.

Examiner's comments

20.1 Most students used a logical approach to the IHT question, with the aid of the standard pro forma, and presented their answers well. The marks most commonly not awarded were for the CGT liability. A significant number did not deal correctly with the fall in value, and a large number deducted the £500,000 charity exemption without first adding the jewellery into the death estate.

20.2 This capital gains tax question was reasonably well answered. Students showed good understanding of chattels and principal private residence relief. The only common error on the PPR was treating part of the let period as exempt under the three year deemed occupation rule. [Note that the part of the question regarding Trinity Traders has been amended since this question was originally set due to syllabus changes]

21 John and Elizabeth (December 2015)

Marking guide

		Marks
21.1	AEA	½
	CGT due	½
	Factory (W1)	2
	Shares in Wilkes Ltd – gain before relief (W2)	1
	Gift relief and no entrepreneurs' relief	1
	CBA/CA	2½
	Painting (W4)	3
	Due date	½
		11
21.2	August 2008 lifetime gift	½
	May 2012 lifetime gift	
	Valuation of Turing plc shares (W1)	1½
	Life tax calculation	2½
	GCT	½
	NRB at death	½
	GCT in 7 years pre gift	½
	Death tax	½
	Less taper relief	½
	Less lifetime tax (in right place)	½
	June 2016 lifetime gift	
	Related property valuation (W2)	2½
	Less 2 x AEs	½
	NRB at death	½
	GCT in 7 years pre gift	½
	Death tax	½
	Death estate	
	Total assets	½
	Less debts and funeral expenses	½
	Less correct spouse exemption	½
	NRB at death	½
	GCT in 7 years pre gift	½
	Death tax	½
		Max **14**
		25

21.1

Capital gains tax payable – 2018/19

	£
Factory (W1)	85,000
Wilkes Ltd (W2)	24,960
Painting (W4)	2,435
	112,395
Less annual exempt amount	(11,700)
Taxable gains	100,695
CGT payable × 20%	20,139

The CGT will be due by 31 January 2020.

WORKINGS

(1) **Factory – sale to connected person**

	£
Proceeds (MV)	205,000
Less cost	(100,000)
	105,000
Gift relief (balancing figure)	(20,000)
Gain chargeable (£185,000 – £100,000)	85,000

(2) **Shares in Wilkes Ltd**

	£
Proceeds (£25 × 6,500) (**Note:** based on actual shareholding disposed of)	162,500
Less cost	(6,500)
	156,000
Less gift relief £156,000 × £210,000/£250,000 (W3)	(131,040)
Gain	24,960

(3) **Chargeable assets and chargeable business assets of Wilkes Ltd**

	CA £	CBA £
Storage unit	40,000	–
Office building	150,000	150,000
Plant	60,000	60,000
	250,000	210,000

Tutorial note

In the Tax Compliance exam, you are expected to include gift relief when it is available, even if the recipient will sell the shares shortly after the gift.

(4) Painting

Disposal of a set of chattels – as total proceeds exceed £6,000 marginal relief applies

	£
March 2019 disposal	
Proceeds	4,200
Less cost £3,100 × $\dfrac{4,200}{4,200 + 4,500}$	(1,497)
Gain	2,703
July 2019 disposal	
Proceeds	5,000
Less cost £3,100 - £1,497	(1,603)
Gain	3,397
Total gains £2,703 + £3,397	6,100
Restricted to: 5/3 × (£4,200 + £5,000 – £6,000)	5,333
	ie, £5,333
Apportionment to March 2019	£2,435

$£5,333 \times \dfrac{4,200}{4,200 + 5,000}$

21.2

	August 2008 CLT £	May 2012 CLT (W1) £	June 2016 PET (W2) £	December 2018 Death (W4) £
Stage 1 - Transfers				
Transfer		133,600	47,500	
Less exemptions				
Annual		(3,000)	(3,000)	
Annual b/f		(3,000)	(3,000)	
		127,600	41,500	975,000
Stage 2 - Lifetime tax				
Less remaining NRB (W3)		(71,000)	No LT tax	No LT tax
		56,600		
IHT@ 20%		11,320		
Gross chargeable transfer	254,000	127,600	41,500	975,000
Stage 3 – Tax on death				
Gross chargeable transfer	More than 7 years	127,600	41,500	975,000
Less remaining NRB (W3)		(71,000)	(197,400)	(155,900)
		56,600	-	819,100
IHT @ 40%		22,640	-	327,640
Taper relief (6-7 yrs)				
20% chargeable		4,528		
Less lifetime tax paid		(11,320)	-	-
Tax payable on death		-	-	327,640

WORKINGS

(1) Valuation of Turing plc shares

The shares are valued at the lower of:
- Quarter up   165 + ¼ × (173 - 165) = 167
- Mid bargain ½ × (166+172) = 169 ie, 167

Transfer 80,000 × £1.67   133,600

(2) Valuation of Sturgeon Ltd shares

June 2016 – Lifetime gift

	£ With RP
Pre transfer (75% with spouse) £150 × 900 (45% without RP – gives £60 so use RP as higher)	135,000
Post transfer (65% with spouse) £125 × 700 (35% without RP gives £60 so use RP as higher)	(87,500)
	47,500

(3) Remaining nil rate band

	August 2008 CLT £	May 2012 CLT £	June 2016 PET £	December 2018 Death £
Stage 2 – Lifetime				
Lifetime NRB		325,000		
Less chargeable in previous 7 years		(254,000)		
Remaining NRB		71,000		
				–
Stage 3 – On death				
NRB at death	N/A	325,000	325,000	325,000
Less chargeable in previous 7 years		(254,000)	(127,600)	
(£127,600 + £41,500)				(169,100)
Remaining NRB		71,000	197,400	155,900

(4) December 2018 – Death estate

Total assets	1,400,000
Less debts and funeral expenses	(100,000)
Less spouse exemption (restricted as spouse non-domiciled)	(325,000)
	975,000

Examiner's comments

21.1 This was a differentiating part of the exam. Some students had a good grasp of the issues and scored well and others only had a vague idea of the issues and scattered calculations about – often it was difficult to know … what their final answer was. The chattels part was probably the least well answered – although many demonstrated knowledge of the special rule involved but struggled with the actual calculations.

21.2 The IHT calculation was usually well answered – with a number of students scoring full marks. The IHT fundamentals were generally understood and answers were presented in a marker friendly format. Most students were able to correctly use the quarter up/average price method for valuing shares, but the related property valuation rules were less well understood – often the husband's holding was included in the valuation (not just used to determine the value per share) and often the correct related property value per share was simply applied to the 200 shares gifted.

22 Mary-Jane (Sample Paper 1)

		Marks
22.1 June 2017 – Lifetime gift		
Gross chargeable transfer	½	
NRB	1	
Tax on death	½	
Less lifetime tax	½	
Death estate – assets	1½	
Less debts	1	
NRB	½	
Tax at 40%	½	
Less QSR	½	
Lifetime tax (W1)		
Cash less AEs	1	
NRB	½	
Lifetime tax	½	
Gross chargeable transfer	½	
Transfer of nil rate band (W2)		
Unused nil rate band	1½	
Valuation of Octo plc shares (W3)	1½	
QSR (W4)		
Death estate less NRB	1	
Tax at 40%	½	
QSR	1½	
		15
22.2 Loss against residential property gain	½	
AEA against residential property gain	½	
CGT	1½	
Gain on Aranas Ltd shares	1	
Gift relief and chargeable gain	2	
Gain on Web Towers	1	
Cherry Tree House		
Gain before reliefs	½	
PPR	1½	
Claim – date and joint election	1½	
		10
		25

22.1

June 2017 – Lifetime gift	£
Gross chargeable transfer (W1)	726,250
Less nil rate band (W2) 125% × £325,000	(406,250)
	320,000
Tax on death £320,000 × 40%	128,000
Less lifetime tax	(80,250)
	47,750

April 2019 – Death estate

	£
London home	550,000
Octo plc shares 10,000 × £1.82 (W3)	18,200
Cash and chattels	180,000
	748,200
Less debts	(9,250)
	738,950
Less remaining nil rate band (fully utilised)	–
Chargeable estate	738,950
Tax @ 40%	295,580
Less QSR (W4)	(2,591)
	292,989

WORKINGS

(1) **Lifetime tax on CLT June 2017**

	£
Cash	652,000
Less annual exemptions	(6,000)
	646,000
Less nil rate band	(325,000)
	321,000
Lifetime tax £321,000 × 20/80	80,250
Gross chargeable transfer £646,000 + £80,250	726,250

(2) **Transfer of nil rate band**
Ben's death July 2008
Unused nil rate band = £(312,000 - 234,000)/£312,000 = 25%

(3) **Valuation of Octo plc shares**
The shares are valued at the lower of:
- Quarter up 180 + ¼ × (188 – 180) = 182
- Mid bargain ½ × (187+179) = 183 ie, 182

(4) **QSR**
February 2017 – Jonah death estate

	£
Death estate	470,000
Less nil rate band	(325,000)
	145,000
Tax £145,000 × 40%	58,000
QSR (2-3 years)	
60% × £58,000 × £35,000/£470,000	2,591

Tutorial note

No residence nil rate band is available as Mary-Jane does not leave her home to direct descendants.

22.2 Capital gains tax payable – 2018/19

	ER £	Non-ER gains £	Residential property gain £
Shares in Aranas Ltd (W1)	48,000		
Web Towers (W2)		34,100	
Cherry Tree House (W3)			614,500
Less brought forward capital loss			(15,352)
Less annual exempt amount			(11,700)
Taxable gains	48,000	34,100	587,448
ER gain = £48,000 × 10%			4,800
Non-ER gains = £34,100 × 20%			
gains utilise BRB)			6,820
Residential property gains = £587,448 × 28%			164,485
Total CGT payable			176,105

The gift relief claim must be a joint claim made by both Harry and his sister, Stacy by 5 April 2023.

WORKINGS

(1) **Sale of Aranas Ltd shares – to connected party**	£
Poceeds (market value)	100,000
Less cost	(12,000)
Chargeable gain	88,000
Less gift relief	(40,000)
Chargeable gain (excess of proceeds over original cost)	48,000

(2) **Commercial property**	£
Proceeds (MV)	454,700
Less cost	(420,600)
Capital gain	34,100

(3) **Cherry Tree House**	£
Proceeds	12,450,000
Less cost	(160,000)
Gain	12,290,000
Less PPR 3 out of 4 years overseas exempt (3 years for any reason)	
19/20 × £12,290,000	(11,675,500)
Chargeable gain	614,500

Tutorial note

There is another form of gift relief, available when a gift also gives rise to an immediate inheritance tax charge. This is outside the Tax Compliance syllabus but students who have knowledge of this and apply it correctly would not be penalised.

23 Jeff (Sample Paper 2)

				Marks
23.1 (a)	Painting	½		
	Necklace	1		
	Sparks Ltd shares	1½		
	Harps plc shares	1½		
	AEA	½		
	BRB remaining	1		
	CGT	1		
				7
(b)	Painting	½		
	PET	½		
	CLT – 1 September 2018			
	Value	2½		
	AE	½		
	NRB	1		
	IHT	½		
	Gross chargeable transfer	½		
	CLT – 31 December 2018			
	NRB	1		
	IHT	½		
	W1			
	AE	½		
	NRB	1		
	IHT	½		
	Gross chargeable transfer	½		
	W2 – share value	2		
		12		
		Max		11
23.2	IHT			
	PET	½		
	BPR	1½		
	Tax and taper relief	1		
	CGT			
	Gift at MV	½		
	Gift relief	2½		
	Election	½		
	Entrepreneurs' relief	½		
	CGT on death	½		
		7½		
		Max		7
				25

23.1 (a) CGT liability for 2018/19

	£
Painting	
Exempt disposal	0
Antique necklace	
Proceeds (connected person so use MV)	212,000
Less cost (probate value as inherited)	(145,000)
	67,000
Sparks Ltd shares	**£**
Proceeds (25% holding = £3 per share)	75,000
Less cost	(25,000)
	50,000
Harps plc shares	**£**
Proceeds (MV)	103,700
Less cost (10,000 × £1.91)	(19,100)
	84,600

Shares valued at:
1,031 + ½ (1,043 – 1,031) = 1,037
10,000 × £10.37 = 103,700

	£
Gains = £67,000 + £50,000 + £84,600	201,600
Less AEA	(11,700)
	189,900
Basic rate band remaining = £34,500 – £8,000 = £26,500	
£26,500 @ 10%	2,650
£163,400 @ 20%	32,680
	35,330

(b)

Painting – Exempt as gift to charity

PET – 1 August 2018 – No lifetime tax as a PET

CLT – 1 September 2018	£	£
Value with related property		
Value based on a 75% holding = 25,000 @ £8		200,000
Value without related property		
Value based on a 25% holding = 25,000 @ £3		75,000
Take higher valuation		200,000
Less AE 2018/19 and 2017/18		
(already allocated to PET on 1 August 2018)		Nil
Less NRB at gift	325,000	
Less chargeable transfers in the previous seven years (W1)	(198,000)	
		(127,000)
		73,000
IHT @ 20/80		18,250
Gross chargeable transfer = £200,000 + £18,250		218,250
CLT – 31 December 2018		
Gift (W2)		103,400
Less NRB at gift	325,000	
Less chargeable transfers in the previous seven years	(218,250)	
		(106,750)
		Nil

No IHT due as covered by nil rate band

CLT – October 2011 (W1)	£	£
Gift		194,000
Less AE 2011/12 and 2010/11 b/f		(6,000)
Chargeable transfer		188,000
Less nil rate band at gift	325,000	
Less GCTs since 1 October 2004	(177,000)	
		(148,000)
		40,000
Lifetime tax at 20/80		10,000
Gross chargeable transfer = £188,000 + £10,000		198,000

Share valuation for IHT (W2)
Shares valued at lower of:
¼ up = 1,031 + ¼ (1,043 – 1,031) = 1,034
Average bargains = 1,035 + 1,042 / 2 = 1,038.5
10,000 × £10.34 = £103,400

23.2 IHT

A lifetime gift to Isabelle is a PET for inheritance tax purposes and will become chargeable on Alexandra's death within seven years.

Only if Isabelle still owns the building at the time of her mother's death (or had sold it but replaced it with a similarly qualifying asset), would the PET be eligible for BPR at 50%.

The balance of the gift after deduction of any BPR, annual exemptions and NRB available would be subject to IHT at 40% and further reduced by taper relief of 40%.

CGT

The gift is subject to CGT as a disposal to a connected person, using deemed proceeds of market value less Alexandra's original cost.

Alexandra and Isabelle could make a joint election for gift relief to apply because the building is used by Alexandra's personal company (>5% holding in a trading company). Alexandra's gain would be reduced to nil, and Isabelle's base cost for a future disposal would be the same as Alexandra's original cost.

The election should be made within four years of the end of the tax year of the gift ie, by 5 April 2023.

Entrepreneurs' relief is not available as the disposal does not amount to the disposal of a business or part of a business.

There are no CGT implications for a lifetime transfer arising from Alexandra's death.

Corporation tax

24 Coe Ltd (June 2012)

	Marks
24.1 Adjusted profit (W1)	
Car lease costs	1
Samples	1
Royalties	½
CAs	½
Gain (W2)	
Proceeds less cost	½
IA	½
Capital loss b/f	1
Property income	1
Corporation tax calculation	½
Due date	½
	7
24.2 Adjusted trading profits	
Interest on loan to buy P&M	½
Interest on loan to buy shares	½
R&D	1
Bank interest	½
CAs	½
Non-trading loan relationships	1
Omit intra group dividend	1
Group relief	1
CAs (W1)	
Additions	½
AIA	1
WDA	½
	8
	15

24.1 Taxable total profits: year ended 31 March 2019

	£
Tax adjusted trading profit (W1)	43,304
Property income (£78,000 × 1/12)	6,500
Chargeable gains (W2)	31,931
Taxable total profits	81,735
Corporation tax (£81,735 × 19%)	£15,530

As Ovett Ltds augmented profits are less than £500,000 (£1,500,00/3) corporation tax will be due 9 months and 1 day after the accounting period ie. 1 January 2020.

WORKINGS

		£
(1)	**Adjusted profit**	
	Adjusted trading profit	579,674
	Less:	
	Lease costs for car	(8,100)
	Gift of samples	(120)
	Patent royalties	(20,000)
		551,454
	Less capital allowances (£190,000 + £318,150)	(508,150)
		43,304

		£
(2)	**Gain on building**	
	Proceeds	551,688
	Less cost	(307,000)
		244,688

Less indexation allowance

$$\frac{278.1-165.6}{165.6} = 0.679 \times £307,000 \qquad (208,453)$$

Gain	36,235
Less capital loss b/f	(4,304)
Chargeable gain	31,931

24.2 Taxable total profits: year ended 31 March 2019

	£	£
Adjusted trading profits per the question		400,190
Add:		
Interest on a loan to purchase P&M	–	
Interest on a loan to purchase shares	790	
		790
Less:		
Research and development (£40,000 × 230%)	92,000	
Bank interest receivable	2,845	
		(94,845)
		306,135
Less capital allowances (W1)		(13,060)
Tax adjusted trading profit		293,075
Non-trade loan relationships (2,845 – 790)		2,055
Total profits		295,130
Less group relief (W2)		(295,130)
Taxable total profits		–

Intra-group dividend of £10,000 is not taxable

WORKINGS

(1) **Capital allowances**	Main pool £	Allowances £
TWDV b/f	7,000	
Additions: Lorry	20,000	
Less AIA £200,000 less £190,000 claimed by Ovett Ltd	(10,000)	10,000
	17,000	
WDA @ 18%	(3,060)	3,060
TWDV c/f	13,940	
Total allowances		13,060

    (2) **Group relief**

        Group relief is the lower of:
        Cram Ltd's loss: £430,600
        Coe Ltd's profit: £295,130

25 Clock Ltd (June 2014)

Marking guide

			Marks
25.1(a)	First accounting period	1	
	Second accounting period	½	
	Third accounting period	½	
			2
(b)	Rules for returns	1½	
	Both returns 31 March 2018	1	
	Fixed penalties for 3 months late	½	
	20% tax geared penalty 24 months	1	
	Penalty based on tax unpaid at 18 months	1	
		5	
	Max		3
25.2	NTLR	1½	
	Cuckoo Ltd shares – SSE	1	
	QCD	1	
	Adjustments for R&D, interest (W1) (½ each)	1	
	Deduction for staff costs	1	
	No other adjustments	½	
	Additional deduction (W2)	1	
	FYA	½	
	Cost (W3)	½	
	Indexation allowance	1	
	Capital loss b/f	1	
			10
			15

25.1(a) Clock Ltd's first three accounting periods are as follows:

- 1 February 2016 to 31 March 2016 – date first acquires a source of chargeable income to date commences to trade

- 1 April 2016 – 31 March 2017 – trade commences to end of first period of account

- 1 April 2017 – 31 December 2017 – same as dates of period of account

(b) The corporation tax returns are due on the later of:

- 12 months after the end of the period of account, as the period of account is <18 months long; and

- 3 months from the date the notice to file a return is issued by HMRC.

Clock Ltd should have filed its first and second return on 31 March 2018.

Both returns are more than three months late so each has an initial fixed penalty of £200.

In addition as both returns will be filed more than 24 months after the end of the return period, a penalty is due in each case of 20% of the tax unpaid at 18 months from the end of the return period ie, 20% of the tax liability as no tax has yet been paid.

25.2 Clock Ltd taxable total profits for year ended 31 December 2018

	£	£
Trading profits (W1)		1,021,785
Non-trading loan relationships		
Interest receivable (£4,350 + £17,500)	21,850	
Interest paid on non-trading transaction	(3,500)	
		18,350
Gains		
Cuckoo Ltd shares – exempt as SSE	–	
Building (W3)	62,500	
		62,500
Less qualifying donations paid		(42,000)
TTP		1,060,635

WORKINGS

(1) **Tax adjusted trading profit**

	£
Trading profit	1,475,823
R&D expenditure (W2)	(220,688)
Interest on overdraft	(20,350)
Staff costs	(213,000)
Trading profit	1,021,785

> **Tutorial note**
>
> Staff costs disallowed in period ended 31 December 2017 as not paid within nine months of end of accounting period. Therefore they are allowable costs in the accounting period in which they are finally paid.

(2) **R&D**

	£
Permitted additional deduction = £118,950 × 130%	154,635
Cost of laboratory = FYA @ 100%	66,053
	220,688

(3) **Gain on disposal of building**

	£
Proceeds	238,000
Less: cost	(156,000)
Indexation = $\dfrac{278.1 - 255.7}{255.7} = 0.088 \times £156,000$	(13,728)
	68,272
Less capital loss b/f	(5,772)
Gain	62,500

Examiner's comments

25.1 (a) Overall, most answers were poor. Common errors were to confuse personal tax rules with corporate tax rules and create accounting periods to 5 April and fiscal years. Lots of students ended up with accounting periods with overlapping dates. Most students did not know when a company's first accounting period starts.

(b) There were some good answers, but also a significant number of poor answers. A fair number of students dealt with deadlines but did not mention penalties suggesting that perhaps where there are two parts to one requirement the second part is too easily overlooked.

Some of the answers to part 25.1 were interesting. Students showed confusion by treating filing and payment interchangeably, although most eventually managed to use the open book to gain sufficient marks. Students should take a moment to think about what they are writing, even in the heat of the exam. For example, it is rather difficult to file a tax return by instalments.

25.2 Overall most students made a good attempt at producing an answer. Although only a few students knew what to do with the bonus as most students either omitted it or added it back.

Most students could correctly calculate the NTLR.

26 Powys Ltd (March 2015)

	Marks	
26.1 Correct periods	½	
Adjusted trading profit prorated	½	
Less capital allowances	½	
Gain in correct period	½	
Corporation tax	1½	
Adjustment to profits – ½ per adjustment	2	
Capital allowances (W2)	2½	
Chargeable gain (W3)	2	
		10
26.2 B/f capital loss offset vs gains in y/e 31.3.18	½	
Current period loss relief	½	
Carry back y/e 31.3.18	½	
Carry forward y/e 31.3.20	1	
Capital loss carried forward	½	
Claim time limit for current year and carry back	1	
Claim for carried forward	1	
		5
		15

26.1 Corporation tax computation: 15 months ended 31 March 2019

	Y/e 31 Dec 2018 £	P/e 31 Mar 2019 £
Adjusted trading profit £2,066,250 × 12:3 (W1)	1,653,000	413,250
Less capital allowances (W2)	(63,580)	(8,411)
Trading profits	1,589,420	404,839
Chargeable gain (W3)		15,000
TTP	1,589,420	419,839
Corporation tax payable:		
CT @ 19%	301,990	79,769

WORKINGS

(1) **Adjusted profits**

	£
Trading profit	2,050,000
Plus:	
Depreciation	151,000
Patent royalties	0
Less:	
Profit on disposal of shop	(53,750)
Dividend received	(81,000)
	2,066,250

(2) **Capital allowances**

	Main pool £	Allowances £
Y/e 31 December 2018		
TWDV b/f	231,000	
Addition – low emission car	22,000	
Less 100% FYA	(22,000)	22,000
	231,000	
WDA @ 18%	(41,580)	41,580
	189,420	63,580
P/e 31 March 2019		
Disposals	(2,500)	
	186,920	
WDA @ 18% × 3/12	(8,411)	8,411
TWDV c/f	178,509	

(3) **Chargeable gain**

	£
Proceeds	125,000
Less cost:	(78,750)
Unindexed gain	46,250
Less IA = 278.1 – 209.8 / 209.8 = 0.326 × £78,750	(25,672)
Indexed gain	20,578
Less rollover relief	(5,578)
Taxable gain	15,000

Proceeds not reinvested (£125,000 – £110,000)

26.2

	Y/e 31.3.18 £	Y/e 31.3.19 £	Y/e 31.3.20 £
Tax adjusted trading profits	45,000	–	2,094,000
Rental income	33,000	–	–
Non-trading loan relationships	–	12,000	6,000
Net gains	195,000	–	–
Taxable total profits	273,000	12,000	2,100,000
Less loss relief	(273,000) [2]	(12,000) [1]	
Less loss relief carried forward			(377,500)
Taxable total profits	–	–	1,722,500

The capital loss incurred in y/e 31.3.20 can only be offset against capital gains and must therefore be left carried forward to be offset against Red Ltd's first available capital gains.

A claim for loss relief must be made within two years of the end of the accounting period in which the loss is made ie, 31 March 2021.

While the unused trade loss is carried forward automatically, when it comes to be used a claim must be made to offset the loss within two years of the accounting period in which the loss is relieved ie 31 March 2022.

Examiner's comments

26.1 Answers were surprisingly well attempted. Only a few students split the period 3 months: 12 months or did a 15 month accounting period. The main errors were to make an adjustment for the patent royalties and to incorrectly calculate the gain on the lease. The lease seemed to cause a lot of problems which is to be expected given it was the most complex part of the question. Although, many students knew enough to use the lease percentages multiplied by the original cost to score one mark. Many students applied indexation to a figure other than the cost they computed and many did not round to three decimal places.

26.2 [This part of the question has been amended since it was originally set due to changes in tax legislation. The examiner comments are no longer relevant.]

27 Homerton Ltd (September 2015)

Marking guide

	Marks
27.1 Adjustment to profits	
Solicitors fees	½
Deduction for profit on disposal of Smith's Plaza	½
No adjustment for interest paid re CT	½
Interest payable re Hughes Tower	1
Deduct CAs	½
CAs (W2)	
Additions	1
Disposal	½
AIA	½
WDAs	1
	6
27.2 Tax-adjusted profit	½
Gain	½
Overseas property income	½
UK property income	½
QCD	½
CT	½
Less DTR	½
Gain (W1)	2½
NTLR (W2)	2
DTR (W3)	1
	9
	15

27.1 Final-tax-adjusted trading profit

	£
Draft tax-adjusted trading profits	339,575
Add	
Solicitors fees – capital	2,000
Less	
Profit on disposal of Smith's Plaza	(24,000)
Interest on late paid corporation tax – not an allowable trading expense	–
Interest payable on Hughes Towers loan 2/3 × £3,750	(2,500)
Capital allowances (W1)	(44,758)
Final tax-adjusted trading profit	270,317

WORKING

(1) **Capital allowances**

	Main pool £	Special rate pool £	Allowances £
TWDV b/f	16,500	25,100	
Additions			
Machinery (£45,000 × 5/6)	37,500		
Car (emissions > 110g/km)		33,000	
AIA	(37,500)		37,500
Disposal	(2,000)		
	14,500	58,100	
WDA @ 18%/8%	(2,610)	(4,648)	7,258
TWDV c/f	11,890	53,452	
Capital allowances			44,758

27.2

	Total £	UK £	Overlandia income £
Final tax-adjusted trading profit (27.1)	270,317	270,317	
Gains (W1)	170,620	170,620	
Overseas property income			
£31,200 × 100/78	40,000		40,000
Non-trading loan relationship (W2)	6,775	6,775	
UK property income (£12,750 + £4,250)	17,000	17,000	
	504,712	464,712	40,000
Qualifying charitable donation	(30,000)	(30,000)	
TTP	474,712	434,712	40,000

Corporation tax payable

FY2018

£474,712 × 19%	90,195
Less DTR (W3)	(7,600)
Corporation tax payable	82,595

WORKINGS

(1) Gain on sale of Smiths Plaza

	£
Proceeds	800,000
Less selling costs	(2,000)
Less cost	(380,000)
Less IA on cost (278.1 – 168.4)/168.4 = 0.651 × £380,000	(247,380)
Gain	170,620
Less rollover relief	(0)
Taxable gain (Proceeds not reinvested) £800,000 – (2/3 × £900,000) = £200,000	170,620

(2) Non-trading loan relationship

	£
Bank deposit interest receivable	10,500
Less: Interest on overdue corporation tax (27.1)	(2,475)
Interest on Hughes Tower loan £3,750 × 1/3 (27.1)	(1,250)
	6,775

(3) Double tax relief

	£
Double tax relief	
DTR = lower of:	
UK tax on overseas income 19% × £40,000	7,600
Overseas tax 22% × £40,000	8,800
	7,600

Examiner's comments

27.1 The adjustment of profits was usually reasonable but not as good as in previous sittings. In the capital allowances many students restricted the car WDA for private use even though this question relates to a company, or dealt with VAT incorrectly.

27.2 This part was generally answered well, as students expect to see a standard calculation – although more errors than in previous sittings on issues such as non-trading loan relationships and property income. The main errors involved some aspect of the overseas income for example, whether overseas dividends should be in the computation of taxable total profits. In addition a number of students struggled to calculate the UK tax on the overseas income.

28 Mallory Ltd (December 2015)

	Marks
28.1 QCD	1
CT	½
Adjustment to profits	
QCD	½
Interest on shares loan	½
No other deductions	½
R&D expenditure	½
Profit on disposal of shares	½
Bank interest receivable	½
Deduct CAs	½
R&D expenditure (W2)	2½
CAs (W3)	2
Gains (W4)	1½
NTLR (W5)	1
	12
28.2 Limit exceeded and in previous year	1
First instalment	1
Second instalment	1
Balancing payment	1
	4
Max	3
	15

28.1 Corporation tax liability

	£
Adjusted trading profit (W1)	720,598
Chargeable gain (W4)	15,716
Non-trading loan relationship (W5)	41,030
Qualifying charitable donation	(18,000)
TTP	759,344
FY2018	
Corporation tax payable £759,344 × 19%	144,275

WORKINGS

(1) Adjusted profit

	£
Draft tax-adjusted trading profits	950,700
Add	
Qualifying charitable donation	18,000
Interest on shares loan	462
Less	
R&D expenditure (W2)	(58,344)
Profit on disposal of shares	(44,200)
Bank interest receivable	(41,492)
Capital allowances (W3)	(104,528)
	720,598

(2) R&D expenditure

	£
Staff costs (£43,600 – £4,350)	39,250
Consumables	5,630
Computer hardware	–
	44,880
Qualifying revenue expenditure × 130%	58,344

> **Tutorial note**
>
> Technically the computer hardware would be added back in the adjustment to profit and then a 100% FYA would be claimed but this has a net £nil impact on the trade profit figure overall.

(3) Capital allowances

	£
Main pool (£100,648 × 18% = £18,117) × 8/12	12,078
New machinery (AIA) £110,940 × 100/120	
(max AIA = £200,000 × 8/12 = £133,333)	92,450
	104,528

(4) Chargeable gains

Lovell Ltd

	£
Sale proceeds	32,000
Less cost	(10,300)
	21,700
Indexation allowance	
(278.1–175.9)/175.9 × £10,300	(5,984)
	15,716

Crompton Ltd

The gain is exempt as this is a disposal of a substantial shareholding (10% ownership for at least 12 months of the last 6 years / trading company).

(5) Non-trading loan relationships

	£
Bank interest receivable	41,492
Less interest on Crompton Ltd share loan	(462)
	41,030

28.2 QIP for short AP

TTP = augmented profits = £759,344

This exceeds the limit of £1,500,000/2 × 8/12 = £500,000, reduced for the short accounting period and because Mallory Ltd had one related 51% group company at the end of the previous accounting period.

Mallory Ltd was also large in the previous accounting period, and so quarterly instalments are due.

First instalment (month 7) – 14 February 2019

3/8 × liability (£144,275) = £54,103

Second instalment (+ 3 months) – 14 May 2019

3/8 × liability = £54,103

Final instalment (month 4 after AP end) – 14 July 2019

Balance = £36,069

Total = £144,275

28.1 Most students demonstrated a good knowledge of the adjustments required in a corporation tax computation, generally dealing well with the main adjustments to the trading profits, the NTLR figure and the qualifying charitable donation. Many also correctly dealt with the more unusual research and development adjustment with many getting the correct answer, or with only one minor error. The errors usually related to the staff costs not directly involved in the R&D project – most however knew that this was not qualifying expenditure but could not think logically through the adjustment required.

28.2 Most students struggled to work out the payments dates for a company with a short accounting period. Some gave dates for a 12 month accounting period – but often these were also wrong stating that they started on 14 Oct 2019 rather than 2018. Some students stated the rules but made no attempt to apply them – the question asked for actual dates and so just stating the rules was not acceptable.

29 Oscoop Ltd (Sample Paper 1)

Marking guide

	Marks
Overseas property income	½
QCD	1
CT	½
DTR deduction	1
Adjusted profit (W1)	
Accounting profits	½
Additions (including ½ for no other adjustment) ½ per item	2
Less property income	1
Less profit on sale of asset	1
Less interest	½
Less dividend	½
Less capital allowances	½
NTLR	1½
Chargeable gains (W3)	
Goblino	
Cost	½
Indexation allowance	½
Electrobe SSE	1
Capital loss b/f offset	1
DTR	1½
	15
	15

	£
Adjusted trading profit (W1)	2,334,144
Overseas property income = £232,875 × 100/75	310,500
Non-trading loan relationship (W2)	81,600
Chargeable gain (W3)	80,766
	2,807,010
Qualifying charitable donation (offset fully against UK income)	(270,000)
TTP	2,537,010

Corporation tax payable for FY2018	
£2,537,010 × 19%	482,032
Less DTR (W4)	(58,995)
Corporation tax payable	423,037

WORKINGS

(1)	**Adjusted profit**	£
	Draft accounting profits	2,586,346
	Depreciation	75,400
	Interest payable – Electrobe share loan	13,700
	Qualifying charitable donation	270,000
	Property income	(232,875)
	Profit on sale of assets (£204,500 – £68,700)	(135,800)
	Bank interest receivable	(95,300)
	Dividend received	(6,327)
		2,475,144
	Capital allowances	(141,000)
	Adjusted trading profit	2,334,144

(2)	**Non-trading loan relationship**	£
	Bank interest receivable	95,300
	Less interest on Electrobe Ltd share loan	(13,700)
		81,600

(3)	**Chargeable gains**	
	Goblino plc	£
	Sale proceeds	254,000
	Less cost	(55,200)
	Indexation allowance	
	(278.1 – 95.21)/95.21 × £55,200	(106,034)
		92,766
	Less capital loss /f	(12,000)
	Net gains	80,766

Electrobe Ltd

The capital loss is not allowable as this is a disposal of a substantial shareholding (10% ownership for at least 12 months of the last 6 years / trading company).

(4)	**Double tax relief**	
	DTR = lower of:	
	UK tax on overseas income	19%
	Overseas tax	25%
	UK tax clearly lower = 19% × £310,500	£58,995

30 C Ltd (Sample Paper 2)

		Marks
30.1	Capital allowance deduction	½
	Capital loss b/f	½
	RDEC above the line	1
	CT	½
	RDEC below the line	½
	Capital allowances (W1)	
	FYA	½
	Disposals	½
	Allowances	1½
	Gain on printing press (W2)	
	Gain calculation made	½
	Cost	½
	Indexation allowance	1
	Gain on shares (W3)	
	Proceeds	½
	Indexation	1
	Share pool	1
		10
30.2	First instalment date	½
	Amount paid on first instalment date	1½
	Second instalment date	½
	Amount paid on second instalment date	1½
	Final instalment date	½
	Amount paid on final instalment date	½
		5
		15

30.1 C Ltd corporation tax liability for year ended 31 March 2019

	£	£
Tax-adjusted trading profits	846,059	
Less capital allowances (W1)	(172,678)	
Trading profits		673,381
Gains		
Printing press (W2)	35,500	
Shares (W3)	174,760	
Loss b/fwd	(25,000)	
		185,260
RDEC (12% x £250,000)		30,000
TTP		888,641
Corporation tax payable:		
CT @ 19%		168,842
Less RDEC		(30,000)
Corporation tax liability		138,842

Capital allowances (W1) Y/e 31 March 2019	Main pool £	SRP £	SLA £	Allowances £
TWDV b/f	423,000	245,600	111,250	
Additions – car	18,800			
FYA	(18,800)			18,800
Disposals – printing press	(12,000)			
Disposals – SLA			(51,000)	
	411,000	245,600	60,250	
Balancing allowance			(60,250)	60,250
WDA @ 18%	(73,980)			73,980
WDA @ 8%		(19,648)		19,648
	337,020	225,952	-	
				172,678

Gain on disposal of printing press (W2)

	£
Proceeds	55,000
Less cost	(12,000)
Less indexation = 278.1 – 171.1 / 171.1 = 0.625 × £12,000	(7,500)
	35,500

Gain on disposal of shares (W3)

	£
Proceeds = 6,000 @ £45	270,000
Less cost	(50,000)
Less indexation = 278.1 – 146.0 / 146.0 × £50,000 (not rounded)	(45,240)
	174,760

C Ltd owned the following shares:	Number	£
January 1995 purchased	10,000	100,000
January 2006 1 for 5 bonus issue	2,000	-
	12,000	100,000
Disposal of 50% of holding	(6,000)	(50,000)

30.2 First instalment

The first instalment was due on the 14th of month 7 – ie, **14 January 2019**

The instalment paid for a short AP = 3 × CT/n = 3 × £910,000/7 = £390,000

Second instalment

The second instalment was due on the 14th of month 10 – ie, **14 April 2019**

The instalment paid for a short AP = 3 × CT/n = 3 × £1,050,000/7 = £450,000

Plus the underpayment of £60,000 relating to instalment 1

Total paid = £510,000

Balancing payment

The final payment cannot be made later than the fourth month following the end of the accounting period – ie, by **14 May 2019**. Therefore a single balancing payment would have been made:

£1,610,000 – £390,000 – £510,000 = £710,000

Income tax and NIC

31 Kim, Lien and Mai

Marking guide

		Marks
31.1 (a) Adjusted profit		
Stock write down	1	
Stock taken for own use	1	
Extension capital expenditure	1	
Replacement double glazing	½	
Legal fees relating to capital expenditure	½	
Lease rental on car	½	
Fines and penalties	½	
Customer entertaining	½	
Gifts	½	
No other adjustments	1	
Capital allowances (W1)		
Additions	2	
AIA	1	
Disposal	½	
FYA 100%	½	
WDA main pool	½	
WDA special rate pool	½	
		12
(b) Salary	½	
Interest on capital	1	
Profit sharing ratio	1	
Total	½	
		3
(c) 2018/19	½	
2019/20	1½	
Overlap profits (W)	2	
NIC	2	
		6
31.2 Fuel benefit	1	
IT on fuel benefit	1	
Number of miles	1	
		3
31.3 Carry forward	1	
Offset against general income	1	
Restriction applied to 2019/20	2	
Restriction applied to 2018/19	1	
		5

31.4 Employment income

Salary	1
Accommodation – exempt	½
Chase's flights – exempt	½
Wife's flights – 2 exempt	1
Employer pension contributions – exempt	½

IT liability

Bank interest and dividends	1
Overseas property income excluded	1
No PA as remittance basis claimed	½
Tax liability	2
Remittance basis charge	1
	9

31.5 Gross up

Gross up	1
NIC	½
Date	½
	2
	40

31.1 (a) Adjusted profits

	£
Trading profit	1,166,911
Clothing stock write down (£125,000 – £108,750)	(16,250)
Stock taken for own use – include as a sale	1,035
Extension capital expenditure	80,600
Replacement double glazing (capital)	12,000
Legal fees relating to capital expenditure	4,150
Lease rental on car disallowed (15% × £2,600)	390
Fines and penalties	750
Non-staff entertaining	200
Gifts of chocolate	400
	1,250,186
Less capital allowances (W1)	(301,004)
	949,182

WORKINGS

(1) Capital allowances

Y/e 30.06.18

	FYA £	Main pool £	Special rate pool £	Allowances £
TWDV b/f		337,115	74,108	
Plant and machinery		34,130		
Machinery		164,000		
Electrical system			118,370	
AIA (max £200,000) (W2)		(81,630)	(118,370)	200,000
Disposal		(1,400)		
Cars	11,400		28,450	
FYA @ 100%	(11,400)			11,400
		452,215	102,558	
WDA @ 18%		(81,399)		81,399
WDA @ 8%			(8,205)	8,205
				301,004
TWDV c/f		370,816	94,353	

(2) **Annual investment allowance**

Allocate to SRP in priority to main pool

(b)

	Kim £	Lien £	Mai £	Total £
Salary	64,000			64,000
Interest on capital @ 6.5%	32,500	48,750	65,000	146,250
PSR 2:4:4	147,786	295,573	295,573	738,932
	244,286	344,323	360,573	949,182
				(from (a))

(c)

Kim's trading income assessments		£
2018/19	CYB (from (b))	244,286
2019/20	Closing year rules	
	Y/E 30.6.19	247,465
	P/E 31.8.19	42,532
	Less overlap from commencement (W)	(18,720)
		271,277

WORKING		£
2002/03	Commencement to next 5 April ie, 1.1.03 – 5.4.03 = 3/18 × £37,440	6,240
2003/04	No AP end so use actual basis ie, 6.4.03 – 5.4.04 = 12/18 × £37,440	24,960
2004/05	12 months to accounting date ie, 1.7.03 – 30.6.04 = 12/18 × £37,440	24,960
		56,160
	Overlap from commencement = £56,160 – £37,440	18,720

NIC

Class 2	= £2.95 × 52	153.40
Class 4	= (244,286 – 46,350) × 2% + (46,350 – 8,424) × 9%	7,372.06

31.2 Berly

Fuel benefit taxed on Berly as employee:

£23,400 × (31% + 4%)	£8,190
Income tax on Berly @ 45%	£3,686
Minimum miles = 3,686/0.12 (rounded up)	30,717

31.3 Paula can relieve the loss as follows:

- Carry forward the trading loss and offset it against future trading profits arising from the same trade

- Offset the loss against her general income for 2019/20 and/or 2018/19

In the case of loss relief against general income, the loss that can be set against income other than the trading income, is restricted to the higher of £50,000 and 25% of Paula's adjusted total income. Therefore if a claim is made against general income in 2019/20, a loss of £50,000 (higher than 25% of £80,000) can be set against Paula's rental income of £80,000. If a claim is made in respect of 2018/19, the loss against other income would be similarly restricted. However, in 2018/19 Paula has trading income of £72,000, and there is no restriction on the loss that can be set against this. Hence the total loss of £60,000 can be relieved in 2018/19.

31.4 2018/19 income tax liability

	£
Income tax (W1)	26,678
Remittance basis charge (resident for at least 12 out of previous 14 tax years)	60,000
Total income tax liability	86,678

WORKINGS

(1) Income tax

	Non savings £	Savings £	Dividend £	Total £
Employment income (W2)	79,695			79,695
Bank interest		4,250		4,250
UK dividends			1,200	1,200
Total income	79,695	4,250	1,200	85,145
Less personal allowance: Lost as claiming Remittance basis	(Nil)			(Nil)
Taxable income	79,695	4,250	1,200	85,145

			Total
Non savings income	£34,500	@ 20%	6,900
	£45,195	@ 40%	18,078
Savings income	£500	@ 0%	0
	£3,750	@ 40%	1,500
Dividend income	£1,200	@ 0%	0
Income tax			26,478

(2) Employment income

	£	£
Salary:		
UK: 9 × £6,250	56,250	
Overseas: 3 × £7,750	23,250	
Total salary		79,500
Accommodation – exempt		–
Chase's flights – both exempt		–
Wife's flights – 2 exempt		195
Employer pension contributions – exempt		–
Total employment income		79,695

> **Tutorial note**
>
> Chase's duties are performed partly in the UK and partly overseas for a UK employer. As a UK resident but non-UK domiciled individual he is taxed on his earnings for both UK and overseas duties on the arising basis.

31.5 Summer party – employer class 1B NIC

	£	£
Party cost	300	
Gross up for additional rate taxpayer @ 45%	245	
	545	
NIC due @ 13.8%		75
Due to be paid by 22 October 2019		

32 Charles (June 2014)

		Marks
32.1 Adjustments to profits		
Depreciation	½	
Office premises	½	
Client entertaining	½	
Lease costs	½	
Drawings	½	
Millie's excess salary	1	
Speeding fine	½	
Stock drawings	½	
Less capital allowances	½	
No other adjustments	1	
Capital allowances (W1)		
AIA	½	
Car	½	
Disposal	½	
Balancing charge	½	
WDA on main pool and SRP	1	
WDA private use	1	
		10
32.2 Salary	½	
Interest	½	
PSR	1	
Reallocation of notional loss	2	
		4
32.3 Salary	½	
Car and fuel benefit, pro-rate	2½	
SMRS	1	
Use of photography equipment	1	
Gift of photography equipment – comparison	½	
MV at gift	½	
MV when provided less benefits	1½	
Beneficial loan	1	
Medical insurance	½	
Medical check up	½	
Employer pension	½	
		10
32.4 Income tax computation		
Trading income	½	
Employment income	½	
Property income	½	
Dividend	½	
Personal allowance	½	
Tax	3	
Tax deducted at source	½	
Due date for property allowance election	½	
Partnership income (W1)	1	
Property income (W2)	2½	
Extend BRB (W3)	1	
		11

32.5 Class 2 ... ½
    Class 4 on trading and partnership income ... ½
    Class 4 @ 9% ... 1
    Class 4 @ 2% ... 1
    Class 1 including SMRS no benefits ... 1
    Class 1 calculation ... 1

    5

    40

32.1 Ducal Traders adjusted trading profits for year ended 31 December 2018

	£
Net profit	155,457
Add:	
Depreciation	15,100
Private use of office premises = £54,500 × 20%	10,900
Client entertaining (£10,180 + £4,000)	14,180
Lease costs (15% × £1,600)	240
Drawings	45,000
Millie's excess salary (£12,000 - £8,000)	4,000
Stock drawings (profit)	600
Less:	
Capital allowances (W1)	(38,801)
Adjusted trading profit	206,676

WORKING

(1) **Capital allowances**

	Main pool £	SRP £	SLA £	Private use £	Allowances £
TWDV b/f	52,400	14,500	3,300	5,100	
Additions	26,700				
Less AIA	(26,700)				26,700
Additions not eligible for AIA	14,000				
Less disposals			(5,000)		
	66,400	14,500	(1,700)	5,100	
Balancing charge			1,700		(1,700)
WDA @ 18% / 8%	(11,952)	(1,160)			13,112
WDA @ 18%				(918) × 75%	689
	54,448	13,340	Nil	4,182	38,801

32.2

	William £	Harry £	Charles £	Total £
Year ended 31.05.19				
Salary		44,000		44,000
Interest on capital @ 7%	7,000	14,000	35,000	56,000
PSR 3:3:4	(13,500)	(13,500)	(18,000)	(45,000)
	(6,500)	44,500	17,000	55,000
Reallocate notional loss				
6,500 × 44,500 : 17,000	6,500	(4,703)	(1,797)	
Total profits for the year	Nil	39,797	15,203	55,000

32.3 Charles employment income for 2018/19

		£	£
Salary (gross amount before IT deducted)			12,000
Company car (capped at 37%)	£31,000 × 37%	11,470	
Fuel	£23,400 × 37%	8,658	
		20,128	
Prorated as unavailable for 2 months	× 10/12		16,773
SMRS (£0.50 – £0.45) × 5,000 miles			250
Photography equipment			
Usage = £10,000 × 6/12 × 20%			1,000
Gift = higher of:			
MV at gift		6,000	
MV when first provided less benefits to date			
= £10,000 – (£10,000 × 20% × 18/12)		7,000	7,000
Beneficial loan			
£20,000 × (2.5% – 1%) × 10/12			250
Medical insurance (cost to Cheval Ltd)			450
Medical check up – exempt benefit			-
Employer pension			-
			37,723

32.4 Charles income tax payable for 2018/19

			NSI £	Dividend £
Trading income (part 32.1) – CYB			206,676	
Partnership income (W1)			12,669	
Employment income (part 32.3)			37,723	
Property income (W2)			200	
Dividend				85,000
Net income			257,268	85,000
Less personal allowance			Nil	
Taxable income			257,268	85,000
Non-savings income	£34,500	× 20%		6,900
Extended BRB (W3)	£62,500	× 20%		12,500
	£53,000	× 40%		21,200
	£107,268	× 45%		48,271
	£257,268			
Dividend income	£2,000	× 0%		0
	£83,000	× 38.1%		31,623
Income tax liability				120,494
Less tax deducted at source				
IT via PAYE				(4,500)
Income tax payable				115,994

WORKINGS

(1) **Partnership income**

	£
Opening years, 1st tax year, tax commencement to next 5 April	
1 June 2018 – 5 April 2019	
= £15,203 × 10/12	12,669

(2) **Property income**

	£
Rental income received £100 × 12	1,200
Less expenses paid	(100)
Property income	1,100
By election, Charles can instead deduct the property allowance	
Rental income received	1,200
Less property allowance	(1,000)
Property income	200

Charles should elect to deduct the property allowance. The election needs to be made by 31 January 2021.

(3) **Extended basic rate band**

	£
Extended by:	
Gift aid	
£30,000 × 100/80	37,500
Personal pension contribution	
£20,000 × 100/80	25,000
	62,500

32.5 Class 2 NIC

	£
52 weeks at £2.95	153
Class 4	
Payable on Ducal Traders and Princely Partners income	
= £12,669 + £206,676 = £219,345	
(£46,350 – £8,424) × 9%	3,413
(£219,345 – £46,350) × 2%	3,460
Class 1 primary	
No NIC on benefits	
NIC on SMRS	
(£12,000 + £250 – £8,424) × 12%	459
	7,485

Examiner's comments

32.1 The adjustment to profits calculation was performed well by most students.

32.2 Answers were generally very good with most students able to deal with the partnership profit allocation including at least an attempt at the reallocation of a notional loss.

32.3 Answers were generally very good. The calculation of employment income, one of the easier parts of the exam, was generally well attempted but too many students could not handle the use, and then gift, of the photographic equipment. Such benefits feature regularly in this exam (and the previous Professional Stage exam), so should not have caused such difficulties.

32.4 Most students did very well. The calculation was well done, although there were many minor errors and omissions in the inclusion of income figures from previous parts of the question. In particular, the need to pro rate the partnership income but not the sole trade figure was a source of confusion.

32.5 There were some decent attempts made at the national insurance calculations, but partnership income was frequently omitted, and some students confused matters by pro-rating amounts or limits.

33 Jasper (March 2015)

			Marks
33.1 (a)	Local charity donation	½	
	Machine	1	
	Leased car	1	
	FRM	1	
	Stock	1	
	Bad debts	½	
	Interest	1	
	Car running costs	1	
			7
(b)	Trading income	½	
	Property income	½	
	Interest and dividends	½	
	BRB extension	1	
	IT on NSI	1	
	IT on SI	1½	
	IT on dividend income	1	
	Rent a room	2	
	Adjusted net income	1	
	Restricted PA	1½	
		10½	
	Max		10
33.2 (a)	Class 1 primary	2	
	Class 1 secondary	1	
	Car and fuel benefit	1	
	Chocolates and loan – exempt	1	
	Annual value	1	
	Additional charge	2	
	Furniture	1	
	Class 1A	1	
			10
(b)	Class 1A payment date	1	
			1
33.3	Lifetime allowance	1	
	Tax free lump sum – 25%	1	
	Balance taxable when received as pension	1	
	Excess	1	
			4
33.4	Cost of employing assistant		
–	Salary	½	
–	Employer NI	1	
–	Lease costs	½	
–	Class 1A NI	1	
–	IT and NI saving	1	
	Cost of employing husband		
–	Salary	½	
–	Mileage allowance	1	
–	Employer NI	2	
–	IT and NI saving	1	
		8½	
	Max		8
			40

33.1 (a) Jasper's draft adjusted trading profits for year ending 31 March 2019

	£
Draft profit	51,000
Less:	
Allowable as a small donation to a local charity	(55)
Machine (no CAs as cash basis)	(5,000)
Leased car (no restriction as cash basis)	(3,000)
New car – FRM scheme instead of CAs = £0.45 × 7,000	(3,150)
Add back:	
Stock for own use – use a just and reasonable amount ie, cost	400
Bad debts	600
Excess interest (£800 - £500)	300
Car running costs = £200 + £1,050	1,250
Adjusted trading profit	42,345

(b) Jasper income tax payable for 2018/19

	NSI £	Savings £	Dividend £
Trading income (part (a)) – CYB	42,345		
Property income (W1)	300		
Interest		28,000	
Dividend			50,000
Net income	42,645	28,000	50,000
Less personal allowance (W2)	(5,278)		
Taxable income	37,367	28,000	50,000

			£
Non-savings income	£34,500	× 20%	6,900
Extended BRB = £6,000 × 100/80 =			
£7,500	£2,867	× 20%	573
Savings income	£500	× 0%	0
(£7,500 - £500 - £2,867)	£4,133	× 20%	827
(£28,000 - £4,133 - £500	£23,367	× 40%	9,347
Dividend income	£2,000	× 0%	0
	£48,000	× 32.5%	15,600
Income tax payable			33,247

WORKINGS

(1) Rent-a-room

	£
Property income rules	
Rental income = £150 × 52	7,800
Less actual expenses	(2,500)
	5,300
Rent-a-room election	
£7,800 – £7,500	300

(2) Personal allowance

	£
Net income (£42,645 + £28,000 + £50,000)	120,645
Less gross personal pension contributions (£6,000 × 100/80)	(7,500)
Adjusted net income	113,145
Less threshold	(100,000)
	13,145
£13,145 × 50% = £6,572	
PA = £11,850 – £6,572	5,278

33.2 (a) National insurance contributions

			£
Dylan			
Class 1 primary			
(£46,350 – £8,424) × 12%			4,551
(£70,000 – £46,350) × 2%			473
			5,024
Pomme Ltd			
Class 1 secondary			
(£70,000 – £8,424) × 13.8%			8,497

Class 1A

		£	£
Company car	£45,000 × 32%		14,400
Fuel	£23,400 × 32%		7,488
Chocolates – exempt as <£50			–
Loan – exempt as <£10,000			–
Accommodation			
Annual value		25,700	
Expensive property charge			
(£345,000 – £75,000) × 2.5%		6,750	
Furniture = 20% × £20,000		4,000	
			36,450
			58,338
Employer NIC @ 13.8%			8,051

(b) Class 1A contributions are paid in one amount by 19 July (22 July if by electronic payment) following the end of the tax year (2018/19). In this case the payment was therefore due by 19 or 22 July 2019.

33.3 Pensions

As Meg's pension scheme exceeds the lifetime allowance of £1,030,000 we will need to consider the tax on the amount up to the lifetime allowance separately to the amount in excess of the allowance.

On up to £1,030,000 of her pension Meg can choose to take up to 25% as a tax free lump sum. Thus £257,500 of the £1,030,000 can be taken as a lump sum with no tax consequences.

The remaining £772,500 (£1,030,000 - £257,500) can then be drawn down by Meg as she wishes. This may include drawing the whole amount as a lump sum, buying an annuity, buying a flexible income drawdown product or leaving the funds in the pension scheme and withdrawing cash as required. Whichever approach is taken, Meg will be taxed on any pension income as it is received and it will be taxed as non-savings income at her marginal rate of tax.

As she draws down therest of her fund in excess of the lifetime allowance there will be additional tax consequences depending on how she draws her benefits.

33.4 Cost of employing assistant

	£
Salary	12,900
Employer's Class 1 national insurance:	
£(12,900 – 8,424) × 13.8% = £618 less employment allowance	-
Leasing cost of van	7,200
Class 1A national insurance on van benefit:	
£3,350 × 13.8%	462
	20,562
Less income tax and Class 4 NI saving £20,562 × 47% (45% + 2%)	(9,664)
Cost to the business of employing assistant	10,898

Cost of employing her husband

	£
Salary	15,000
Mileage allowance (5,000 miles × 50p)	2,500
Employer's Class 1 NIC (W1) £942 covered by employment allowance	-
	17,500
Less income tax and Class 4 NI saving £17,500 × 47%	(8,225)
Cost to the business of employing husband	9,275

WORKING

Class 1 earnings

	£
Salary	15,000
Mileage allowance – 5,000 × (50p – 45p)	250
	15,250
Less secondary threshold	(8,424)
	6,826
Class 1 contributions @ 13.8%	942

Examiner's comments

33.1 (a) The answers were unexpectedly poor. Most students revealed that they were not well prepared for a question on the cash basis, although this particular requirement tested the basic principles in a simple form. Those students who had learnt the rules gained full or nearly full marks. However, most students produced answers that were simply awful. There were many who added rather than deducted and vice versa when doing the adjustments. Most did a leased car restriction; calculated capital allowances on the car as well as the fixed rate mileage figure; applied private use percentage to the tyres; added back £500 for the stock taken for own use etc.

(b) Some aspects were attempted well, others less so. When dealing with the rental income, there were many who either deducted rent a room [and expenses] or compared £5,300 to £7,500 or just ignored rent a room altogether. The personal allowance was well attempted and the tax liability calculations were good with most extending the basic rate band by the gross pension. The main error in the personal allowance calculations was to forget to adjust the net income for the pension contributions.

33.2 (a) Some students were able to correctly quantify benefits and the associated class 1A NIC. However, in general, there were far too many mistakes in this very straightforward question. Students should be able to determine the benefits on accommodation without difficulty, but this was not the case.

(b) Most students knew and stated in full (ie, day, month, year) the correct date.

33.3 and 4 [No examiner comments as these requirements were not part of the original exam.]

34 Selwyn (September 2015)

		Marks
34.1 Selwyn		
Salary	½	
Car benefit	2	
Laptop	½	
Employer pension contribution	½	
Childcare payments	1	
Edmund		
Salary	½	
Bonus	½	
Subscriptions	½	
		6
34.2 (a) Selwyn		
Employment income	½	
Bank interest	½	
Qualifying interest	1	
Personal allowance	½	
IT liability	2½	
Child benefit charge	½	
PAYE	½	
Child benefit tax charge (W1)	1½	
Edmund		
Income (½ per income)	2	
Personal allowance	½	
NSI @ 20%	½	
SI @ 0%	½	
Marriage allowance	1	
Tax repayable after tax credits	½	
Property income (W1)	2	
Basic rate band	½	
		15
(b) National insurance		
Selwyn	1	
Edmund	1	
		2
34.3 If rent for 8 weeks – no property income	1	
If rent for 12 weeks		
– Taxed on normal property income	1	
– Property allowance	1	
– Elect to use property allowance	1	
		4

		Marks
34.4 (a)	Adjustments (½ per adjustment)	2
	Note (½ per note)	1½
	Car lease costs	<u>1½</u>
		5
(b)	2018/19	1
	2019/20	1½
	2020/21	1
	Overlap profits	<u>1½</u>
		5
34.5	Income tax/grossing up	1
	Class 1B	1
	Due date	<u>1</u>
		3
		40

34.1

Employment income – Selwyn

	£
Salary £2,500 × 12	30,000
Car benefit (£21,000 – £5,000) × (28 + 4)% = £5120 × 9/12	3,840
Use of laptop 20% × £540	108
Employer pension contribution	–
Childcare payments £(60 – 55) × 52	260
	34,208

Employment income – Edmund

	£
Salary £2,500 × 12	30,000
Bonus – December 2018	6,500
Professional subscription	(300)
	36,200

34.2 (a)

Selwyn – Income tax payable	Non-savings £	Savings £	Dividend £	Total
Employment income (34.1)	34,208			
Bank interest £18,445 – £345		18,100		
Dividend			5,750	
Less qualifying interest	(220)			
Net income	33,988	18,100	5,750	57,838
Less personal allowance	(11,850)			(11,850)
Taxable income	22,138	18,100	5,750	45,988

	£		£
Non-savings income	22,138	× 20%	4,428
Savings income	500	× 0%	0
	11,862	× 20%	2,372
	34,500		
	5,738	× 40%	2,295
Dividend income	2,000	× 0%	0
	3,750	× 32.5%	1,219
Tax liability			10,314
Add child benefit tax charge (W1)			1,395
			11,709
Less: tax credits			
PAYE			(4,630)
Tax payable			7,079

WORKING

Child benefit tax charge	£
Net income	57,838
Less threshold	(50,000)
Excess	7,838
Excess/£100 (rounded down to nearest whole number)	78
Charge 1% × £1,788 × 78	1,395

Edmund – income tax payable	Non-savings £	Savings
Employment income (34.1)	36,200	
State pension	5,881	
Property income (W1)	300	
Interest income £1,200 × 50%		600
Net income	42,381	
Less personal allowance	(11,850)	
Taxable income	30,531	600

			£
Non-savings income (W2)	£30,531	× 20%	6,106
Savings income	£600	× 0%	0
Less marriage allowance	£1,190	× 20%	(238)
Less tax credits			
PAYE			(6,950)
Tax repayable			(1,082)

WORKINGS

(1) **Property income – rent-a-room**
   Normal calculation

	£
Rental income (£150 × 52)	7,800
Less allowable expenses	(2,670)
	5,130

   Rent-a-room election

	£
Alternative assessment (£7,800 – £7,500)	300

   Hence Edmund should make a rent-a-room election

(2) **Basic rate band**

Extended BRB £34,500 + £14,200 × 100/80	£52,250

(b) **National insurance contributions - Selwyn**

Class 1 primary

($30,000 - 8,424) × 12%   £2,589

National insurance contributions - Edmund

As Edmund is over state pension age he does not pay national insurance contributions.

34.3 Gertie will be taxed on property income based on the rental income she receives during 2018/19.

If she rents the hut out for 8 weeks in 2018/19 her rental receipts will be £800 and her propery income will not be charged to tax due to the property allowance.

If she rents the hut out for 12 weeks in 2018/19 her rental recepts will be £1,200 and she will be taxed on her property income:

	£
Rent received £100 × 12	1,200
Less allowable expenses	(0)
Property income	1,200

However, if Gertie elects, she can instead deduct the property allowance of £1,000 from her property receipts:

	£
Rent received £100 × 12	1,200
Less property allowance	(1,000)
Property income	200

If Gertie is sucessul in renting the hut out for 12 weeks she should make the election to deduct the property allowance.

34.4 (a)

	£
Draft tax-adjusted trading profits	14,500
Add	
Car lease costs £3,000 – £765 (W1)	2,235
Running expenses £700 × 70%	490
Less	
Legal advice	(1,394)
Computer purchase (AIA)	(2,150)
Revised tax-adjusted trading profit	13,681

Notes

1   Legal advice - within seven years before trading commenced is treated as incurred on the first day of trading, and is deductible.

2   Purchase of the computer - an AIA is available as similarly this is treated as purchased on the first day of trading.

3   Entertaining - not allowable as would not have been allowable had trading commenced.

WORKING

Car lease costs

Allowable proportion (£300 × 10) = £3,000 × 85% × 30% = £765

34.4 (b) Trading income assessments

		£
2018/19	Actual basis 1 July 2018 to 5 April 2019	
	£13,681 × 9/10	12,313
2019/20	Accounting period less than 12 months	
	First 12 months ie, 1 July 2018 – 30 June 2019	
	10 months ended 30 April 2019	13,681
	1 May 2019 – 30 June 2019 2/12 × £51,000	8,500
		22,181
2020/21	CYB – 1 May 2019 – 30 April 2020	51,000
	Overlap profits	
	1 July 2018 to 5 April 2019	12,313
	1 May 2019 to 30 June 2019	8,500
		20,813

34.5

	Basic rate £	Higher rate £	Total £
Gifts £70 × 36; £70 × 14	2,520	980	3,500
Income tax (× 20/80; × 40/60)	630	653	1,283
	3,150	1,633	4,783
Class 1B NIC × 13.8%	435	225	660

Class 1B is payable by 19 October 2019 (22 October 2019 if electronic)

Examiner's comments

34.1   This part was well answered and many scored close to full marks. When errors were made, these usually related to the childcare costs.

34.2 (a) Students were well prepared for the income tax computations. However they did not perform child benefit charge calculations well, if at all. Many used taxable income or employment income, rather than net income, as the basis for any restriction.

34.2 (b) The national insurance contributions were poorly attempted. There were only two marks available, which should have indicated that students did not need a whole page or more of workings. Few realised Edmund was too old to pay NIC and so performed further calculations for him. Many made errors on the calculation of Selwyn's NICs as they included additional amounts of income in the calculation.

34.3   [There are no examiner comments for this part of the question as it has been rewritten due to syllabus changes since this question was originally set.]

34.4 (a) Students had some difficulty with the leased car calculation, although often gained most of the marks. Most dealt with the pre-trading expenditure correctly but did not provide correct explanations of the pre-trading expenditure rules – either ignoring them and answering with normal adjustment of profit explanations, or mixing the rules up with the VAT pre-registration rules.

34.4 (b) Students were often poor at accurately stating the basis periods. Many ended the 2018/19 period on 1 April, 6 April, 4 April, 31 March. Many did not correctly state the second basis period, often thinking that it was only up 30 April 2019, or that it was the tax year itself (6/4/19 to 5/4/20). Few stated the periods for the overlap profits although the majority could calculate the amount.

34.5   Most students struggled with at least one aspect of the PAYE settlement agreement.

35 Pierre (December 2015)

				Marks
35.1		Domicile of origin	1	
		Domicile of choice	½	
		Sever ties	½	
		UK as permanent home	½	
			2½	
		Max		2
35.2	(a)	Salary	½	
		Bonus	1	
		SMRS	2	
		Bicycle	2	
		Private medical insurance	½	
				6
	(b)	Bonus	½	
		SMRS	1	
		Omitting insurance and bicycle	½	
		Class 1 primary	1	
				3
	(c)	Employment and dividend income	½	
		Interest	½	
		Property income	½	
		Personal allowance	½	
		IT	2½	
		DTR	1	
		PAYE	½	
		Extend BRB (W1)	1	
		DTR on property (W2)		
		Highest rate first	½	
		Net income	½	
		Personal allowance	½	
		Tax	2	
		DTR	1½	
		DTR on interest income (W3)	1	
				13
35.3	(a)	Deduct CAs from adjusted profits	½	
		Machinery added to main pool	½	
		Nissan car	½	
		AIA	½	
		Disposal	½	
		WDA @ 18%	½	
		WDA @ 8%	1	
		Balancing charge	1	
				5
	(b)	Jan-Sept basis period	½	
		Jan-Sept profits	½	
		Prorated salary	½	
		PSR	½	
				2
	(c)	Class 2 NIC	1	
		Class 4 NIC	1	
				2

			Marks
35.4	(a)	Election	½
		Adjustments required	½
		Debtors	½
		Adjustment expense	½
		Accountancy fees	½
		Adjustment income	½
			3
	(b)	Just and reasonable amount	½
		Cost	½
		Market value	½
		Computer is allowable expense	½
		Computer under accruals	½
		Capital allowances for car	1
			3½
		Max	**3**
	(c)	VAT cash accounting	1
			1
			40

35.1 Pierre has a 'domicile of origin' in Erehwon, which he acquired at birth from his father, who was presumably domiciled in Erehwon.

In order to become UK domiciled he would have to become UK 'domicile by choice':

- Sever ties with Erehwon

- Take steps to make the UK his permanent home, including making burial arrangements in the UK

Tutorial note

Note that Pierre will not be deemed domicile for income tax purposes as he has not been resident in the UK for 15 of the previous 20 tax years. This is not mentioned in the marking grid as when this question was originally set the concept of deemed domicile only existed for inheritance tax and so was not relevant here. If this question were to be set now then consideration of deemed domicile would be a valid point and marks would be available in the marking guide for this.

35.2 (a)

	£
Employment income	
Salary	27,000
Bonus – ie, date determined after the year end (at AGM)	9,100
Statutory mileage rate scheme (W1)	1,000
Bicycle (W2)	90
Private medical insurance	410
Total employment income	37,600

WORKINGS

(1) **Statutory mileage rate scheme**

		£
Amount received 12,000 × 50p		6,000
Less statutory allowance	10,000 × 45p	(4,500)
	2,000 × 25p	(500)
		1,000

(2) **Bicycle**

	£
Use of bicycle – no benefit as scheme open to all employees	–
Transfer of bicycle:	
MV at transfer	130
Less employee contribution	(40)
	90

(b)

Class 1 NIC – primary

Earnings

	£
Salary	27,000
Bonus	9,100
Statutory mileage rate scheme £6,000 – (12,000 × 45p)	600
	36,700

Medical insurance or bicycle not included in earnings calculation

Annual basis for director

Class 1 primary (£36,700 – £8,424) × 12%	3,393

(c)

	Total £	NSI £	Savings £	Dividend £
Employment income (a)	37,600	37,600		
Dividends	5,650			5,650
Interest £3,444 × 100/70	4,920		4,920	
Property income £6,160 × 100/55	11,200	11,200		
Net income	59,370	48,800	4,920	5,650
Less personal allowance	(11,850)	(11,850)		
Taxable income	47,520	36,950	4,920	5,650
Non-savings income (W1)	£36,950	× 20%		7,390
Savings income	£500	× 0%		0
	£2,250	× 20%		450
	£2,170	× 40%		868
Dividend income	£2,000	× 0%		0
	£3,650	× 32.5%		1,186
Income tax liability				9,894
Less DTR				
Property income (W2)				(3,686)
Interest (W3)				(784)
Less PAYE				(5,000)
Income tax payable				424

WORKINGS

(1) **Extended basic rate band**

	£
Basic rate band	34,500
Personal pension contributions £4,160 × 100/80	5,200
	39,700

(2) **DTR – Property income**

Highest rate first

	Total £	NSI £	Savings £	Dividend £
Employment income (bi)	37,600	37,600		
Dividends	5,650			5,650
Interest	4,920		4,920	
Net income	48,170	37,600	4,920	5,650
Less personal allowance	(11,850)	(11,850)		
Taxable income	36,320	25,750	4,920	5,650
Non-savings income	£25,750	× 20%		5,150
Savings income	£1,000	× 0%		0
	£3,920	× 20%		784
Dividend income	£2,000	× 0%		0
	£3,650	× 7.5%		274
Income tax liability				6,208

DTR = lower of
- UK tax on property income £9,894 – £6,208 3,686
- overseas tax on property income £11,200 × 45% 5,040

ie, £3,686

(3) **DTR – Interest income**

Interest is clearly taxed at 0% (£1,000 of savings income nil rate band) and 20% in UK

	£
DTR = lower of	
• UK tax on interest £3,920 × 20%	784
• overseas tax on interest £4,920 × 30%	1,476
	ie, £784

Tutorial note

The short cut can be used in working (3), as removing the overseas interest from the calculation would not change the way in which the remaining income, including the dividends, would be taxed. That is, the UK tax on the overseas interest is that shown on that income in working (2).

35.3 (a)

	£
Tax-adjusted trading profits	53,194
Less	
Capital allowances (W)	(2,146)
Final tax-adjusted trading profit	51,048

WORKING
Capital allowances

	Main pool £	Ford car £	Nissan car £	Allowances £
TWDV b/f	2,490	1,524		
Additions				
Machinery	1,560			
Nissan car			9,200	
AIA	(1,560)			1,560
Disposal		(1,800)		
	2,490	(276)	9,200	
WDA @18%	(448)			448
WDA @ 8%			(736) ×30%	221
Balancing charge		276 × 30%		(83)
TWDV c/f	2,042	-	8,464	
Capital allowances				2,146

(b) **Trading income assessments 2018/19**

2018/19 – Y/e 31 December 2018	Total £	Emmeline £	Richmal £
1 Jan 2018 – 30 Sep 2018 (9/12)			
£51,048 × 9/12 = £38,286	38,286	19,143	19,143
1 Oct 2018 – 31 Dec 2018			
£51,048 × 3/12 = £12,762			
Salary (3/12)	2,000	2,000	-
PSR (55:45) £12,762 – £2,000	10,762	5,919	4,843
Trading income assessments	51,048	27,062	23,986

(c)

Emmeline

	£
2018/19 Taxable trading income (b)	27,062
National insurance contributions	
Class 2 52 × £2.95	153
Class 4 (£27,062 – 8,424) × 9%	1,677
	1,830

35.4 (a)   The election to use the cash basis is made by ticking the 'cash basis' box on the tax return.

On the change from the accruals basis to the cash basis, adjustments are required in the first accounting period of the cash basis ie, year ended 31 December 2019.

The debtors of £598 relates to income which was included in the accounts to 31 December 2018 (and so taxed in 2018/19). However it also falls within the cash basis for y/e 31 December 2019.

Hence an 'adjustment expense' is required to reduce the taxable profits.

Similarly the accountancy fees are deducted in both accounting periods under the alternative bases.

'Adjustment income' is required to increase the taxable profits.

(b) **Goods for own use**

Under the cash basis a 'just and reasonable' amount should be added to taxable profits.

This would often be the cost of the goods ie, £350.

Under the accruals basis the goods are treated as sold at their market value (ie, £670).

Purchase of computer

The purchase of the computer is treated as an allowable expense under the cash basis.

Under the accruals basis this would not have been allowable and instead eligible for capital allowances.

Purchase of car

Capital allowances are calculated on cars irrespective of the basis of accounting, dependent on the level of the emissions.

(c) Where the cash basis is used for income tax purposes then the VAT cash accounting scheme must also be used.

Examiner's comments

35.1 Many students answered as if the question related to domicile for IHT purposes and not income tax purposes, discussing the concept the IHT election which can be made by a non-domiciled spouse of a UK domiciled individual –which is not relevant. When originally set many students also incorrectly considered the concept of deemed domicile which, at the time the question was set, was not relevant. As explained in the tutorial note above the consideration of deemed domicile would now be valid.

Only a minority correctly explained the concept of domicile of origin – the majority thought it is where an individual is born, one even believed that it is where an individual is conceived. This could be a difficult concept to prove.

35.2 (a) The employment income calculation was generally well attempted – especially the statutory mileage rate scheme. The most common errors related to the bonus, where the special rules for directors were ignored, and the transfer of the bicycle, where the normal rules for transfer of assets, which do not apply to bicycles, were used.

(b) Many students were unable to correctly calculate the earnings relevant for class 1 and either included all of the employment income or only included the salary and bonus. Those who tried to include the SMRS used the taxable benefit figure of £1,000 rather than the correct figure of £600. Many also wasted time incorrectly performing monthly NIC calculations rather than the annual calculation for a director.

(c) The income tax calculation was well attempted although less well prepared students struggled with the double tax relief (DTR) calculation. Some students lost a significant number of marks because they believed that DTR was not relevant as there was no double tax treaty in place.

35.3 (a) This part was well answered and many scored close to full marks. When errors were made, these usually related to the balancing charge on the car, VAT aspects or the private use element.

(b) This part caused much confusion mainly due to the salary. Many incorrectly deducted £8,000 salary from the profit figure, pro rated the remainder and then applied the relevant PSRs. A large number of students ignored the change in the partnership agreement part way through the period, gave £8,000 salary to Emmeline and then split the remainder of the profit for the year 55:45.

(c) Many students scored well on this part, although a number did try to calculate class 1 on the 'salary' element.

35.4 (a) Students were poorly prepared for any of the cash basis parts. They could not explain what adjustments needed to be made on a change of basis. They were very competent at explaining the treatment under the cash basis of a receipt and payment but did not answer the question asked ie, the transition between accruals basis and cash basis.

(b) Students were slightly better at this part, especially in relation to the assets purchased. Some understood the rules and explained them well. Others provided confused explanations and did not distinguish the cash basis from the accruals basis. With regards to the drawings many missed the fundamental point that an amount needed to be added back to profit.

(c) This part was often not answered and rarely answered correctly. Common answers included accruals, flat rate scheme or cash accounting scheme with only the latter being correct.

36 Peter (Sample Paper 1)

Marking guide

			Marks
36.1 (a)	Salary	½	
	Mobile phone	½	
	Loan benefit	1	
	Loan write off	½	
	Business entertaining expenses	½	
	Employer pension contribution	½	
	Car benefit (W1)	1½	
	Accommodation (W2)		
	Annual value	½	
	Additional benefit	1	
	Furniture	½	
	Pro-rate	½	
	Less rent paid	½	
			8
(b)	Monthly calculation for six months	2	
	Earnings in loan write off month	½	
	Calculation for month with loan w/o	1½	
			4
36.2 (a)	Capital allowances on pre-trading expenditure	1	
	VAT recoverable in the four years before registration	1	
	AIA on VAT exclusive amount	1	
		3	
		Max	2
(b)	Deduct CAs	½	
	Additions	1½	
	AIA	½	
	WDA	1½	
			4

				Marks
(c)	2018/19 basis period		½	
	2018/19 assessment		1	
	Class 2		½	
	Class 4		1	
				3
36.3 (a)	Rental income		1	
	Repairs		½	
	Refrigerator		1	
	Fee		½	
	Insurance		1	
				4
(b)	Property income		½	
	Employment income		½	
	Personal allowance		½	
	IT		1	
	PAYE		½	
				3
(c)	Money laundering – ½ mark per procedure	Max	1	
	Fundamental principle		1	
	Steps to mitigate – ½ mark per step	Max	2	
			4	
		Max		3
36.4	Relevant earnings		1	
	Greater than £3,600		½	
	ANI – less gift aid donation		1	
	Less PPC		1	
	Excess over threshold		1½	
	PA		1½	
	Tax reduction due to increased PA		1	
	Tax reduction due to BRB extension		1	
	No annual allowance charge		½	
				9
				40

36.1 (a)

	£
Employment income	
Salary £2,500 × 7	17,500
Mobile telephone	–
Interest free loan – loan benefit £16,000 × 2.5% × 7/12	233
Loan write off – 31 October 2018	16,000
Car benefit (W1)	4,840
Living accommodation (W2)	8,327
Business entertaining expenses	–
Employer pension contribution	–
	46,900

WORKINGS

(1)	**Car benefit**	£
	Car £25,000 × 20% × 6/12	2,500
	Fuel £23,400 × 20% × 6/12	2,340
		4,840

		£
(2)	**Living accommodation**	
	Annual value	15,000
	Additional yearly rent £(250,000 − 75,000) × 2.5%	4,375
	Furniture = £12,000 × 20%	2,400
		21,775
	Prorate × 7/12	12,702
	Less actual rent paid = £625 × 7	(4,375)
		8,327

(b)

	£
National insurance contributions	
Class 1 primary	
For 6 months	
(£2,500 − £702) × 12% × 6	1,295
For 1 month	
Earnings = £18,500 (£2,500 + £16,000)	
(£3,863 − £702) × 12%	379
(£18,500 − £3,863) × 2%	293
	1,967

36.2(a) Capital expenditure on plant and machinery before a business starts is eligible for capital allowances, with the expenditure treated as incurred on the first day of trading, and so included in the capital allowances computation for the first accounting period.

As the capital expenditure is incurred within the four years before registration and the equipment is still held at registration, the input VAT is recoverable and so the cost for capital allowances purposes is the VAT exclusive amount of £8,200 (£9,840 × 5/6).

The expenditure is eligible for the annual investment allowance.

(b)

	£
Tax-adjusted trading profit	
Draft tax-adjusted trading profits	45,095
Less capital allowances	(10,938)
	34,157

WORKING
Capital allowances

	Main pool £	Special rate pool (BU 40%) £	Allowances £
Additions			
1 Oct 2018 – computer equipment (£9,840 × 5/6)	8,200		
10 Jan 2019 – car (emissions >110g/km)		14,880	
14 Feb 2019 – furniture (£3,000 × 5/6)	2,500		
AIA (clearly less than max)	(10,700)		10,700
WDA @ 8% × 6/12		(595) × 40%	238
TWDV c/f	−	14,285	
Capital allowances			10,938

(c) **Taxable trading income**

		£
2018/19	1 November 2018 – 5 April 2019	
	5/6 × £34,157	28,464
National insurance contributions		
Class 2	52 × £2.95 × 5/12	64
Class 4	(£28,464 − 8,424) × 9%	1,804
		1,868

36.3 (a)

Property income (cash basis)	£
Rental income received £1,200 × 10	12,000
Repairs	(1,306)
Refrigerator (replacement element and disposal fee)	(250)
Property management fees	(605)
Insurance paid £300 + £550	(850)
Property income	8,989

(b)

Income tax liability	Non-savings £		
Property income (a)	8,989		
Employment income	40,000		
Less personal allowance	(11,850)		
Taxable income	37,139		

	£		£
Non-savings income	34,500	× 20%	6,900
	2,639	× 40% β	1,056
Tax liability			7,956
Less PAYE			(5,630)
Tax payable			2,326

(c) Before agreeing to accept Peter's brother, Liam, as a new client we must carry out new customer due diligence to ensure the client is known and establish any areas of risk. We must also verify Liam's identity and maintain evidence of identification.

The fundamental principle threatened by taking on Liam will be confidentiality as he is Peter's brother.

This potential conflict of interest can be managed by: ensuring that both Peter and Liam are made aware that we are working with each party; the use of separate engagement teams; secure data filing; clear guidelines and confidentiality and security for the engagement team; the use of confidentiality agreements and regular review of the application of safeguards by a senior individual not involved with Peter and Liam.

36.4

	£
Maximum possible pension contribution	
Employment income	12,500
Relevant earnings	12,500
Greater than minimum of £3,600	

	No PPC £	With PPC £
Adjusted net income		
Total income	115,000	115,000
Less gross GA donation = £2,000 × 100/80	(2,500)	(2,500)
Less gross PPC (max)		(12,500)
	112,500	100,000
Less threshold	(100,000)	(100,000)
Excess	12,500	0
PA available		
Maximum PA	11,850	11,850
Less restriction – excess × 50%	(6,250)	0
	5,600	11,850

Tax liability reduces by:

	£
Amount Mildred's PA increases by at her marginal rate of tax:	
£6,250 @ 40%	2,500
Plus: saving due to amount taxed at the basic rate rather than the higher rate because the PPC extends the BRB:	
£12,500 @ 20%	2,500
Total income tax reduction	5,000

Mildred has an annual allowance of £40,000 in 2018/19 and so she would have no annual allowance charge for a pension contribution of £12,500.

37 Sunil (Sample Paper 2)

			Marks
37.1 (a)	Class 1 primary	1½	
	Class 1 secondary	1	
	Class 1A	1½	
			4
(b)	Less interest received	½	
	Less NIC	1	
	Add backs and no adjustment for repairs (½ per item)	4	
	Less capital allowances	½	
	Car expenses (W1)	2½	
	Capital allowances (W2)		
	AIA	1	
	WDA	1½	
			11
(c)	Interest including from business account	½	
	Dividend not including overseas	½	
	Personal allowance	½	
	IT – ½ per income stream	1½	
	IT – dividend nil rate band	½	
	IT – additional rate tax	½	
	RBC	1	
	DTR	1	
	Trading income (W1)	1	
	FHL (W2)	1	
	Extension of BRB (W3)	2	
			10
37.2	Salary	½	
	Car benefit	2	
	Fuel benefit	1½	
	Employer pension contribution	½	
	Vouchers	½	
	Clock	½	
	Social events	1	
	Employee pension contribution	½	
			7

		Marks
37.3 (a) Period prior to 5 April	1	
Period from 6 April	1	
		2
(b) TLR	2	
Claim	1	
		3
(c) Current year and/or prior year	1	
Against net income	1	
Extension of loss relief to gain	1	
Remaining loss	1	
	4	
Max		3
		40

37.1 (a)

	£
Class 1 Primary NIC	
(£12,500 – £8,424) × 12%	489
Class 1 Secondary NIC	
(£12,500 – £8,424) × 13.8% = £562 covered by £3,000 employment allowance	–
Class 1A	
NIC on benefits	
Van = £3,350	
Training = exempt	
£3,350 × 13.8%	462

(b)

Sunil's tax adjusted trading profits for 15 months ended 31 March 2019	£
Draft profit	144,975
Less:	
Interest received	(150)
NIC for Marwan (part (a))	(462)
Add back:	
Client entertaining	2,556
New hot water heating system	1,500
Decoration – repair not improvement	0
Replacement windows – repair not improvement	0
Depreciation	5,500
Car expenses (W1)	21,400
Charitable donation	500
Gift – assume not trade gifts as is a publisher	8,340
Less capital allowances (W2)	(11,388)
Adjusted trading profit	172,771

Car expenses (W1)	£
Disallowed costs	
Cost of car	18,500
Servicing plan (£3,000 × 25% × 15/36)	312
Servicing plan (£3,000 × 21/36)	1,750
Fuel × 25%	500
Running costs × 25%	338
	21,400

Capital allowances (W2) P/e 31 March 2019	Main pool	SRP	PUA – 75%	Allowances
Van	8,500			
AIA	(8,500)			8,500
Hot water heating system		1,500		
AIA		(1,500)		1,500
Sunil's new car			18,500	
	-	-		
WDA @ 8% × 15/12			(1,850) ×75%	1,388
	-	-	16,650	11,388

(c)

Sunil income tax payable for 2018/19			NSI £	Savings £	Dividend £
Trading income (W1)			138,217		
Property income (W2)			20,350		
Interest on business account				150	
Interest				17,855	
Dividends					163,000
Swiss dividend income exempt as not remitted					-
Net income			158,567	18,005	163,000
Less personal allowance (as RB claimed)			-		
			158,567	18,005	163,000
Taxable income					
Non-savings income (W3)	£45,124	× 20%			9,025
	£113,443	× 40%			45,377
Savings income	£2,058	× 40%			823
	£15,947	× 45%			7,176
Dividend income	£2,000	× 0%			0
	£161,000	× 38.1%			61,341
Plus RBC (resident for at least 7 but fewer than 12 years)					30,000
Less DTR (Norwegian tax clearly lower than UK tax)					(500)
Income tax payable					153,242

Trading income (W1) £
Opening year rules – 12 months to accounting date for year 2
£172,771 × 12/15   138,217

Property income (W2) £
Income   34,000
Less expenses   (7,400)
Less replacement furniture   (6,250)
    20,350

Extended bands (W3) £
Gift Aid donation = £500 × 100/80   625
PPC = £8,000 × 100/80   10,000
    10,625

BRB = £10,625 + £34,500   45,125
HRB = £10,625 + £150,000   160,625

37.2 Employment income for 2018/19

		£	£
Salary			15,000
Company car (List price – capital contribution)	£10,500 × 19%	1,995	
Less contribution for use of car	£50 × 12	(600)	
		1,395	
Prorate for part year	× 9/12		1,046
Fuel benefit	£23,400 × 19% × 9/12		3,335
(No deduction for partial payment)			
Employer pension contribution			-
Vouchers			2,069
Clock – non-cash long service award –exempt			-
Social events – maximise the tax free amount			
Year-end ball			130
Summer ball – exempt			
Barbecue – exempt			
Together the summer ball and the barbecue add up to more than the cost of the year- end ball but less than the maximum permitted of £150			
			21,580
Less employee pension contribution	£15,000 × 5%		(750)
Total employment income			20,830

37.3 (a)

Terminal loss relief	£	£
1 November 2018 – 5 April 2019		
Allocated profits £7,000 × 5/12	2,917	
		0
6 April 2019 – 31 October 2019		
P/E 31 October 2018	(105,000)	
Overlap profits	(23,450)	
		(128,450)
Total amount eligible for terminal loss relief		128,450

(b)

Terminal loss relief use	2016/17 £	2017/18 £	2018/19 £	2019/20 £
Assessable trading profits	31,000	10,000	7,000	0
TLR	(31,000)	(10,000)	(7,000)	
Rental income	14,000	14,000	14,000	14,000
Net income	14,000	14,000	14,000	14,000

A claim for TLR must be made within four years of the end of the last tax year of trade ie, 5 April 2024.

(c) **Other loss relief options**

£80,450 (£128,450 – £31,000 – £10,000 – £7,000) of the amount eligible for terminal loss relief is unrelieved.

This could be set off against the current year and or the prior year in any order.

Relief would be against net income so could offset the rental income in both 2018/19 and 2019/20.

If Dhruthi made a claim to offset the loss against her current year income (ie, 2019/20) she could then offset her trading losses against her chargeable gain.

The remaining loss would be unrelieved.

March 2016 exam answers

38 Amy and Kath (March 2016)

		Marks
38.1 Appoint MLRO	½	
Implement internal reporting procedures	½	
Train staff	½	
On relevant legislation	½	
To recognise ML	½	
Internal procedures re risk assessment	½	
Customer due diligence	½	
Verify identify of new clients	½	
Report to NCA	½	
SAR	½	
	5	
Max		4
38.2 Client disclose or authorise	½	
Amendment	½	
Check engagement letter for authority	½	
Set down in writing	½	
Consequences	½	
Do not inform HMRC	½	
Cease to act	½	
Inform client in writing	½	
Inform HMRC that no longer act but not why	½	
Consider ML disclosure	½	
	5	
Max		3
		7

38.1 Anti-money laundering procedures

Amy should do the following to ensure compliance with anti-money laundering regulations:

Appoint a Money Laundering Reporting Officer (MLRO).

Implement internal reporting procedures.

Train staff and herself to ensure that they are aware of the relevant legislation, know how to recognise and deal with potential money laundering, how to report suspicions to the MLRO, and how to identify clients.

Establish appropriate internal procedures relating to risk assessment and management to deter and prevent money laundering, and make relevant individuals aware of the procedures.

Carry out customer due diligence on any new client and monitor existing clients to ensure the client is known and establish areas of risk.

Verify the identity of new clients and maintain evidence of identification and records of any transactions undertaken for or with the client.

Report suspicions of money laundering to the National Crime Agency (NCA), using a suspicious activity report (SAR).

38.2 Misrepresenting income and expenses

Explain to Kath that she should disclose these figures to HMRC or give authorisation for you to disclose and she will then be required to pay the tax due.

Disclose via an amendment to Kath's 2017/18 self-assessment return as the deadline for this has not passed (31 January 2020).

Check if engagement letter gives automatic authority to disclose.

Set down in writing: the likely consequences of the failure to disclose (including interest, penalties and possible criminal prosecution).

Do not inform HMRC yet as no duty to disclose.

If Kath refuses to authorise full disclosure, you should:

- cease to act for Kath
- inform Kath in writing
- inform HMRC that no longer act for the taxpayer (without disclosing why)
- consider disclosure under anti-money laundering regulations

Examiner's comments

38.1 Most students only gained the basic marks for appointing a money laundering reporting officer, training staff, and reporting to the NCA using a SAR.

38.2 Most students gained two marks out of three for this question which given there were five marks available is, although adequate, not a stellar performance on what should be a classic ethics question.

39 Pict Ltd (March 2016)

Marking guide

	Marks	
39.1 VAT re taxable supplies	1	
VAT re exempt supplies	½	
VAT on overheads	½	
Recoverable amount %	2	
Allocation to taxable and exempt supplies	1	
Van	½	
De minimis test	1	
VAT on standard-rated sales	½	
No VAT on exempt supplies	½	
Sales to EU VAT registered customers	½	
Sales to non VAT registered EU customers	1	
Deduct recoverable input VAT	½	
Car	½	
		10
39.2 SDLT (½ mark per %)	2	
Date	1	
		3
		13

39.1

Q/e 31 December 2018	Taxable £	Exempt £	Total £
Standard-rated costs = (£89,150 – £2,500) × 20%	17,330		17,330
Exempt input VAT = £8,875 × 20%		1,775	1,775
Non-attributable input VAT = £26,290 × 20% = £5,258			
Recoverable amount = T / T+E			
T = £345,150 + £75,000 / £445,410 = 95%			
95% × £5,258	4,995		4,995
5% × £5,258		263	263
Delivery van = £28,800 × 20%	5,760		5,760
	28,085	2,038	30,123

As £2,038 is more than £625 per month on average (although not more than 50% of total input tax), the exempt input tax is not recoverable.

VAT return	£
Standard-rated UK sales = £345,150 × 20%	69,030
No VAT on exempt supplies	-
Sales to EU VAT registered customers = zero rated	-
Sales to non-registered customers within the EU = £75,000 × 2/3 × 5%	2,500
	71,530
Input VAT	
Recoverable input tax	(28,085)
Purchase of car	-
Net VAT payable	43,445

39.2 SDLT on residential property

- The first £125,000 at 0% = £0
- The next £125,000 at 2% = £2,500
- The next £675,000 at 5% = £33,750
- The next £325,000 at 10% = £32,500

Total SDLT due is £68,750.

The SDLT should be paid within 30 days of completion ie, 30 July 2018.

> **Tutorial note**
>
> Despite this being Edith's first home she will not benefit from first time buyer relief as the property costs more than £500,000.

Examiner's comments

39.1 Answers to this part were surprisingly poor. A large number of students did not read the question properly and therefore did not realise that they had to work out the VAT on the figures given. Some presumed that the sales figures required VAT to be computed but that the costs were already VAT figures. Some just mixed and matched throughout. Students were not able to correctly compute the partial exemption percentage (often treating only £50,000 of the £75,000 sales to EU customers as taxable supplies on the top of the fraction). There were also lots of very convoluted partial exemption tests performed, sometimes running to two pages. Also many students worked everything out using the figures in the question and then somewhere at the end applied 20% to the total which was very confusing to mark.

It was also common for answers to completely ignore the partial exemption calculation and simply claim the whole of the non-attributable input tax.

Lots of students lost very easy marks by not reading the question properly and failing to clearly show their treatment of all items – ie, including the exempt sales and sales to VAT registered EU customers.

The general layout of the answers was poor with little regard to the examples/guidance in the learning materials.

39.2 Most students achieved full marks for the calculation of the SDLT but lots then just stated the rule for when the SDLT was payable rather than giving the date. If a date is requested, then it must be given to achieve the marks available.

40 Tracey, Fred and Matthew (March 2016)

Marking guide

	Marks
40.1 Land costs of disposal	½
Land cost	2½
Car	½
AEA	½
Taxable income	½
BRB remaining	½
Tax at 10%	½
Tax at 20%	½
	6
40.2 February lifetime gift – death tax	
Gross chargeable transfer	½
FIV	½
NRB	1
Tax on death	½
Taper relief	½
Less lifetime tax	½
Small gifts	1
School fees	1
Death estate	
Shares less BPR	1
Cash	½
NRB at death	½
Less GCTs	1
Tax at 40%	½
February lifetime gift – lifetime tax	
MV at date of gift	½
AEs	½
NRB	1
Lifetime tax	½
Gross chargeable transfer	½
	12

40.3 IHT

PET	½
Chargeable within 7 years	½
Still own or replace	1
BPR means no IHT	1
IHT on value at gift	½
Taper relief	½
CGT	
Market value	½
Joint election	½
Gift relief	½
Unquoted trading company	½
Gain reduced to nil	½
Base cost	½
No CGT on death	½
If discuss ER instead of GR	
Worked for company	½
5%	½
Trading company	½
One year	½
Taxable @ 10%	½
Base cost	½
	10½

Max $\dfrac{7}{25}$

40.1

CGT liability for 2018/19

	£
Part disposal of land	
Proceeds	42,000
Less costs of disposal	(1,450)
Less cost = (£76,000 + £2,400) × (£42,000 / £42,000 + £60,000)	(32,282)
Gain	8,268
Car – exempt asset	Nil
Total gains = £147,000 + £8,268	155,268
Less AEA	(11,700)
Taxable gains	143,568
Taxable income = £25,615 – £11,850	13,765
BRB remaining = £34,500 – £13,765	20,735
CGT liability:	
£20,735 @ 10%	2,074
(£143,568 – £20,735 = £122,833) @ 20%	24,567
	26,641

	April 2011 CLT £	February 2018 CLT £	December 2024 Death (W3) £
Stage 1 - Transfers			
Transfer		240,000	
Less exemptions			
Annual		(3,000)	
Annual b/f		(3,000)	
		234,000	1,000,000
Stage 2 – Lifetime tax			
Less remaining NRB (W2)		(18,000)	N/A
		216,000	
IHT @ 20/80		54,000	
Gross chargeable transfer	307,000		–
(£234,000 + £54,000)		288,000	
Stage 3 - Tax on death			
Gross chargeable transfer	More than 7 years	288,000	1,000,000
Less fall in value relief		(121,000)	
(£240,000 – £119,000)			
Less remaining NRB (W2)		(18,000)	(37,000)
		149,000	963,000
IHT @ 40%		59,600	385,200
Taper relief (6-7 yrs) 20% chargeable		11,920	
Less lifetime tax paid		(54,000)	
Tax payable on death		–	385,200

WORKINGS

(1) **Gift to grandchildren**

Exempt as covered by small gift exemption

School fees

Exempt as constitutes normal expenditure out of income.

(2) **Remaining nil rate band**

	April 2011 CLT £	February 2018 CLT £	December 2024 Death £
Stage 2 – Lifetime			
Lifetime NRB		325,000	–
Less chargeable in previous 7 years		(307,000)	
Remaining NRB		18,000	–
Stage 3 – On death			
NRB at death	N/A	325,000	325,000
Less chargeable in previous 7 years		(307,000)	
(ignore FIV relief)			(288,000)
Remaining NRB		18,000	37,000

(3) **Death estate**

Shares less BPR	0
Cash etc	1,000,000
	1000,000

40.3 IHT

A lifetime gift to his daughter will be a PET for inheritance tax purposes and will become chargeable on Matthew's death within seven years.

Assuming the daughter still owned the shares (or had sold but replaced them), the shares would be eligible for BPR and no IHT would be payable.

Otherwise IHT would be due on the value at the date of the gift (£10 million). IHT would be charged at 40% subject to taper relief of 60%.

CGT

The lifetime transfer would be subject to CGT as a disposal to a connected person, using deemed proceeds of market value of £10 million less Matthew's original cost.

Matthew and his daughter could make a joint election for gift relief to apply because the shares are in an unquoted trading company. Matthew's gain would be reduced to nil, and his daughter's base cost for a future disposal would be the same as Matthew's original cost.

There are no CGT implications for a lifetime transfer arising from Matthew's death.

Additional credit available if discuss ER

Alternatively Matthew could make a claim for entrepreneurs' relief to apply because he has worked for the company, held at least 5% of the shares, and it has been a trading company, for at least one year. Matthew's gain would then be taxable at 10% and his daughter's base cost for any future disposals would be £10 million.

> **Tutorial note**
>
> No marks were awarded for a purely computational answer.

Examiner's comments

40.1 This requirement was very well answered with lots of students achieving full or nearly full marks. The most common errors were deducting the costs of acquisition from the purchase price paid rather than adding, and not using a part disposal working.

40.2 This requirement was very well answered on the whole. The layout of the answers was generally logical and easy to follow. The more unusual parts of the question ie, the small gifts, school fees and the fall in value were also generally dealt with well. The majority of students understood that the fall in value was not included in the value of accumulated gross chargeable transfers.

Students could do better if they showed their workings. This is most often an issue with the nil rate band where it is not uncommon for students just to put a dash where they think there is no nil rate band remaining. Where this is incorrect it is difficult to award marks without knowing how they have reached that conclusion.

40.3 There were many good answers to this part that were written in short, clear and succinct sentences, that covered many aspects and that were presented in different sections using headings eg, CGT at time of gift, IHT at time of gift. This was a challenging part covering two taxes, where it is common to mix up the reliefs, and it was encouraging to see so many students produce good answers.

41 Pietra Ltd (March 2016)

		Marks
41.1	Depreciation	½
	Profit on disposal warehouse	½
	Rental income	½
	Interest relating to rental	1
	Interest and costs re loan on fixed assets	1
	Charitable donations	½
	Deduct capital allowances	½
	Capital allowances (W1)	
	Additions not eligible for AIA	½
	Additions eligible for AIA	1
	AIA – amount and use against SRP first	1
	WDAs	1
		8
41.2	Rental income	½
	NTLR calculation	1
	NTLR calculation	½
	Qualifying charitable donations	½
	Corporation tax payable	½
	Gain (W1)	4
		7
		15

41.1 Pietra Ltd tax adjusted trading profit for year ended 31 December 2018

	£
Accounting profit	4,000,000
Depreciation	130,000
Less profit on disposal of warehouse	(340,000)
Less rental income	(20,000)
Less interest income	(800)
Add back interest expense relating to rental = £23,400 × 1/5	4,680
Interest and incidental costs re loan to purchase fixed assets	0
Charitable donations	50,000
Capital allowances (W1)	(425,800)
Trading profit	3,398,080

WORKINGS

(1)	Capital allowances Y/e 31 December 2018	Main pool £	SR pool £	Allowances £
	TWDV b/f	386,000	283,000	
	Additions – not eligible for AIA		135,000	
	Additions – eligible for AIA	664,000	242,000	
	AIA = max £200,000		(200,000)	200,000
		1,050,000	460,000	
	WDA @ 18% / 8%	(189,000)	(36,800)	225,800
	TWDV c/f	861,000	423,200	
	Total allowances			425,800

41.2 Pietra Ltd corporation tax liability for year ended 31 December 2018

	£	£
Trading profits (part 1)		3,398,080
Rental income		20,000
Gain (W1)		15,000
Non-trading loan relationships (W2)		(3,880)
Less qualifying charitable donations paid		(40,000)
TTP		3,389,200
Corporation tax payable:		
CT @ 19%		643,948

WORKING

(1) **Gain**	£
Proceeds	550,000
Less cost	(210,000)
Less enhancement expenditure	(124,000)
Unindexed gain	216,000
Less IA on cost = 278.1 – 207.3 / 207.3 = 0.342 × £210,000	(71,820)
IA on enhancement = 278.1 – 223.6 / 223.6 = 0.244 × £124,000	(30,256)
Gain	113,924
Less rollover relief	(98,924)
Taxable now	15,000

(Proceeds not reinvested)
£550,000 – £535,000 = £15,000

(2) **NTLR income**	£
Interest income	800
Less interest paid on factory rented out	(4,680)
Non-trading loan relationship deficit	(3,880)

Examiner's comments

41.1 Corporation tax was not as well understood as income tax, CGT and IHT. There was confusion over what the adjustment should be for the charitable donations. Luckily the capital allowances were very well attempted and many scored the full three marks here. Most students did follow the instructions to show all items in the computation; those who did not, lost easy marks. [Note that this question has been amended due to syllabus changes from as it was originally set.]

41.2 The calculation of the tax liability was generally not dealt with very well, quite often there was not much in the answer apart from the trading profit. It was very common for students to add rather than deduct the NTLR figure in the computation. In relation to the gain indexation was commonly not rounded. [Note that this question has been amended due to syllabus changes from as it was originally set.]

42 Anka (March 2016)

Marks

42.1	Depreciation	½	
	Drawings	1	
	Client entertaining	½	
	Leased car costs	1	
	Loss on disposal	½	
	Small donation to local charity	½	
	Legal and professional costs	1½	
	Stock for own use	1	
	Less capital allowances	½	
	Bad debts (W1) (½ per item)	2	
	Capital allowances (W2)		
	Disposal	½	
	WDA on main pool	½	
	WDA on PU asset	1	
			11
42.2 (a)	Salary only (no mileage)	1	
	Vouchers	1	
	ST	½	
	NIC @ 13.8%	½	
			3
(b)	Car parking	½	
	Employer pension contribution	½	
	NIC @ 13.8%	½	
	Company car (W1)		
	List price	1	
	Car benefit %	1	
	Fuel benefit	1	
	Use of sound equipment (W2)		
	Use	½	
	Prorate	½	
	Less contribution	½	
			6
(c)	Pension contribution	½	
	Total employment income	½	
	Income tax @ 45%	½	
	Class 1 primary NIC		
	Earnings @ 12%	1½	
	Earnings @ 2%	1½	
	Net disposable income		
	Salary	½	
	Pension contribution	½	
	Fuel contribution	½	
	Contribution for sound equipment	½	
	Less class 1 primary NIC	½	
			7

		Marks
42.3 (a)	Gross overseas income (½ per source)	1
	Personal allowance	½
	IT on non-savings income	½
	IT on savings income	1
	IT on dividend income	<u>1</u>
		4
(b)	Taxable income excluding o/s rental income	½
	IT on non-savings income	½
	IT on savings income	1
	IT on dividend income	1
	UK income tax on overseas rental income	½
	Taxable income excluding all overseas income	½
	IT on non-savings income	½
	IT on savings income	1
	IT on dividend income	1
	UK income tax on overseas interest	½
	DTR is lower of	½
	Source by source basis	½
	DTR on rental income	½
	DTR on interest	<u>½</u>
		<u>9</u>
		<u>40</u>

42.1 Anka's tax adjusted trading profits for year ended 31 December 2018

	£
Draft profit	112,000
Add back:	
Depreciation	8,450
Drawings = £80 × 12	960
Client entertaining	550
Disallowed leased car costs = £3,000 × 15%	450
Loss on disposal of machine	2,000
Small donation to local charity	0
Legal and professional costs	400
Bad debt expense disallowed (W1)	150
Stock taken for own use	1,000
Less capital allowances (W2)	(8,568)
Adjusted trading profit	<u>117,392</u>

Bad debts (W1)	£
Trade debts written off is allowable	0
Loan to former employee written off is not allowable	250
Increase in provision for specific debts is allowable	0
Recovery of loan	(100)
Add back	<u>150</u>

Capital allowances (W2)	Main pool £	PUA – 80% £		Allowances £
TWDV b/f	44,000	12,000		
Disposal	(6,000)			
WDA @ 18%	(6,840)			6,840
WDA @ 18%		(2,160)	× 80%	1,728
	<u>31,160</u>	<u>9,840</u>		<u>8,568</u>

42.2 (a) Gandalf – employer class 1 NIC

	£
Salary	50,000
Mileage scheme – no NIC deduction for payment < £0.45 per mile	0
Vouchers – exchangeable for goods	2,400
	52,400
Less ST	(8,424)
	43,976
NIC due @ 13.8%	6,069

(b) Xanthe's taxable benefits

	£
Company car (W1)	12,844
Use of sound equipment (W2)	85
Car parking	Nil
Employer pension contribution	Nil
	12,929
Class 1A NIC due @ 13.8%	1,784

WORKINGS

(1) Company car

	£
Car benefit	
List price – capital contribution = £31,000 – £5,000 = £26,000	
Benefit % = 4% + 22% = 26%	
Car benefit = 26% × £26,000	6,760
Fuel benefit = 26% × £23,400	6,084
	12,844

(2) Use of sound equipment

	£
£5,520 × 20%	1,104
Prorated for actual use × 5/12	460
Less contribution = £75 × 5	(375)
	85

(c) Income tax liability

	£
Salary	60,000
Benefits	12,929
Less occupational pension contribution £60,000 × 10%	(6,000)
Total taxable employment income	66,929
Income tax due on employment income at 45%	30,118

Class 1 primary NIC

	£
(£46,350 – £8,424) × 12%	4,551
(£60,000 – £46,350) × 2%	273
	4,824

Net disposable income

	£
Salary	60,000
Less Xanthe's pension contribution	(6,000)
Less fuel contribution £20 × 12	(240)
Less contribution for sound equipment (part (b))	(375)
Less income tax	(30,118)
Less Class 1 primary NIC	(4,824)
	18,443

42.3(a) Mack income tax liability for 2018/19

	NSI £	Savings £	Dividend £
Employment income	25,385		
Dividend			13,000
Bank interest		2,680	
Gross debenture interest		9,450	
Gross rental income	15,000		
Net income	40,385	12,130	13,000
Less personal allowance	(11,850)		
Taxable income	28,535	12,130	13,000
Non-savings income	£28,535	× 20%	5,707
Savings income	£500	× 0%	0
	£5,465	× 20%	1,093
	£6,165	× 40%	2,466
Dividend income	£2,000	× 0%	0
	£11,000	× 32.5%	3,575
Income tax liability			12,841

(b) Mack double taxation relief for 2018/19

	NSI £	Savings £	Dividend £
Taxable income excluding overseas rental income	13,535	12,130	13,000
Non-savings income	£13,535	× 20%	2,707
Savings income	£500	× 0%	0
	£11,630	× 20%	2,326
Dividend income	£2,000	× 0%	0
	£6,835	× 7.5%	513
	£4,165	× 32.5%	1,354
Income tax liability excluding overseas rental income			6,900

UK income tax on overseas rental income
= £12,841 – £6,900 → 5,941

	NSI £	Savings £	Dividend £
Taxable income excluding all overseas income	13,535	2,680	13,000
Non-savings income	£13,535	× 20%	2,707
Savings income	£1,000	× 0%	0
	£1,680	× 20%	336
Dividend income	£2,000	× 0%	0
	£11,000	× 7.5%	825
Income tax liability excluding both sources of overseas income			3,868

UK income tax on overseas debenture interest
= £6,900 – £3,868 → 3,032

DTR is the lower of UK tax and overseas tax on a source by source basis
Rental income is the lower of £8,000 and £5,941 → 5,941
Debenture interest is the lower of £2,200 and £3,032 → 2,200
→ 8,141

Examiner's comments

42.1 The adjustment of profit was generally handled well and most students followed the instructions to show the treatment of all items. The main errors were not adding back the pension contributions, the incorrect calculation of the leased car adjustment (where it was very common to take a further adjustment for the 50% private use) and the stock taken for own use adjustment (most commonly £300 added back).

42.2 (a)   Answers were mixed for this part. It was quite common to include the mileage payments and to use an incorrect voucher figure. The actual NIC was normally correct.

(b)   It was quite common to award full marks for this part. Most students showed they were very familiar with the calculation of employee benefits. Common errors were to use the price paid for the car, the actual capital contribution, to deduct a contribution for private fuel and incorrectly prorate the use of the sound equipment.

(c)   A lot of students performed badly on this part because they did not consider the cash items – many simply calculated taxable income (which included many non-cash benefits) and then deducted the income tax liability. Many also lost marks for not calculating the class 1 primary NIC, although when it was calculated, it usually scored full marks.

Some students still dislike having to work at the marginal rate and persist in producing a full income tax computation in this type of question.

It is also interesting to see that so many students still do not understand the difference between cash and the notional value attributed to a taxable benefit in kind.

42.3 (a)   It was very common to award full marks for this part. A minority of students lost easy marks for the overseas income even though the gross figures were quite clearly given in the question.

(b)   Some students scored full marks on this part but the majority performed quite poorly and it was often difficult to follow the calculations, as they were often not very logical or clearly presented. Most students calculated the DTR on a source by source basis and recognised that it was the lower of the overseas and UK tax but most used an incorrect method to calculate the UK tax. Most dealt with the debenture interest first rather than the rental income, some appeared to deal with the rental income first but then did not exclude it from taxable income when calculating the UK tax on debenture interest. It was also common to incorrectly calculate the UK tax by reference to the tax rate paid on the source in part 3a, but this is too simplistic where there is dividend income [and a varying savings income nil rate band].

43 Lyra (June 2016)

	Marks
Advise client to disclose	½
Advise to pay back	½
Check engagement letter for authority to disclose	1
Warn of consequences	½
Resign	½
Document advice	½
Criminal offence eg, under Theft Act	1
Anti-money laundering	½
SAR to NCA	1
Principle of confidentiality prevents disclosure	½
Unless legal or professional right or duty to disclose	1
Do not disclose to HMRC why cease to act	½
ML disclosure not a breach of confidentiality	½
	8½
Max	7
	7

Despite the finance director's statement, Lyra should advise him to disclose the error to HMRC and pay back the £1 million.

Lyra should check whether the engagement letter gives her authority to disclose the error to HMRC (or ask Hat plc for authority to disclose).

Lyra should warn Hat plc of the possible legal consequences of refusal to allow her to disclose the error, including interest and penalties.

Lyra should advise Hat plc that if it refuses to allow her to advise HMRC of the error then she will have to resign.

Lyra should document the advice given to Hat plc.

A deliberate attempt to benefit from an error made by HMRC may constitute a criminal offence under UK law. For example, the client may face a prosecution under the Theft Act 1968.

If a crime is committed it brings the non-disclosure of the error into the scope of anti-money laundering legislation. This may then require Lyra to make a SAR to the NCA.

The fundamental principle of confidentiality prevents Lyra from disclosing confidential information acquired as a result of professional or business relationships.

However, client information may be disclosed without the client's consent if there is an express legal or professional right or duty to disclose:

- If Lyra ceases to act, she may not disclose to HMRC why she has ceased to act.

- However, if a crime has been committed then it is not a breach of her duty of confidentiality as anti-money laundering legislation is in point.

44 Hammer Ltd (June 2016)

		Marks
44.1 Common control	½	
So Tack Ltd not eligible	½	
Fixed establishment in UK so Nail GmbH not eligible	1	
Advantages of VAT group	1½	
Nut Ltd sales standard rated as customers not VAT-registered	1	
Bolt Ltd – benefits from cash flow of monthly repayments	1½	
Screw Ltd – group partially exempt	½	
Except if *de minimis*	½	
	7	
Max		6
44.2 (a) Commercial property – recoverable VAT on costs	½	
Residential property supply – zero rated	1	
So recoverable VAT on costs	½	
		2
(b) SDLT on commercial property	2	
SDLT on residential property	1	
		3
(c) Group	1	
No SDLT	1	
		2
		13

44.1 VAT group

To be in a VAT group companies must be under common control/51% group companies. Therefore Tack Ltd is not eligible to be included in a VAT group.

Nail GmbH does not have a fixed establishment in the UK so is not eligible to be included in the group registration.

Hammer Ltd makes standard-rated supplies and should be included in the group to reduce administration as intra-group sales will not be subject to VAT with only one return required.

As an exporter to private individuals in the EU, given the nature of Nut Ltd's customers its sales will be standard rated (ie, they're unlikely to be VAT registered) and Nut Ltd should be included in the group.

As a zero-rated trader, Bolt Ltd is a repayment trader. It should be excluded from the VAT group otherwise the cash flow advantage of a monthly VAT repayment will be lost.

Screw Ltd is exempt so including it in the group will make the whole group partially exempt. Screw Ltd should be excluded from the group unless the level of exempt input VAT is *de minimis* such that it would not affect the recoverability of input tax for the whole group.

44.2 (a) **Input VAT recoverable on commercial property**

As a standard-rated taxable supply, the input VAT is fully recoverable.

Input VAT recoverable on residential property

As a zero-rated supply which is a taxable supply, the input VAT is fully recoverable.

(b) **SDLT on commercial property**

SDLT due on VAT inclusive amount:

£150m × 1.2 = £180m

- The first £150,000 at 0% = £0
- £100,000 at 2% = £2,000
- £179,750,000 at 5% = £8,987,500

Total SDLT due is £8,989,500

SDLT on residential property

- The first £125,000 at 0% = £0
- £125,000 at 2% = £2,500
- £575,000 at 5% = £28,750

Total SDLT due is £31,250

(c) **Group relief for SDLT**

As the two companies would constitute a group (minimum 75% ownership) then no SDLT would be due on the transfer.

Examiner's comments

44.1 Answers to this part were surprisingly poor. A lack of explanation was common. For example students would simply state that as Bolt Ltd was a zero-rated trader it should be excluded from the group. This scored no marks as the question had clearly stated both that Bolt Ltd was zero rated and that it should not be included in the group. What was required was for students to explain what it is about a zero-rated trader that means it should be excluded from the group. Students demonstrated that they appeared to have learned aspects of this question without understanding it.

In addition, a significant minority just stated that in order to form a group, all the members had to make the same type of supplies and simply stated this as reason for only including Hammer Ltd and Nut Ltd.

Many who attempted to do more than simply regurgitate the facts were often confused about the implications of making zero-rated or exempt supplies on VAT recovery. Many also thought that a VAT group required a shareholding of 75%.

44.2 (a) Quite a lot of students either do not understand the differences between input VAT and output VAT or did not read the question properly as they gave explanations as to whether the purchasers could reclaim their input VAT rather than whether the supplier could recover its input VAT.

Other students thought the supplier recovered the output VAT charged to the customer or thought that the supplier could recover its input VAT only if the purchaser were VAT registered.

There was also a distinct lack of understanding of the difference between an exempt supply and a zero-rated supply.

(b) Most gained at least half marks on this part.

45 Emma and Tom (June 2016)

Marking guide

		Marks
45.1 Clock	½	
AEA against residential property gain first	1	
Taxable income	½	
BRB remaining	½	
CGT	1	
House (W1)		
Cost	½	
SDLT	½	
Legal fees	½	
PPR	½	
Letting relief	1½	
PPR (W2)		
Periods of occupation and absence (½ per period)	3	
		10
45.2 Lifetime gift – death tax		
Gross chargeable transfer	½	
NRB	1	
Tax on death	½	
Taper relief	½	
Less lifetime tax	½	
Death estate		
Cash and personal effects	½	
Life assurance policy	1	
Unit trusts	1	
Less bank loan	½	
Less tax liability	½	
Less political donation	1	
NRB	1	
Tax at 40%	½	
Less QSR	½	
Lifetime tax – life tax		
AEs	½	
NRB	1	
Lifetime tax	½	
Gross chargeable transfer	½	
QSR (W3)		
Death estate less NRB	½	
Tax at 40%	½	
QSR	2	
		15
		25

45.1

CGT liability for 2018/19

	Gains on other assets £	Gains on residential property £
House (W1)		5,618
Commercial property	50,000	
Antique clock – exempt as a wasting asset (a clock is plant and machinery, so predictable life is always treated as < 50 years)		–
Less AEA	(6,082)	(5,618)
Taxable gain	43,918	–
Taxable income = £22,500 – £11,850		10,650
BRB remaining = £34,500 – £10,650		23,850
£23,850 @ 10%		2,385
£20,068 @ 20%		4,014
CGT liability		6,399

WORKINGS

		£
(1)	**Gain on house**	
	Proceeds	330,000
	Less cost	(153,000)
	Less SDLT	(1,530)
	Less legal fees	(600)
		174,870
	Less PPR (W2) = £174,870 × 102/138	(129,252)
		45,618
	Less letting exemption – lowest of:	
	£40,000	
	Gain when let = £45,618	
	PPR already given = £129,252	
		(40,000)
		5,618

(2) **Periods of occupation and absence for PPR**

Dates	Reason	Occupied (Months)	Deemed (Months)	Absent (Months)
1.1.07 – 30.6.08	Actual occupation	18		
1.7.08 – 30.6.12	Working elsewhere in the UK – max 4 years deemed		48	
1.7.12 – 30.6.13	Up to 3 years absence for any reason		12	
1.7.13 – 31.12.13	Actual occupation	6		
1.1.14 – 31.12.16	Travelling overseas – no deemed occupation as not followed by actual occupation			36
1.1.17 – 30.6.18	Last 18 months – always exempt		18	
		24	78	36

Total ownership = 138 months
Actual and deemed occupation = 102 months

	January 2010 CLT £	February 2012 CLT £	January 2019 Death (W2) £
Stage 1 - Transfers			
Transfer		250,000	
Less exemptions			
Annual		(3,000)	
Annual b/f		(3,000)	
	275,000	244,000	473,500
Stage 2 – Lifetime tax			
Less remaining NRB (W1)		(50,000)	
		194,000	
IHT @ 20/80		48,500	
Gross chargeable transfer			
(£244,000 + £46,500)	275,000	292,500	473,500
Stage 3 - Tax on death			
Gross chargeable transfer	More than 7 years	292,500	473,500
Less remaining NRB (W1)		(50,000)	(32,500)
		242,500	441,000
IHT @ 40%		97,000	176,400
Taper relief (6-7 yrs)		19,400	
20% chargeable			
Less lifetime tax paid		(48,500)	
Less QSR (W3)			(48,160)
Tax payable on death		-	128,240

WORKINGS

(1) **Remaining nil rate band**

	January 2010 CLT £	February 2012 CLT £	January 2019 Death £
Stage 2 – Lifetime			
Lifetime NRB		325,000	
Less chargeable in previous 7 years		(275,000)	
Remaining NRB		50,000	
Stage 3 – On death			
NRB at death	N/A	325,000	325,000
Less chargeable in previous 7 years		(275,000)	(292,500)
Remaining NRB		50,000	32,500

(2) **Death estate**

	£
Cash + personal effects	350,000
Life assurance policy – payable proceeds as on own life	150,000
Unit trusts = 10,000 × £1.55	15,500
Less bank loan	(20,000)
Less outstanding tax liability	(17,000)
Less donation to qualifying political party	(5,000)
	473,500

(3) **QSR on father's estate**

	£
Chargeable estate	500,000
Less NRB 2016/17	(325,000)
Chargeable transfer	175,000
IHT on £175,000 @ 40%	70,000
QSR = £70,000 × £430,000 / £500,000 × 80%	48,160

Examiner's comments

45.1 Most students knew how to apply the tax rates and correctly calculated the remaining basic rate band. The presentation of answers has improved and assisted candidates particularly in the calculation of tax. It was noticeable that those students who had a separate working to calculate the remaining basic rate band tended to get the correct answer whereas those who tried to combine all the calculations into the tax payable calculation tended to fall into the trap of deducting the full basic rate band when calculating the tax at the higher rate.

A minority of students deducted the SDLT and legal fees from the cost rather than increasing the cost for the gain calculation. Some applied the PPR fraction to the cost rather than the gain.

Application of PPR and letting relief rules was often weak. Very few students gained all marks for working 1. The most common errors were not identifying deemed occupation for the final 12 months of working elsewhere in the UK (ie, missing the three years any reason rule) and assuming deemed occupation for the period of overseas travel (ie, missing the lack of occupation post travel). Some students seemed unable to use words to describe their workings and so lost marks if their numbers were wrong and had no labels attached to them to allow follow through marks to be awarded.

Many students were unable to correctly identify the three numbers to compare in letting relief. Also many students just stated that letting relief was the gain remaining after PPR – in this case this was correct – but this is often not the case and therefore candidates should not get into the habit of approaching the calculation of letting relief in this way.

Most students calculated a gain on the antique clock.

45.2 On the whole, answers to the IHT question were excellent and very well presented. Where mistakes were made, they were in relation to the valuation of the unit trusts and the life insurance policy. I was very pleased that almost all students made an excellent attempt at calculating QSR and the majority got it correct. It is interesting that students can correctly calculate QSR but not deal with more basic parts of tax law such as the correct application of basis periods to an unincorporated business (see part 47.1(c)).

46 Bagno Ltd (June 2016)

		Marks
46.1	Disposal	
	LLA in SRP	½
	AIA in SRP	½
	Balancing charge	1
	WDA @ 8%	½
	WDA @18%	½
	FYA	1
	Capital allowances	½
		5
46.2	Loss relief group	1
	Gains group	1
		2
46.3	Gain on shares	
	Cost	½
	Indexation allowance	½
	No reliefs	½
	Capital loss set against gains	1
	Elect to reallocate gains and capital losses	1½
	Capital loss c/f	½
	Trading loss b/f	1
	No gains in TTP	½
	Group relief – right companies and position	1½
	Trading loss c/f	½
		8
		15

46.1

	Main pool £	SRP £	SLA £	Allowances £
TWDV b/f	875,450	345,600	42,000	
Disposal			(76,000)	
Additions				
Machine – LLA		300,000		
Machine	100,000			
AIA – against SRP		(200,000)		200,000
	975,450	445,600	(34,000)	
Balancing charge			34,000	(34,000)
WDA @ 8%		(35,648)		35,648
WDA @ 18%	(175,581)			175,581
				377,229
TWDV c/f	799,869	409,952	–	

	£
Trading profits	2,200,000
Less FYA at 100% for R&D related capex excluding land	(150,000)
Less capital allowances	(377,229)
Tax-adjusted trading profits	1,672,771

46.2 Bagno Ltd, Doccia Ltd and Onda Ltd form a loss relief group.

Bagno Ltd, Doccia Ltd, Onda Ltd and Ponte Ltd form a chargeable gains group.

46.3

Gain on disposal of shares in Tappo SpA	**£**
Proceeds	860,000
Less cost	(265,000)
IA = 278.1 – 146.0 / 146.0 × £265,000	(239,770)
Chargeable gain (ie, no SSE as holding < 10%)	355,230

Group gains

The capital loss of £900,000 can only be offset against capital gains, not against any other profits. Therefore not all of the capital loss can be offset this year.

It is possible to make an election to reallocate the group gains and/or Onda Ltd's capital loss within the group. This would allow the gains to be offset by the capital loss in the current year and would give a net gain for the group of £nil.

	£
Gains = £355,230 + £160,000	515,230
Capital loss for the current year	(900,000)
Onda Ltd's capital loss carried forward	384,770

Taxable total profits for the year ended 31 March 2019

	Acqua Ltd £	Bagno Ltd £	Doccia Ltd £	Onda Ltd £	Ponte Ltd £
Tax adjusted trading profits	1,000,000	–	1,000,000	1,000,000	1,672,771
Property income				1,900,000	
Gains		–	–		
Total profits	1,000,000	–	1,000,000	2,900,000	1,672,771
Less trade loss b/f				(500,000)	
Total profits	1,000,000	–	1,000,000	2,400,000	1,672,771
QCD				(400,000)	
TTP pre group relief	1,000,000	–	1,000,000	2,000,000	1,672,771
Less CY group relief from Bagno			(1,000,000)	(2,000,000)	
TTP	1,000,000	–	–	–	1,672,771

Trading loss carried forward in Bagno Ltd is £2,000,000 (£5,000,000 – £1,000,000 – £2,000,000) + £200,000 = £2,200,000. These losses will be available to offset against Bagno Ltd's future total profits or for group relief.

Examiner's comments

46.1 Many students scored at least three out of five marks, with the R&D being the area where marks were commonly lost – in a variety of ways: the whole £500,000 receiving a FYA; being omitted completely; being given an AIA/WDA; or simply being treated as R&D revenue expenditure. The other most common error was to include the long life asset in the main pool.

46.2 Many students scored full marks but a significant number either included Acqua Ltd in the group or reversed the definitions and so included Ponte Ltd in the loss group rather than the gains group.

Interestingly a number of students included John Smith in the groups.

46.3 Students seemed to forget their answer to part 2 when it came to answering part 3.

Most students calculated the gain on the share disposal, although it was very common to round the indexation allowance.

However, the application of the capital and trading losses rules was atrocious. Students seemed to be confused concerning the basic rules re offsetting trading and capital losses. The most common mistakes were:

- offsetting any loss in any company irrespective of which company was in which group
- offsetting the trading loss brought forward in Onda Ltd incorrectly
- offsetting capital losses against other income
- offsetting group relief only against trading profits

Often the explanations regarding the loss offset, if there were any at all, referred to income tax rules.

The confused nature of many answers and the erratic nature of their presentation, gave the impression that many students did not know how to approach the question. A columnar approach rather than multiple taxable total profits workings is much easier to mark and much easier for the candidates to follow what has been allocated where. Students are strongly encouraged to use a columnar layout (ie, one column per company) in a single taxable total profits working. [Note that due to the introduction of new rules regarding corporate loss relief this question has been amended since it was originally set.]

47 Indira (June 2016)

Marking guide

			Marks
47.1 (a)	Annual rent	1	
	Interest on loan to buy lease	1	
	Windows	1	
	Legal fees	½	
	Adverts	½	
	Staff party	1	
	NIC on staff party	½	
	Corporate hospitality	½	
	Parking fine	½	
	Goods taken for own use	1	
	Trade samples	½	
	Less capital allowances	½	
	Capital allowances (W1)		
	P&M and AIA	1	
	WDA @18%	½	
	WDA on Indira's car	1	
	WDA on Sanjeev's car	1	
			12
(b)	Allocation for first 5 months	1	
	Salary	1	
	Allocation of remaining profits	1	
			3
(c)	Existing partners - CYB	1	
	New partner - opening year rules	1	
	(W1)	1	
			3

(d) Class 2 ½
Class 4 NIC @9% 1½
Class 4 NIC @2% <u>1</u>
3

47.2 (a) Vouchers ½
Beneficial loan interest on loan 1½
General round sum allowance 1
SMRS deduction ½
Subscription 1
GAYE 1
SMRS calculation (W1) <u>1½</u>
7

(b) Lottery ½
Personal allowance ½
IT on non-savings income ½
IT on savings income 1
IT on dividend income 1
Property income (W1) 1½
Extension of basic rate band (W2) <u>1</u>
6

47.3 Amount on which interest is charged
Lower of ½
Two amounts for comparison 2
Less payment actually made ½
First POA
Due date ½
Interest period ½
Interest ½
Second POA
Due date ½
Interest period for late payment ½
Interest amount 1
Interest period for excessive reduction in POA ½
Interest amount <u>½</u>
7½

Max <u>6</u>
<u>40</u>

47.1 (a) Partnership tax adjusted trading profits for year ended 31 December 2018

	£
Draft profit	171,000
Less:	
Annual rent = £24,000 × 7/12	(14,000)
Interest on loan to fund expansion = £200,000 × 5% × 7/12	(5,833)
Windows – capex as building was not useable until done	0
Legal fees – as a new lease, disallowed as capex	0
Newspaper adverts	(7,012)
Staff party – £150 is for employment income purposes only	(1,000)
NIC on staff party = own figure × 13.8%	(138)
Corporate hospitality	0
Parking fine	0
Goods taken for own use (selling price)	500
Trade sample of silk scarves	(982)
Less capital allowances (W1)	(41,850)
Adjusted trading profit	100,685

Capital allowances (W1)	Main pool £	PUA – 75% £	PUA – 60% £	Allowances £
TWDV b/f	76,500	18,000		
Acquisition – No FYA/AIA			25,000	
Acquisition – AIA	12,000			
AIA	(12,000)			12,000
WDA @ 18%	(13,770)			13,770
WDA @ 8%		(1,440)	× 75%	1,080
FYA @ 100%			(25,000) × 60%	15,000
	62,730	16,560	–	41,850

(b)

	Indira £	Chakor £	Sanjeev £	Total £
1.1.18 to 31.5.18 (5 months)				
PSR = 1:1	20,976	20,976		41,952
1.6.18 to 31.12.18 (7 months)				
Salary x 7/12	8,750			8,750
β PSR = 2:2:1	19,993	19,993	9,997	β49,983
	49,719	40,969	9,997	100,685

(c)

Indira and Chakor's trading income assessment		£
2018/19	CYB (from part 1(b))	
	Indira	49,719
	Chakor	40,969

Sanjeev's trading income assessment		£
2018/19	Opening year rules	
	1.6.18 – 31.12.18 = 7 months	9,997
	1.1.19 – 5.4.19 = 3/12 × 20,000 (W)	5,000
		14,997

WORKING		
Sanjeev's share of profits for y/e 31.12.19		£
	(£115,000 – £15,000) × 1/5	20,000

(d)

	£
Class 2 NIC	
£2.95 × 52	153
Class 4	
(£46,350 – £8,424) × 9%	3,413
(£49,719 – £46,350) × 2%	67
	3,480

47.2 (a) **Meera's employment income**

	£
Salary	45,000
Vouchers	2,250
Loan = £100,000 × (2.5% – 1%) × 3/12	375
General round sum allowance	8,000
SMRS (W)	(2,000)
	53,625
Less subscription	(250)
GAYE = £50 × 12	(600)
	52,775

WORKING

SMRS

	£	£
Meera received 12,000 × £0.25		3,000
Meera was entitled to		
10,000 × £0.45	4,500	
2,000 × £0.25	500	
		(5,000)
		(2,000)

(b)

Meera income tax liability for 2018/19	NSI £	Savings £	Dividend £
Employment income (part (a))	52,775		
Property income (W1)	7,700		
Lottery – exempt	0		
Bank interest		8,125	
Dividend			7,800
Net income	60,475	8,125	7,800
Less personal allowance	(11,850)		
Taxable income	48,625	8,125	7,800

Non-savings income (W2)	£36,000	× 20%	7,200
	£12,625	× 40%	5,050
Savings income	£500	× 0%	0
	£7,625	× 40%	3,050
Dividend income	£2,000	× 0%	0
	£5,800	× 32.5%	1,885
Income tax liability			17,185

WORKINGS

(1) **Property income** (cash basis)	£
Rent received	15,000
Less costs	(7,300)
	7,700

(2) **Extended band**	£
BRB	34,500
PPC × 100/80	1,500
	36,000

47.3

Sunil claim to reduce POA	£
Interest will be charged on lower of:	
Reduced POA plus 50% of the balancing payment = £10,000 + (50% × £19,000)	19,500
Original POA (£25,000 + £3,000) × 50%	14,000
Ie, £14,000 less payment actually made of £10,000 = £4,000	

First POA	£
Due 31 January 2018	
Interest due from 1 February 2018 to 31 May 2019	
£4,000 × 3% × 16/12	160

Second POA	
Due 31 July 2018	
Interest on late paid POA	
Interest due from 1 August 2018 to 31 August 2018	
£10,000 × 3% × 1/12	25

Interest on excessive reduction in POA	
Interest due from 1 August 2018 to 31 May 2019	
£4,000 × 3% × 10/12	100

Examiner's comments

47.1 (a)   There were some very good and some very poor answers. The poorer answers often did not understand how to make the correct adjustments to the draft profit figure eg, adding back hospitality instead of not deducting it – but they were normally inconsistent so it was not because they had misunderstood the question.

Common errors in the adjustment of profits included allowing the expenditure on the new windows and the legal fees for the new lease; using the employment income limit of £150 for the staff entertaining; and allowing the parking fine.

A very small number of students did misread the question and assumed that the items listed had already been included in the draft profit figure. Students must read the question carefully to see what information they have been given.

(b)   Many students made a reasonable attempt at allocating profits, although some omitted the salary or included a full 12 months of salary.

(c)   This was by far the worst answered question on the exam. Students did not seem to know that the continuing partners would use the current year basis while the new partner would need to use opening year rules.

Most students attempted various forms of apportionment or allocated profits of the wrong accounting period.

(d)   Many students did well on this part of the question, although as always, a significant number also tried to calculate class 1 NIC on the partner's 'salary'.

47.2 (a)   Many students gained good marks on this question. Common errors included an incorrect valuation of the shopping vouchers, deducting some costs from the round sum allowance and not deducting the payroll giving to arrive at an employment income figure.

(b)   Students generally produced good answers to this question.

47.3 Answers to this question were generally poor. Many students made little attempt but could still have scored easy marks by answering the question and stating due dates of payment for the payments on account. Those who did make an attempt at the question usually only considered whether the actual payments made were made on time (and could as a result get 2½ of the marks). Only a very small number considered that the payments on account were too small and so they could gain marks for late payment interest on the excess.

The vast majority of those making calculations also considered the balancing payment but the question only asked for consideration of the payments on account.

A lot of marks could have been gained by judicious use of the open book, but not the sections on quarterly CT payments or PAYE for a question about an individual's payments on account.

Students are reminded that where a date is requested they must state the day, month and year.

September 2016 exam answers

48 Teresa (September 2016)

		Marks
48.1 Unlimited fine	½	
Custodial sentence	½	
Five years	½	
ICAEW disciplinary action	½	
		2
48.2 No knowledge or suspicion of ML	1	
Privilege reporting exemption	1	
Reasonable excuse such as threat to safety	1	
ML occurring outside UK where not unlawful in that country	1	
	4	
Max		2
48.3 Check engagement letter for permission to disclose	½	
Accountant contact HMRC if permission	½	
Ask client permission to contact HMRC	½	
Document conversations	½	
Resign	½	
SAR	½	
To NCA	½	
	3½	
Max		3
		7

48.1 If found guilty of a failure to disclose an ICAEW Chartered Accountant could face an unlimited fine and a custodial sentence of up to five years.

In addition the accountant is likely to face disciplinary action by ICAEW and could face further fines, or a possible striking off.

48.2 **Potential defences**

The possible defences for failure to disclose are:

- the accountant did not know or suspect money laundering had occurred.

- the accountant has a suspicion or reasonable grounds for knowing/suspecting that the client was engaged in money laundering, but the knowledge came to him/her in privileged circumstances (the privilege reporting exemption).

- there is reasonable excuse for not making a report (extreme circumstances such as a threat to personal safety).

- it is known or believed that the money laundering is occurring outside of the UK, and is not unlawful under the criminal law of the country where it is occurring.

48.3 Teresa should have checked her engagement letter to see whether she has permission to contact HMRC directly, without a breach of confidentiality. If so she should have contacted HMRC to check whether the repayment was correct. Otherwise she should have asked the client's permission to contact HMRC.

All of her conversations with her client and her advice to him should have been documented.

If she was not given permission to disclose then she should have resigned.

To avoid a charge for failure to disclose under POCA 2002 Teresa, as the money laundering reporting officer, should have submitted a suspicious activity report (SAR) to the National Crime Agency (NCA).

Examiner's comments

48.1 Many students answered this part well and often scored three of the four half marks available.

48.2 Students had some worrying ideas for possible defences against a charge of failure to report money laundering. They included the accountant only acting as agent and so taking no responsibility, and, most commonly, the accountant not being allowed to breach client confidentiality. Students also listed professional indemnity insurance as a defence. This suggestion that a potential breach of confidentiality overrides the need to report money laundering is worrying.

48.3 Many students knew some of the actions an ICAEW Chartered Accountant should take regarding a repayment made in error by HMRC. Rather strangely given the flags towards money laundering in the question, some did not address actions in relation to this. While many recognised that a sole practitioner would not be able to refer to a money laundering reporting officer, some thought the only course of action was to refer to ICAEW or HMRC.

49 Star Ltd (September 2016)

Marking guide

		Marks
49.1 VAT payable		
Output tax (½ per entry)	3	
Input tax (½ per entry)	2½	
VAT payable	½	
China materials – correct output tax treatment	½	
	6½	
Max		6
49.2 (a) New residential property – zero rated	½	
Letting residential property – exempt	½	
OTT – for commercial property only	½	
New commercial property – standard rated	½	
Input VAT – at 20% and irrecoverable	1	
Letting – exempt	½	
Rent standard rated if OTT	½	
Recover input tax on purchase and rental costs	1	
	5	
Max		4
(b) SDLT – residential property (½ per band)	1	
SDLT on VAT inclusive amount	1	
SDLT – commercial property (½ per band)	1	
		3
		13

49.1 VAT payable for quarter ended 31 March 2019

Output tax		£	£
Sales in the UK	£385,000 × 20%		77,000
Sales elsewhere in the EU:			
To other businesses			0
To individuals	£15,400 × 20%		3,080
Overseas sales outside the EU:			
To other businesses			0
To individuals			0
Professional services – reverse charge			1,440
			81,520

Input tax			
Materials – all standard-rated goods:			
• UK suppliers	£105,000 × 1/6	17,500	
• suppliers in China	£78,000 × 20%	15,600	
Car	Blocked	–	
Other overhead costs	£42,000 × 1/6	7,000	
Professional services (China)	£7,200 × 20%	1,440	
			(41,540)

VAT payable by Star Ltd   39,980

Note: Star Ltd paid customs duty of £15,600 at point of entry into the UK on the materials from China.

49.2 (a) Residential property

The supply of new residential property is a zero-rated supply. VAT will be charged at 0%.

The letting of residential property is an exempt supply so no VAT will be charged.

The option to tax cannot be made on residential property.

New commercial building

The purchase of the new (less than 3 years) freehold commercial property will be a standard-rated supply.

Hence Caitlin will suffer irrecoverable input tax of £40,000 (£200,000 × 20%).

The letting of the property is an exempt supply, so no VAT will be charged.

Option to tax

If Caitlin makes an option to tax when letting the commercial building, she must charge VAT at 20% on the rents that she charges her tenants.

She will also be able to recover input tax on her costs of renting and also on the purchase of the new building.

(b) SDLT payable

Residential property

	£
£125,000 × 3%	3,750
£75,000 × 5%	3,750
£200,000	7,500

New freehold commercial property

SDLT on VAT inclusive price of £240,000 (£200,000 × 120%)

	£
£150,000 × 0%	0
£90,000 × 2%	1,800
£240,000	1,800

49.1 Many students performed the calculations well, with most scoring at least 4 out of 6. The main points that were missed were how to deal with the overseas sales outside the EU (many thinking that output VAT would be charged) and not knowing that the professional services would have a reverse charge and where it was included, included inputs and outputs of £1,200 instead of £1,440. The point that few got right was how to deal with the materials from the suppliers in China. Some incorrectly included a reverse charge of £15,600 although the majority calculated the input and output at £13,000.

49.2 (a) There were some good answers in which students made it quite clear which property they were dealing with and which logically covered the different transactions of purchase, renting and opting to tax.

However, there were many poor answers. This was partly because students had not learned the basic technical knowledge ie, that the supply of new residential property is zero rated and new commercial property is standard-rated. Other students did not set out answers well, so it was not clear which property was being discussed. They used vague, non-technical language, for example no VAT charged as opposed to zero-rated or exempt.

Quite a common misconception was that Caitlin opting to tax would affect the VAT charged on the purchase, rather than just the rent.

(b) Most students made a reasonable attempt at this part.

50 Carmen (September 2016)

Marking guide

		Marks
50.1 (a) Share proceeds	½	
Share cost	½	
No gift relief on share gain	½	
Land gross proceeds	½	
Less selling costs	½	
Less land cost	1	
UK gains taxed whether claim or not	½	
Overseas gains only taxed if no claim	1	
AEA only if no claim	1	
CGT at 20%	½	
DTR calculation	1½	
DTR only if no claim	1	
RBC	½	
Share pool initial purchase (W1)	½	
Rights issue	1	
Disposal	½	
	11½	
Max		11
(b) Gain over period from 5 April 2015	1	
PPR	½	
PPR – periods from 5 April 2015	1½	
		3

		Marks
50.2 June 2010 gift – no IHT on death	½	
PET – June 2012		
AE	½	
Fall in value relief	½	
NRB	1	
Tax on death	½	
Taper relief	½	
Death estate		
House	½	
Cash	½	
BPR shares	1	
Less debts	½	
Residence nil rate band (including wife's)	1	
NRB	1½	
Tax at 40%	½	
Lifetime tax on June 2010 gift		
Cash less AEs	½	
NRB	½	
Lifetime tax	½	
Gross chargeable transfer	½	
		11
		25

50.1 (a) Tax liability for 2018/19 in respect of disposals

Widmore Ltd shares

	£
Proceeds (market value to brother) £45 × 4,500	202,500
Less cost (W1)	(72,000)
	130,500

Land in Ruritania

	£
Proceeds	520,000
Less selling costs 3% × £520,000	(15,600)
	504,400
Less cost	

$$\frac{520,000}{520,000+150,000} \times £120,000$$

	(93,134)
	411,266

UK liability in respect of disposals

	No claim £	RB claim £
Total UK gains	130,500	130,500
Ruritanian gains	411,266	–
	541,766	130,500
Less annual exempt amount	(11,700)	N/A
Taxable gains	530,066	130,500
CGT @ 20% as taxable income in excess of BRB	106,013	26,100
Less double tax relief – lower of:		
UK tax on overseas gains 20% × £411,266 = £82,253		
Overseas tax £63,100		
Ie, £63,100	(63,100)	N/A
Add remittance basis charge (12 out of 14 years)		60,000
Tax payable in respect of disposals	42,913	86,100

WORKING

Share pool	Number	Cost £
August 2007 – purchase	6,000	90,000
July 2009 – Rights issue 1-for-4	1,500	30,000
£20 × 1,500		
	7,500	120,000
Disposal (4,500/7,500)	(4,500)	(72,000)
	3,000	48,000

(b) **Chargeable gain on sale of house after becoming non-UK resident**

Proceeds	450,000
Less market value at 5 April 2015	(375,000)
Gain over period from 5 April 2015	75,000
Less PPR £75,000 × 78/84	(69,643)
Chargeable gain	5,357

WORKING
PPR

Only consider periods from 5 April 2015
6 April 2015 – 5 April 2020 – actual occupation = 60 months exempt
6 April 2020 – 5 October 2020 – no occupation so 6 months taxable
6 October 2020 – 5 April 2022 – last 18 months exempt

Total period = 60 + 6 + 18 = 84

50.2

	June 2010 CLT £	January 2012 PET £	December 2018 Death (W1) £
Stage 1 – Transfers			
Transfer	342,000	98,000	
Less exemptions			
Annual	(3,000)		
Annual b/f	(3,000)	(3,000)	
	336,000	95,000	784,700
Stage 2 – Lifetime tax			
Less remaining NRB (W2)	(325,000)	No LT tax	
	11,000		
IHT @ 20/80	2,750		
Gross chargeable transfer			
(£336,000 + £2,750)	338,750	95,000	784,700
Stage 3 – Tax on death			
Gross chargeable transfer	More than 7 years	95,000	784,700
Less fall in value relief		(20,000)	
Less residence NRB (including Kate's)			(250,000)
Less remaining NRB (W2)		-	(230,000)
		75,000	304,700
IHT @ 40%		30,000	121,880
Taper relief (6-7 yrs) 20% chargeable		6,000	
Tax payable on death		6,000	121,880

WORKINGS

(1) **Death estate**

House less mortgage (860,000 – £350,000)		510,000
Cash and personal effects		290,000
Shares in Lapidus Ltd	140,000	
Less 100% BPR	(140,000)	
		Nil
Less debts		(15,300)
		784,700

(2) **Remaining nil rate band**

	June 2010 CLT £	January 2012 PET £	December 2018 Death £
Stage 2 – Lifetime			
Lifetime NRB	325,000		
Less chargeable in previous 7 years	-		
Remaining NRB	325,000		
			-
Stage 3 – On death			
NRB at death	N/A	325,000	325,000
Less chargeable in previous 7 years (use value pre-FIV relief)		(338,750)	(95,000)
Remaining NRB		-	230,000

Examiner's comments

50.1 (a) Students had obviously prepared well for a capital gains tax question with overseas elements. Many students achieved full, or nearly full marks, on this requirement.

Only a handful of students thought that the land would only be taxed if the remittance basis applied. The main areas for candidates losing marks were the following:

- Applying gift relief to the disposal of shares.

- Calculating the part disposal of the land incorrectly. This involved taking the net sale proceeds as A or more commonly confusing the cost of £120,000 and the value of the remainder B £150,000.

- Ignoring the DTR or taking as £63,100 without comparing it to the UK tax.

- Ignoring the RBC or taking it as £30,000 or £90,000.

(b) Students were clearly not prepared for this new topic of legislation. However it was possible to gain marks with a knowledge of some aspects of PPR, for example the 18 month rule.

50.2 Students generally performed well on this part, with common errors being the failure to identify business property relief and a large number of students incorrectly calculating QSR. [Note that the residence nil rate band was not initially in this question when set but has been added in due to the finance act update on the syllabus.]

51 Faraday Ltd (September 2016)

		Marks
51.1 Loss relief group	1	
Gains group	1	
		2
51.2 Taxable total profits	½	
CT at 19%	½	
Adjusted profit (W1)		
R&D expenditure at 100%	1	
Qualifying R&D expenditure	1½	
Enhanced deduction	½	
Less arrangement fee	½	
Less capital allowances	½	
Capital allowances (W2)		
WDA	½	
AIA	½	
FYA	½	
NTLR (W3)		
Interest on loan stock	½	
Profit on loan stock	1	
Less interest on shares loan	½	
Gain (W4)		
Unindexed gain	½	
Indexation allowance	½	
Rollover relief	1	
Less capital losses	1	
Proceeds not reinvested (W5)		
Burke Place	½	
Group assets	1	
		13
		15

51.1 Faraday Ltd and Straume Ltd form a loss relief group.

Faraday Ltd, Straume Ltd and Rutherford Ltd form a chargeable gains group.

51.2

	£
Tax-adjusted trading profit (W1)	452,590
Non-trading loan relationship (W3)	8,460
Chargeable gains (W4)	101,000
Taxable total profits	562,050
Corporation tax payable	
FY2018 – £562,050 × 19%	106,790

WORKINGS

		£	£
(1)	**Tax-adjusted trading profit**		
	Draft tax-adjusted trading profits		621,400
	Less		
	R&D expenditure (100%)		
	Staff costs		(48,000)
	Computer software		(3,700)

	£	£
Qualifying R&D expenditure		
Staff costs (65% for agency workers) £48,000 × 65%	31,200	
Computer software	3,700	
	34,900	
Additional R&D deduction £34,900 × 130%		(45,370)
Arrangement fee		(400)
Capital allowances (W2)		(71,340)
		452,590

(2) **Capital allowances**	£
Main pool £158,000 x 18%	28,440
Machinery addition – AIA	40,000
R&D computer hardware – FYA	2,900
	71,340

(3) **Non-trading loan relationship**	
Interest receivable on loan stock	1,560
Profit on sale of loan stock (£46,000 – £38,000)	8,000
Less Interest on shares loan	(1,100)
	8,460

(4) **Gain on Austen Towers**	
Sale proceeds	580,000
Less cost	(210,000)
	370,000

Less indexation allowance $\dfrac{278.1 - 163.0}{163.0} = 0.706 \times £210,000$	(148,260)
	221,740
Less rollover relief β	(91,740)
Remaining gain (proceeds not reinvested (W5)	130,000
Less Rutherford Ltd capital losses transferred – gains group	(29,000)
	101,000

(5) **Proceeds not reinvested**	
Sale proceeds	580,000
Less cost of Burke Place	(300,000)
Less cost of Straume factory	(150,000)
Proceeds not reinvested	130,000

Examiner's comments

51.1 Most students answered this part well.

51.2 Students' answers were rarely excellent or very poor but revealed some misunderstandings, in particular in relation to groups. If students understood capital allowances and R&D, they could still score well enough but would have been in danger, had the group, particularly the loss, elements been more crucial to the question. In this case, the trading loss of another company could not be used as the two companies concerned were not in a loss group. However, even when erroneously used, students set trading losses against trading income only, or even against a tax liability figure. Conversely, they set capital losses against TTP in a number of cases. Few students understood the relevance of the figures given for capital investments by other group companies. Students were generally weak on the interaction of group aspects within a single company calculation and were fortunate that it only amounted to 3 out of the 13 marks available.

52 Omar, Pierre and Sayid (September 2016)

			Marks
52.1 (a)	Depreciation	½	
	Car lease cost	½	
	Fines	½	
	Legal and professional fees	1½	
	Repairs	1½	
	Goods taken for own use – selling price	1½	
	Business expenditure paid by Pierre	½	
	Less capital allowances	½	
	Car lease (W1)	1½	
	Capital allowances (W2)		
	Purchases (½ per item)	2½	
	AIA	1	
	WDA at 18%	½	
	WDA at 8%	½	
	WDA on private use car	1	
			14
(b)	Period to 31 July		
	Profit for period	½	
	Salary	½	
	Interest	½	
	PSR	1	
	Period from 1 August		
	PSR	1	
	Total	½	
			4
(c)	2018/19	1	
			1
(d)	Unincorporated business	½	
	Receipts not exceed £150,000	1	
	Not eligible as receipts must exceed this	1	
		2½	
		Max	2
52.2 (a)	Salary	½	
	Round sum allowance	½	
	Car benefit	1	
	Fuel benefit	½	
	Private medical insurance	½	
	Vouchers	½	
	Pension contributions	1	
	Professional subscription	½	
			5
(b)	11 months		
	Monthly earnings	½	
	NIC	1	
	1 month		
	Earnings	½	
	NIC	1	
			3

(c) Dividends — ½
Personal allowance — ½
IT on non-savings income — ½
IT on dividend income — ½
Property income (W1) — 2
Extended bands — ½
20% tax reduction for remaining finance costs — ½
5

(d) Cash received (½ mark per item) — 2
Cash paid (½ mark per expense) — 4
6
40

52.1 (a) Partnership tax adjusted trading profits for year ended 31 January 2019

	£
Draft profit	413,633
Add:	
Depreciation	42,100
Car lease cost (W1)	2,980
Fines – breach of health and safety	2,500
Legal and professional fees – factory purchase	2,100
No adjustments for fees re debt recovery and cost of registering patent	-
Repairs – chimney (capital as required)	10,000
Repairs – redecoration	-
Repairs – double glazing (capital)	6,000
Goods taken for own use (selling price) £1,200 × 140%	1,680
Business expenditure paid by Pierre	(500)
Less:	
Less capital allowances (W2)	(214,372)
Adjusted trading profit	266,121

WORKINGS

(1) **Car lease**

	£
Allowable lease cost = £4,000 × 85% × 30%	1,020
So disallowable amount is £4,000 – £1,020	2,980

(2) **Capital allowances**

	Main pool £	Special rate pool £	PUA – 40% £	Allowances £
TWDV b/f	35,000	23,000		
Purchases – AIA				
Ford van	15,000			
Machinery	140,000			
Wall – not qualifying				
Thermal insulation		75,000		
AIA – restricted, SRP first	(125,000)	(75,000)		200,000
Purchases – non-AIA				
Omar car			26,000	
	65,000	23,000	26,000	
WDA @ 18%/8%	(11,700)	(1,840)		13,540
WDA @ 8%			(2,080) × 40%	832
	53,300	21,160	23,920	214,372

(b)

	Omar £	Pierre £	Sayid £	Total £
To 31 July 2018 (6/12 × £266,121) £133,060				
Salary (6/12)	10,000			10,000
Interest on capital (4% × 6/12)	1,000	1,000	2,000	4,000
PSR = 30:50:20	35,718	59,530	23,812	119,060
				133,060
From 1 August 2018				
PSR =1:1	66,530	66,531		133,061
£266,121 × 6/12				
	113,248	127,061	25,812	266,121

(c) **Sayid taxable trading profit for 2018/19**

Final period 1 Feb 2018 to 31 July 2018	25,812
Less overlap profit	(5,000)
	20,812

(d) The cash basis of accounting can be used by unincorporated businesses ie, sole traders and partnerships.

To be eligible to join the receipts of the business must not exceed £150,000.

As profits are expected to be over £400,000 pa then receipts must exceed £150,000 and the partnership is not eligible to use the cash basis of accounting.

52.2 (a) **Regina's employment income**

	£
Salary £3,200 × 12	38,400
Round sum allowance	2,400
Car (£25,000 – £5,000) × 19%	3,800
Fuel benefit £23,400 × 19%	4,446
Private medical insurance	400
Vouchers – cost to employer	230
Employer pension contributions – exempt	-
	49,676
Less	
Professional subscription	(200)
	49,476

(b)

Class 1 NIC	£
11 months	
Monthly earnings £3,200 + £200 = £3,400	
(3,400 – 702) × 12% = £324 × 11	3,564
1 month – December	
Earnings £3,400 + £230 = £3,630	
(3,630 – 702) × 12%	351
	3,915

(c)

Regina's income tax liability 2018/19			NSI £	Dividend £
Employment income (part 2a)			49,476	
Property income (W1)			10,390	
Dividend (£610 – £110)				500
Net income			59,866	500
Less personal allowance			(11,850)	
Taxable income			48,016	500
Non-savings income (W2)	£37,380	× 20%		7,476
	£10,636	× 40%		4,254
Dividend income	£500	× 0%		0
Less 20% tax reduction for remaining finance costs (W3) 20% × £200				(40)
Income tax liability				11,690

WORKINGS

(1) **Property income** (cash basis)	£
Rent received	12,000
Less insurance paid	(240)
50% x interest on the mortgage (50% × £400)	(200)
Sofa replacement	(1,170)
	10,390

(2) **Extended bands**	£
BRB	34,500
PPC = (6% × £38,400) = × 100/80	2,880
	37,380

(3) The 20% tax reduction is based on the lower of:

- 50% of finance costs (£400 × 50% = £200)

- property income (£10,390)

- adjusted total income that exceeds the PA (£59,866 – 11,850 = £48,016)

So the deduction will be 20% × £200

(d) **Regina's cash available in 2018/19**

	£	£
Cash received		
Salary		38,400
Round sum allowance less entertaining expenses (£2,400 – £2,170)		230
Rental income		12,000
Dividends		610
		51,240
Cash paid		
Pension contributions paid 6% × £38,400 (2c)	2,304	
Subscriptions paid	200	
Rental expenses paid in the year – insurance	240	
Rental expenses paid in the year – interest	400	
Rental expenses paid in the year – sofa	1,170	
Household bills	16,000	
Income tax liability (2c)	11,690	
National insurance contributions (2b)	3,915	
		35,919
Cash available		15,321

Examiner's comments

52.1 (a) Students usually scored quite well on this part. Most difficulties arose in the treatment of the car lease and aspects of the capital allowances computation. The van often had its own pool, or was in the special rate pool and was not given the AIA.

(b) Students often struggled with the allocation of profits for the first six months by not pro rating the salary and interest on capital and/or using the PSR on the whole of the six months of profits rather than remaining profits. Markers also noted that students rarely showed clear workings on this part.

(c) This one easy mark was frequently lost. Common errors included adding overlap profits or prorating the profit share from part (b).

(d) Most students knew that the cash basis could not apply but thought the limit was based on profits not receipts. Many hedged their bets and used the word 'earnings'. A small number of students answered the question as if it related to cash accounting for VAT purposes.

52.2 (a) Many students produced excellent answers. However a significant number made a least one of the following errors; treated the medical insurance as exempt, deducted the £5,000 limit after the 19% charge on the car benefit, deducted the entertaining costs from the round sum allowance and incorrectly treated the pension payments.

(b) Most students performed poorly on this part. The vast majority calculated the NIC on annual sums not monthly and either included total employment income, deducted the entertaining expenses from the round sum or missed the vouchers.

(c) Most students used the standard income tax pro forma and presented their answer very well.

(d) Students very occasionally omitted this part although most attempted it, some with significant success. Students either made a decent, sometimes excellent, attempt, or took a single income figure from their income tax computation and deducted tax and one other expense figure. They needed to start again and think of all items of income and expenditure from a cash, rather than tax, perspective. Those who did so usually scored well.

December 2016 exam answers

53 Johanna (December 2016)

		Marks
53.1 Identify objectivity	1	
Explanation	1	
		2
53.2 Johanna retains responsibility	½	
DB LLP acts as agent	½	
Accountants responsible for accuracy of return	½	
Not required to audit the figures	½	
Take reasonable care	½	
Professional scepticism	½	
Accountant not normally liable to HMRC	½	
	3½	
	Max	3
53.3 Advice from ICAEW/legal advisors	1	
Document discussions	1	
Consider resigning	1	
	3	
	Max	2
		7

53.1 The fundamental principle of objectivity is threatened.

This is an intimidation threat, arising from the pressure applied by Johanna about reporting the firm to ICAEW.

53.2 Johanna retains responsibility for the accuracy of her own VAT return.

DB LLP is acting as an agent rather than a principal when preparing and submitting the VAT return.

The accountants are responsible to Johanna for the accuracy of the return based on the information provided by her. They are not required to audit the figures provided. However, they must take reasonable care and exercise appropriate professional scepticism.

The accountants would not normally be liable to HMRC if any of the information proves to be incorrect.

53.3 DB LLP may obtain advice from ICAEW or legal advisors on legal and ethical issues without breaching confidentiality. The firm could contact ICAEW confidential helpline.

Details of any discussions/decisions concerning this issue should be documented in writing.

DB LLP should consider resigning from the engagement.

53.1 Many candidates answered this part well with many scoring at least 1.5 of the two marks available.

53.2 Candidates making a good attempt at this part quoted verbatim what they had been taught on principal v agent role and most then applied this knowledge. However a significant number sat on the fence stating 'If an agent….. or if acting as principal'. Another significant number incorrectly identified the accountant's role as that of principal. These did not score well.

53.3 Many candidates knew the actions an ICAEW Chartered Accountant should take regarding the threat. This part was generally well answered.

54 Yemi Ltd group (December 2016)

Marking guide

		Marks
54.1 Fixed establishment in UK	½	
Controls	½	
Explanation of control	1	
		2
54.2 no VAT on intra-group supplies	½	
Save administration time and costs	½	
Aldo – cause whole group to be partially exempt	½	
– unless below *de minimis*	½	
Kwon – no UK fixed establishment	1	
Dorrit – lose cashflow benefit of monthly repayments	1½	
	4½	
	Max	4
54.3 Eko in VAT group	½	
Eko not in VAT group	2	
	2½	
	Max	2
54.4 Purchase by Dorrit	2	
Purchase by Eko		
- Not in SDLT group so SDLT payable	1½	
- Assuming in a VAT group	1	
- Assuming not in a VAT group	1½	
	6	
	Max	5
		13

54.1 Two or more companies can be in a VAT group together if each has a fixed establishment in the UK and:

- one controls the other;
- one person (individual or company) controls them all; or
- two or more persons in partnership control all of them

where control means there is a shareholding of more than 50%.

54.2 Yemi Ltd and Eko Ltd should be included in a group VAT registration so that intra-group supplies can be made without accounting for VAT, and to save on administrative time and costs.

Aldo Ltd makes exempt supplies and could cause the whole group to become partially exempt. It should not be in a group with Yemi Ltd unless the level of exempt input VAT is *de minimis* such that it would not affect the recoverability of input tax for the whole group.

Kwon SA does not have a UK fixed establishment and so cannot be in a group for VAT purposes.

Dorrit Ltd should not be in a VAT group with Yemi, as it would lose the cashflow benefit of monthly VAT repayments.

54.3 Eko Ltd in the VAT group:

If Eko Ltd is in a VAT group with Yemi Ltd then no VAT is charged on the intra-group supply of the building.

Eko Ltd not in the VAT group:

The sale of the building is standard rated as it is a sale of a 'new' building, ie less than three years old.

Input tax of £40,000 (£200,000 × 20%) will be suffered by Eko Ltd. This cannot be recovered as Eko Ltd will be making exempt supplies from the building (ie renting it out).

As the original cost was below £250,000 the capital goods scheme does not apply.

54.4 **Purchase by Dorrit Ltd**

As Yemi Ltd directly owns at least 75% of Dorrit Ltd they are in the same group for SDLT purposes.

Therefore an exemption applies and there is no SDLT on sale.

Purchase by Eko Ltd

Although the direct shareholdings to Eko Ltd are at least 75%, the indirect shareholding from Yemi Ltd to Eko Ltd is less than 75% (80% × 80% = 64%), so they are not in a group for SDLT purposes.

So SDLT will be payable by Eko Ltd.

The amount payable will depend on whether Eko Ltd is in a VAT group with Yemi Ltd.

Assuming Eko Ltd is in a VAT group with Yemi, no VAT is charged.

The SDLT payable by Eko Ltd is £1,000.

$$£150,000 \times 0\% = \quad 0$$
$$£90,000 \times 2\% = \quad \underline{1,000}$$
$$\underline{£1,000}$$

If they are not in a VAT group, as the building is less than 3 years old VAT should be charged at the standard rate on the sale.

The SDLT payable by Eko Ltd is based on £240,000 (£200,000 × 1.2).

$$£150,000 \times 0\% = \quad 0$$
$$£50,000 \times 2\% = \quad \underline{1,800}$$
$$\underline{£1,800}$$

The SDLT is payable within 30 days of the sale of the building ie, by 19 February 2020.

54.1 Many candidates lost marks for inaccurate use of language. 'Control' is a key word in relation to VAT groups. Many candidates stated that companies should be UK resident which is not the same as having a UK fixed establishment.

54.2 It appeared that many candidates had learned the answer to requirement 54.2 without understanding the reason behind the answer. So for example a lot of students knew that traders making wholly zero-rated or wholly exempt supplies should not be included in the group but could not give the correct reason, or in some cases could not give any reason. This lack of understanding also led to some contradictory answers between 54.2 and 54.3 re the implications of supplies between group members.

54.3 Many candidates incorrectly stated that transactions within a group are 'exempt'. Some candidates thought that the difference was in whether VAT was recoverable rather than whether it was actually charged, with only a few identifying that VAT is non-recoverable for Eko Ltd as it makes an exempt supply by leasing the building. A number of candidates discussed the differences if an option to tax has been made, even though the question clearly states that no option to tax is made.

54.4 Very few candidates discussed the SDLT group and thought that Dorrit Ltd would pay SDLT. A significant number incorrectly stated that no SDLT would be payable if Eko Ltd was in the VAT group. Most candidates stated that the purchaser would pay but often struggled to get the easy half mark relating to the payment date.

55 Ruby and Todd (December 2016)

Marking guide

		Marks
55.1 AEA (non-ER/Residential Property gains first)	1	
CGT payable	1	
Gain on sale of her home (W1)	2	
Crust sale proceeds (W2)	1½	
Crust gain (W3)	1½	
Crust CBA/CA (W4)	2	
		9
55.2 (a) August 2014 gift – no death tax	½	
March 2019 CLT (ABC shares) – death tax		
– Gross chargeable transfer	½	
– NRB available	1	
– Death tax at 40%	½	
– Less lifetime tax	½	
March 2019 PET (XYZ shares)– death tax		
– Related property valuation	1½	
– Business property relief	½	
– IHT on death	½	
Death estate		
– 100% BPR on XYZ shares	½	
– Spouse exemption	½	
– NRB available	1	
– No RNRB	½	
– Death tax at 40%	½	

	Marks
Lifetime tax on March 2019 gift	
- Value less AE	1
- NRB at gift less GCTs	1
- Lifetime tax	½
- Gross chargeable transfer	½
CLT share valuation	
- Lower of	½
- Quarter up	½
- Mid bargain	½
	13

55.2 (b)		Marks
	BPR no longer available	½
	Revised death tax on lifetime gift	1½
	PET now accumulates into NRB for death estate calculation	1
	FIV relief could be available	½
	No IHT on sale of shares	½
		4
	Max	3
		25

55.1

CGT liability for 2018/19	ER £	Non-ER (Residential property) £
Commercial property (W1)		24,571
Crust plc shares (W3)	250,192	
Less AEA (non-ER gains first)		(11,700)
Taxable gains	250,192	12,871
CGT payable @ 10%/28% = £28,623	25,019	3,604

WORKINGS

(1) **Sale of her home**

	£
Proceeds	458,000
Less cost	(200,000)
Gain	258,000
Less PPR relief ((6.5 + 3)/10.5 × £258,000) (deemed 3 years for any reason)	(233,429)
	24,571

(2) **Crust plc sale proceeds**

Lower quoted price + ½ × (Higher quoted price – lower quoted price)

560 + ½ × (574-560) = 567

So proceeds are 300,000 × £5.67	1,701,000

(3) **Crust plc**

	£
Proceeds (W2)	1,701,000
Less cost	(400,000)
	1,301,000
Less Gift relief (W4) £1,301,000 x 21,000/26,000	(1,050,808)
	250,192

(4) **Crust plc – CBA/CA**

	CBA £'000	CA £'000
Freehold property	20,000	20,000
Leasehold property	-	5,000
Plant and machinery	1,000	1,000
Other assets	-	-
Total	21,000	26,000

55.2 (a)

	31 August 2014 CLT £	16 March 2019 CLT (W1) £	24 March 2019 PET (W2) £	December 2021 Death (W4) £
Stage 1 – Transfers				
Transfer		185,600	114,500	
BPR			(114,500)	
Less exemptions				
Annual		(3,000)		
Annual b/f		(3,000)		
		179,600	-	500,000
Stage 2 – Lifetime tax				
Less remaining NRB (W3)		(25,000)	No LT tax	No LT tax
		154,600		
IHT @ 20/80		38,650		
Gross chargeable transfer (£179,600 + £38,650)	300,000	218,250	-	500,000
Stage 3 – Tax on death				
Gross chargeable transfer	More than 7 years	218,250	-	500,000
Less remaining NRB (W3)		(25,000)	-	(106,750)
		193,250	-	393,250
IHT @ 40%		77,300	-	157,300
Less lifetime tax paid		(38,650)	-	
Tax payable on death		38,650	-	157,300

WORKINGS

(1) **16 March 2019 CLT share valuation**

Shares valued at the lower of
Quarter up 460 + ¼ (476 – 460) = 464
Mid bargain ½ (461 + 471) = 466
Shares £4.64 × 40,000   185,600

(2) **24 March 2019 PET XYZ shares**

Related property valuation
Pre-transfer related holding (85%) £45 × 5,500   247,500
Post transfer related holding (65%) £38 × 3,500   (133,000)
                                                        114,500

(3) **Remaining nil rate band**

	31 August 2014 CLT £	16 March 2019 CLT £	24 March 2019 PET £	December 2021 Death £
Stage 2 – Lifetime				
Lifetime NRB		325,000		
Less chargeable in previous 7 years		(300,000)		
Remaining NRB		25,000		-
Stage 3 – On death				
NRB at death	N/A	325,000		325,000
Less chargeable in previous 7 years (£218,250 + £0)		(300,000)		(218,250)
Remaining NRB		25,000		106,750

(4) **Death estate**

Shares in XYZ Ltd (from W2)	133,000	
Less 100% BPR	(133,000)	-
Other assets		2,000,000
Less spouse exemption		(1,500,000)
		500,000

(b)

If Finn sells his shares in XYZ Ltd prior to Todd's death the BPR on the PET will not be available. IHT will therefore be payable by Finn on the gift of the XYZ Ltd shares.

Hence there will be IHT at death on the PET

	£	£
Transfer		114,500
Nil rate band	325,000	
Less GCTs since 25 March 2012 (£300,000 + £218,250)	(518,250)	Nil
		114,500
IHT @ 40%		45,800

The transfer of £114,500 is also accumulated for the death estate to offset against the nil rate band.

The chargeable death estate will be £500,000 leading to IHT on the death estate of £200,000 (£500,000 × 40%).

If the shares are sold for less than the market value at the date of the PET then fall in value relief will be available on Todd's death.

There is no IHT on a sale of shares.

Examiner's comments

55.1 Candidates produced a wide variety of answers but generally they seemed to struggle more with CGT in this session than previously. Most candidates identified the correct method of calculating the value of the quoted shares however the vast majority then gave 100% gift relief. They generally did not know how to deal with the asset information – many ignored it but others brought the value of the assets into the CGT computation as though there had been a disposal of the assets as well as the shares. This was also then often combined with entrepreneurs' relief adjustments. Those who recognised that an adjustment to gift relief was required generally only adjusted for the leasehold property ignoring the cars and the non-chargeable assets. However most candidates recognised the benefit of setting the annual exempt amount against non-ER gains in priority to ER gains. [Note that the residential property disposal was not in the question as it was originally set but has been added in due to syllabus updates.]

55.2 (a) This part was generally well answered and presented well. Common errors included not recognising that the 'gross chargeable transfer' value of the first CLT was given in the question so that additional calculations were not required (ie, many reduced the £300,000 by £6,000 for annual exemptions) and not recognising that 100% BPR applied to the XYZ Ltd shares. The valuations of the two share disposals were generally dealt with well including the more difficult related property valuation where there were many correct answers.

(b) The quality of answer to this part depended on whether BPR had been identified in the previous part – if so most candidates correctly recognised that the relief would be withdrawn if the donor sold the shares. There were many good answers to this part that demonstrated a very thorough understanding of the implications of the sale both on the gift and the death estate. If candidates failed to identify the BPR issue in the previous part they could still get one out of the three marks available. This was a discriminating part of the exam.

56 Scissor Ltd (December 2016)

Marking guide

		Marks
56.1 Gain exempt	½	
Substantial shareholding explanation	1½	
Explanation of degrouping charge	3	
Calculation of degrouping charge (W)	1½	
	6½	
	Max	5
56.2 Adjustment to profit		
– Interest on loan to purchase Brush Ltd shares	1	
– Computer hardware	½	
– Profit on disposal of shares	½	
– Capital allowances	1	
		6
56.3 Gross up overseas income	½	
RDEC into TTP	1	
TTP	½	
Corporation tax calculation	½	
Deduct RDEC from CT	½	
Double tax relief	1½	
Non-trading loan relationship (W1)	1	
Qualifying R&D (W2)	1½	
		4
		15

56.1 The substantial shareholding exemption applies so the gain on the disposal of Crop Ltd is exempt as Scissor Ltd has owned at least 10% of the shares in Crop Ltd for at least 12 months out of the last 6 years, and Crop Ltd is a trading company.

In addition Crop Ltd and Scissor Ltd were in a gains group when a property was transferred from Scissor Ltd to Crop Ltd under nil gain/ nil loss in November 2014.

When Crop Ltd left the group within six years of the transfer whilst still owning the asset a degrouping charge of £126,480 (W) arose.

The degrouping charge is added to the proceeds on disposal of the shares to give total sale proceeds of £809,480 (£683,000 + £126,480).

As the gain on the shares is exempt, the degrouping charge is also exempt.

WORKING	£
Sale proceeds (MV at time of transfer)	240,000
Less cost	(80,000)
	160,000
Less indexation allowance (Apr 2003 – Nov 2014)	
$\dfrac{257.1 - 181.2}{181.2} = 0.419 \times £80,000$	(33,520)
Degrouping gain	126,480

56.2 Final tax-adjusted trading profits for year ended 31 March 2019

	£
Draft profit	20,795,000
Add:	
Computer hardware (100% FYA)	3,000
Interest on loan to purchase Brush Ltd shares (NTLR)	11,900
Less:	
Profit on disposal of shares	(241,000)
Less capital allowances (£29,850 + £3,000)	(32,850)
Adjusted trading profit	20,536,050

56.3

	Total £	UK £	Elixia income £
Final tax-adjusted trading profit (part 2)	20,536,050	20,536,050	
Non-trading loan relationship (W1)	4,300	4,300	
Overseas property income			
£77,900 × 100/82	95,000		95,000
RDEC (12% × £108,500) (W2)	13,020	13,020	
TTP	20,648,370	20,553,370	95,000

Corporation tax payable

FY2018

£20,648,370 × 19%	3,923,190
Less RDEC	(13,020)
Less: DTR	
DTR = lower of:	
UK tax on overseas income 19%	
Overseas tax 18% = 18% x £95,000	(17,100)
Corporation tax payable	3,893,070

WORKING

(1) Non-trading loan relationship

Non-trading loan relationship	
Bank deposit interest receivable	16,200
Less Interest on Brush Ltd loan	(11,900)
	4,300

(2) RDEC- Qualifying expenditure

Salaries	92,000
Computer software	4,500
Consumables	12,000
	108,500

Examiner's comments

56.1 This was the least well answered part of the exam. The majority of candidates did not identify that the substantial shareholding exemption applied and calculated a gain on the disposal of the shares. Many candidates did not identify the degrouping charge. Many candidates produced three calculations, a gain on the shares and two gains in respect of the property often with no explanation. Candidates on the whole did not have the skills to recognise the tax issues relevant to the given scenario.

56.2 Generally the question was answered quite well. [Note that due to syllabus changes Note 3 of this question has been rewritten.]

56.3 Candidates generally answered this question well, with many scoring full marks.

57 Nellie, Ben and Judd (December 2016)

Marking guide

			Marks
57.1 (a)	Capital allowance deduction	1	
	Capital allowances (W1)		
	– Lift	½	
	– AIA in priority to lift	½	
	– Machinery and AIA	1	
	– BMW car	½	
	– Ford car disposal	½	
	– Balancing allowance re Ford	1	
	– Small pool write-off	1	
	– Mail pool allowance	½	
	– BMW allowance	1	
	– No capital allowance for small building	½	
			8
(b)	Carry forward (s83)	1½	
	Current year and/or prior year (s64)	4½	
	Extension against gains in 2017/18	2	
	Net income before loss relief (W1)	2	
		10	
		Max	8

		Marks
57.2 (a)	Salary	½
	Relocation allowance	½
	Use of equipment	1
	Transfer of equipment (W1)	2½
	Employer pension contribution	½
	No adjustment for employee pension contribution	½
	Loan	½
	SMRS adjustment	½
	SMRS (W2)	1½
	Subscription to ISMM	1
		9
(b)	Class 1 secondary	2½
	Class 1A	1½
	Deadlines	1
		5
57.3 (a)	Trading income or capital gain	1
	Explanation of each badge of trade (max 5)	5
		6
(b)	Trading receipts £800	1
	Trading receipts £1,200- tax adjusted profit	½
	Election to use trading allowance	1
	Recommend make election	1
	Deadline	½
		4
		40

57.1 (a) Tax adjusted trading loss for year ended 31 March 2019

	£
Trading loss before capital allowances	(24,000)
Less:	
Less capital allowances (W)	(132,740)
Tax-adjusted trading loss	(156,740)

WORKING

Capital allowances

	Main pool	Special rate pool	PUA – 25%	PUA – 30%	£ Total
TWDV b/f	96,500	900	4,220		
Purchases					
Lift		61,700			
5/6 x £74,040					
AIA		(61,700)			61,700
Machinery					
5/6 x £62,400	52,000				
AIA	(52,000)				52,000
BMW car				24,600	

	Main pool	Special rate pool	PUA – 25%	PUA – 30%		£ Total
Disposal						
Ford car			(3,500)			
	96,500	900	720	24,600		
Bal allowance			(720)		× 25%	180
Small pool		(900)				900
WDA @ 18%	(17,370)					17,370
WDA @ 8%				(1,968)	× 30%	590
	80,770	–	–	22,632		
Capital allowances						132,740

No capital allowances available for the small building

(b) The options for relief of trading loss are:

s83

To carry forward the trading loss of £156,740 against the first available trading profits of the same trade.

This applies unless an alternative claim is made.

s64

Relieve the trading loss of £156,740 against net income of 2017/18 and/ or 2018/19. It is possible to fully relieve the net income of £12,950 in 2018/19.

Relief against non-trading income in 2017/18 is restricted to the higher of:
- £50,000; and
- 25% × adjusted total income ie, 25% × £192,850 = £48,213

Hence the total loss relief available in 2017/18 is £132,000 (£82,000 + £50,000)
A s.64 claim must be made within 12 months from 31 January following the end of the tax year in which the loss arose.

s 261B

If Nellie made a claim to offset the loss against her net income of 2017/18 she could then offset the remaining trading loss of £24,740 against her substantial chargeable gain of the same tax year.

A s.261B claim must be made within 12 months from 31 January following the end of the tax year in which the loss arose.

WORKING

Net income before loss relief

		2017/18	2018/19
Trading income		82,000	–
Property income			
Rent	13,650		
Less rent-a-room	(7,500)		
		6,150	6,150
NS&I interest		6,500	6,800
REIT income 100/80 × £78,560		98,200	
Net income		192,850	12,950

57.2(a)

Ben's employment income

	£
Salary	45,000
Relocation allowance – up to £8,000 exempt	-
Use of photographic equipment 20% × £4,000 × 6/12	400
Transfer of photographic equipment (W1)	1,100
Employer's pension contributions – exempt	-
No adjustment of employee's own 4% PPC contributions	-
Loan £11,000 × 2.5%	275
SMRS (W2)	1,250
	48,025
Less subscription to ISMM	(148)
	47,877

WORKINGS

(1) **Transfer of photographic equipment**

	£	
Higher of		
– MV at transfer	3,000	
– Cost	4,000	
Less benefits charged	(400)	
	3,600	
ie		3,600
Less employee contribution		(2,500)
		1,100

(2) **SMRS**

	£	
Ben received 13,000 × £0.50		6,500
Less allowable		
10,000 × £0.45	4,500	
3,000 × £0.25	750	
		(5,250)
Taxable amount		1,250

(b)

Class 1 secondary

	£
Earnings	
Salary	45,000
SMRS using only 45p limit for NIC 13,000 × (50p – 45p)	650
	45,650
Class 1 (45,650 – 8,424) × 13.8%	5,137

Class 1A

Earnings £(400 + 1,100 + 275) = £1,775

	£
Class 1A £1,775 × 13.8%	245

The Class 1 secondary NIC is collected under the PAYE system on a monthly basis. Class 1A contributions are paid in one amount by 19 July (22 July if by electronic payment) following the end of the tax year. So 19 July 2019 for 2018/19.

57.3(a) The tax treatment of the profit from the sale of books will depend on whether Judd is carrying on a trade of selling second hand books or whether he is selling capital assets. If it is deemed that he is trading he will need to pay income tax on the trading profits whereas if it is deemed to be a capital asset sale then capital gains tax will be due.

In order to determine this HMRC will consider the 'badges of trade.' The most relevant in this case are as follows:

- Number of transactions

  Given that Judd has inherited a 'large' collection of books and plans to sell them on quickly the high number of transactions will make it more likely he is considered to be trading. However, if Judd is only selling the books which he inherited it could be considered that these are isolated transactions and thus not trading transactions.

- Existence of similar transactions or interests

  If there is an existing trade, then a similarity to the transaction being considered may point to that transaction having a trading character. As Judd does not have an existing trade this will not apply here.

- Way in which the assets were acquired

  As the assets were acquired unintentionally, by inheritance, their later sale is unlikely to be considered trading.

- Changes to the assets

  When work is done to make an asset more marketable, or steps are taken to find purchasers, a transaction is more likely to be considered trading. The rebinding of the books and the advertising are both more likely to make the transactions appear to be of a trading nature.

- Interval between purchase and sale

  Judd's plan to sell the books as soon as possible may make it more likely that the transactions are deemed to be trading.

(b) If Judd's trading receipts for 2018/19 are £800 then his trading profits will be treated as nil and there will be no charge to income tax as a result of his trade due to the trading allowance.

If his trading receipts, however, are £1,200 then he will be taxed on his tax adjusted trading profits. Given that he is expecting minimal costs this will give him taxable trading income of £1,200. However, he can make an election to apply the trading allowance instead. He will then be charged to income tax on his trade income of £1,200 less £1,000 giving £200 taxable trading income. He should therefore make the election to use the trading allowance. This election must be made by the first anniversary of the normal self-assessment filing date for the tax year so 31 January 2021 for 2018/19.

Examiner's comments

57.1 (a) Although answers were generally comprehensive, surprisingly some candidates seemed to struggle with the capital allowances computation – this was evidenced not just by the mark attained but by the poor presentation often involving many crossings out. Uncertainty over the treatment of VAT appeared to be an issue with many candidates obviously changing their minds part way through the calculations. However, candidates often correctly allocated the AIA but then made mistakes in other easier areas such as private use restrictions. It was a common error to claim an AIA on the building.

(b) This part was not answered well – some candidates produced mainly numbers and no explanation, others produced lengthy explanations that did not score well because the technical language used was too imprecise. Some candidates wasted time by detailing irrelevant options such as early year loss relief or terminal loss relief. A minority of candidates suggested the taxpayer should cease to trade in order to use the latter relief, without addressing the loss reliefs for an ongoing business, and so conveniently answered the question they wanted rather than the one set. Many candidates lost easy calculation marks as they seemed to think, incorrectly, that the interest on the NS&I Direct Saver account was exempt from income tax. They also calculated the property income incorrectly by deducting both rent-a-room relief and property expenses from the rental income.

57.2(a) This was generally answered well – the main errors were in relation to the photographic equipment. A common error was not including a use benefit in employment income. The transfer benefit was poorly answered. Whilst the basic structure of how to calculate the benefit looked correct often the actual figures used were so incorrect that it was hard to give much credit for demonstrating any real understanding. Other errors included no deduction for the subscription or including either income or a deduction in relation to pension contributions.

(b) This part was generally well answered, although a common error was to include the same figure for SMRS as in the previous part.

57.3 [This part of the question has been re-written due to changes in the syllabus and thus there are no examiner comments.]

March 2017 exam answers

58 Mita and Ruth (March 2017)

		Marks
58.1 Receives internal information/ report	1	
Deciding whether information needs to be relayed to NCA	1	
Compiling and despatching SAR	1	
Offences for MLROs failing to make report	<u>1</u>	
Max	4	3
58.2 Integrity	½	
Professional behaviour	½	
False/misleading statement or information omitted/obscured	1	
Should not make exaggerated claims	1	
Self-interest threat as wants job/ money	<u>1½</u>	
Max	4½	<u>4</u>
		<u>7</u>

58.1 The money laundering reporting officer (MLRO) receives any internal information/report where there is knowledge or suspicion of money laundering.

The MLRO is then responsible for deciding whether the information contained in an internal report needs to be relayed to the NCA in the form of an external report, a SAR, and if so, for compiling and despatching the SAR.

There are specific offences applying to MLROs failing to make a report where one is needed.

58.2 Integrity is threatened if Ruth submits false information.

Ruth should not knowingly be associated with any information that she knows:

- contains a materially false or misleading statement; or

- omits or obscures information required to be included where such omission or obscurity would be misleading.

Professional behaviour will be breached if Ruth submits false information.

Ruth should not make exaggerated claims for the services she is able to offer, the qualifications she possesses, or the experience she has gained.

The threat here is a self-interest threat which affect's Ruth's objectivity because she wants a job/money on the team and the financial reward, but if she tells the truth she may not be given one.

58.1 Generally well-answered with students able to identify at least some of the reporting responsibilities of a money laundering reporting officer.

58.2 Generally well-answered with students able to identify the fundamental principles under threat when a professional accountant misrepresents her skills or qualifications for personal gain.

59 Andy, Jim and Lamb Ltd (March 2017)

Marking guide

		Marks
59.1 Identifying single/composite versus multiple/mixed supply	1	
Depends on circumstances	½	
Is single supply/all exempt	1	
Reasons – 1 mark per reason	3	
Max	5½	4
59.2 Stamp duty on lease premium	1½	
Stamp duty on NPV of lease rentals	1	
Total stamp duty	½	
		3
59.3 Input tax attributable to taxable/exempt supplies	1	
Calculation of % non-attributable tax to recover	1½	
Apportionment of non-attributable input VAT	1	
Consider *de minimis*	1	
Conclude and annual adjustment	1½	
Max		6
		13

59.1 Single and multiple supplies

How the VAT should be calculated depends on whether the supply is a single/composite supply with a single VAT rate, or a multiple/mixed supply with multiple VAT rates.

Whether a supply is in fact a single or a multiple supply depends on the circumstances.

This is a single supply/all exempt because of the following:

- The supply is a single supply because to split the healthcare supply into two parts would be 'artificially splitting the transaction'.

- The supply is in essence a supply of healthcare, with an ancillary/minor/incidental supply of medicine. Where a supply is ancillary there is a single supply.

- The supply is a single economic supply as the customer was not offered a lower price if no medicines were required.

59.2 SDLT on non-residential lease

SDLT is payable on both the lease premium and the net present value of the lease rentals:

On the grant of a non-residential lease with a premium of £261,500:

- The first £150,000 at 0% = £0
- The next £100,000 at 2% = £2,000
- The remaining £11,500 at 5% = £575

In addition a lease is liable to SDLT on the NPV of the lease rentals over the life of the lease:

- £5,500 × 30 = £165,000
- £165,000 – £150,000 = £15,000 × 1% = £150

The total SDLT due is £2,000 + £575 + £150 = £2,725.

59.3 Lamb Ltd – year ended 31 March 2019

	Taxable supplies £	Exempt supplies £	Total supplies £
Wholly attributable input tax:			
Taxable supplies	100,100		100,100
Exempt supplies		12,600	12,600
Non-attributable input tax:			
Recoverable amount % is			
£562,562 / £631,383 = 90% (rounded up)			
Attributable to taxable supplies: 90% × £26,780	24,102		24,102
Attributable to exempt supplies: 10% × £26,780		2,678	2,678
Input VAT	124,202	15,278	139,480

Tests for *de minimis* limit:

(1) Is the monthly average attributable to exempt supplies £625 or less?

Monthly average is £15,278 / 12 = £1,274 per month – fails this test

(2) Is the proportion of VAT on exempt supplies not more than 50% of input VAT for the year?

£15,278 / £139,480 = 11% – passes this test

As at least one of the tests is not passed, input tax on exempt supplies exceeds *de minimis* limits.

Conclusion

Only input VAT attributable to taxable supplies is recoverable ie, £124,202

Therefore the annual adjustment is:

£125,532 – £124,202 = £1,330 is payable to HMRC

Examiner's comments

59.1 Most students identified that this question concerned single versus multiple supplies, although a small number thought this concerned the partial exemption rules. While not all students correctly concluded that the single supply treatment was appropriate, they were able to achieve good marks for their analysis of the factors involved. Students are reminded that, while an analysis of opposing factors may be required, giving two conflicting conclusions is counterproductive as neither conclusion will then score marks.

59.2 This question, requiring calculations of stamp duty land tax, was not well answered as usual. There was confusion between SDLT on the premium, and on the rental payments, with many students confusing the rules for residential and commercial leases. It was quite common for the lease premium to be taxed as though it were a lease rental. Also often the lease rental was not taxed at all.

59.3 This question involving the partial exemption calculation was very well-answered by most students. Often the only mistake was not rounding the partial exemption fraction. The minority of students that did not perform so well did not show their workings and/or fully explain the *de minimis* tests.

60 Clara and Simon (March 2017)

Marking guide

			Marks
60.1 (a)	31 January 2022	<u>1</u>	
			1
(b)	Shares in ISA-exempt	1	
	Gain on jewellery	1½	
	Gain on lease	1½	
	Total gains	½	
	Deduct b/f cap loss and AEA	1	
	Calculation of converted trading losses and offset	2	
	Calculation of CGT	2½	
			10
60.2 (a)	15 out of last 20 years	1	
	Domiciled from 6 April 2015/ 2015/16	<u>1</u>	
			2
(b)	May 2018 PET	½	
	June 2018 CLT		
	- Diminution in value	1½	
	- BPR	2½	
	- AE, NRB available	1½	
	- IHT	½	
	August 2018 CLT		
	- APR	1½	
	- No BPR	½	
	- NRB available	1	
	- IHT due	½	
	W1 CLT July 2011	2½	
	Max		12
			25

60.1 (a) Time limit for converted trading losses claim

The claim must be made within 12 months from 31 January next following the tax year in which the loss arose. As the loss arose in 2019/20, the anniversary of the next 31 January is: 31 January 2022.

(b)

CGT liability for 2018/19
Shares

Exempt disposal as ISA (must show)	0

Jewellery

	£
Proceeds less fees = £23,000 × 95%	21,850
Less cost (probate value as inherited)	(16,000)
	5,850

Garden Ltd shares

	£
Proceeds (MV)	260,000
Less cost	(150,000)
	110,000
Less Gift relief	(60,000)
Taxable now (Actual proceeds – cost) (£200,000 – £150,000)	50,000

CGT liability

	£
Gains = £75,000 + £5,850 + £50,000	130,850
Less converted trading losses (W)	(17,400)
Less b/fwd capital loss	(8,450)
Less AEA	(11,700)
	93,300
£34,500 @ 10% (Clara has no income as the loss fully offsets her income)	3,450
£58,800 @ 20%	11,760
	15,210

WORKING

Converted trading losses

Relevant amount = £34,500 – £13,500 – £3,600	17,400
Maximum amount = £130,850 – £8,450	122,400

60.2 (a) **Deemed domicile for IHT**

Simon will be treated as deemed domiciled for IHT purposes once he has been resident in the UK for at least 15 of the previous 20 years and including at least one of the four tax years ending with the current tax year. In Simon's case he will therefore be treated as domiciled in the UK for IHT purposes from 6 April 2017 onwards.

(b)

PET – May 2018
No lifetime tax as a PET. (Uses 2018/19 and 2017/18 AEs)

CLT – June 2018	£	£
Diminution in value:		
Prior to gift = 60% holding = 60,000 × £36	2,160,000	
Post gift = 40% holding = 40,000 × £25	(1,000,000)	
		1,160,000
Less BPR @ 100%		
£1,160,000 × (£5.4m – £0.6m / £5.4m) × 100%		(1,031,111)
Less AE 2018/19 and 2017/18 (already allocated to PET)		nil
		128,889
Less NRB at gift	325,000	
Less chargeable transfers in the previous seven years (W1)	(133,250)	
		(191,750)
		0
IHT is nil		0

CLT - August 2018	£	£
Value of transfer		850,000
Less APR @ 100% on agricultural value		(500,000)
No BPR as held as investment		nil
Less AE 2018/19 and 2017/18 (already allocated to PET)		nil
		350,000
Less NRB at gift	325,000	
Less chargeable transfers since August 2011	(128,889)	
		(196,111)
		153,889
IHT @ 20/80		38,472

WORKING

CLT - July 2011	£	£
Gift		125,000
Less AE 2011/12 and 2010/11 b/f		(6,000)
Chargeable transfer		119,000
Less nil rate band at gift	325,000	
Less GCTs since 1 July 2004	(263,000)	
		(62,000)
		57,000
Lifetime tax at 20/80		14,250
Gross chargeable transfer = £119,000 + £14,250		133,250
(£119,000 + tax at 20/80)		

Examiner's comments

60.1 (a)   Answers to this administration requirement (claim for loss relief against gains) were poor throughout, despite the rule being stated in the open book. Only a very small minority of students got this correct. In addition a large number of students did not attempt this part. The most common incorrect answer was 31 January 2021.

(b)   Most students scored decent marks for this capital gains tax calculation but few realised that the disposal of shares which had been held within an ISA would not give rise to a chargeable gain. Despite clear instructions with regard to the use of the trading loss (and the emphasis given to this in part (a), most students were obviously ill-prepared for this loss relief and chose to ignore it. [Note that the question has been amended to include the Garden Ltd shares disposal due to syllabus updates.]

60.2 (a)   Answers to this question on deemed domicile were almost always wrong. Students could not even identify the concept, and either omitted this or gave a guess based on one of the transactions within the question. The guess was sometimes based on the rules for the remittance basis or the election available for a non-UK domiciled spouse.

(b)   Performance on this inheritance tax calculation was a little disappointing. The question was slightly unusual in that it focussed only on lifetime inheritance tax and some students always seem to struggle where an IHT question does not involve a death. Some students went so far as to state their assumption that Simon had died on an arbitrary date and/or they created a death estate in order to calculate the death tax due. It is worth reiterating that if the question does not mention a death then nobody has died.

Aside from an absence of death, there were some tricky elements, such as the restriction on business property relief for excepted assets which few correctly addressed. The simpler agricultural property relief, was better dealt with. However, more concerning were some basic errors such as charging a potentially exempt transfer to lifetime tax, and failing to correctly apply the cumulation rules when calculating nil rate bands.

As usual, some students did not show full workings for the nil rate band making it more difficult to give marks.

61 Cup Ltd (March 2017)

			Marks
61.1 (a)	Adjustment to profit		
	– Interest on rental property	1	
	– Each other adjustment – ½ mark	3½	
	Capital allowances (W1)	3½	
			8
(b)	Gain calculation (W1)	1	
	TTP calculation	2½	
	Corporation tax calculation	½	
			4
61.2	QIPs if AP exceed £1.5 million	½	
	Else 9 months and 1 day	½	
	Pro rate for related 51% group companies	½	
	Application to Teaspoon	1½	
	4 QIP dates for Teaspoon	1	
	No exceptions as large in prior year	1	
		5	
	Max		3
			15

61.1 (a) Saucer Ltd tax adjusted trading profit for nine months ended 31 December 2018

	£
Trading profit	5,298,000
Profit on disposal of copyright	0
Goodwill impairment is specifically disallowed	57,000
Dividends received	(800,000)
Profit on disposal of land	(145,000)
Rent – adjust for the amount included in profit	(72,000)
Interest on shares	75,750
Interest on rental property = £18,000 × 4/9	8,000
Capital allowances (W1)	(309,158)
Trading profit	4,112,592

WORKING

(1) **Capital allowances** **P/E 31 December 2018**	Main pool £	SR pool £	Total £
TWDV b/f	648,500	256,000	
Additions	250,000	525,000	
AIA = max £200,000 × 9/12		(150,000)	150,000
	898,500	631,000	
WDA @ 18% / 8% × 9/12	(121,298)	(37,860)	159,158
TWDV c/f	777,202	593,140	
Total allowances			309,158

(2) **Capital allowances (alternative layout)**

P/E 31 December 2018	AIA £	Main pool £	SR pool £	Total £
TWDV b/f		648,500	256,000	
Additions	775,000			
AIA = max £200,000 × 9/12	(150,000)			150,000
Trfr to pools	(625,000)	250,000	375,000	
		898,500	631,000	
WDA @ 18% / 8% × 9/12		(121,298)	(37,860)	159,158
TWDV c/f		777,202	593,140	
Total allowances				309,158

(b) **Saucer Ltd corporation tax liability for nine months ended 31 December 2018**

Trading profits (part (a))		4,112,592
Property income		
Rent × 4/12 = £72,000 × 4/12		24,000
Gain (W)		0
Non-trading loan relationships		
Interest paid on shares	(75,750)	
Interest paid on rental property loan	(8,000)	
		(83,750)
TTP		4,052,842

Corporation tax payable:

CT @ 19%	770,040

WORKING

Gain

Proceeds	450,000
Less cost	(305,000)
Less IA = 278.1-166.6 / 166.6 = 0.669 × £305,000	(204,045)
	0

61.2 A company will pay its corporation tax liability by quarterly instalment payments (QIPs) where it has augmented profits in excess of £1.5 million. Otherwise corporation tax is payable nine months and one day after the end of the accounting period/1 December 2020.

This limit is pro rated by the number of related 51% group companies a company has. For this purpose the company must have been a related 51% group company on the last day of the previous accounting period.

As at 28 February 2019 Teaspoon Ltd had two related 51% group companies. Therefore for the year ended 29 February 2020 the £1.5 million limit becomes £0.5 million and with augmented profits of £685,000 it is liable to pay its corporation tax liability in four equal QIPs on the following dates. (All the dates below need to be a day, month and year)

- 14 September 2019
- 14 December 2019
- 14 March 2020
- 14 June 2020

As Teaspoon Ltd was clearly large in the previous accounting period (augmented profits were > £1.5m) no exceptions to QIPs apply in the current accounting period.

Examiner's comments

61.1 (a) Most students were able to make a decent attempt at part (a) to adjust trading profits, with errors mainly relating to intangible fixed assets and/or interest payments. In addition some students did not follow the instructions in the requirement to show their treatment of all items.

(b) Students often produced poor answers for part (b) even if their answer to part (a) had been good. Some merely charged corporation tax on their answer to part (a). Too many students used indexation to create a loss on disposal of land, suggesting they are not thinking through the numbers they calculate. Many also calculated indexation incorrectly in any case. Many also did not use, or in some cases even calculate, the non-trading loan relationship deficit.

61.2 This question involved quarterly instalment payments. There were some confused answers and the requirement was one which was occasionally omitted. However, those students who pushed on did manage to achieve some marks, for comparison of profits and (a reduced) limit, and possibly some marks for the payment dates although these were frequently incorrect by a year. Very few students correctly referred to related 51% group companies, many still referred to the old associated companies rule. Generally students are not confident applying the rules for instalments, even for twelve month periods (a skill required for the Principles of Taxation exam).

Many students continue not to give a full date (ie, a day, a month and a year) when asked to do so.

62 Chitra (March 2017)

Marking guide

		Marks	
62.1 (a)	Adjustment to profit		
	- Interest payable	1	
	- Staff costs (must be shown)	½	
	- Niece's salary	1	
	- Stock write off	1	
	- Fine (must be shown)	½	
	- Gifted stock	1	
	- CAs	½	
	Capital allowances (W1)	2½	
			8
(b)	Taxable income	2	
	IT liability	3	
	Extended bands (W1)	1	
			6
(c)	Class 2	½	
	Class 4	2½	
	Due date	1	
			4

		Marks
62.2(a)	Flat (W1)	3½
	Company car (W2)	1½
	Training course	1
		6
(b)	Company car cost	1½
	Leased car cost	2½
		4
62.3	Calculation of overlap profits (W1)	2
	2018/19 Assessment calculation	2
		4
62.4	Maximum possible pension contribution	
–	Higher of relevant earnings and £3,600	1½
–	Annual allowance calculation	1
–	ANI and PA thus available	2
	Reduction in tax liability	3½
		8
		40

62.1(a) Chitra's tax adjusted trading profits for year ended 31 December 2018

	£
Draft profit	121,500
Less:	
Interest payable £14,000 × 85%	(11,900)
Chitra's staff costs	0
Niece's salary – allow what is reasonable for work done	(15,000)
Stock write off = £15,600 – £10,100	(5,500)
Fine	0
Gifted stock – allowable expense	(2,300)
Less capital allowances (W1)	(13,568)
Adjusted trading profit	73,232

Capital allowances (W1)	Main pool	SRP	PUA – 65%	Total
TWDV b/f	56,755	895	21,000	
Small pools write off		(895)		895
WDA @ 18%	(10,216)			10,216
WDA @ 18% × 65%			(3,780) × 65%	2,457
	46,539	–	17,220	13,568

(b)

Chitra income tax payable for 2018/19		NSI £	Savings £	Dividend £
Trading income (part (a)) – CYB		73,232		
BSI			3,600	
Dividend				9,440
Net income		73,232	3,600	9,440
Less personal allowance		(11,850)		
Taxable income		61,382	3,600	9,440
Non-savings income (W)	£39,500 × 20%			7,900
	£21,882 × 40%			8,753
Savings income	£500 × 0%			0
	£3,100 × 40%			1,240
Dividend income	£2,000 × 0%			0
	£7,440 × 32.5%			2,418
Income tax liability				20,311

WORKING

Extended bands	£
BRB	34,500
Gift Aid donation = £4,000 × 100/80	5,000
	39,500

(c) **Class 2 NIC**

	£
£2.95 × 52	153

Class 4

	£
(£46,350 – £8,424) × 9%	3,413
(£73,232 – £46,350) × 2%	538
	3,951

The Class 2 NIC will be due on 31 January 2020 and the class 4 will be collected through two payments on account (31 January 2019, 31 July 2019) with any balancing payment due 31 January 2020.

62.2 (a) **Saina's employment income**

	£
Salary	86,000
Company flat (W1)	33,650
Company car (W2)	5,670
Training course – not job related	2,400
	127,720

WORKINGS
(1) **Company flat**

	£
Annual value	18,000
Additional yearly rent	
(£425,000 + £68,000 – £75,000) × 2.5%	10,450
Use of furniture = £26,000 × 20%	5,200
	33,650

(2) **Company car**

	£
£21,000 × 27%	5,670
Ignore repair costs	0
	5,670

(b) **Company car cost**

	£	£
Value of benefit per part (a)	5,670	
Income tax and NIC = 45% + 0% (no employee NIC on benefits)		(2,552)

Leased car cost

	£	£
Additional salary	12,000	
Less income tax and NIC = 47%	(5,640)	
		6,360
Private lease cost		(8,100)
Running costs		(1,750)
		(3,490)

62.3 Arun's trading income assessments

		£
2018/19	Closing year rules	
	Y/E 31.05.18	30,264
	P/E 30.11.18	7,156
	Less overlap from commencement (W)	(34,100)
		3,320

WORKING

		£
2003/04	Commencement to next 5 April ie, 1.8.03 – 5.4.04 = 8/22 × £75,020	27,280
2004/05	No AP end so use actual basis ie, 6.4.04 – 5.4.05 = 12/22 × £75,020	40,920
2005/06	12 months to accounting date ie, 1.6.04 – 31.5.05 = 12/22 × £75,020	40,920
		109,120
	Overlap from commencement = £109,120 – £75,020	34,100

62.4 Maximum possible pension contribution

	£
Employment income	62,000
Partnership income	15,000
	77,000

Greater than minimum of £3,600

Maximum tax relievable is annual allowance + unused allowances brought forward:

	£
2018/19	40,000
Unused annual allowance brought forward	5,000
Total	45,000
Thus maximum possible pension contribution	45,000

With PPC

Adjusted net income

	£
Total income	148,000
Less gross PPC (max)	(45,000)
	103,000
Less threshold	(100,000)
Excess	3,000

PA available

	£
Maximum PA	11,850
Less restriction – (103,000 – 100,000) × 50%	(1,500)
	10,350

Without PPC

Clearly without making a PPC Rajiv's adjusted net income will exceed £123,700 and he will have no personal allowance. The increase in the PA is therefore £10,350.

Reduction in tax liability

Tax liability reduces by the amount Rajiv's PA increases by at his marginal rate of tax:
£10,350 @ 40%   4,140

Plus

The amount taxed at the basic rate rather than the higher rate because the PPC extends the BRB:

£45,000 @ 20%   9,000
Total income tax reduction   13,140

Examiner's comments

62.1 (a) The scenario reflected a common situation in practice where a sole trader provides their accountant with a partial set of accounts, ignoring entries they do not understand. Most students read the information correctly, and deducted items they thought to be allowable, and showed nil for the remaining costs (so addressing the instruction in the requirement to show their treatment of each item). Most students made some errors, although not always the same ones. The gift of stock to a local school caused some problems, as did the required write-down of damaged stock. Some treated the trader's own salary (drawings) as allowable. Most students missed the fact that the balance on the special rate pool was small and could be taken as an allowance in full in the year.

(b) The income tax computations were very well answered with many students achieving full or nearly full marks. Occasionally, drawings were added to trading profit showing a fundamental misunderstanding of a sole trader business.

(c) The NIC computations were very well answered with many students achieving full or nearly full marks. The main reason for loss of marks in the NIC calculations, where this did occur, was failure to show workings.

62.2 (a) Surprisingly, the accommodation benefit caused some difficulties to most students, although the extent of errors varied. This demonstrates that students must learn the precise rules, for example, of costs/values to be included in the additional benefit, and not just pick out a figure they see in the question. Whilst it might have been expected that the treatment of the refurbishment would have proved difficult I was surprised to see such a lot of difficulties with the basic elements of the annual value and additional yearly rent calculations. Similarly, the car benefit, although handled better, revealed where students had not learned the actual rules, for example using cost rather than list price, and including repair costs.

(b) This requirement asked for an after-tax cost. It was one of the requirements most frequently omitted by students, although those who attempted it usually scored at least 2.5 marks. The common errors included not using the additional rate of tax, despite it being stated clearly in the question that the taxpayer paid at this rate, and a failure to consider national insurance contributions. Most students did not identify the after-tax cost of the options and the majority assumed that the lease and running costs were tax deductible.

62.3 A small number of students omitted this question. Of those who completed it, most students performed well on this requirement, calculating and subtracting overlap profits.

Again, the main reason marks were lost was a failure to show workings; marks could not be awarded for incorrect answers with no evidence of how they were calculated.

62.4 A small number of students omitted this question. Of those who completed it, many managed to score reasonable marks on a fairly difficult requirement, although students rarely covered all the main elements. A decent number of students considered relevant earnings, although not always correctly. Most understood the extension of the basic rate band and the subsequent tax saving. Many recognised that the personal allowance was not available without a pension contribution, but few realised the effect of the contribution on adjusted net income ie, that the personal allowance would be partially restored, leading to a further tax saving. [Note that this requirement has been simplified since originally set due to syllabus changes.]

63   Liz, Kira and Jane (June 2017)

Marking guide

		Marks
63.1 At least two years	1	
Preferably six years	1	
Minimum level of cover (mark for any one of three points)	$\frac{1}{3}$	
Max		2
63.2 Conflicts carefully managed	½	
Removed from situation where conflict of interest	½	
Whilst on secondment must serve interests of HMRC	½	
Not be involved in matters relating to her employer	1	
Not be involved in matters relating to any of its/her clients	1	
After secondment must not be involved in affairs of taxpayer involved with whilst at HMRC	$\frac{1}{4½}$	
Max		3
63.3 Privilege reporting exemption	1	
Legal advice so legally privileged	$\frac{1}{2}$	
		$\frac{}{7}$

63.1 As a qualified member of ICAEW in public practice and resident in the UK, Liz should maintain cover for at least two years after her retirement, preferably for at least six years.

The minimum recommended level of cover is:

- £100,000;
- 2.5 times fee income if cover then exceeds £100,000; or
- preferably higher if Liz's recent fee income has exceeded £600,000 pa.

63.2 Any potential conflict of interest, actual or perceived, should be carefully managed and Kira should be removed from any situation where there is a conflict between HMRC's and her employer's interests.

Whilst on secondment Kira needs to be aware that she must serve the interests of HMRC/duty to HMRC/act for HMRC/responsible to HMRC.

Whilst working for HMRC Kira should not be involved in any matters relating to her employer or any of its/her clients.

For a significant period after the end of the secondment, Kira should not be involved in the affairs of any taxpayer she was involved with whilst at HMRC.

63.3 The privilege reporting exemption applies if knowledge or suspicion of money laundering came to Jane in privileged circumstances.

As Jane learnt about the tax evasion whilst giving legal advice the knowledge came to her as legally privileged information which she cannot disclose via a money laundering report.

63.1 Students had either studied this topic and therefore knew the answer and scored well or had not studied it and therefore normally scored zero.

63.2 Students could normally score quite well by giving 'a common sense' answer. Often however answers were not always easy to understand and could be quite long and repetitive.

63.3 Few students scored well. Only a relatively small percentage identified the privilege reporting exemption and of those only a handful linked this to providing legal advice. Many students identified other acceptable defences for not reporting money laundering eg, happening overseas and not illegal in that country but could not identify the one appropriate to the given scenario. Others appeared not to have studied this topic at all and often gave quite inappropriate answers.

The number of students who suggested that the accountant should essentially make up a story in defence (ie, lie) was astonishing.

This requirement certainly elicited the most varied range of answers. For example, that professional incompetence or professional scepticism (ie, the adviser had not believed the client's confession) might be a valid defence.

Overall students that appeared to have studied ethics scored well but there were a reasonable number of students that scored zero for the whole of question one.

64 Mela Ltd and Pesca Ltd (June 2017)

Marking guide

		Marks
64.1 Group treated as single taxable entity	½	
Mela, as representative member, responsible for paying VAT and submitting returns	½	
How total VAT due calculated	½	
No VAT due on intra-group supplies/ outside scope of VAT	½	
Only one VAT return required	½	
Including Pear could make whole group partially exempt	½	
Explanation of whole group becoming partially exempt	1	
All companies jointly and severally liable and impact if Quince Ltd became insolvent	1	
Difficulty collating information	$\frac{1}{6}$	
Max		5
64.2 (a) £400,000 input VAT suffered recoverable	1	
Y/e 31 December 2016 – no adjustment	½	
Y/e 31 December 2017 and 18		
- 70% taxable use so some VAT repayable	1	
- Calculation	2	
Sale adjustment		
- Normal adjustment	½	
- Sale adjustment	$\frac{2}{7}$	
Max		6

		Marks
64.2(b) Calculation of stamp duty	1½	
Payment date	½	
		$\frac{2}{13}$

64.1 The group is treated as being a single taxable person/thing/entity.

Mela Ltd, as the representative member, will be responsible for paying VAT on behalf of the group and submitting the VAT returns.

The total VAT due will be based on the total output VAT for the group less the total input VAT suffered by the group.

No VAT will be charged on intra-group supplies/outside scope of VAT – therefore no need to consider tax point or amount of VAT due.

Only one VAT return required.

Including Pear Ltd in the group would make the group partially exempt, affecting recoverability of input for the whole group unless it was *de minimis*.

All companies in the group are equally/jointly and severally to pay the VAT due – eg, if Quince Ltd were to become insolvent, the other companies would be responsible for paying its VAT liability.

Given the companies have decentralised finance functions it may be administratively difficult to collate the information in time to file a single return.

Tutorial note

No marks were awarded for phrases such as exempt, disallowed or zero rated. Students must ensure that they use the correct technical language if they are to score marks.

64.2(a) **VAT on purchase**
All input VAT (£2,000,000 × 20% = £400,000) recoverable

VAT adjustments on usage
Y/E 31 December 2016
100% taxable use, so no adjustment required

Y/E 31 December 2017 and 31 December 2018
Only 70% taxable use so some VAT repayable to HMRC
£400,000 / 10 × 30% = £12,000
£12,000 repayable to HMRC each year

VAT adjustments on sale
As it is still within CGS, an adjustment on disposal applies:
Normal adjustment for usage = repay VAT of £12,000

Adjustment for sale = six years remaining and no tax chargeable on/exempt disposal
£400,000 / 10 × 6 = £240,000 VAT repayable

(b) **SDLT on 2019 sale**

£150,000 × 0% = 0
£(250,000 – 150,000) × 2% = 2,000
£(3,500,000 – 250,000) × 5% = 162,500
Total SDLT = £164,500

The SDLT must be paid to HMRC within 30 days of the transaction ie, 30 March 2019.

64.1 Lots of students did very well on one or two elements of this part, but failed to address adequately each of the different aspects of the requirement: implications, advantages and disadvantages. However, other students did not perform so well at all. Many students could not explain the issues clearly enough to demonstrate their understanding or relate it sufficiently well to the scenario. Many were confused about the implications of traders making zero-rated and exempt supplies. Comments about being able to offset losses against other group company profits were not relevant. Few discussed the implications of the joint and several liability and when they did thought it was positive as Quince Ltd would not have to pay the VAT.

In addition some students gave the answer to a question that they were expecting, but not the actual question ie, in a group they expect there to be a partial exemption issue and a repayment trader – so they made the facts of the question suit the answer they wanted to give. They also wasted time justifying why the companies qualified for inclusion in a VAT group. Hence, only the better students dealt well with the more unusual facts eg, decentralised finance functions and the possibility of Quince Ltd becoming insolvent.

64.2 (a) Many students gained an excellent mark. They were obviously very familiar with the technical content of the capital goods scheme and both applied their knowledge well to the given situation and also explained the issues very well.

Many students think that a trader reclaims the appropriate percentage each year rather than making an initial claim and then subsequently adjusting eg, £40,000 reclaim in year 1 (one tenth of the VAT) but then only a reduced £28,000 reclaim in year 2 etc, or even a repayment of £12,000 in year 2 after only reclaiming £40,000 initially.

(b) Many students scored full marks on this part. The most common mistake was including the VAT but it was good to see that the date was identified correctly. A small number of candidates identified the wrong transaction despite this being clearly indicated in the question but were still able to gain almost all the marks on follow-through.

65 Anne and Johan (June 2017)

Marking guide

			Marks
65.1 (a)	7 out of last 9 tax years	1	
			1
(b)	Gain on Mast Ltd shares	1	
	Gain on Petal Ltd shares	2½	
	Gain qualifying for entrepreneurs relief	1	
	No foreign gain as proceeds not remitted	1	
	Offset capital loss brought forward (versus non-ER gains in priority)	1	
	No AEA as remittance claim	1	
	Calculation of CGT	1	
	Due date	½	
			9

		Marks
65.2 (a)	House – UK	½	
	Cash – branch located – UK	½	
	Shares- register located – USA	1	
	Life assurance – proceeds payable – UK	<u>1</u>	
			3
(b)	July 2012 PET		
	– Exemptions	1	
	– NRB available	1	
	– Death tax due	1	
	Death estate		
	– House	½	
	– Cash	½	
	– Shares	2	
	– Life insurance policy	1	
	– Spouse exemption	½	
	– No residential NRB as estate exceeds £2.25 million	1½	
	– Remaining NRB	1	
	– Charitable exemption	½	
	– IHT due	1	
	Charitable exemption calculation (W1)	<u>½</u>	
			<u>12</u>
			<u><u>25</u></u>

65.1 (a) Remittance basis claim

No remittance basis charge as does not pass the 7-year test (ie, not UK resident for 7 out of the last 9 tax years).

(b) CGT liability for 2018/19

	£
Mast Shares	
Proceeds	125,000
Less cost	(34,000)
	91,000
Petal Shares	
Proceeds	83,000
Less cost (W1)	(20,500)
	62,500

CGT liability	£ ER	£ Non-ER
Gains – ER	91,000	
Gains – non-ER = £152,000 + £62,500		214,500
Foreign gains on commercial property – not remitted		0
Less capital loss b/fwd		(7,950)
Less AEA – not available as remittance basis user	0	0
	91,000	206,550
ER gains @ 10% = £91,000 @ 10%		9,100
Non-ER gains @ 20%		41,310
		50,410

The CGT will be due by 31 January 2020.

(1) **Share pool**	**No**	**Cost (£)**
June 2005 Acquisition	1,000	20,000
June 2005 1 for 2 bonus issue	500	0
	1,500	20,000
December 2010 1 for 3 rights issue at £42	500	21,000
	2,000	41,000
July 2018 Disposal	(1,000)	(20,500)
	1,000	20,500

65.2 (a) **Location rules**

- London house – located where physically situated, so UK
- Cash – located where branch situated, so UK
- Shares – located where register situated, so USA
- Life assurance policy – located where proceeds payable, so UK

(b) If Johan is UK domiciled he is liable to UK IHT on his worldwide assets.

Failed PET – July 2012	£	£
Gift		100,000
Less ME		(5,000)
Less AE 2012/13 and 2011/12		(6,000)
		89,000
Less NRB at death	325,000	
Less chargeable transfers since 1 July 2005	(400,000)	
		Nil
		89,000
Death tax due at 40%		35,600
Death tax due after taper relief (6-7 years ie, at 80%)		7,120

Death estate		
House less mortgage (£3.5m – £1.5m)		2,000,000
Cash		
		1,000,000
Shares – lower of:		
255p + ¼ × (274p – 255p) = £2.5975		
258p + 273p / 2 = £2.655		
= 50,000 × £2.5975		
		129,875
Life insurance policy – market value as not own life		48,000
Less exempt gift to spouse		(500,000)
		2,677,875
Residential NRB – not available as estate (before exemptions) exceeds £2.25 million and thus RNRB is tapered to £nil		–
Less NRB at death	325,000	
Less chargeable transfers since 1 March 2012	(89,000)	
		(236,000)
Chargeable death estate before gift to charity		2,441,875
Less exempt gift to charity		(425,000)
Chargeable death estate		2,016,875
IHT @ 36% (W)		726,075

WORKING

Charitable exemption

Charitable exemption % = £425,000 / £2,441,875 = 17%

Examiner's comments

65.1 (a) Answers to this administration requirement (7 year test for remittance basis charge to apply) were good.

However, lots of answers were not precise enough (ie, they just stated needed to be resident for seven years) despite the rule being stated in the open book. A substantial number of students suggested that the remittance basis charge would not be due because income is not remitted.

(b) On the whole students performed well on the capital taxes question. For both CGT and IHT there is a relatively straightforward approach and useful proformas that can be learned which enable a number of marks to be picked up fairly easily and students seem to have taken this on board. Students also demonstrated the ability to adapt the approach to the specifics of the CGT question, which involved the implications of using the remittance basis. Recognising that the Mast Ltd shares qualified for entrepreneurs' relief but that the Petal Ltd shares did not and the optimal use of the capital losses were also important in scoring a good mark. This was not a problem for most students, although a significant number gave the substantial shareholding exemption for the share disposal. [Note that the question has been adapted due to syllabus changes and the Petal Ltd shares were not in the original exam question.]

65.2 (a) Most students scored very well. The only common error was not to correctly identify the reason that the shares were located in the USA. A small minority of students did not answer the actual question by either giving a city rather than a country as a location or by stating where the assets were taxable rather than where they were located.

(b) This part was also generally answered very well. Presentation of the answer in a clear and logical manner was very good. Most students recognised the availability of the marriage exemption and were able to correctly value the assets. The only issue with presentation was some students did not give details of the formula used to value the shares, just the rounded end result, which did not give sufficient information to be able to decide if the correct valuation formula had been used. Most students identified that the lower 36% rate was appropriate and used it correctly just on the death estate but did not provide correct workings to justify the rate.

As usual, some students did not show full workings for the nil rate band making it more difficult to give marks.

66 Sedia Ltd and Tog Ltd (June 2017)

			Marks
66.1 (a)	Adjustment to profit		
	- Amortisation of patents	½	
	- Loss on sale of patent	½	
	- Profit on sale of shares	½	
	- Loan finance costs	1	
	- Charitable donations	½	
	- Capital allowances	½	
	Capital allowances (W1)	3½	
			7
(b)	SSE	1	
	Trade loss b/f	½	
	QCDs	½	
	Group relief – current year and carried forward	1	
	Corporation tax	½	
	Capital loss to carry forward	½	
			4
66.2	Split into two APs	1	
	Payment		
	- Nine months and one day for each AP	1	
	- Apply to dates	1	
	Filing returns	1½	
		4½	
	Max		4
			15

66.1 (a) Letto Ltd tax adjusted trading profit for year ended 31 March 2019

	£
Trading profit	6,500,000
Amortisation of patents	0
Loss on sale of patent	0
Profit on sale of shares	(379,000)
Loan finance costs (incidental costs of £52,500 and interest costs of £420,000)	0
Charitable donations	60,000
Capital allowances (W)	(270,158)
Trading profit	5,910,842

WORKING

Capital allowances Y/E 31 March 2019	FYA £	Main pool £	SR pool £	Total £
TWDV b/f		850,233	443,000	
Zero-emissions good vehicles × 5/6	75,000			
Addition – integral feature in SR pool			83,450	
No AIA as allocated to group				
			526,450	
FYA @ 100%	(75,000)			75,000
WDA @ 18% / 8%		(153,042)	(42,116)	195,158
TWDV c/f	0	697,191	484,334	
Total allowances				270,158

(b)   **Letto Ltd corporation tax liability for year ended 31 March 2019**

	£
Trading profits (part (a))	5,910,842
Gain on sale of shares exempt as SSE	0
Total profits	5,910,842
Less trade losses brought forward	(100,000)
Less qualifying charitable donations paid	(50,000)
TTP	5,760,842
Group loss – current year	(4,500,000)
Group loss – of carried forward losses	(225,000)
Revised TTP	1,035,842

Corporation tax payable:

CT @ 19%	196,810

The capital loss in Letto Ltd can only be offset against capital gains. As Letto Ltd has none the capital loss will be carried forward to be offset against gains in the year ended 31 March 2020.

66.2 A company cannot have an accounting period exceeding 12 months. Therefore for tax purposes Tog Ltd has two APs:

- The year ended 31 December 2018
- The three months ended 31 March 2019

A company which does not pay corporation tax by instalments must pay its corporation tax within nine months and one day after the end of the accounting period.

Tog Ltd's CT liability is payable nine months and one day after the end of each accounting period:

- 1 October 2019
- 1 January 2020

A return is due for each AP but both returns must be filed within 12 months of the period of account end – ie, by 31 March 2020, or three months after the notice to deliver a return is issued, if later.

Examiner's comments

66.1 (a)   There were quite a lot of disappointing answers to this question. The majority of students treated the patents as capital ie, disallowed the amortisation and loss on sale and calculated a capital loss on disposal which was brought into part (b). Instead of adjusting for the profit on the shares many adjusted for an actual gain that they calculated. It was also common to disallow some or all of the loan finance costs. The charitable donation adjustments were evenly split between adding £50K, deducting £50K, adding £60K and deducting £60K.

Generally though the capital allowances computation was good, the only mistake being the VAT treatment of the assets.

(b)   It was quite common for the SSE not to be identified. [Note that the group relief and losses section of this question has been amended since it was originally set due to syllabus changes. Consequently the examiner comments which are no longer relevant have been removed.]

Most students did not identify that there were two accounting periods and therefore were limited in the number of marks they could score. As a result many just gained 1½ marks for stating the rules and dates for payment and filing for a period to 31 March 2019.

Many students continue not to give a full date (ie, a day, a month and a year) when asked to do so.

67 Anushka (June 2017)

Marking guide

			Marks
67.1(a)	Adjustment to profit		
	- Samples	½	
	- Food	½	
	- Subscription	½	
	- General provision	½	
	- Interest received	½	
	- Legal fees	1	
	- Repair	1	
	- CAs	½	
	Capital allowances (W1)	3	
			8
(b)	Interest on business bank account	½	
	Shares donated to charity	1	
	PA and BPA	1	
	IT liability	3½	
			6
67.2(a)	Phone	½	
	Safety clothing	1	
	Job related accommodation	3	
	Employment income	½	
	W1 loan benefit	2½	
		7½	
	Max		7
(b)	Exempt amount	1	
	IT on taxable amount	1½	
	No NIC	½	
			3
67.3	Rental income	1	
	Management expenses	½	
	Interest on loan	1	
	Capital repayment	½	
	Council tax and water rates	½	
	Insurance	½	
	AIA on lawnmower	½	
	Replacement sofa	1	
	Brought forward property loss	½	
			6

67.4 (a)	2016/17	1	
	2017/18	1½	
	2018/19	½	
			3
(b)	Foreign dividend in 2018/19	½	
	Prior year loss offset	½	
	Current year loss offset	½	
	Carried forward loss offset	1	
	Personal allowance	½	
			3
(c)	Calculation of trade profit on which Class 4 calculated	2	
	NIC at 9%	1½	
	NIC at 2%	1	
		4½	
	Max		4
			40

67.1 (a) Anushka's tax adjusted trading profits for year ending 31 March 2019

	£
Draft profit	63,000
Samples allowable	0
Food – drawing	2,400
Subscription allowable	0
General provision increase	2,650
Interest received	(200)
Legal fees – capital related	925
December's repair cost	(2,100)
Less capital allowances (W1)	(4,843)
Adjusted trading profit	61,832

Capital allowances (W1)	Main pool	SRP	PUA – 70%		Total
TWDV b/f	26,879	12,450	6,420		
Disposal in main pool	(10,000)				
WDA @ 18% / 8%	(3,038)	(996)			4,034
WDA @ 18%			(1,156)	× 70%	809
	13,841	11,454	5,264		4,843

(b) Anushka income tax for 2018/19

	NSI £	Savings £	Dividend £
Trading income (part (a))	61,832		
Interest on business bank account		200	
BSI		20,175	
Dividend			9,960
Shares donated to charity	(12,000)		
Net income	49,832	20,375	9,960
Less personal allowance + BPA = £11,850 + £2,390	(14,240)		
Taxable income	35,592	20,375	9,960
Non-savings income			
	£34,500	× 20%	6,900
	£1,092	× 40%	437

	NSI £	Savings £	Dividend £
Savings income			
Savings income NRB	£500 × 0%		0
	£19,875 × 40%		7,950
Dividend income			
Dividend NRB	£2,000 × 0%		0
	£7,960 × 32.5%		2,587
Income tax liability			17,874

67.2 (a) Jasminder's employment income

	£
Salary	18,000
Phone	0
Loan (W)	1,167
Less safety clothing	(500)
	18,667

Plus JRA expenses, max = 10% of net earnings
Lower of:

Job related accommodation

	£	£	£
Furniture = £4,000 × 20%	800		
Expenses (£750 + £2,080 + £950)	3,780		
		4,580	
Employment income × 10%			
£18,667 × 10% = £1,867		1,867	
			1,867
			20,534

WORKING
Loan
Use average method

	£
[(£60,000 + £40,000) / 2] = £50,000 @ 2.5%	1,250
Or	
Strict method	
£60,000 × 4/12 = £20,000 @ 2.5%	500
£40,000 × 8/12 = £26,667 @ 2.5%	667
	1,167

Elect for strict method

(b) Relocation package

	£	£
Allowance	15,000	15,000
Less exempt amount	(8,000)	
Taxable amount	7,000	
IT at 20%		(1,400)
No Class 1 primary NIC		0
Net cash		13,600

67.3 Daniel's taxable property income

	£
As cash receipts < £150,000 the cash basis applies.	
Rental income received £1,400 × 11	15,400
Less:	
Management expenses paid	(1,000)
50% × interest on loan (50% × £500)	(250)
Capital repayments – not deductible	–
Council tax and water rates paid	(1,000)
Insurance paid	(550)
AIA on the lawnmower (100% × £200)	(200)
Replacement sofa (£950 + £20)	(970)
	11,430
Less brought forward property loss	(300)
Taxable property income	11,130

67.4(a) Roger's trading income assessments

		£	£
2016/17	Opening year rules		
	Commencement to next 5 April		
	1.1.17 – 5.4.17 = 3/12 × £43,500		(10,875)
2017/18	Year ended 31 December 2017		
	Loss for the period	43,500	
	Less loss already used in 2016/17	(10,875)	
			(32,625)
2018/19	Year ended 31 December 2018		117,000

(b) Steve's total taxable income

	2016/17 £	2017/18 £	2018/19 £
Trading profits	2,000	0	78,000
Less trading loss b/fwd			(3,000)
Property income	12,000	12,000	12,000
Foreign dividend = (£3,000 + £1,500)			4,500
Total income	14,000	12,000	91,500
Less prior year loss	(14,000)		
Less current year loss		(12,000)	
Total income	0	0	91,500
Less personal allowance			(11,850)
Taxable income	0	0	79,650

(c) Class 4

	£
Income subject to NIC Class 4 = £78,000 – £3,000 – £12,000 – £12,000	£51,000
Only trading profits are subject to NIC	
The loss of the prior year set-off against non-trading income is treated as carried forward for NIC purposes	

	£
(£46,350 – £8,424) = £37,926 × 9%	3,413
(£51,000 – £46,350) × 2%	93
	3,506

Examiner's comments

67.1 (a) Students generally performed much better on the adjustment of profit for the sole trader than they did for the company in question 66 (Sedia Ltd and Tog Ltd). The only common mistake was not adding back the whole of the legal fees. The capital allowances computation was performed well apart from the disposal of the low emission car which was normally incorrect. Students do not appear to understand that a low emission car addition is a main pool item on which FYAs are claimed and thus they really had no idea how to treat its disposal.

   (b) The calculation of income tax was generally excellent with the vast majority demonstrating a good understanding of how the tax bands and the savings and dividend nil rate bands operate. The majority of students however forgot to include the business bank account interest and a large number treated the shares donated to charity as a Gift Aid payment. The blind person's allowance was also often forgotten or treated as a deduction from the tax liability.

67.2 (a) Overall performance on the employment income calculation was poor – often also by students that had performed well on the rest of the exam. Most students however, correctly treated the phone as exempt and gave a deduction for the safety clothing. Most also correctly calculated a loan benefit, but only used one method, normally the strict method. The accommodation benefit caused the most problems with many students scoring nil. Commonly the rent was treated as a benefit but not the redecoration. Only a handful recognised that there was a restriction of the taxable expenses but then calculated the restriction by reference to the salary only. The furniture benefit was often correct but it was also quite common for 20% of the expenses to be treated as taxable.

   (b) This requirement was often entirely correct demonstrating not only knowledge of the tax issues but also the concept of net cash.

67.3 [This requirement has been rewritten due to syllabus changes and there are therefore no examiner comments.]

67.4 (a) It was surprising how many students really had no idea how to calculate basis periods for opening years and clearly did not understand the difference between basis periods and years of assessment. This was one of the parts of the exam that was most commonly not answered. Many students really just wrote out the question ie, just gave the results for each accounting period and made no attempt to allocate to tax years. Students who did note that there was an amount of loss that had already been allocated to the first year, often then stated that it would be relieved in the final year as an 'overlap loss' and did not deduct it from the second year's loss as unavailable.

   (b) There were some good answers but also some appalling answers. This part was not answered well mainly because it was not presented well so it was often difficult to know what income losses were being offset against and in which years. There appeared to be little understanding of what losses can be relieved against. In addition, easy marks for including the correct foreign income and the personal allowance were lost by most students. Again, the question tested loss relief in a fairly simple form, suggesting that as for corporate losses, students are not adequately prepared for loss relief questions involving individuals.

   (c) The NIC part was generally answered well, although only a handful of students deducted the losses offset in prior years from the profits subject to NIC. This part was also one of the parts that was often not answered at all.

September 2017 exam answers

68 Flash LLP (September 2017)

	Marks
68.1 Contact Iris, relevant facts, check demand correct	1½
Document issue	½
Check engagement letter for permission to contact HMRC, ask client for permission, contact HMRC	1½
Legal advice, contact PII providers, penalties and interest	1½
	5
Max	**3**
68.2 Self-interest threat to objectivity, integrity and professional behaviour	1
Tax evasion	1
Discussion of tax evasion and consequences	2½
Actions for firm	1½
	6
Max	**4**
	7

68.1 Flash LLP should immediately contact Iris to inform her that the matter is being investigated.

The firm should ascertain the relevant facts relating to the termination payment and the advice given at that point in time, and check that HMRC's demand is correct.

It is advisable to document the current issue in writing, including any discussions with the client.

The firm should check the engagement letter for permission to contact HMRC if needed, or if not ask the client for permission. The firm should contact HMRC to confirm/refute the discovery assessment.

The firm may wish to obtain professional advice from ICAEW or legal advisors.

It may be appropriate to contact the firm's providers of PII to let them know that there may be a claim.

Flash LLP may be required to pay any penalties or interest.

68.2 **Eddie**

By preparing his own P11D in this way, Eddie has allowed a self-interest threat to affect his objectivity, integrity and professional behaviour in submitting an incorrect form in order to pay less tax.

Eddie's actions amount to tax evasion as he has deliberately withheld information from HMRC/provided HMRC with false information by understating his employment income/omitting his car benefit.

It would not be tax evasion if this was simply a mistake, but it is likely it was deliberate. Eddie could be the subject of a criminal prosecution which may lead to fines and/ or imprisonment. This could also constitute money laundering.

ICAEW may take action against him.

The firm

The firm should contact HMRC immediately to correct the P11D and pay any underpaid employer NICs.

The firm should follow its own internal disciplinary procedures in relation to Eddie's wrong doing.

Examiner's comments

68.1 Many students did not correctly understand the facts of the question and accused the client of money laundering. The suggested treatment of the client in many cases was inappropriate and only a small number of students indicated they would actually contact the client to reassure her that the issue was being investigated.

68.2 A significant number of students answered assuming that Eddie was a client of the firm rather than an employee, so there were references to reviewing the engagement letter and resigning from the engagement. Where students did answer appropriately they generally focussed on the legal rather than ethical issues.

69 Fleet Ltd (September 2017)

		Marks
69.1 VAT on original purchase	½	
Initial recovery	1	
No adjustment for y/e 31 March 2017,2018 and 2019	½	
Y/e 31 March 2020 – normal adjustment	1½	
Y/e 31 March 2020 – sale adjustment	2	
	5½	
	Max	5
69.2 Lopp	½	
Pemmican	2	
	2½	
	Max	2
69.3 Stamp duty	1	
		1
69.4 Total received	½	
Operational costs	½	
Corporation tax on gain	½	
Capital goods scheme adjustment	½	
Purchase of Lopp Ltd	½	
Stamp duty on Lopp Ltd	½	
Stamp duty reserve tax	1	
Calculation of number of shares	1	
		5
		13

69.1 Capital goods scheme: 10-year period of adjustment

VAT on original purchase £1.5 million × 20% = £300,000
Year ended 31 March 2016 – initial recovery £300,000 × 60% = £180,000

	£
No adjustment required in years ended 31 March 2017, 2018 and 2019 – ie prior to disposal	
Y/e 31 March 2020 – year of disposal Normal adjustment	
Adjustment = recoverable from HMRC £300,000 × 1/10 × (85 – 60)%	7,500
Adjustment for sale (exempt) Adjustment = payable to HMRC £300,000 × (0 – 60)% = £180,000 × 5/10	(90,000)
Total adjustment = payable to HMRC	(82,500)

69.2 Lopp Ltd

The stock transfer form must be presented to HMRC within 30 days of execution and the stamp duty paid at that time.

Pemmican plc

SDRT is payable on the 7th day of the month following the month of agreement for a paper transaction. However if the transfer can be made by CREST it should be paid over by 14 calendar days after the trade date.

69.3 Lopp Ltd

Stamp duty is payable at ½%. £514,600 × ½% = £2,573 rounded up to £2,575.

69.4 Fleet Ltd will receive £2.5 million for the building but then in addition to legal/rent costs must pay the following:

- Corporation tax on the gain
- Purchase cost of the Lopp Ltd shares (including stamp duty)
- Stamp duty reserve tax on the Pemmican plc share purchase
- Additional VAT relating to the capital goods scheme

	£
Total received (no VAT)	2,500,000
Operational costs	(140,000)
Corporation tax on gain 19% × £760,000	(144,400)
Capital goods scheme adjustment (part 1)	(82,500)
Purchase of Lopp Ltd	(514,600)
Stamp duty on Lopp Ltd (part 3)	(2,575)
	1,615,925
Stamp duty reserve tax 0.5/100.5 × £1,615,925	(8,039)
	1,607,886
The maximum number of shares is £1,607,886/ £50.24 = 32,004.1 ie	32,004 shares

Examiner's comments

69.1 This question was quite a differentiator – with some students performing extremely well and others poorly. The capital goods scheme was not handled as well as in previous sessions, particularly the adjustment on sale, but most students managed to pick up enough marks here.

69.2 Few students correctly identified the stamp taxes payment dates for both sets of shares – usually being correct for one or the other.

69.3 Many students picked up half a mark on this one mark question but very few rounded the amount up to the next £5 point.

69.4 Those students who attempted the calculation of the number of shares that could be purchased usually scored decent marks, but with some errors. Common errors included starting with the gain rather than the cash received and the omission of stamp duty reserve tax on the shares themselves, a higher level point.

70 Nora and Linda (September 2017)

Marking guide

			Marks
70.1	Gain on Snart Ltd shares after gift relief (W1)	2	
	CBA/CA calculation (W2)	3½	
	Painting (W3)	2	
	Ramon shares (W4) and (W5)	2½	
	Gains summary calculation	2	
			12
70.2 (a)	Domicile of origin	½	
	Not established UK domicile of choice	½	
	Deemed UK domicile	1	
			2
(b)	Home in the UK	½	
	Holiday home	1	
	Nimbus shares	1	
	Cash and other personal effects	½	
	Residence nil rate band (including spouse's)	1	
	NRB at death (including spouse's)	1	
	IHT at 40%	½	
	DTR	½	
	Spouse's unused NRB (W1)	2	
	DTR (W2)	2	
			10
(c)	Who pays	½	
	Date	½	
			1
			25

70.1 CGT liability for 2018/19

	ER £	Non-ER £
Snart Ltd shares (W1)	55,210	
Painting (W3)		(3,100)
Ramon plc shares (W4)		10,333
	55,210	7,233
Less annual exempt amount	(4,467)	(7,233)
Taxable gains	50,743	-
CGT liability £50,743 × 10%		5,074

WORKINGS

(1) Snart Ltd

	£
Sale proceeds (market value)	254,000
Less cost	(35,000)
	219,000
Less gift relief	
$219,000 \times \dfrac{890,000}{1,190,000}$ (W2)	(163,790)
	55,210

(2) CBA/CA

	CBA	CA
Office building – held as an investment	–	300,000
Factory – used by Snart Ltd	600,000	600,000
Goodwill	250,000	250,000
Plant and machinery		
Items over £6,000 each	40,000	40,000
Items less than £6,000 each	–	–
Other net current assets	–	–
	890,000	1,190,000

(3) Painting

	£
Sale proceeds (deemed)	6,000
Less selling costs £5,000 × 2%	(100)
	5,900
Less cost (probate value)	(9,000)
	(3,100)

(4) Ramon plc

	£
Sale proceeds	24,000
Less cost (W5)	(13,667)
	10,333

(5) Share pool

	No	Cost
June 2010	4,000	10,000
April 2013	2,000	6,400
	6,000	16,400
September 2018	(5,000)	(13,667)
	1,000	2,733

70.2 (a) On her arrival into the UK Linda's domicile of origin was Italy, inherited from her father.

As it had been her intention to return to Italy she had not made the UK her domicile of choice.

At her death Linda had been resident in the UK for at least 15 out of the previous 20 years, including one of the four tax years ending with the current tax year, so she is deemed to be UK domiciled for IHT purposes.

(b)

	£	£
Death estate		
Free estate		
Home in UK		600,000
Holiday home in Italy		250,000
Shares in Nimbus Ltd – related property (55%) £80 × 4,000		320,000
Cash and other personal effects		270,000
		1,440,000
Less residence nil rate band (including Ronnie's)		(250,000)
		1,190,000
Less nil rate band at death		
Own	325,000	
Spouse unused (W1)	81,250	
		(406,250)
		783,750
IHT due at 40%		313,500
Less DTR (W2)		(54,427)
IHT payable		259,073

WORKINGS

(1) **Spouse nil rate band**

NRB at death in June 2008	312,000
Less used on death	(234,000)
Unused NRB	78,000

Percentage unused 78,000 / 312,000 × 100 = 25%

Available for Linda £325,000 × 25%   81,250

(2) **DTR**

Lower of: UK tax on overseas estate 313,500 / 1,440,000 × £250,000	54,427
Overseas tax	80,000
	le £54,427

(c) The IHT due on the estate is payable by the executors/personal representatives and will be due by 30 September 2019 in order to avoid interest.

Examiner's comments

70.1 The calculation of the loss on the painting was invariably incorrect often with more than one computation being presented. The majority made an attempt at gift relief on the relevant share disposal as adjusted for the non-business asset. It was very common however, for the non-chargeable assets eg net current assets to be treated as chargeable assets. A surprising number did not recognise that entrepreneurs' relief was available on the Snart Ltd shares, and so missed some of the marks for use of losses and the annual exempt amount. Many students correctly calculated the gain on disposal of the pooled shares.

70.2 (a) Many students did not answer the question set and only looked at her domicile status on death rather than since her arrival.

(b) The death estate calculation was generally well answered. The main error was in the valuation of the Nimbus Ltd shares where students tried to perform a diminution in value calculation and did not correctly identify the related parties. Most students incorrectly calculated the UK tax on the overseas property using a 40% tax rate. However, many did recognise that DTR is available and put it in the correct place. The calculation of the spouses nil rate band was generally performed well.

(c) Most students incorrectly stated who suffered the tax, Henry, rather than who paid it, the executors/personal representatives. [The due date requirement has been added to the question from when originally set and so there is no Examiner comment.]

71 Bolt Ltd (September 2017)

		Marks
71.1 Adjustment to profit (½ per item)	3½	
R&D deduction (W1)	2½	
Capital allowances (W2)	1	
		7
71.2 Property income	½	
Group relief	½	
Tax at 19%	½	
Non-trade loan relationship (W1)	1	
Gain – calculation (W2)	1	
Gain – elect to transfer to Girder to offset b/f capital loss (W2)	½	
Gain – group rollover claim (W2)	2	
Group relief (W3)	2	
		8
		15

71.1 Tax adjusted trading profits for year ended 31 March 2019

	£	£
Draft profit		683,000
Add:		
Loan interest re: Mardon Place £5,000 × 20%		1,000
Other interest allowable		–
Professional fees – Mardon Place		12,000
Professional fees – new machinery		1,500
Less:		
Profit on disposal of factory	234,000	
130% R&D deduction (W1) £34,200 × 130%	44,460	
Capital allowances (W2)	11,520	
		(289,980)
Adjusted trading profit		407,520

WORKINGS

	£
(1) Qualifying R&D	
Salaries	32,000
Software	600
Consumables	1,000
Power, water and fuel	600
	34,200

	Main pool	Total
(2) Capital allowances		
TWDV b/f	45,000	
Purchase	19,000	
	64,000	
WDA @ 18%	(11,520)	11,520
	52,480	11,520

71.2

	£
Tax-adjusted trading profit (part 1)	407,520
Non-trading loan relationship (W1)	4,700
Property income	8,300
Chargeable gains (W2)	42,368
Taxable total profits	462,888
Less group loss relief	(100,000)
Taxable total profits	362,888
Corporation tax @ 19%	68,949

WORKINGS

(1) **Non-trading loan relationship**	
Interest receivable	5,700
Less Interest on Mardon Place loan (part 1)	(1,000)
	4,700

(2) **Gain on Mardon Place**	
Sale proceeds	300,000
Less selling costs	(12,000)
	288,000
Less cost	(110,000)
	178,000

Less indexation allowance $\dfrac{278.1-149.8}{149.8} = 0.856 \times £110,000$ (94,160)

	83,840

Bolt Ltd should elect to transfer £22,000 of the capital gain to Girder Ltd where it can be offset by Girder Ltd's capital loss carried forward   (22,000)

	61,840
Group rollover against Girder Ltd's warehouse (W3)	(19,472)
Taxable now	42,368

(3)   Rollover relief with non-business use

	Business 80%	NB 20%	Total
Gain	49,472	12,368	61,840
Group ROR β	(19,472)	-	(19,472)
Taxable now	30,000	12,368	42,368

(Proceeds not reinvested: 300,000 × 80% – 210,000)

Examiner's comments

71.1 Most students understand the need to show clear workings to support particular figures in cells, despite the ability to use formulae in the spreadsheet function of the software. However, some students are now not referencing their workings (W1, W2) as clearly as they did when answering on paper, and so risk losing marks if the marker cannot easily follow these. This was particularly evident in questions 71 (Bolt Ltd) and 72 (Martin Stein and Pattie). Some students had difficulty in preparing a corporation tax computation and knowing what adjustments to make in the adjusted profit computation and which to make in the calculation of taxable total profits. This was particularly true of the gain computation which was often adjusted for in arriving at the adjusted trading profit. In addition adjustments were often deducted when they should have been added and vice versa demonstrating a lack of understanding of how to adjust profits.

71.2 The quality of answers to this part was a cause for concern. Many students put very little other than their trading profit into the computation which they then taxed (correctly) at 19%. The calculations of the gain were frequently wrong, particularly indexation, a basic skill at the Principles of Taxation exam. The treatment of losses was poor. [Note that the part of this question regarding losses and groups has been rewritten due to syllabus changes.]

72   Martin Stein and Pattie (September 2017)

Marking guide

		Marks
72.1 (a) Depreciation	½	
Staff costs	½	
Gifts – food hampers to customers	1	
PAYE settlement agreements	½	
Capital allowances	½	
PAYE settlement agreement (W1)	2½	
Capital allowances (W2)	7½	
		13
(b) 2017/18	1	
2018/19	2	
		3
(c) Class 2	1	
Class 4	2	
		3

		Marks
72.2 (a) Salary	½	
Round sum allowance	½	
Employer pension contributions	½	
Train travel	½	
No deduction for entertaining costs	½	
Payroll giving	½	
Car benefit (W1)	½	
Fuel benefit (W2)	1½	
		5
(b) Net income calculation (½ per item)	3	
Personal allowance	½	
IT calculation	3	
DTR deductions	½	
Extended bands (W1)	1½	
Adjusted net income (W2)	1½	
DTR calculations (W3) and (W4)	3	
		13
(c) Reduced contributions	½	
Increased income taxed at higher rate	2	
Adjusted net income (W1)	1½	
	4	
Max		3
		40

72.1 (a) Tax-adjusted trading profits for 15 months ended 31 March 2019

	£
Draft profit	361,700
Add: depreciation	70,860
Staff costs – Martin's drawings (no other staff cost adjustments)	50,000
Gifts – food hampers to customers	800
Less:	
PAYE settlement agreement (W1)	(1,156)
Less capital allowances (W2)	(284,855)
Adjusted trading profit	197,349

WORKINGS

(1) **PAYE settlement agreement**

	BR	HR	Total
Small benefit	2,100	300	2,400
Tax on benefit 20/80; 40/60	525	200	725
	2,625	500	3,125
Class 1B NIC £3,125 × 13.8%			431
Total payable to HMRC £725 + £431			1,156

(2) **Capital allowances**	**Main pool**	**Special rate**	**Short life**	**Allowances**
TWDV b/f	120,300	48,000	1,465	
Purchases – AIA (note)				
Van (£21k × 5/6)	17,500			
Electrical system (£282K × 5/6)		235,000		
AIA	(15,000)	(235,000)		250,000
Purchases non-AIA				
Car		15,600		
Disposal (£720 × 5/6)			(600)	
	122,800	63,600	865	
Balancing allowance			(865)	865
WDA @ 18% × 15/12	(27,630)			27,630
WDA @ 8% × 15/12		(6,360)		6,360
	95,170	57,240		
Total allowances				284,855

Note: AIA for the 15-month period is £250,000 (£200,000 × 15/12)

AIA to the special rate pool purchases in priority

(b)

		£
2017/18	1 January to 31 December 2017	40,000
2018/19	Year of change	
	1 January 2018 to 31 March 2019 (a)	197,349
	Less overlap profits	(9,500)
		187,849

(c)

	£
Class 2 NIC	
£2.95 × 52	153
Class 4	
(£46,350 – £8,424) × 9%	3,413
(£187,849 – £46,350) × 2% (b)	2,830
	6,243

72.2 (a)

Pattie's employment income

	£
Salary	80,000
Round sum allowance	2,400
Company car (W1)	2,175
Fuel benefit (W2)	4,680
Employer pension contributions	-
	89,255
Less	
Train travel	(695)
No deduction for entertaining costs paid from a general RSA	-
Payroll giving	(480)
Employment income	88,080

WORKINGS

		£
(1)	**Car benefit**	
	£10,875 × 20%	2,175
(2)	**Fuel benefit**	
	£23,400 × 20%	4,680

Tutorial note

If private fuel is not available for part of a tax year (eg, the employee opts out of an arrangement), the fuel benefit is time apportioned. However, this does not apply if private fuel again becomes available to the employee later in the tax year.

(b)

Pattie income tax payable for 2018/19

	Total £	NSI £	Savings £	Dividend £
Employment income (a)		88,080		
Repayment interest – exempt			–	
UK Interest (£6,240 – £40)			6,200	
UK Dividend				8,400
French property income (£8,000 × 100/80)		10,000		
Spanish interest (£2,000 + £200)			2,200	
Net income	114,880	98,080	8,400	8,400
Less personal allowance (W2)	(11,850)	(11,850)		
Taxable income	103,030	86,230	8,400	8,400
Non-savings income (W1)	59,500	× 20%		11,900
	26,730	× 40%		10,692
Savings income	500	× 0%		–
	7,900	× 40%		3,160
Dividend income	2,000	× 0%		–
	6,400	× 32.5%		2,080
				27,832
Less DTR on property income (highest overseas tax rate) (W3)				(2,000)
Less DTR on interest income (W4)				(200)
Income tax liability				25,632

WORKINGS

	£
(1) Extended bands	
BRB	34,500
PPC (£20,000 ×100/80)	25,000
	59,500

(2) Adjusted net income (PA)

	£
Net income	114,880
Less personal pension contributions £20,000 × 100/80	(25,000)
	89,880

Adjusted net income – less than £100,000 so full personal allowance available

(3) Remove overseas property income

The overseas income clearly falls into the higher rate tax band thus no need for a full income tax computation.

DTR is the lower of:

UK tax on overseas property income	10,000	× 40%	= 4,000
Overseas tax			=2,000

So, DTR £2,000

(4) Remove overseas interest income

DTR is the lower of:

UK tax on overseas interest income	2,200	× 40%	= 880
Overseas tax			= 200

So, DTR £200

(c)

Pattie total cash saving

	£
Reduced pension contributions £20,000 - £10,000	10,000
Increased income taxed at higher rate (W1) £1,190 × 40%	(476)
Increased income taxed at higher rate (W1) (40-20)% × £12,500	(2,500)
Total cash saving	7,024

WORKINGS

(1) Adjusted net income

	£
Net income (b)	114,880
Less personal pension contributions £10,000 × 100/80	(12,500)
	102,380

As this exceeds £100,000 the PA is abated by ½ × (£102,380 - £100,000) = £1,190. So, a further £1,190 of income will be taxed at 40%.

In addition, the BRB is extended by £12,500 rather than £25,000 meaning an additional £12,500 will be taxed at 40% rather than 20%.

Examiner's comments

72.1 (a) Many students picked up good marks on this part of the question, particularly in relation to capital allowances. The exceptions were the treatment of the PAYE settlement agreement which was largely ignored. Better prepared students frequently lost marks for grossing up the relevant benefit, but could gain marks for national insurance payable. There were some tricky elements to the capital allowances calculation for a 15 month period, with a small number of students adopting a corporate approach and splitting this into two periods. The necessary VAT adjustments were also omitted by some, although this did not cost many marks.

(b) This part was not answered well. Many students showed no knowledge at all in this area. This is fundamental to the understanding of the taxation of unincorporated businesses and should offer easy marks to students.

(c) Having performed badly in the previous part, a significant number of students then gained full marks on this 3 mark part.

72.2 (a) This was generally answered well – most employment income adjustments were correctly made apart from the fuel benefit which was invariably time apportioned.

(b) Most students performed well in the main aspects of this part. However, many did not consider the pension contribution beyond the effect on the basic rate band, not considering the effect on adjusted net income. [Note that the overseas element to this question has been added in due to syllabus changes and thus there are no Examiner's comments relating to this.]

(c) This part was a discriminating element of the exam. A common approach was to recalculate the income tax liability, which gained marks but used a lot of time compared to the approach taken in the model answer. A reasonable number however, did attempt the model answer approach and usually gained the marks for the increased tax at the higher rate. Surprisingly, not many students gained marks for the cash savings from reducing the pension contributions. This mark was more likely to be gained by those taking the model answer approach as they were more focussed on the main issue (ie the cash savings) than those that got involved in detailed income tax computations. Whilst the recalculation of the income tax liability is an acceptable, if not preferred, method of attempting this part, it will not be acceptable in the Business Planning: Taxation exam where the focus will be on discussing the individual aspects making up the cash savings and making recommendations. [Note that the detail tested in this requirement has been amended due to syllabus changes although these examiner comments remain appropriate.]

December 2017 exam answers

73 Sherazi LLP (December 2017)

Marking guide

		Marks
73.1 Objectivity	½	
Confidentiality	½	
Safeguards – ½ mark per safeguard	$\frac{4}{5}$	
Max		4
73.2 1 mark per step	$\frac{4}{4}$	
Max		$\frac{3}{7}$

73.1 The fundamental principles threatened by Sherazi LLP accepting Javadi Ltd as a client are objectivity and confidentiality.

Sherazi LLP should do the following:

- Notify Higgins Ltd and Javadi Ltd of the potential conflict in acting for them both.

- Obtain consent from each party to act for both.

- If consent is not obtained then Sherazi LLP should not accept Javadi Ltd as a client.

- Assuming consent is obtained, use separate engagement teams for each client.

- Apply procedures to prevent access to information (physical separation of teams, secure data filing).

- Issue clear guidelines to the engagement teams/ provide training on issues of security and confidentiality.

- Use confidentiality agreements for employees and partners.

- Arrange a regular review of safeguards by a senior individual not involved in either engagement.

73.2 Before accepting the client Sherazi LLP should do the following:

- Carry out customer due diligence to establish areas of risk
- Verify the identity of Javadi Ltd and its directors and keep evidence of identification
- Obtain professional clearance from their previous advisors
- Prepare an appropriate engagement letter explaining the scope of responsibilities

73.1 This part was generally well answered although students were unclear which part of their answer related to 73.1 and which to 73.2. Students addressed the specific scenario in the question and had learned the safeguards to deal with this situation.

73.2 Surprisingly few students gained all three marks on this part. Many students got the marks for due diligence and client identification. A significant number mentioned the engagement letter but very few mentioned professional clearance.

74 Virgil Ltd (December 2017)

Marking guide

		Marks
74.1 B2B	½	
Supplied in the UK	½	
Reverse charge system	½	
Treatment for VAT	1½	
Treatment if solicitor in USA	1	
	4	
Max		3
74.2 Output VAT	3	
Input VAT	2½	
VAT payable	½	
		6
74.3 Calculation of stamp duty on Virgil Ltd shares	1	
Calculation of stamp duty on property	2	
Due date and by whom	1	
	4	
		13

74.1 Legal fees

The supply of legal services to Virgil Ltd is a business-to-business (B2B) service.

The supply is treated as taking place in the UK (ie the place of the customer) and is charged under the reverse charge system.

Virgil Ltd should account for output tax on the VAT return, as it is treated as making the supply. The same amount can also be recovered as input tax on the same VAT return as the company makes only taxable supplies.

The same treatment would have applied had the solicitor been located in the USA.

74.2

	£	£
Output tax		
UK customers £258,000 × 20%		51,600
Supplies to Italian registered customers zero rated		-
Supplies to Italian individuals £32,000 × 20%		6,400
Supplies to USA (businesses and individuals) - zero rated		-
Reverse charge £8,400 × 20%		1,680
Input tax		
Purchases and expenses in UK £135,000 × 20%	27,000	
Rent paid	-	
Legal fees – reverse charge	1,680	
Purchase of car – blocked input tax	-	
Purchase of machinery £12,000 × 20%	2,400	
		(31,080)
VAT payable		28,600

74.3

	£
Stamp duty on the shares	
£874,600 × ½% = £4,373 rounded up to	4,375
Stamp duty land tax on the building	
£150,000 × 0%	-
(£250,000 – £150,000) × 2%	2,000
(£400,000 – £250,000) × 5%	7,500
	9,500

Both stamp duty and SDLT are payable by the purchaser by 29 April 2019

Examiner's comments

74.1 Students were not clear in their descriptions of how to deal with the legal fees. Comments appeared such as 'there would be output and input' but not explaining the reverse charge and not making it clear who would be paying this VAT. Very few knew that the treatment is the same whether the service was from Italy or the US.

74.2 Many students were clear on how to account for reverse charge, even if they could not explain it in words in part 74.1. The overseas aspects, particularly the supplies to the US, were the only thing causing difficulty.

74.3 Stamp duty land tax calculations were well attempted. However students seemed to get confused with what 0.5% actually means when calculating stamp duty on the shares and many did not round to the next £5. Few students correctly identified the stamp taxes payment dates for both assets – usually being correct for one or the other. It was not sufficient to just state 'within 30 days' – the requirement asked for a date.

75 Carrie

		Marks
75.1	Cash to Otto	½
	AEA	½
	CGT	½
	No CGT on death estate	½
	Brody plc (W1)	2½
	Share valuation (W2)	1
		5 ½
	Max	5
75.2	June 11 CLT	1
	May 18 PET – GCT	1
	– Avail NRB	1
	– IHT	½
	Sept 18 PET – Value (W1)	3½
	– Available NRB	1
	– IHT	½
	March 2019 – Death estate valuation (W3)	3
	– RNRB	½
	– Available NRB	1
	– IHT including (W4)	1
	– QSR	½
	– QSR (W5)	2
		16½
	Max	16
75.3	Increase in charitable giving	½
	Change in IHT due	2
	Presentation cash cost/saving	1½
		4
		25

75.1 CGT payable for 2018/19

	£
Cash to Otto – exempt	–
Shares in Brody plc (W1)	70,000
	70,000
Less annual exempt amount	(11,700)
Taxable gains	58,300
CGT liability £58,300 × 20%	11,660

No CGT on death estate

WORKINGS

	£
(1) Brody plc	
Sale proceeds (market value, W2) £3.12 x 100,000	312,000
Less cost	(80,000)
	232,000
Less gift relief β	(162,000)
Remaining gain (excess cash £150,000 - £80,000)	70,000

(2) Share valuation

Valuation = lower quoted price + ½ (Higher price – lower price)

308 + ½ (316-308) = 312p

The marked bargain should not be considered.

75.2

	June 2011 CLT £	May 2018 PET £	September 2018 PET (W1) £	March 2019 Death (W3) £
Stage 1 - Transfers				
Transfer	256,000	220,000	159,000	1,158,840
Less exemptions				
Marriage		(5,000)		
Annual	(3,000)	(3,000)		
Annual b/f	(3,000)	(3,000)		
	250,000	209,000	159,000	1,158,840
Stage 2 – Lifetime tax				
Less remaining NRB (W2)	(325,000)	No LT tax	No LT tax	
	0			
IHT@ 20%	0			
Gross chargeable transfer	250,000	209,000	159,000	1,158,840
Stage 3 – Tax on death				
Gross chargeable transfer	More than 7 years	209,000	159,000	1,158,840
Less residence NRB				(125,000)
Less remaining NRB (W2)		(75,000)	(116,000)	–
		134,000	43,000	1,033,840
IHT @ 40% (W4)		53,600	17,200	413,536
Taper (<3 yrs)		53,600	17,200	413,536
100% chargeable				
Less QSR (W5)				(39,417)
Tax payable on death		53,600	17,200	374,119

WORKINGS

(1) Valuation of Brody plc shares

Valuation = lower of

> Quarter up valuation 308 + ¼ (316 – 308) = 310p
> Mid bargain = 309p

Ie, 309p

	£
Value 100,000 × £3.09	309,000
Less amount paid	(150,000)
Diminution in value	159,000

(2) **Remaining nil rate band**

	June 2011 CLT £	May 2018 PET £	September 2018 PET £	March 2019 Death £
Stage 2 – Lifetime				
Lifetime NRB	325,000			
Less chargeable in previous 7 years				
Remaining NRB	325,000			–
Stage 3 – On death				
NRB at death	N/A	325,000	325,000	325,000
Less chargeable in previous 7 years		(250,000)	(209,000)	
£(209,000 + 159,000)				(368,000)
Remaining NRB	N/A	75,000	116,000	–

(3) **Death estate – March 2019**

Total assets	1,300,000
Less expenses	
Income tax	(20,000)
Capital gains tax (75.1)	(11,660)
Funeral expenses	(9,500)
Chargeable estate before exemptions	1,258,840
Less gift to charity - exempt	(100,000)
Chargeable death estate	1,158,840

(4) **Rate of IHT**

Chargeable estate before charity exemption × 10%
  (Note this is after any remaining NRB of £nil but before any RNRB)

£1,258,840 × 10%	125,884

As £100,000 is less than this amount IHT is charged at 40%

(5) **Quick succession relief (QSR)**

Tax on 1st transfer × Increase in Carrie's estate/
  Decrease in Simon's estate × %

£62,000 × £240,000/(£240,000 + £62,000) × 80% (1-2 years)	39,417

75.3

Cash cost/saving	£
Increase in charitable donation (£162,000 – £100,000)	62,000
Decrease in IHT liability (before QSR) (W)	(63,654)
Net cash saving	(1,654)

WORKING

IHT calculation

The charitable donation is now greater than £125,884 (part 2)
So IHT is charged at 36% on the death estate

Chargeable estate before exemptions	1,258,840
Less gift to charity – exempt	(162,000)
Less RNRB	(125,000)
Chargeable death estate	971,840
IHT @ 36%	349,862
IHT saving £413,516 - £349,862	63,654

Examiner's comments

75.1 Most students were able to value the Brody plc shares using the correct method, and calculate the CGT liability at the correct rate after deducting the annual exempt amount. However, a significant number did not identify that gift relief was available. Many students also incorrectly calculated a gain on the painting left in the estate (treating death as a chargeable event). It was encouraging to see that many addressed the specific requirement to show the treatment of every event and stated that the cash transfer was exempt.

75.2 The standard of answers to the IHT part was good, although perhaps not as good as in previous sessions. CGT and IHT were combined in the same scenario and candidates had to consider each transaction first in terms of CGT for part 1 and then in terms of IHT in this part, which made the question marginally more difficult not least as the value of shares differs for the two taxes. In fact, this did not seem to deter many students who correctly valued the shares. But it was perhaps this combined scenario that contributed to the main error, the treatment of the sale of the shares at undervalue. A significant number of students did not treat the disposal as an IHT event, presumably because it was described as a 'sale' and they could justify to themselves the inclusion of the information given as being for part 1 only. When the 'sale' was treated as an IHT transfer only a handful of students correctly deducted the amount paid. This was a distinguishing aspect of the exam.

Students also lost marks for not showing workings, especially in relation to the available nil rate band. Students had previously improved at showing workings but that trend has reversed at this session. On a positive note, most students clearly demonstrated the overall procedure for calculating IHT payable on gifts and the estate as a result of death. QSR was usually identified and deducted in the correct place, but most treated £240,000 (the value of the asset), as the gross transfer.

75.3 Most students made a reasonable attempt at this fairly demanding part demonstrating that they understood the issues even if some of the figures were incorrect. Common errors included not deducting the increase in the donation from the estate before recalculating the tax at 36%, and not netting off the additional cost of the increased donation from the tax saving. Another, less common, error was recalculating the tax at 36% on the gifts as well as the estate. Supporting workings/descriptions could generally have been improved, but this was a discriminating element of the exam and it was pleasing that many students made a decent attempt.

76 Mathison Ltd

			Marks
76.1(a)	Proceeds and cost (½ each)	1	
	Indexation	1	
			2
(b)	Trading profits	½	
	NTLR income	1	
	Gains	½	
	Trade loss offset	½	
	QCDs	1	
	Corporation tax at 19%	½	
	Working – Gain on sale of Galvez Ltd	3	
			7
76.2(a)	AP exceed £437,500	2	
	Large in previous period	½	
	Tax liability not less then £5,833	½	
	AP calculation	½	
		3½	
	Max		3
(b)	Calculation of tax due	½	
	3 Dates	1 ½	
	Calculation of instalments	1	
			3
			15

76.1(a) Degrouping charge

		£
Sale proceeds (market value at transfer)		340,000
Less cost		(60,000)
Less indexation allowance	$\dfrac{261.4 - 126.7}{126.7} = 1.063 \times £60,000$	(63,780)
		216,220

(b)

	£
Tax-adjusted trading profit	980,000
Non-trading loan relationship	20,000
Chargeable gains (W)	424,162
Total profits	1,424,162
Less trade loss carried forward	(37,200)
Less QCD	(4,500)
Taxable total profits	1,382,462
Corporation tax payable × 19%	262,668

WORKING

Gain on sale of Galvez Ltd

	£
Sale proceeds	400,000
Add degrouping charge (a)	216,220
	616,220
Less cost	(150,000)
	466,220

Less indexation allowance (no rounding)

$$£150,000 \times \frac{278.1 - 217.2}{217.2}$$

	(42,058)
	424,162

76.2 (a) Lockhart Ltd is required to pay corporation tax in instalments for the seven months ended 31 October 2019 as:

(1) it has augmented profits exceeding £437,500 (£1.5 million × ½ × 7/12)

ie, it had one other related 51% group company at the end of the previous accounting period and the period is seven months long.

(2) it was a large company in the previous accounting period (ie augmented profits exceeded £750,000 (£1.5 million × 1/2).

(3) the tax liability is not less than £5,833 (£10,000 × 7/12).

WORKING

	£
Taxable total profit	775,000
Exempt ABGH distribution	12,000
Augmented profit	787,000

(b)

	£
The company has a corporation payable of (£775,000 × 19%)	147,250

Payments are due by:

14 October 2019 (3/7 × £147,250)	63,107
14 January 2020	63,107
14 February 2020	21,036

Examiner's comments

76.1 (a) A significant number of students could not calculate the degrouping charge. Many calculated a gain on the investment property but did not recognise it as a degrouping charge.

(b) Answers to this part were generally poor. A lot of students lost easy marks for basic errors, such as positioning of the trading loss brought forward, adjusting the trading profit before using it in the computation, not including their gains in the actual computation, treating the charitable donation and the political donation in the same way. The quality of corporation tax computations is showing a general downward trend with too many students unable to construct a computation from various types of income and gains.

(a) Most students made a reasonable attempt at this part. However many failed to mention augmented profits and a significant number failed to calculate them (or deducted dividends rather than added them) and confused the current period's profits with last year's. Very few showed any knowledge of the £10,000 exemption.

(b) One marker described this part as 'a little bit of a black hole'. It was rare for the total tax payments to equal the tax liability of £147,250 for the period. Many students used the TTP figure as the tax payable, but others based the payments on last year's liability or an invented figure for a 12 month accounting period. It was most common to see four payments or three equal payments. Students also lost marks for not giving precise dates which should include the year. A lot of answers also just stated the rules for the payment dates rather than applying the rules to the situation.

77 Saul

Marking guide

			Marks
77.1 (a)	Bonus	1	
	Loan write off	1	
	Each other item ½ mark for 7 items	3 ½	
	Working SMRS	2 ½	
			8
(b)	Interest, dividend income and PA (½ each)	1 ½	
	Calculation of IT	3	
	Less DTR	2	
	Property income (W1)	2	
	Calculation of IT excluding overseas income (W2)	3	
	Max	11 ½	
			11
77.2 (a)	Good for own use	1	
	Each other item in adjustment to profit (½ mark each × 8)	4	
	Capital allowances (W1)	6	
			11
(b)	Salary	1	
	Balance using PSR	1	
	Reallocation of notional profit	1	
			3
(c)	2018/19	1 ½	
	2019/20	1 ½	
			3
(d)	2018/19	½	
	2019/20	1 ½	
			2
(e)	½ mark per point	3	
		3	
	Max		2
			40

77.1 (a) Saul's employment income

	£
Salary	25,000
Bonus (£800 + £790)	1,590
Entertaining expenditure	–
Statutory mileage payments (W)	1,360
Employer pension contributions	–
Loan interest – exempt (loan less than £10,000)	–
Loan write off	1,500
	29,450
Less	
Occupational pension scheme payment £25,000 × 2%	(500)
Subscriptions	(320)
Employment income	28,630

WORKING

Statutory mileage payments

		£
Use of own car (12,000 × 52p)		6,240
Less allowable deductions		
10,000 × 45p		(4,500)
2,000 × 25p		(500)
		1,240
Passenger payment (12,000 × 6p)	720	
Less allowable deduction (12,000 × 5p)	(600)	
		120
		1,360

(b)

Saul income tax liability for 2018/19	Total £	NSI £	Savings £	Dividend £
Employment income (a)		28,630		
Interest			1,400	
Dividend				6,000
Property income (W1)		11,150		
Net income	47,180	39,780	1,400	6,000
Less personal allowance	(11,850)	(11,850)		
Taxable income	35,330	27,930	1,400	6,000
Non-savings income	£27,930	× 20%		5,586
Savings income - HR taxpayer	£500	× 0%		–
	£900	× 20%		180
Dividend income	£2,000	× 0%		–
	β£3,170	× 7.5%		238
	£34,500			
	£830	× 32.5%		270
				6,274
Less DTR (W2)				
Lower of				
UK tax on overseas income (£6,274 – £3,736)			2,538	
Overseas tax			1,900	(1,900)
Income tax liability				4,374

WORKINGS

(1) **Property income**

	£
Rental income	13,000
Less allowable expenditure	
Repairs and insurance	(1,100)
Cleaning	(450)
Furniture – replacement value not enhancement	(300)
	11,150

(2) **Double tax relief –Income tax excluding overseas income**

	Total £	NSI £	Savings £	Dividend £
Taxable income (35,330 – 11,150)	24,180	16,780	1,400	6,000
Non-savings income	£16,780	× 20%		3,356
Savings income - BR taxpayer	£1,000	× 0%		-
	£400	× 20%		80
Dividend income	£2,000	× 0%		-
	£4,000	× 7.5%		300
				3,736

77.2 (a) Tax-adjusted trading profit/ (loss) for six months ended 30 June 2019

	£
Draft profit	22,000
Less:	
Pre trading expenditure	
Legal advice re contracts	(20,000)
Legal advice re lease – capital	-
Rent payable £6,000 × 6/12	(3,000)
Gifts to customers (less than £50 per client, including advert)	(1,000)
Small donation to local charity	(300)
Insurance bill £340 × 6/12	(170)
Goods for own use	
(as nothing recorded in accounts at all the profit needs to be taxed)	40
Staff entertaining (3/10 × £1,000)	(300)
Capital allowances (W1)	(112,952)
Tax-adjusted trading loss	(115,682)

WORKING

Capital allowances	Main pool	Special rate	Private use car 10% bus	Private use car 20% bus		
Purchases – AIA						
Computer equipment	170,000					
AIA β	(65,000)					65,000
Air conditioning		35,000				
AIA		(35,000)				35,000
Purchases non-AIA						
Car - David			25,400			
Car – Mike (FYA)				17,000		
£17,000 × 20%				(17,000)	20%	3,400
	105,000	–	25,400			
WDA @ 18% × 6/12	(9,450)					9,450
WDA @ 8% × 6/12			(1,016)		10%	102
	95,550	–	24,384	–		
Total allowances						112,952

Note: AIA for the six month period is £100,000 (£200,000 × 6/12)
AIA to the special rate pool purchases

(b)

Six months ended 30 June 2019	David £	Mike £	Nicholas £	Total £
Salary (6/12)	45,000	5,000		50,000
PSR 20:40:40	(33,136)	(66,273)	(66,273)	(165,682)
	11,864	(61,273)	(66,273)	(115,682)
Reallocation of notional profit				
Mike 61,273/127,546 × £11,864	(5,699)	5,699		
Nicholas 66,273/127,546 × £11,864	(6,165)		6,165	
	–	(55,574)	(60,108)	

(c)

			£
2018/19	1 January 2019 to 5 April 2019		–
	3/6 × £(55,574) = £(27,787)		
2019/20	12 months ended 1 December 2019		
	Six months ended 30 June 2019	(55,574)	
	Less already used above	27,787	
		(27,787)	
	1 July 2019 to 31 December 2019		
	6/12 × £140,000	70,000	
			42,213

(d)

Class 4	£
2018/19 – loss making so no class 4 liability	–
2019/20 – the loss of 2018/19 is deducted from the 2019/20 earnings	
(£42,213 – £27,787 – £8,464) × 9%	537

(e) As Nicholas does not spend a 'significant' amount of time working within the partnership ie at least 10 hours per week, his loss relief is restricted to a maximum of £25,000 when claiming against total income or gains.

There is no restriction against trading income.

As the loss is also within the first four years it is restricted to the amount of his capital contribution.

Loss relief against total income is also restricted to the higher of £50,000 and 25% of adjusted total income. However this is not relevant in this situation as Nicholas only has £35,000 of income.

Examiner's comments

77.1(a) Many students produced excellent answers to this part. The most common errors were not including both bonuses and the loan write off. The calculation of the statutory mileage payments was particularly good.

(b) Most students performed well on this part and it was not uncommon to award close to full marks. The most common errors were treating the NS&I income as exempt and giving a savings nil rate band of £1,000 when the taxpayer was higher rate (even when the same student taxed dividends at the higher rate). Many students appeared to think that because the savings income was not in the higher rate band then the savings nil rate band was not reduced. It was pleasing to see that a significant number of students calculated the UK tax on the overseas income using the correct method. A short cut method only seemed to be attempted by weaker students. The calculation of the property income was very good – most students recognising the replacement furniture relief.

77.2 (a) This was generally answered well. Many students were awarded full marks in this part and scored very well in the subsequent parts. Others seemed to struggle and often did not answer parts 2c onwards. Common errors included forgetting to deduct the rent payable and not knowing how to treat the legal advice – either deducting both or ignoring both.

(b) The apportionment of the loss after accounting for salaries proved to be difficult for a lot of students. The reapportionment of the notional profit was either ignored or done incorrectly by a significant number.

(c) This part was one of the poorest answered on the exam. Very few students knew how to apply the opening year rules at all, before even considering the loss element.

(d) Students generally performed well on this part, although only a very small number brought forward the loss from the previous tax year to calculate earnings.

(e) This part was a discriminating element of the exam. It was not uncommon for students to score '0' or 0.5 marks. Very few students identified being a non-active trader as the key point.

March 2018 exam answers

78 Janet and John

		Marks
78.1 Nature of conflict	2	
– Managing the conflict		
– Safeguards	½	
– Separate teams and impartial advice	1 ½	
– Act for only one party but probably not viable for joint wills	1	
– If cannot manage conflict cease to act	1	
	6	
Max		4
78.2 Authorise disclosure and repay	1	
Legal consequence and example of consequence	1	
Advise if consent not given will cease to act	1	
Maintain written record	½	
Consideration error not *de minimis*	½	
Money laundering	½	
	4 ½	
Max		3
		7

78.1 Nature of conflict

This conflict presents a self-interest threat to objectivity

Janet and John are two separate clients/two individuals/act for both and should be advised accordingly.

Managing the conflict

Unless the potential conflict is clearly insignificant, safeguards should be put in place to mitigate the conflict.

Assuming we continue to act for both clients we could use separate engagement teams and separate meetings to ensure that each spouse receives impartial advice/without bias/without favouring either party without undue influence from the other part affecting their decisions.

Normally we would consider acting for only one party, but that is probably not a viable option in the preparation of joint wills.

If the conflict cannot be managed to an acceptable level we should cease to act for both parties.

78.2 HMRC error in client's favour

The client should be:

- asked to authorise disclosure of the error to HMRC and to repay the amount

- warned of the possible legal consequences of non-disclosure, including interest and penalties and possibly criminal prosecution (2nd ½ is for any example)

- advised that if consent is not given we will need to **cease to act**.

We should maintain a written record of all advice given.

Strictly, all errors should be disclosed. However, if the error is below a *de minimis* limit (PCRT suggests £200), then it may be reasonable to not disclose it. The £1,000 in this case is not *de minimis*.

If our client will not repay the £1,000, we should cease to act and consider that this amount becomes criminal proceeds so falls within money laundering.

Examiner's comments

78.1 Most students identified that there were two separate clients but then failed to appreciate the specific nature and practicalities of a conflict of interest between a married couple – so the majority concentrated on issues of confidentiality and relatively few mentioned the need to provide impartial advice or the impracticalities of just acting for one client in the preparation of joint wills.

78.2 This was answered very well with the majority of students getting all the key points. Students that performed less well tended to describe the issues rather than answer the question ie, in answering "what action should you take" students would explain "that the matter should be disclosed/penalties would apply" but did not actually state that they would tell the client to disclose etc.

79 Skate Ltd

Marking guide

		Marks
79.1 Benefits of VAT group (½ each)	1½	
Why Whale Ltd is not included	1	
Why Velvet Ltd is not included	1½	
Consideration of Unicorn Ltd	1½	
	5½	
Max		4
79.2 75% direct/indirect	½	
Why Whale Ltd cannot be in group	½	
Why Unicorn Ltd cannot be in group	1	
		2
79.3 VAT on sale	1	
SDLT on sale	2	
If sold to Tuna Ltd	2	
		5

	Marks

79.4 Recover VAT if

VAT registered trader	½
Uses to make taxable supplies	½
Has a VAT invoice	1
If rent only recover if opt to tax	1
	3
Max	2
	13

79.1 VAT group

Skate Ltd and Tuna Ltd makes standard-rated supplies have been included in the group to reduce VAT administration as intra-group sales will not be subject to VAT. Only one VAT return is required.

Whale Ltd cannot be included in the VAT group because the holding is only 49% which is less than the requirement of more than 50%/control/51% company

As a zero-rated trader, assuming its inputs are standard rated, Velvet Ltd is a repayment trader. Velvet Ltd has been excluded from the VAT group because otherwise the cashflow advantage of a monthly VAT repayment would be lost.

As an exporter within the EU to private individuals Unicorn Ltd's customers are unlikely to be VAT registered. Therefore its sales will be standard rated/subject to VAT and Unicorn Ltd has been included in the group for the same reasons as Skate Ltd and Tuna Ltd.

79.2 SDLT group

A group relationship for SDLT purposes exists where there is 75% ownership directly or indirectly between companies.

The direct holding in Whale Ltd is below 75% and therefore it cannot be in the SDLT group.

Unicorn Ltd is not in a group with Skate Ltd for SDLT purposes as the indirect holding is less than 75%/only 71.25% (95% × 75%).

79.3 VAT on sale

As the warehouse is a commercial building which **is less than three years old**, it is a standard-rated supply.

The VAT due is £200,000 × 20% = £40,000 (or £33,333 if taken as inclusive of VAT)

SDLT payable by purchaser

SDLT is payable on the VAT inclusive amount ie £200,000 × 1.2 = £240,000

The first £150,000 at 0% = £0
The next £90,000 at 2% = £1,800

Sold to Tuna Ltd

As Tuna Ltd is in a VAT group with Skate Ltd, no VAT would be charged

As Tuna Ltd is in a SDLT group with Skate Ltd, no SDLT would be charged

79.4 Recovering VAT

The VAT is recoverable in full if Cat plc is a VAT-registered trader, uses the warehouse for the purposes of its trade/making taxable supplies, and has a VAT invoice for the purchase.

If Cat plc intends to rent out the warehouse it can only recover the input VAT if it opts to tax the warehouse.

Examiner's comments

79.1 Most students mentioned the administrative savings and VAT return points. Re the intra group transactions quite a few students thought that there was no VAT because it effectively cancels out on the VAT return – not that the transactions are not subject to VAT.

A lot of students used '50%' or 'at least 50%' when referring to the VAT group ownership requirement.

The position of zero-rated traders, as in previous sittings, appears to be confusing to some students. It was quite common for Velvet Ltd to be discussed as though it were an exempt trader – thus mentioning partial exemption issues. Other students used quite vague language ie, 'they can reclaim input VAT' which is not the same as being in a repayment position and generally used a lot of words but never quite got to the main points.

Very few students were awarded the marks for Unicorn Ltd.

79.2 This part was answered very well by most students, although surprisingly, a number of students thought that the reason Unicorn Ltd could not be in the SDLT group was that it was making sales outside the UK.

79.3 This part was answered well by most students.

79.4 This part was answered particularly poorly, even by students that answered the rest of the question well. A significant number of students thought the only way to recover the VAT was to opt to tax the building and others described the capital goods scheme, even where they had already indicated it did not apply. Only 1%–2% of students mentioned the requirement for a VAT invoice to recover input VAT.

80 Simon and Graham

		Marks
80.1 Car	1	
Part disposal		
– Proceeds less fees	½	
– Cost	2	
Residential sale	1	
Taxing land gain as "other assets" at 10/20% not as residential property	½	
Capital loss brought forward (½ deducting and ½ vs res property)	1	
AE (½ deducting and ½ vs res property)	1	
CGT calculation	2	
Basic rate band remaining (W1)	1	
		10
80.2 CLT Jan 16 – Lifetime tax	2	
CLT Jan 16 – Death tax		
– GCT	½	
– Fall in value	½	
– NRB available	½	
– IHT	½	
– Less lifetax	½	
Death estate		
– House	½	
– Sparks plc shares	2	
– Farmland	2	
– Flhim Flam	1	
– Holiday home	1	
– Unpaid tax	½	
– RNRB	1	
– NRB available	1	
– IHT	½	
– DTR	2	
	16	
Max		15
		25

80.1 CGT liability for 2018/19

Vintage car

Exempt   0

Part disposal of land

	£
Proceeds less fees = £50,000 × 97.5%	48,750
Less cost £18,000 + £1,500 × [£50,000 / (£50,000 + £43,000)]	(10,484)
	38,266

Residential sale

	£
Proceeds	250,000
Less cost	(150,000)
Less SDLT	(1,500)
	98,500

CGT liability

	Residential property £	Other assets £
Residential property	98,500	
Other assets = £100,000 + £38,266		138,266
(½ is for taxing the land at 10% and 20%)		
Less b/fwd capital loss	(23,450)	
Less AEA	(11,700)	
	63,350	138,266

     or

£21,350 @ 18% (W) = £3,843	£21,350 @ 10% (W) = £2,135
£42,000 @ 28% = £11,760	£116,916 @ 20% = £23,383
£138,266 @ 20% = £27,653	£63,350 @ 28% = £17,738
	43,256

WORKING

Basic rate band remaining

	£
Taxable income = £25,000 – £11,850	13,150
BRB remaining = £34,500 – £13,150	21,350

80.2

CLT – January 2016

	£
Gross transfer value (W)	1,315,000
Less fall in value relief (£1,123,000 – £235,000)	(888,000)
	427,000
Less NRB at death	(325,000)
	102,000
IHT @ 40%	40,800
Less lifetime tax paid	(198,000)
	0

Death estate	£	£
House		400,000
Sparks plc shares valued at lower of:		
410p + ¼ × (418p – 410p) = 412p		
407p + 414p / 2 = 410.5p		
1,000 × £4.105		4,105
Farmland	1,000,000	
Less APR @ 100% on agricultural value	(500,000)	
Less BPR @ 100%	(500,000)	
		0
Flhim Flam partnership	20,000	
No BPR as binding agreement for sale	(0)	
		20,000
Holiday home	347,000	
Less additional expenses (max 5%)		
(£21,000 = ½, deduct anywhere)	(17,350)	
		329,650
Less unpaid taxes		(148,000)
Death estate		605,755
Less RNRB		(125,000)
Less NRB at death	325,000	
Less chargeable transfers since May 2011	(1,315,000)	
		(0)
		480,755
IHT @ 40%		192,302
Less DTR lower of UK and overseas tax, UK tax clearly lower:		
UK tax at average rate = £192,302 / £605,755 = 31.7%		
UK tax = £329,650 @ 31.7%		(104,499)
		87,803

WORKING

CLT – January 2016	£
Gift	1,123,000
Less AE 2015/16 and 2014/15 b/f	(6,000)
Chargeable transfer	1,117,000
Less NRB at gift	(325,000)
	792,000
Lifetime tax at 20/80	198,000
Gross chargeable transfer = £1,117,000 + £198,000	1,315,000

Examiner's comments

80.1 It was not unusual to award full marks in the CGT part and close to full marks on the IHT. The majority of students had no problems calculating the gains in part 1. The flat was a straightforward calculation but the students' calculations on the harder part disposal of land were outstandingly good. The overall performance on this question then depended on whether they knew the different treatment for calculating tax on residential and non-residential assets. A majority of students had learned these rules and were very comfortable with the tax rates and the treatment of capital losses and the annual exempt amount.

80.2 The majority of students also performed very well on part 2 including the more unusual aspects such as fall in value relief. The RNRB was dealt with correctly by most students ie, it was treated separately from the normal nil rate band. This again may have been because it is a relatively new change and therefore potentially expected. The only common error was not claiming BPR on the farmland. Overall the majority of students have learned the steps required and the logical format required to achieve a good mark in this type of IHT question.

81 Salt Ltd

Marking guide

		Marks
81.1 Trading profit		
– Less trade related interest	½	
– Capital allowances	1 ½	
Non-trading loan relationships	2	
Les QCDs	1 ½	
CT at 19%	½	
		6
81.2 (a) Nil gain nil loss	½	
Chargeable gains group	1	
Cost plus indexation	½	
		2
(b) Proceeds	½	
Degrouping charge	½	
Cost	½	
Indexation allowance	1	
W1 Degrouping charge	2½	
		5
(c) Identifying and explaining why SSE applies	2	
Consequences of SSE	1	
	3	
	Max	2
		15

ICAEW 2019

81.1 Salt Ltd corporation tax liability for the year ended 31 December 2018

		£
Trading profit		622,000
Less trade related interest		(15,000)
Less capital allowances		
AIA @ 100%		(150,000)
WDA @ 18% × (£485,000 – £1,200)		(87,084)
Tax adjusted trading profit		369,916
Non-trading loan relationships		
Bank interest received	42,000	
Profit on sale of debenture stock (£32,400 – £16,000)	16,400	
Interest paid on loan to purchase shares	(12,000)	
		46,400
Less qualifying charitable donations paid		
£34,000 + £5,000 – £19,000		(20,000)
TTP		396,316
Corporation tax payable:		
CT × 19%		75,300

81.2 (a) The sale in February 2016 would have been treated as a nil gain, nil loss transfer as at that time Asp Ltd and Boa Ltd formed a chargeable gains group as Asp Ltd owned at least 75% of Boa Ltd.

The building will have transferred at an amount equal to cost plus indexation from acquisition to the date of transfer ie from May 1995 to February 2016.

(b)

	£
Gain on sale of shares	
Proceeds	1,500,000
Plus degrouping charge (W)	1,421,246
Less cost = £236,000 × 50%	(118,000)
Less IA = 278.1-171.1 / 171.1 × £118,000	(73,793)
	2,729,453

WORKING

Degrouping charge

	£
Deemed proceeds (OMV as at date of transfer)	2,000,000
Less original cost	(333,000)
Less IA May 1995 – February 2016	
260.0 – 149.6 / 149.6 = 0.738 × £333,000	(245,754)
	1,421,246

(c) The substantial shareholding exemption (SSE) applies as Asp Ltd held at least a 10% holding for at least 12 months in the 24 months prior to disposal, and both are trading companies.

The full gain is exempt including the degrouping gain.

Examiner's comments

81.1 The answers to part 1 were quite difficult to follow as often there was no distinction between the different sources of profits eg, trading profits, NTLR. Very common errors included treating the profit on the debenture stock as a gain and the calculation of the donations paid. It was quite unusual to see the correct figure for donations - workings very commonly showed that accruals were added instead of deducted and *vice versa* - I'm not sure if this was a confusion re the tax treatment or problems of accounting knowledge as to how you get a paid figure from payables and accruals figures.

On the basis of some answers to this part, it did appear that some students had not studied corporation tax at all.

81.2 Part 2 was answered well by those students that recognised the main issues - the related calculations were then performed very well. It was however, very common for the full cost rather than 50% of the cost of the shares to be used. These students almost always also scored full marks on part (c). A significant number of students however, did not attempt parts (a) and (c) or discussed completely irrelevant points.

82 Amy

Marking guide

			Marks
82.1	Occupational pension scheme deduction	½	
	Property income	1	
	Betting winnings- exempt	½	
	Personal allowance	½	
	Income tax liability	3½	
	Extended BRB (W1)	1	
			7
82.2 (a)	Drawings	1	
	Fixed rate expenses	1	
	Each other item in adjustment to profit – ½ mark each x 9	4½	
	NIC (W1)	3½	
	Capital allowances (W2)	4	
			14
(b)	2017/18	1	
	2018/19	1	
			2
82.3 (a)	Why eligible	1½	
	How long election applies for	1½	
			3
(b)	Office rent	1	
	Car running costs	1	
	Capital allowances	1	
	Each other entry ½ mark each x 6	3	
			6

82.4 Net disposable income
- Salary ½
- Self employment ½
- Less tax ½

Income tax if employed (W1)	1½
Income tax if self employed (W1)	1
NIC if employed (W2)	1½
NIC if self employed (W3)	2½
	8
	40

82.1

Amy income tax liability for 2018/19		NSI £	Savings £	Dividend £
Employment income = £30,000 – £1,000		29,000		
Property income – excess over rent-a-room limit		2,500		
BSI			2,000	
Dividends				17,000
Betting winnings – exempt				
Net income		31,500	2,000	17,000
Less personal allowance		(11,850)		
Taxable income		19,650	2,000	17,000
Non-savings income	£19,650	× 20%		3,930
Savings income nil rate band	£500	× 0%		0
Savings income	£1,500	× 20%		300
Dividend nil rate band	£2,000	× 0%		0
Dividend income – extended BRB (W1)	£12,725	× 7.5%		954
	£36,375			
Dividend income	£2,275	× 32.5%		739
Income tax liability				5,923

WORKING

Extended BRB	£
BRB	34,500
Plus gross PPS contribution = £1,500 × 100/80	1,875
	36,375

82.2(a)

Fred's tax-adjusted trading profits for 16 months ending 31 March 2019	£
Draft profit	545,504
Depreciation	36,000
Staff costs	
Drawings	15,000
Running costs for car	3,000
Fixed rate expenses for car = 10,000 × 45ppm + 1,250 × 25ppm	(4,813)
Staff salary costs paid	0
Accrued pension	400
Employer NIC (W1)	(2,168)
Advertising	
Donation - small and local so allowable	0
Customer gifts - cost > £50 each	5,500
Client entertaining	3,780
Less capital allowances (W2)	(284,337)
Adjusted trading profit	317,866

WORKINGS

(1)

NIC	£
No NIC on pension - exempt benefit	
Class 1 secondary	
£24,000 - £8,424 = £15,576 × 13.8% × 2	4,299
Less employment allowance	(3,000)
Class 1a	
£15,000 × 1.2 × 35% × 13.8%	869
	2,168

(2)

Capital allowances	Main pool	SRP	Total
Additions - eligible for AIA	292,292	40,000	
Additions - SRP car + irrecoverable VAT		18,000	
Less AIA (Max £200,000 × 16/12)	(226,667)	(40,000)	266,667
	65,625	18,000	
WDA @ 18% × 16/12	(15,750)		15,750
WDA @ 8% × 16/12		(1,920)	1,920
	49,875	16,080	284,337

(b)

Fred's trading income assessments		£
2017/18	Opening year rules	
	Commencement to next 5 April ie 1.12.17 - 5.4.18	
	= 4/16 × £317,866	79,467
2018/19	Opening year rules	
	12 months to accounting date ie 1.4.18 - 31.3.19	
	= 12/16 × £317,866	238,400

82.3 (a) Saj can make an election for the cash basis because he is trading as a sole trader (companies are not eligible) and his total cash basis receipts for 2018/19 do not exceed £150,000.

Saj will remain in the scheme until he is required to leave, or chooses to leave/is no longer appropriate because his commercial circumstances change.

Saj will be required to leave the cash basis if his receipts in the previous tax year exceed £300,000 for that previous year and receipts for the current year exceed £150,000.

(b)

Saj's tax-adjusted trading profits for year ended 31 December 2018	£
Invoices paid in cash = £27,840 + £4,500	32,340
Invoices issued on credit terms paid during the year = £28,000 – £12,000	16,000
Materials paid	(21,000)
Bank interest received – not trade related	0
Office rent paid = 6 × £300	(1,800)
Public liability insurance paid	(980)
Car running costs paid relating to business use = £1,350 × 3/5	(810)
Machinery – capex allowable under cash basis	(2,500)
Less capital allowances on car relating to business use = £8,000 × 18% × 3/5	(864)
Adjusted trading profit	20,386

82.4 **Leroy net disposable income**

	Employee £	Self-employed £
Salary	35,000	
Net cash received if self-employed = £60,000 – £5,500		54,500
Less income tax (W1)	(17,258)	(25,515)
Less NIC – employee (W2)	(3,189)	
Less NIC – self-employed (W3)		(3,773)
	14,553	25,212

WORKINGS

(1)

Income tax	£
Salary	35,000
Van	3,350
	38,350
Income tax due = £38,350 at 45%	17,258
Fee income	60,000
Less allowable van cost = £5,500 × 60%	(3,300)
	56,700
Income tax due = £56,700 at 45%	25,515

(2)

NIC employee	£
= £35,000 – £8,424 = £26,576 × 12%	(3,189)

(3)

NIC self-employed	**£**
= £46,350 – £8,424 = £37,926 × 9%	(3,413)
= £56,700 – £46,350 = £10,350 × 2%	(207)
= £2.95 × 52	(153)
	(3,773)

Examiner's comments

82.1 The standard of answers to this part was generally very good. Most students correctly extended the basic rate band and applied the different rates of tax well. A relatively common error however, was giving a savings nil rate band of £1,000 when the taxpayer was a higher rate taxpayer. A minority of students treated the savings and dividends nil rate amounts as allowances which do not use up the basic rate band.

The treatment of pension contributions was better than in previous sittings. The majority of students treated the personal pension contributions correctly and although it was very common to ignore the occupational scheme contributions they were at least not treated incorrectly.

Surprisingly, the property income figure was the figure most likely to be incorrect – it was very common to deduct the expenses as well as the rent-a-room relief.

82.2 (a) Most students gave good enough answers, although these were rarely excellent. There were 14 marks available, which means that students should have spent 21 minutes on this part. If they had, they may not have omitted the national insurance calculation, or may have realised that this required consideration of the employment allowance (and, for very well-prepared students, NIC on the employee car benefit).

Common errors involved the calculation of car fixed rate expenses (the 10,000 limit for 45p applies despite the longer period of account) and failing to disallow the entire amount of the cost of gifts (many students allowed the first £50 per customer, or the entire amount). In respect of capital allowances, there were some good calculations with most errors involving the car provided for the employee. Here, VAT was not included in the cost and often there was an attempt to treat this separately as a private use asset, despite this only being used privately by an employee and not the proprietor.

(b) This part was not answered well – the common issue was not being able to correctly identify the dates of the basis periods. On the plus side students were better at writing dates out in full (ie a day, a month, and a year) – even if they were wrong.

Students are reminded that "31 March 2018" is not the same as "5 April 2018", despite the rounding to the nearest month that is permissible in the actual calculations.

82.3 (a) This part was generally very well answered. Use of the open book should have enabled every student to gain full marks for this part.

(b) This part was not answered very well and some students did not attempt it. The cash receipts side was rather better understood than the expenses which were frequently pro-rated in an attempt to reflect the accruals basis, and the treatment of the car (in terms of capital allowances and running costs) was usually incorrect. Students seemed ill-prepared for this fairly simple cash basis calculation.

82.4 This part was a discriminating element of the exam. This disposable income question was generally done much better than in previous sittings. The presentation of the answers in particular was much better – the discipline of keeping the workings separate from the disposable income calculations seemed to help students focus better on cash/non-cash items.

Students who failed to appreciate that national insurance would be suffered, lost many marks. Some students insisted on applying the personal allowance, and lower rates of income tax, despite being told that the taxpayer was already paying at the additional rate.

83 John

		Marks
83	Tax planning arrangements	4
	Client specific	2
	Lawful	3
		9
	Max	7

83 Compliance with tax planning Standards

Tax planning arrangements

Members must not create, encourage or promote tax planning arrangements or structures that:

- set out to achieve results that are contrary to the clear intention of Parliament in enacting relevant legislation and/or

- are highly artificial/contrived and seek to exploit shortcomings within the relevant legislation.

Client Specific

Tax planning must be specific to the particular client's facts and circumstances.

Clients must be alerted to the wider risks and the implications of any courses of action.

Lawful

Tax planning should be based on a realistic assessment of the facts and on a credible view of the law.

The requirement to advise clients on material uncertainty in the law (including where HMRC take a different view) applies even if the practical likelihood of HMRC intervention is considered low.

Members should consider taking further advice appropriate to the risks and circumstances of the particular case, for example where litigation is likely.

Examiner's comment

83 The majority of students demonstrated that they were familiar with the content of the Standards for Tax Planning, even though it was less common for the actual standards to be named. There was also however, a significant minority who demonstrated no knowledge of the specific Standards for Tax Planning and instead answered the question by reference to the general ethics fundamental principles or general knowledge. In almost all cases however the answers supported the conclusion that the tax planning scheme went against ethical standards.

This question was occasionally not attempted with 4.4% of students making no attempt to answer the main ethics question on the exam.

84 Kavitha

		Marks
84.1 (a)	Rules to determine whether a limited cost trader	2	
	Application with VAT inclusive purchases of £240	3½	
	Application with VAT inclusive purchases of £450	1	
		6½	
	Max		5
(b)	Description of evasion	2	
	Conclusion	1	
			3
84.2	Bertie	1	
	Jeeves	2½	
	Madeline	2	
		5½	
	Max		5
			13

84.1 (a) VAT Flat Rate for a Limited Cost Business

Kavitha's flat rate will depend on whether she is a limited cost trader. She will be a limited cost trader if her VAT inclusive costs for the quarter are less than:

- £1,000 / 4 = £250 or
- 2% of VAT inclusive turnover for the quarter = £15,000 × 1.2 × 2% = £360

With VAT inclusive purchases of £240, as this is less than £360 she will be a limited cost trader and her VAT liability will be: £15,000 × 1.2 × 16.5% – 0 = £2,970

If Kavitha's purchases exceed £360 then her VAT liability will be:
£15,000 × 1.2 × 11% = £1,980

(b) Tax evasion is the deliberate:

- suppression of information; or
- provision of false information.

This is clearly not tax evasion.

84.2 SDLT on transfer from spouse

No VAT chargeable.

No SDLT as a transfer is exempt from SDLT where the transfer forms part of a divorce settlement.

On the purchase of a commercial property

- VAT = £1m × 20% = £200,000
- The first £150,000 at 0% = £0
- The next £100,000 at 2% = £2,000
- The remaining £950,000 at 5% = £47,500
- Total SDLT = £49,500

On the grant of a commercial lease

- No VAT as leasehold
- SDLT due on NPV of rent = £12,000 × 30 = £360,000
- £150,000 at 0% = £0
- The remaining £210,000 at 1% = £2,100

Examiner's comments

84.1 (a) Generally, there were quite poor and confusing answers to this question. This question was occasionally not attempted.

It was very common for the two limited cost tests to be stated. From the precise wording used it would appear that these were copied from Hardman's and also because it was unusual for students to demonstrate they understood what the words in the tests actually meant. The 'business's VAT flat rate turnover' was taken to mean numerous and various things, often involving input tax and the limited cost % (16.5%). It was also unusual for the 'amount spent on relevant goods' to be taken as the VAT inclusive input tax. Most students that tried to apply the tests, even if incorrectly, did however, conclude that in the first instance the business was a limited cost trader, but not in the second case. A lot of students then stopped at that point and did not answer the question in terms of calculating the VAT payable. Those answers that did apply their conclusion in a VAT calculation were not very good and it was unusual to get a correct answer. The best of the rest applied the correct percentage but to the VAT exclusive turnover, but it was not uncommon to see a calculation combining the 20% and 16.5% rates and input tax.

Lots of students thought that if not a limited cost trader a trader could not be in the flat rate scheme and instead that VAT paid to HMRC would be at 20% rather than 11%.

(b) Almost all students correctly recognised that this was not an example of tax evasion, although not all were able to explain why.

84.2 Generally, students' answers were good for both the VAT and stamp duty land tax parts of this question. It was not unusual to award full marks. However, it was noted that marginal students in particular had a tendency to only answer the SDLT part of the question and omit the VAT part. The lease was more difficult for some students with VAT sometimes being charged at 20% and a reasonable number of students either applying residential bands or applying the bands just to £12,000 rather than £360,000.

85 Denzel and Marwan

			Marks
85.1(a)	Gain on shares	2	
	Gain on land	1½	
	Car	1	
	AE	½	
	Tax	½	
	DTR	2½	
	W1 Basic rate band remaining	1	
			9
(b)	Remittance basis charge	1½	
	Lose PA	1½	
	Lose AEA	1½	
	Only remitted gains chargeable	1	
	Changes DTR	½	
		6	
	Max		4
85.2(a)	PET January 2014 – Death tax		
	- BPR	1	
	- AE	½	
	- NRB available	1	
	- IHT	½	
	- Taper	½	
	CLT January 2017 – Lifetime tax		
	- Diminution in value	1½	
	- AE	½	
	- NRB available	1	
	- Gross chargeable transfer	1	
	- Death tax		
	- CGT	½	
	- NRB available	1	
	- IHT	½	
	- Less life tax	½	
			10
(b)	IHT on PET	1	
	IHT on CLT	1	
			2
			25

85.1 (a) CGT liability for 2018/19

Shares		£
Proceeds		55,000
Less cost		(21,000)
		34,000

	Number	Cost
	£	£
Purchase – December 2010	12,000	15,000
Rights issue – December 2014	3,000	7,500
	15,000	22,500
Disposal	(14,000)	(21,000)
	1,000	1,500

Land	£
Proceeds	1,500,000
Less cost	
£125,000 × (£1,500,000 / (£1,500,000 + £750,000))	(83,333)
	1,416,667

CGT liability	UK	Foreign
	£	£
Sculpture	45,200	
Shares	34,000	
Car – exempt	0	
Land		1,416,667
Less AEA	(11,700)	
	67,500	1,416,667
Gains in BRB = £29,850 @ 10% (W)	2,985	
Gains exceeding BRB = £67,500 – £29,850 = £37,650 @ 20%	7,530	
Foreign gains (exceed BRB) @ 20%		283,333
	10,515	283,333
Total CGT		293,848
Less DTR: Lower of:		
UK tax = £1,416,667 × 20%	283,333	
Overseas tax = 15% × £1.5 million	225,000	
Less DTR		(225,000)
		68,848

WORKING

Basic rate band remaining	£
Taxable UK income = £16,500 – £11,850	4,650
BRB remaining = £34,500 – £4,650	29,850

(b) Remittance basis claim

If Denzel makes a claim for the remittance basis to apply, then:

- as he has been resident for more than 7 years out of the last 9 years, he will be liable to pay a remittance basis charge of £30,000 in addition to the tax due.

- he will lose entitlement to the personal allowance for IT purposes which will increase his income tax liability and reduce the amount of basic rate band available for his gains.

- he will also lose entitlement to the AEA for CGT purposes, which will increase the amount subject to CGT.

- however, only the gains remitted to the UK will then be chargeable rather than the full gain.

- changes DTR.

85.2(a)

	January 2012 CLT £	January 2014 PET £	January 2018 CLT (W1) £	April 2019 Death £
Stage 1 - Transfers				
Transfer		2,000,000	222,500	
BPR		(1,000,000)		
50% × £2,000,000				
Less exemptions				
Annual		(3,000)	(3,000)	
Annual b/f		(3,000)	(3,000)	
		994,000	216,500	
Stage 2 - Lifetime tax				
Less remaining NRB (W2)		No LT tax	(150,000)	
			66,500	
IHT @ 20/80			16,625	
Gross chargeable transfer	175,000	994,000	233,125	
Stage 3 - Tax on death				
Gross chargeable transfer	More than 7 years	994,000	233,125	
Less remaining NRB (W2)		(150,000)	-	
		844,000	233,125	
IHT @ 40%		337,600	93,250	
Taper relief (5-6 yrs)		135,040		
40% chargeable				
Taper (<3 yrs)			93,250	
100% chargeable				
Less lifetime tax paid			(16,625)	
Tax payable on death		135,040	76,625	

WORKINGS

(1)

		£	£
Lifetime tax on CLT in January 2017			
Diminution in value			
Prior to gift = 45% holding		472,500	
Post gift = 25% holding		(250,000)	
			222,500

(2) **Remaining nil rate band**

	January 2012 CLT £	January 2014 PET £	January 2018 CLT £	April 2019 Death £
Stage 2 – Lifetime				
Lifetime NRB			325,000	
Less chargeable in previous 7 years			(175,000)	
Remaining NRB			150,000	
Stage 3 – On death				
NRB at death		325,000	325,000	
Less chargeable in previous 7 years		(175,000)		
£(175,000 + 994,000)			(1,169,000)	
£(46,500 + 17,750)				
Remaining NRB		150,000		-

(b) **IHT Admin**

The IHT due on the failed PET is payable by Marwan's son and should be paid within six months of the end of the month of death ie 31 October 2019.

The IHT due on the CLT is payable by the trustees and should be paid within six months of the end of the month of death ie 31 October 2019.

Examiner's comments

85.1(a) On the whole the majority of students made a very good attempt at this question. Most students seemed confident in their approach to the question, preparing workings for the individual gains and then using a logical approach and standard layout to calculate the CGT payable. Almost all students recognised the car was exempt and correctly calculated the gain on the shares. In most cases students considered the available basic rate band and DTR in the calculation of the tax payable. It was relatively common to ignore the personal allowance in the basic rate band calculation but students were much better at calculating the higher rate tax on the balance of the gain – rather than on the gain less the full basic rate band, which has been a common error in the past. Most students who considered DTR understood how to calculate it, although the calculation of UK tax was often incorrectly calculated using an average tax rate.

(b) Part (b) was also answered very well – it was quite common to award full marks. This was pleasing as students usually prefer numerical questions, whereas this was a written answer. It also involved more than one tax (there were some marks available for income tax, as well as CGT, implications) and students coped well.

85.2(a) Weaker students lost marks for performing computations in the wrong order or completely omitting either lifetime tax or death tax computations. As would be expected BPR and the diminution in value calculations were the areas which caused the most problem. Whilst overall students were good at providing workings to support their answers the exception continues to be in relation to the nil rate band. It is common to see 'NRB fully used'. This is normally insufficient as it is usually important to see that the student understands which previous transfers have used the nil rate band.

(b) Part (b) was not answered very well. Most students failed to actually state an accurate date, consisting of a day, a month and a year. Often students explained how to calculate the date, probably copied from Hardman's, or only included a month or year. Students who did manage to give a day, a month and a year were often unaware that there are in fact 31 days in October. Students of a professional exam really should have sufficient general knowledge to know how many days there are in a given month. Getting this wrong when working on tax compliance in practice could lead to significant penalties for clients.

In addition, students often answered this part without considering the facts of the question – because the question related to tax payable on death they automatically stated the personal representatives paid the tax – even though there was no death estate and the tax payable related to lifetime transfers.

86   H Ltd

			Marks
86.1 Direct holding		1	
Indirect holding		1	
Application		$\frac{1}{3}$	
	Max		2
86.2 Related 51% group companies		1½	
End of previous accounting period		$\frac{1}{2½}$	
	Max		2
86.3 Revised trade profit (½ mark each x 6)		3	
Gain		1	
Non trade loan relationship		1	
QCD		1	
Group relief		1	
Tax		½	
Due dates		3½	
			$\frac{11}{15}$

86.1 Loss relief group

To be in a loss relief group there must be both:

- a direct holding of at least 75% at every level – ie, H Ltd holds 75% of Y Ltd and Y Ltd holds 75% of Z Ltd; and

- an indirect/effective holding of at least 75% – ie, H Ltd should have an indirect holding in Z Ltd of at least 75%.

As H Ltd's indirect holding in Z Ltd is only 56.25% or 75% × 75%, H Ltd cannot claim losses from Z Ltd.

86.2 Related 51% group companies

To be a related 51% group company of H Ltd, H Ltd must own 51%/more than 50% either directly (ie, A Ltd and Y Ltd) or indirectly/effectively (ie Z Ltd) ie 56.25% or 75% × 75%.

When considering payment date(s), the relevant number of related 51% group companies depends on shareholdings as at the end of the previous accounting period. So for the year ended 30 June 2018 H Ltd's holdings as at 30 June 2017 are relevant. As A Ltd was still owned on 30 June 2017, it remains a related 51% group company for due dates for the year ended 30 June 2018.

There are therefore four related 51% group companies for the year ended 30 June 2018.

86.3 H Ltd corporation tax liability for the year ended 30 June 2018

Trading profits		496,450
Depreciation – correctly added back, no correction required		0
Amortisation – allowable expense		(15,000)
Client entertaining – correctly added back		0
Staff entertaining – allowable expense		(5,000)
Overdraft interest – allowable expense		(1,450)
Non- trading loan interest – correctly added back		0
		475,000
Chargeable gain	60,000	
Loss on disposal of A Ltd – not allowable as SSE applies	0	
		60,000
Non-trading loan relationships	48,550	
Remove overdraft interest	1,450	
		50,000
QCD – political party so not deductible		0
Less group relief – not eligible		0
TTP		585,000
Corporation tax payable:		
(585,000 × 19%)		111,150

Due dates

With four related 51% group companies, corporation tax is due by quarterly instalment payments (QIPs) if augmented profits exceed £1.5m / 4 = £375,000

Corporation tax will be due in four equal instalments of £27,788 (ie £111,150 / 4)

Payments will be due as follows:

14 January 2017	27,788
14 April 2017	27,287
14 July 2017	27,788
14 October 2017	27,787
	111,150

As H Ltd was clearly large in the previous accounting period (augmented profits were > £375,000) no exceptions to QIPs apply in the current accounting period.

Examiner's comments

86.1 This part was often answered well, with most correctly calculating the effective holding in Z Ltd. In answering this part though it was important to use accurate terminology to describe the ownership of the companies. A common term that was used this sitting was 'strict relationship' which is not a sufficiently accurate description.

86.2 There was a distinct lack of accuracy in the answers to this part with relatively few defining a related 51% group company and even fewer students making a comment about the company that left the group during the accounting period ie that it is the number of such companies at the end of the previous accounting period which is relevant. The general issue seemed to be that students did not answer the question set. They often explained when tax was payable or why 51% group companies were important in determining when tax was payable.

86.3 Students showed a distinct lack of skill in joining up the answers to the different parts. Part 1 specifically stated that group relief was not available and asked students to explain why. Despite this students gave group relief time and again in part 3, sometimes with a helpful note explaining why. The question said no group relief. There was no mystery. Students are reminded that if the question specifically states that something is not available, then it really is not available.

Students were also confused how to apply their knowledge, for example, they correctly stated that political donations were not allowed, but then either deducted them anyway, or added them to trading profit despite the donations not having been deducted here. This suggests students learn pro formas and adjustments, but without understanding why they should make such adjustments.

Students also seemed to lack confidence in applying their knowledge, for example, with regard to SSE. A number stated that SSE was relevant to the disposal of shares but then felt this could not be true when a loss arises. Some thought the error in respect of the loss was failure to deduct indexation allowance to make the loss bigger.

Some students lost easy marks for not showing their treatment of each item. Part 2 stated that there were four related 51% group companies and yet students divided the limit by three when determining the payment dates in part 3. In addition, admin knowledge was generally weak as students were unable to determine the correct dates for payment or how much should be paid at each date. On the whole students do not seem to like corporation tax questions.

87 Ellie

			Marks
87.1 (a)	Salary	½	
	School fees	1	
	Parking space	½	
	Car and fuel benefit (W1)	4	
	Expenses	1	
	Pension contributions	1	
	Subscription	1	
			9
(b)	Adjustment to profit		
	- Car expenses	1 ½	
	- Each other adjustment ½ each × 7	3 ½	
	Capital allowances	4	
			9
(c)	Trade income (W1)	1	
	Property income (W2)	2	
	Each other income ½ each × 4	2	
	Personal allowance	1	
	Tax calculation	2 ½	
	Finance deduction	½	
	Extended band (W3)	1	
	Relief for finance cost (W4)	2 ½	
		12 ½	
	Max		12
87.2 (a)	Option 1	1 ½	
	Option 2	2 ½	
			4
(b)	Option 1		
	- Salary	½	
	- NIC	½	
	- Lease	½	
	- Running costs	½	
	- Tax savings	1 ½	
	Option 2		
	- Salary	½	
	- Voucher	½	
	- Mileage	½	
	- NIC	½	
	- Tax savings	½	
			6
			40

87.1 (a) **Ellie's employment income**

	£
Salary = £5,000 × 5	25,000
School fees – marginal cost to employer	530
Parking space – exempt	0
Company car (W1)	9,021
Expenses reimbursed – exempt	0
Less Ellie's contribution to OPS = £25,000 × 3%	(750)
Employer contribution	–
Less institute subscription	(300)
	33,501

WORKING

Company car	£
List price + optional extras = £36,616 + £1,000	37,616
Less capital contribution	(2,500)
	35,116
Car benefit % = 35% + 4% = 39% but capped at 37%	
Taxable car benefit = £35,116 × 37%	12,993
Fuel benefit = £23,400 × 37%	8,658
	21,651
Prorated for five months usage	9,021

(b) **Ellie's tax adjusted trading profits for nine months ended 31 May 2019**

		£
Draft profit		57,269
Add back:		
Salary – drawings		4,000
Repairs and renewals – solar shading is a capital item		2,400
Repairs and renewals – partition walls are capital		7,900
Repairs and renewals – no adjustment for redecorating (revenue)		0
Car expenses		
– Amount deducted	845	
– Allowable amount is £845 × 9/12 × 70% =	(444)	
– Disallowed amount		401
Rent allowed in next period = £8,100 × 3/12		2,025
Other expenses		
– Speeding fine		100
Less capital allowances (W1)		(15,946)
Adjusted trading profit		58,149

WORKING

Capital allowances	FYA	Main pool	SRP	PUA - 70%	Total
Solar shading			2,400		
Partition walls		7,900			
Car				13,000	
Office equipment		4,100			
Energy saving equipment	1,000				
	1,000	12,000	2,400	13,000	
100% FYA	(1,000)				1,000
AIA		(12,000)	(2,400)		14,400
WDA @ 8% × 9/12				(780)	×70% 546
	-	-	-	12,220	15,946

(c)

Ellie income tax liability for 2018/19		NSI £	Savings £	Dividend £
Trading income (W1)		45,227		
Employment income		33,501		
Property income (W2)		2,700		
Invigilation – covered by trading allowance	(	-		
BSI			1,200	
Dividend				8,000
Net income		81,428	1,200	8,000
Less personal allowance		(11,850)		
Taxable income		69,578	1,200	8,000
Non-savings income (W3)	£36,125	× 20%		7,225
	£33,453	× 40%		13,381
Savings income nil rate band	£500	× 0%		0
Savings income	£700	× 40%		280
Dividend nil rate band	£2,000	× 0%		0
Dividend income	£6,000	× 32.5%		1,950
				22,836
Relief for finance costs relating to residential property businesses (W4)				(400)
Income tax liability				22,436

WORKINGS

(1)

Basis periods	£
Commencement to next 5 April = 1 September 2018 – 5 April 2019	
= £58,149 × 7/9	45,227

(2)

Property income (cash basis)	£
Rent	5,000
Allowable expenses	(300)
Mortgage interest = £4,000 × 50%	(2,000)
	2,700

(3)

	£
Extended bands	
BRB	34,500
PPS contribution = £1,300 × 100/80	1,625
	36,125

(4)

Relief for finance costs for residential property £

The 20% tax reduction is based on the lowest of:

- 50% of the finance costs for the tax year plus any finance costs brought forward = £4,000 × 50% — 2,000
- Property income for the tax year (after using any brought forward property losses) — 2,700
- Adjusted total income (excluding savings and dividend income) that exceeds the personal allowance for the tax year — 69,578

Relief = 20% × £2,000 = £400

87.2 (a)

	£	£
Option One		
Employer's class 1 NIC		
(£13,500 - £8,424) × 13.8%		700
Class 1A NIC on car benefit = £3,000 × 13.8%		414
Total NIC		1,114
Option Two		
Salary		8,300
Shopping vouchers = £100 × 52		5,200
Mileage allowance = 6,000 × (60p – 45p)		900
		14,400
Less secondary threshold		(8,424)
		5,976
Class 1 contributions @ 13.8%		825

(b)

	£	£
Option One		
Salary		13,500
Employer NIC (part (a))		1,114
Allowable leased car cost = £4,000		4,000
Car running costs		2,300
		20,914
Less income tax and NIC saving = £20,914 × 47% (45% + 2%)		(9,830)
Cost to the business of option one		11,084
Option Two		
Salary		8,300
Shopping vouchers (part (a))		5,200
Mileage allowance = 6,000 × 60p		3,600
Employer NIC (part (a))		825
		17,925
Less income tax and NIC saving = £17,925 × 47% (45% + 2%)		(8,425)
Cost to the business of option two		9,500

Examiner's comments

87.1 (a) Many students achieved close to full marks on this part. Common errors included not using the marginal cost for the school place, calculating a benefit on the car parking space, not restricting the car benefit to 37% and pro rating the institute subscription.

(b) Many students did well on this part. However there were some difficult aspects. In general most students scored some marks on the more difficult aspect of the car expenses. The capital allowances should not have caused any difficulties but a number of less well prepared students introduced first year allowances, calculated the car at 18% or did not prorate for business use.

(c) Many students gained good marks on this part. The presentation was generally very good as were supporting workings. Students were much better at this sitting at showing how much income was taxed at the different rates. Almost all students correctly extended the basic rate band and gave the correct savings and dividend nil bands. The most common error was not adjusting the trading income calculated in part (b) to reflect the opening year basis period. The majority of students restricted the deduction of interest in the property income calculation but only a minority claimed a tax reduction for the balance of the interest.

87.2 (a) This part was performed well with many students gaining full marks.

(b) Students have clearly been practising questions of this type and many gained at least four out of the six marks available. However, the majority of students ignored the tax saving. Students often considered the employer NIC from part (a) to be the tax saving and deducted it in part (b) to calculate the after tax cost to the employer.

ICAEW 2019

September 2018 exam answers

88 Gustavo and Mike

			Marks
88	Money laundering	4	
	Professional Indemnity Insurance	3	
	Data Protection	1½	
	Max	8½	7

88 Money laundering

- Register for anti-money laundering (AML) supervision with ICAEW as the appropriate supervisory body

- Appoint a Money Laundering Reporting Officer (MLRO)

- Train the partners and staff in relation to money laundering legislation

- Establish appropriate AML procedures to risk assess and deter money laundering

Other regulatory requirements:

Professional Indemnity Insurance

- In order to obtain a Practising Certificate they must have a minimum level of Professional Indemnity Insurance (PII):

  - If gross fee income is less than £600,000 the minimum cover is two and a half times gross fee income (minimum £100,000)

  - Otherwise the minimum is £1.5 million

Data Protection

- They must register as a data controller with the Information Commissioner's Office (ICO) under data protection legislation

Examiner's comments

88 Most students were able to score good marks for the regulatory requirements in respect of money-laundering. Some also considered the need for professional indemnity insurance, although giving it a variety of names. Those who did, often gave detailed answers of the level of coverage needed. A smaller number of students also recognised the need for data protection although few suggested registering with the ICO.

89 Shrayder Ltd

Marking guide

			Marks
89.1	Simplified test 1	1½	
	Simplified test 2	1½	
		3	
	Max		2
89.2	Output VAT	1	
	Net VAT payable	½	
	Working	4	
	De minimis tests	1½	
			7
89.3	VAT	3	
	Stamp duty	2½	
		5½	
	Max		4
			13

89.1 Simplified test 1

Fully recoverable if both:

- exempt supplies no more than 50% of total supplies – clearly less than 50% so ok
- monthly total input tax of £625 or less (£12,100/3) = £4,033 > £625 – so test failed

Simplified test 2

Fully recoverable if both:

- exempt supplies no more than 50% of total supplies – clearly less than 50% so ok

- monthly total less taxable input tax of £625 or less ((£12,100 – £8,400)/3) = £1,233 > £625 – so test failed

89.2

	£
VAT payable	
Output tax £90,000 × 20%	18,000
Input tax (W)	(12,100)
Net VAT payable	5,900

WORKING	Taxable supplies £	Exempt supplies £
Wholly attributable to taxable	8,400	
Wholly attributable to exempt		1,400
Non-attributable:		
(90,000 – 9,000 + 10,000)/(124,000 – 9,000) = 79.1%		
Attributable to taxable: round up to 80% × £2,300	1,840	
Attributable to exempt: (£2,300 – £1,840)		460
Input tax	10,240	1,860

De minimis tests

Monthly average input tax attributable to exempt supplies £625 or less?
£1,860/3 = £620 – yes
VAT on exempt supplies no more than 50% of all input VAT
1,860/12,100 × 100 = 15.4% – yes
So all input tax recoverable £10,240 + £1,860 = £12,100

89.3 VAT implications

The purchase of the new freehold factory is a standard-rated supply so the vendor will charge VAT of £240,000 (£1.2m × 20%).

As the factory is used 90% for taxable and 10% for exempt purposes, Schrayder Ltd can initially recover 90% of the input tax, ie, £216,000 (£240,000 × 90%).

The factory is subject to the capital goods scheme and so adjustments to the amount recovered may be required over the 10-year adjustment period if the use changes.

SDLT is payable on the VAT-inclusive amount £1.44m (£1.2m × 120%)

	£
Stamp duty land tax on the building	
£150,000 × 0%	–
(£250,000 – £150,000) × 2%	2,000
(£1,440,000 – £250,000) × 5%	59,500
	61,500

SDLT is payable by Schrayder Ltd by 8 June 2019

Examiner's comments

89.1 Students often scored full marks on this part of the question, perhaps helped by the information required being in the tax tables.

89.2 There were some very good answers to this part, usually where students set the answer out in a table as in the model answer. Using this format made it more likely that they would pick up the correct figures. Having prepared calculations for the non-attributable VAT however, many students did not then apply the de minimis tests. It was also very common, even on the best scripts for the net VAT payable not to be calculated. A common error included not rounding up the partial exemption fraction. Some students calculated the fraction in relation to the exempt element, rather than the taxable element, which is fine provided they then remember to round this fraction down – which most did not.

89.3 Many students achieved full marks for this requirement combining VAT and SDLT on the purchase of a new commercial building. A notable error concerned the date SDLT was due which was often wrong and sometimes omitted despite the specific request for this in the requirement.

90 Walter

		Marks
90.1 Deduction of AEA	1	
CGT calculation	1	
(W1)		
- Gain on house	½	
- PPR	½	
- Letting relief	2½	
(W2)	2½	
		8
90.2 Normal expenditure out of income	½	
Reasons – 1 mark each	3	
	3½	
	Max	3
90.3 CLT – June 2011	½	
Valuation of Froing shares (W1)	3	
PET – October 2015 – AE	½	
PET – October 2015 – Death tax calculation	2	
Death estate valuation (W3)	4½	
Death estate – Death tax calculation	2	
Reduced rate of IHT (W4)	1½	
		14
		25

90.1 CGT payable for 2018/19

	Tax at 20% £	Tax at 28% £
Antique furniture	38,000	–
House in London (W1)		86,000
Less annual exempt amount		(11,700)
Taxable gains	38,000	74,300
CGT liability 20%/28%	7,600	20,804
Total		28,404

WORKINGS

(1) **Sale of house in London**

Sale proceeds	1,500,000
Less cost	(240,000)
	1,260,000
Less PPR (W2) £1.26m × 31.5/35	(1,134,000)
	126,000

Less letting relief
Lowest of:
- PPR relief £1,134,000
- Gain relating to letting 3/3.5 × £126,000 = £108,000
- £40,000

	(40,000)
Gain	86,000

(2) **Principal private residence relief**

	Taxable	Exempt
Feb 1984–Feb 1996 occupied		12
Feb 1996–Feb 2000 employed elsewhere in UK		4
Feb 2000–Feb 2003 three years any reason		3
Feb 2003–Feb 2006 not occupied	3	
Feb 2006–Feb 2017 occupied		11
Feb 2017–Feb 2019 last 18 months exempt	0.5	1.5
Total 35 years	3.5	31.5

90.2 School fees

The lifetime payment of school fees by Walter is exempt as it is 'normal expenditure out of income'.

It is treated as such because:

- it is paid out of his income.

- he is left with sufficient income to maintain his usual lifestyle since he has surplus income of £150,000 pa.

- it is part of a regular pattern of giving as it has been happening since 2010.

90.3

	June 2011 CLT £	October 2015 PET (W1) £	March 2019 Death (W3) £
Stage 1 – Transfers			
Transfer		168,000	1,115,796
Less exemptions			
Annual		(3,000)	
Annual b/f		(3,000)	
	300,000	162,000	1,115,796
Stage 2 – Lifetime tax			
Less remaining NRB (W2)	(325,000)	No LT tax	No LT tax
	0		
Gross chargeable transfer	300,000	162,000	1,115,796
Stage 3 – Tax on death			
Gross chargeable transfer	More than 7 years	162,000	1,115,796
Less remaining NRB (W2)		(25,000)	(163,000)
		137,000	952,796
IHT @ 40%		54,800	
IHT @ 36% (W4)			343,007
Taper relief (3-4 yrs)			
80% chargeable		43,840	
Tax payable on death		43,840	343,007

WORKINGS

(1) Shares in Froing Ltd - related property

£

Value shares at the higher of the related and unrelated values. The related values (including Marie) are clearly the higher figures and so have been used in the diminution in value calculation.

Value before transfer - 100% related property

6,000 × £60 | 360,000

Value after transfer - 80% related property

4,000 × £48 | (192,000)

| | 168,000

(2) Remaining nil rate band

	June 2011 CLT £	October 2015 PET (W1) £	March 2019 Death £
Stage 2 - Lifetime			
Lifetime NRB	325,000		
Less chargeable in previous 7 years			
Remaining NRB	325,000		
Stage 3 - On death			
NRB at death	N/A	325,000	325,000
Less chargeable in previous 7 years		(300,000)	(162,000)
Remaining NRB		25,000	163,000

(3) Death estate - March 2019

Total assets	1,900,000
Less expenses	
Income tax	(23,600)
Capital gains tax (part 1)	(28,404)
Credit card bills	(2,000)
Gaming debt	0
Funeral expenses	(10,200)
Chargeable estate before exemptions	1,835,796
Less gift to spouse - exempt	(550,000)
Less gift to charity - exempt	(170,000)
Chargeable death estate	1,115,796

(4) Reduced rate of IHT

Chargeable estate	952,796
Add charitable donation	170,000
Net chargeable estate	1,122,796

Chargeable donation exceeds 10% of NCA so reduced rate of IHT

Examiner's comment

90.1 The majority of students made a very good attempt at this question. Better students prepared a PPR working setting out the taxable and exempt periods. This meant it was easy to identify the periods the students thought were exempt and more likely that they would calculate PPR using the correct number of years. Most students identified that the last 18 months were exempt but it was more unusual for the 7 exempt years to be identified.

Often either the 4 or 3 years exemptions were identified, but not both and quite commonly the whole 10 years were treated as exempt.

Letting relief was often considered. Most identified the £40,000 and PPR limits but it was quite rare for the gain relating to letting to be correct. The letting gain was often incorrectly treated as the gain after PPR – being described as the 'gain remaining'. Another common error was to calculate the letting gain as the gain for the whole let period (including periods that had been treated as exempt under PPR). The calculation of the tax, correctly using the AEA and the appropriate tax rates was generally very good, although some stated that the antique furniture was exempt as a chattel.

90.2 Most students seemed to be aware of the relevant exemption but there were a lot of imprecise explanations from which it was often difficult to determine if they understood the three key elements required for the exemption.

90.3 There were some very good answers to the inheritance tax computation. Many students correctly calculated the related property transfer of value. A common mistake was using the combined ownership in the number of shares. A number of students gave business property relief to shares in an investment company.

Most identified the reduced rate on the death estate, although fewer provided a correct supporting calculation normally incorrectly treating the nil rate band. Noticeably more students provided workings for the available nil rate band than in previous sittings.

There were a number of very poor answers to this question from students who appeared to have little understanding of the IHT calculations required.

91 Heissen Ltd

		Marks
91.1 Unindexed gain	½	
Indexation allowance	½	
Rollover relief	1	
Base cost of new factory	<u>1</u>	
		3
91.2 Corporation tax computation		
- Capital allowances	½	
- Gain	½	
- Property income	½	
- QCDs	1½	
- Corporation tax	½	
- DTR deduction	½	
Overseas dividend income (W1)	2	
DTR (W2)	3½	
CAs (W3)	3	
	<u>3½</u>	
	13	
Max		<u>12</u>
		<u><u>15</u></u>

91.1

Gain on sale freehold premises

	£
Sale proceeds	250,000
Less cost	(180,000)
Less indexation allowance (to December 2017)	70,000

$$\frac{278.1-219.2}{219.2} = 0.269 \times £180,000$$

	£
	(48,420)
	21,580
Less rollover relief β	(11,580)
Gain chargeable – cash not reinvested (£250,000 – £240,000)	10,000
Base cost of new leasehold factory (unchanged)	240,000

91.2 Corporation tax computation – year ended 31 March 2019

	UK £	O'seas div £	O'seas prop £	Total £
Tax-adjusted trading profit	86,000			
Less capital allowances (W3)	(69,160)			
	16,840			16,840
Chargeable gains (part 1)	10,000			10,000
Dividend income (W1)		21,600		21,600
Property income £90,000 x 100/90			100,000	100,000
Less QCD	(26,840)		(8,160)	(35,000)
Taxable total profits	Nil	21,600	91,840	113,440
Corporation tax @ 19%				
Less DTR (W2)				21,554
Dividend income				(4,104)
Property income				(10,000)
Corporation tax payable				7,450

WORKINGS

(1) Overseas dividend income

	£
Dividend received	16,000
Add withholding tax (£16,000 × 20/80)	4,000
	20,000

Add underlying tax $\dfrac{9,600}{120,000} \times £20,000$

	£
	1,600
Gross dividend income	21,600

(2) Double tax relief

	£
Dividend income – lower of:	
UK tax £21,600 × 19%	4,104
Overseas tax (£4,000 + £1,600)	5,600
ie,	4,104
Property income – lower of:	
UK tax £91,840 × 19%	17,450
Overseas tax (£100,000 – £90,000)	10,000
ie,	10,000

(3) Capital allowances

	Main pool £	Special rate £	Allowances £
TWDV b/f	90,000	12,000	
Purchases – AIA			
Machinery (£47K + £3K)	50,000		
AIA β	(50,000)		50,000
Purchases non-AIA			
Car – SRP		25,000	
	90,000	37,000	
WDA @ 18%	(16,200)		16,200
WDA @ 8%		(2,960)	2,960
Total allowances	73,800	34,040	69,160

Examiner's comment

91.1 The calculation of a gain eligible for rollover relief proved surprisingly difficult for many students. The proceeds were only partially reinvested in a depreciating asset and so many students unsurprisingly reduced the base cost of the new asset by rollover relief. However, more of a concern was errors made in calculating indexation, and confusions between the costs etc of the old and new assets. Some students even produced different gains calculations in their answers to part 2.

91.2 Students again produced poor answers to the corporation tax question. This will cause difficulties as they progress to the Business Planning: Taxation exam. There were difficult elements such as the inclusion of overseas income (particularly a taxable dividend with underlying tax) and the treatment of a qualifying charitable donation to maximise DTR. However, most students could have ignored these issues and still scored good marks. They often made more basic errors including failing to include all additions in capital allowances, restricting allowances for private use despite this being a company and deducting allowances from total profits, rather than trading income. The calculations of DTR were often the better elements of many students' answers, with many follow-through marks awarded despite earlier mistakes. Some students confused the approach required for DTR for corporation tax with that needed for income tax (removing sources of overseas income, and recalculating computations), not appreciating that there is only one UK corporation tax rate and so an easy calculation of UK CT on each amount of overseas income. These students could gain all the DTR marks but obviously wasted time.

92 Jessie and Saul

		Marks
92.1 (a)	Property income (W1)	3
	Employment income (W2)	6½
	Interest and dividends	1
	Personal allowance	½
	Tax calculation	2
	Child benefit charge	1
	20% deduction for remaining finance charges (including W3)	2½
	PAYE	½
		17
(b)	Class 1 secondary	2
	Class 1A	2
		4
92.2 (a)	Legal advice	1½
	Insurance	1½
	Entertaining	½
		3½
	Max	**3**
(b)	Actual cost basis	2½
	Fixed rate expenses	1½
		4
(c)	Adjustment to profit – ½ mark each item	1½
	Capital allowances (W)	3½
		5
(d)	Salary and property figures	1
	Property income (W)	2½
	Use of loss	3
	Personal allowance	1
	Taxable income	½
		8
	Max	**7**
		40

92.1 (a) Jessie income tax payable for 2018/19

	NSI £	Savings £	Dividend £
Property income (W1)	9,490		
Employment income (W2)	78,053		
Interest		600	
Dividends			838
Net income	87,543	600	838
Less personal allowance (NSI)	(11,850)		
Taxable income	75,693	600	838

	£	£
Non-savings income	34,500 × 20%	6,900
	41,193 × 40%	16,477
	75,693	-
Savings income - HR taxpayer	500 × 0%	-
	100 × 40%	40
Dividend income	838 × 0%	-
		23,417
Add child benefit tax charge (100% as ANI greater than £60,000)		1,076
Less tax credits:		
20% tax reduction for remaining finance costs (W3)		
20% × £800	160	
PAYE	14,100	
		(14,260)
Income tax liability		10,233

WORKING

(1) **Property income**

	£
Cash basis	
Rental received £1,000 × 11	11,000
Less finance costs (50% × £1,600)	(800)
management fee	(100)
insurance	(500)
replacement washing machine (£100 + £10)	(110)
Property income	9,490

(2) **Employment income**

		£
Salary		59,000
Car park permit – not exempt as salary sacrifice		1,000
Car benefit (£36,000 – £5,000) × (28% + 4%)		9,920
Fuel benefit £23,400 × 32%		7,488
Round sum allowance	1,200	
Less deductions		
car parking	(400)	
entertaining – not allowable	-	
		800
Less expenses		
Subscriptions		(155)
		78,053

(3) The 20% tax reduction is based on the lower of:

- 50% of the finance costs for the year (£1,600 × 50% = £800)
- Property income for the year (£9,940)
- Adjusted total income (excluding savings and dividends) that exceed the PA (£75,693)

(b)

National insurance contributions	Class 1	Class 1A
	£	£
Salary	59,000	
Car parking annual season ticket		1,000
Round sum allowance profit	800	
Car benefit		9,920
Fuel benefit		7,488
	59,800	18,408
Class 1 secondary (£59,800 – £8,424) × 13.8%		7,090
Class 1A £18,408 × 13.8%		2,540

92.2 (a) Pre trading expenditure

		£
Feb 2018	Legal advice on sales contracts is an allowable expense as it was incurred in the seven years before trading and would have been allowable if incurred whilst trading.	800
Jun 2018	Insurance is an allowable expense for the period from being taken out ie,1 June 2018 to 31 March 2019. £1,200 × 10/12.	1,000
August 2018	Entertaining customers is disallowable as it would not be allowable once trading commenced.	-
		1,800

(b)

	£
Car – actual cost basis	
Lease cost – allowable amount	
Emissions greater than 110g/km £2,000 × 85%	1,700
Private use £1,700 × 3,000/15,000	(340)
	1,360
Fuel costs £2,800 × 12,000/ 15,000	2,240
Total allowable	3,600
Car – fixed rate expenses	
10,000 × 45p	4,500
2,000 × 25p	500
Total allowable	5,000

(c)

Tax-adjusted trading loss for six months ended 31 March 2019

	£
Draft profit	13,000
Less:	
Pre trading expenditure (part (a))	(1,800)
Fixed rate car expenses (part (b))	(5,000)
Capital allowances (W)	(105,750)
Tax-adjusted trading loss	(99,550)

WORKING

Capital allowances	Main pool £	Special rate £	
Purchases – AIA			
Office furniture	15,000		
Lift		210,000	
AIA (£200,000 × 6/12)	_____	(100,000)	100,000
	15,000	110,000	
WDA @ 18% × 6/12	(1,350)		1,350
WDA @ 8% × 6/12	_____	(4,400)	4,400
	13,650	105,600	
Total allowances			105,750

Note: AIA for the six-month period is £100,000 (£200,000 × 6/12)
AIA to the special rate pool purchases first

(d)

Loss relief	2014/15 £	2015/16 £	2016/17 £	2017/18 £	2018/19 £
Trading profits					-
Salary	38,000	35,000	39,000	40,000	20,000
Property income (W)	3,100	3,200	3,000	2,900	2,700
	41,100	38,200	42,000	42,900	22,700
Less loss relief	-	(1)(38,200)	(2)(42,000)	(3)(19,350)	
Personal allowance	(10,000)	-	-	(11,500)	(11,850)
Taxable income	31,100	-		12,050	10,850

WORKING

Property income 2018/19

Rental income (cash basis) (£4,200 × 10/12)	3,500
Less expenses:	
Mortgage interest (£900 × 50%) (Note)	(450)
Repairs	(350)
	2,700

Note: In 2018/19 50% of the mortgage interest is treated as a deduction in calculating property income. The remaining 50% of mortgage interest gets 20% tax relief (ie, £90) as a deduction from Saul's income tax liability.

Examiner's comment

92.1 (a) Most students performed well on this part. The income tax computation was generally good but the child benefit charge was often omitted or treated as income. In the employment income calculation, most students did not understand the salary sacrifice rules, and many did not restrict the employee's contribution to the purchase of the company car. The round sum allowance was usually either taxed in full (ie, without deduction of allowable parking expense), or only the entertaining element was taxed.

(b) Many student produced good answers to this part, although there was some confusion about how and where to include the season ticket and round sum allowance.

92.2 (a) Many students confused VAT pre-registration expenditure rules with income tax pre-trading expenditure rules. Some students then discussed VAT recoverability rather than deductibility of costs ie they answered the wrong question.

(b) Students usually produced reasonable answers to this discriminating part of the question. Most could do the correct calculations based on business mileage (although many added additional costs to this), but the actual allowable costs were rarely calculated entirely correctly, often with only one cost (if any) being restricted for private use. Some students also calculated fuel benefits, confusing this with an employment scenario.

(c) This part was generally well answered with many students remembering to pro-rate both the AIA and the WDA.

(d) The quality of answers to this part varied significantly. The most common approach was to offset the loss against current and prior year net income. Where the early years loss relief rules were applied it was often applied from the current year on a LIFO basis. The loss relief was normally offset against net income however some students tried to apply the £50,000 or 25% loss relief restriction rules. The personal allowance was often forgotten and many students did not restrict the mortgage interest in the property income calculation.

REVIEW FORM – TAX COMPLIANCE QUESTION BANK

Your ratings, comments and suggestions would be appreciated on the following areas of this Question Bank

	Very useful	Useful	Not useful
Number of questions in each section	☐	☐	☐
Standard of answers	☐	☐	☐
Amount of guidance on exam technique	☐	☐	☐
Quality of marking guides	☐	☐	☐

	Excellent	Good	Adequate	Poor
Overall opinion of this Question Bank	☐	☐	☐	☐

Please return completed form to:
The Learning Team
Learning and Professional Department
ICAEW
Metropolitan House
321 Avebury Boulevard
Milton Keynes
MK9 2FZ
E learning@icaew.com

For space to add further comments please see overleaf.

REVIEW FORM (continued)

TELL US WHAT YOU THINK

Please note any further comments and suggestions/errors below.